SHOP

MIKAMOTO

三家本礼

REIKO ZOMBIE SHOP

① 1

CONTENTS

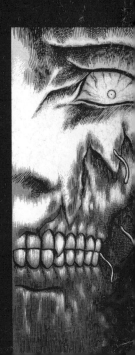

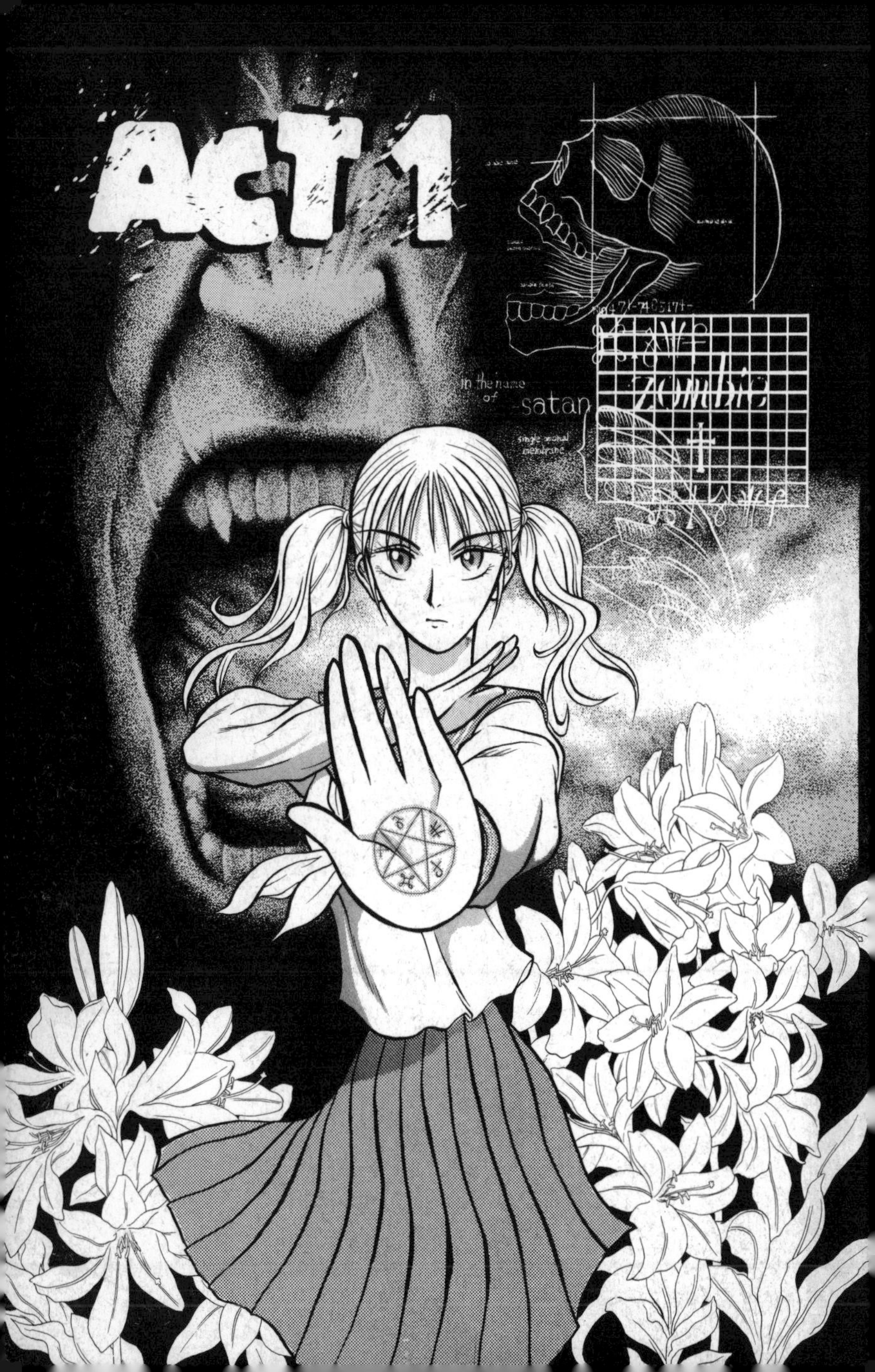
ACT 1
in the name of satan
zombie

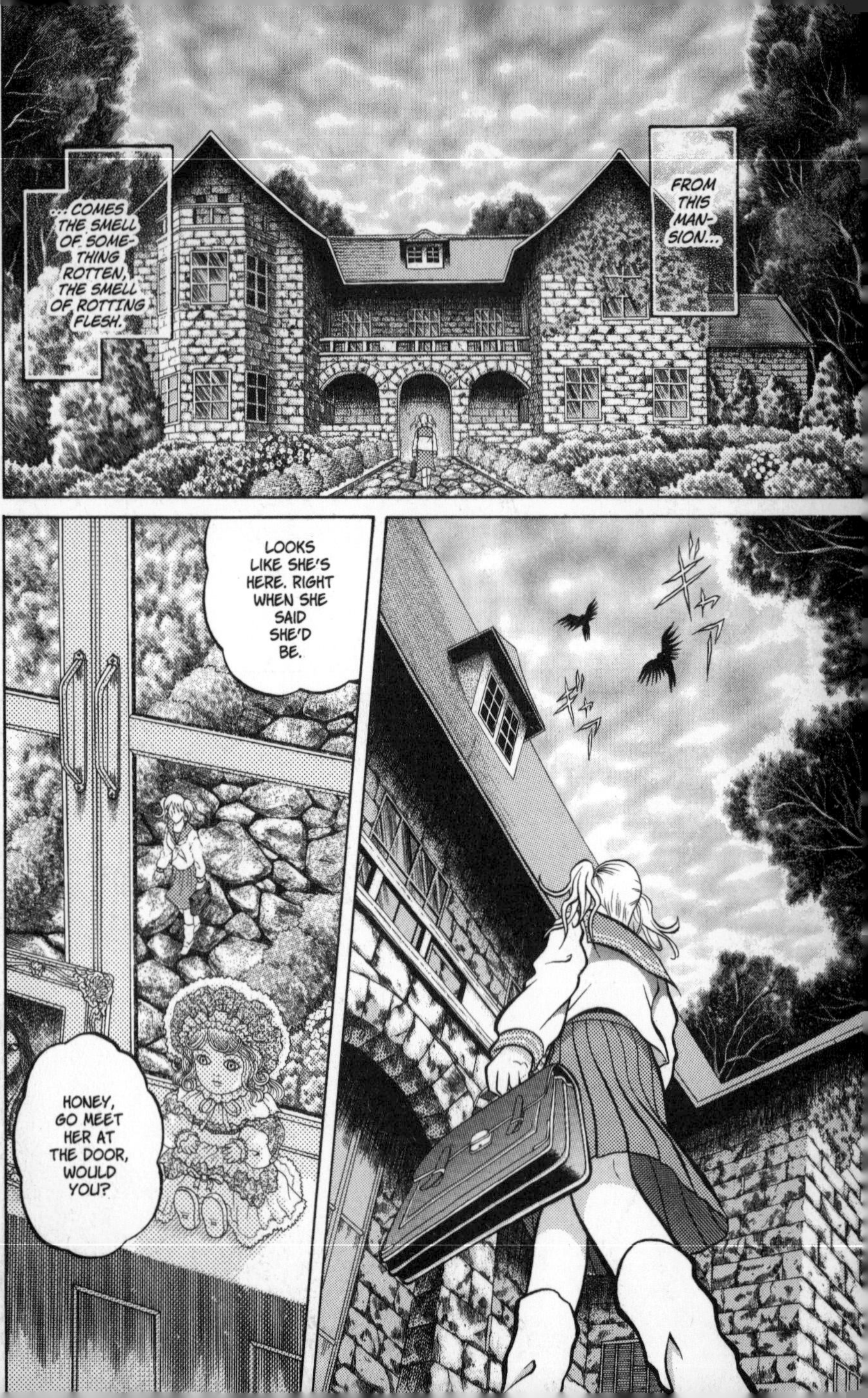
FROM THIS MANSION...
...COMES THE SMELL OF SOMETHING ROTTEN, THE SMELL OF ROTTING FLESH.
ギャア
ギャア
LOOKS LIKE SHE'S HERE. RIGHT WHEN SHE SAID SHE'D BE.
HONEY, GO MEET HER AT THE DOOR, WOULD YOU?

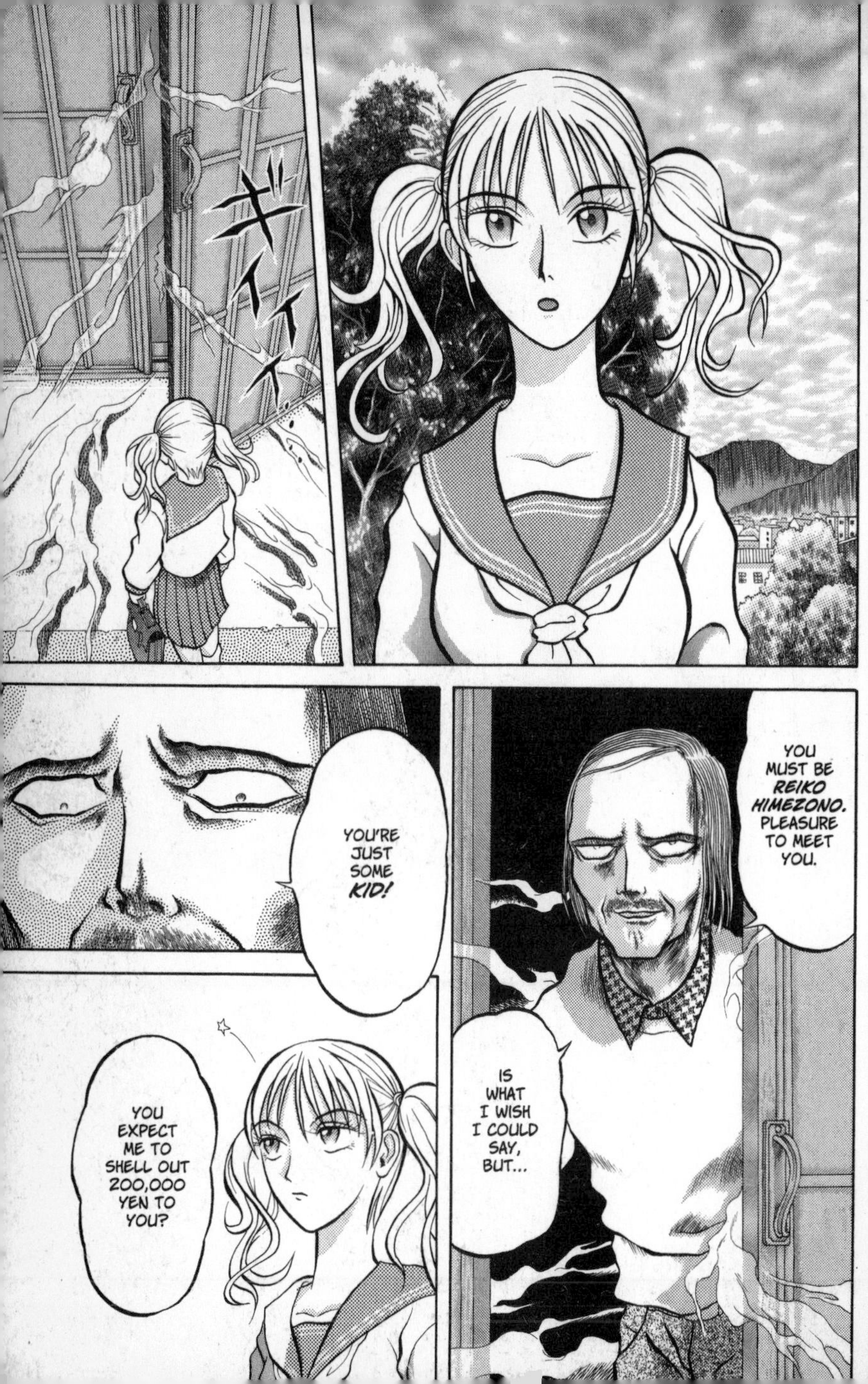
YOU MUST BE REIKO HIMEZONO. PLEASURE TO MEET YOU.
IS WHAT I WISH I COULD SAY, BUT...
YOU'RE JUST SOME KID!
YOU EXPECT ME TO SHELL OUT 200,000 YEN TO YOU?

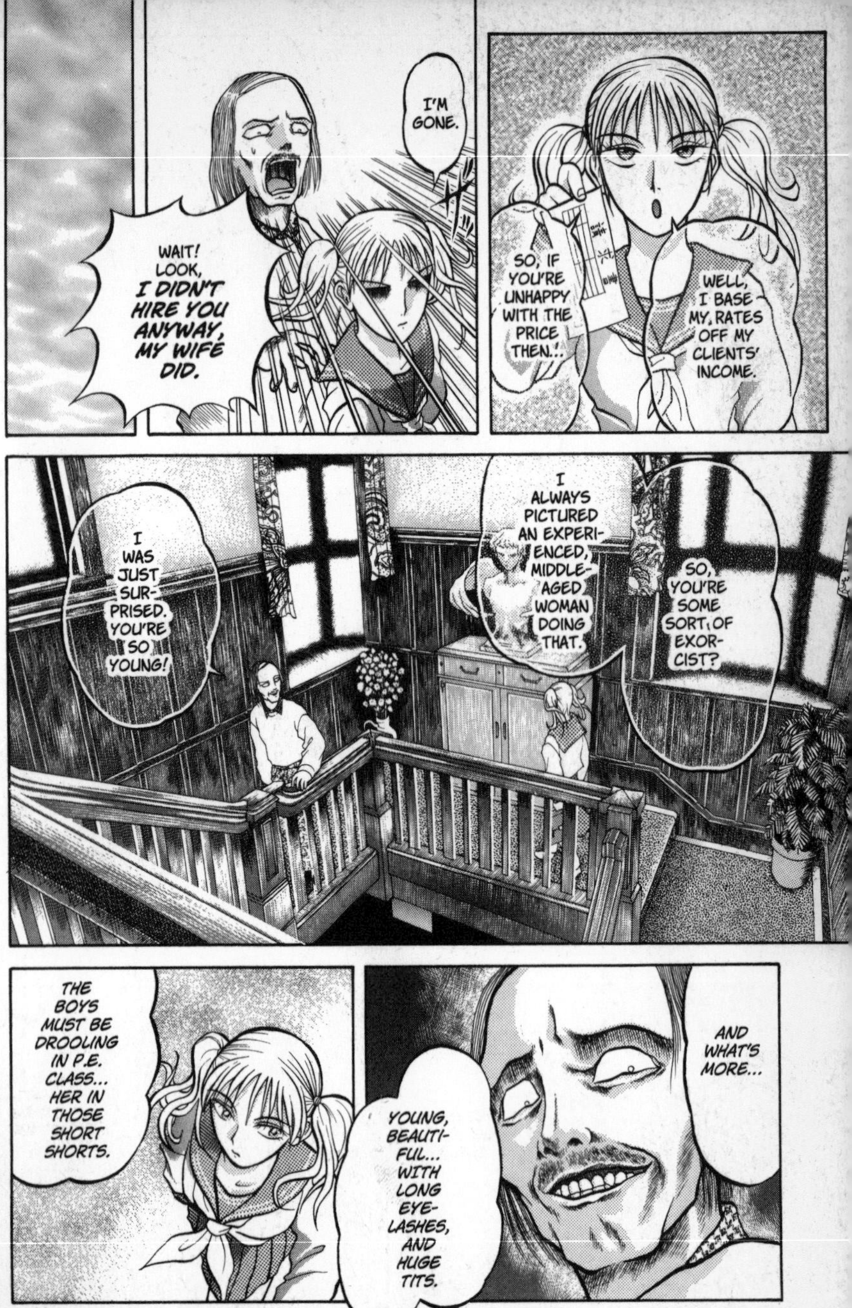
WELL, I BASE MY RATES OFF MY CLIENTS' INCOME.
SO, IF YOU'RE UNHAPPY WITH THE PRICE THEN...
I'M GONE.
WAIT! LOOK, I DIDN'T HIRE YOU ANYWAY, MY WIFE DID.
SO, YOU'RE SOME SORT OF EXORCIST?
I ALWAYS PICTURED AN EXPERIENCED, MIDDLE-AGED WOMAN DOING THAT.
I WAS JUST SURPRISED. YOU'RE SO YOUNG!
AND WHAT'S MORE...
YOUNG, BEAUTIFUL... WITH LONG EYELASHES, AND HUGE TITS.
THE BOYS MUST BE DROOLING IN P.E. CLASS... HER IN THOSE SHORT SHORTS.

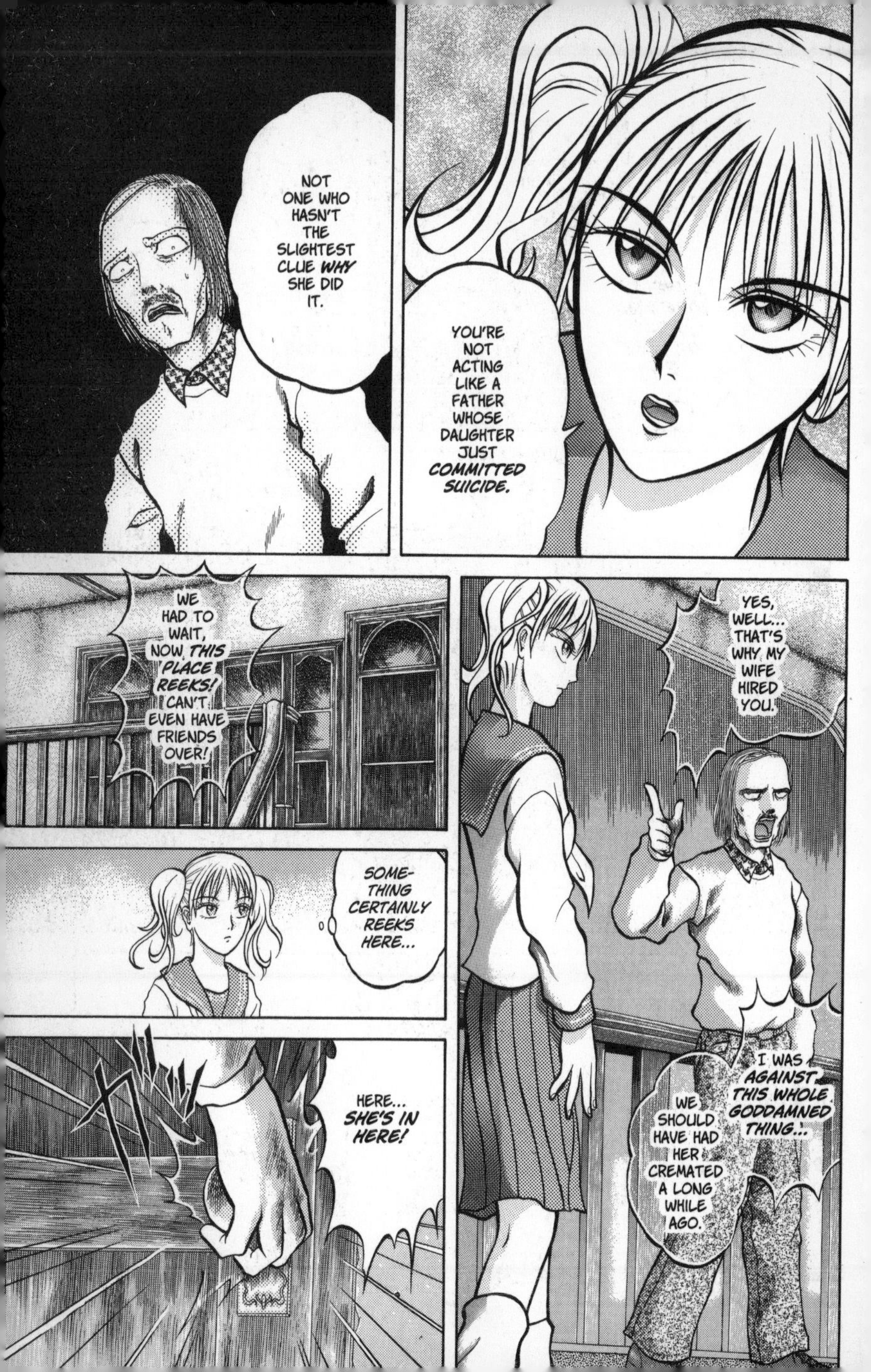
YOU'RE NOT ACTING LIKE A FATHER WHOSE DAUGHTER JUST *COMMITTED SUICIDE.*
NOT ONE WHO HASN'T THE SLIGHTEST CLUE *WHY* SHE DID IT.
YES, WELL... THAT'S WHY MY WIFE HIRED YOU.
I WAS *AGAINST THIS WHOLE GODDAMNED THING...*
WE SHOULD HAVE HAD HER CREMATED A LONG WHILE AGO.
WE HAD TO WAIT, NOW *THIS PLACE REEKS!* CAN'T EVEN HAVE FRIENDS OVER!
*SOME-THING CERTAINLY REEKS HERE...*
HERE... *SHE'S IN HERE!*

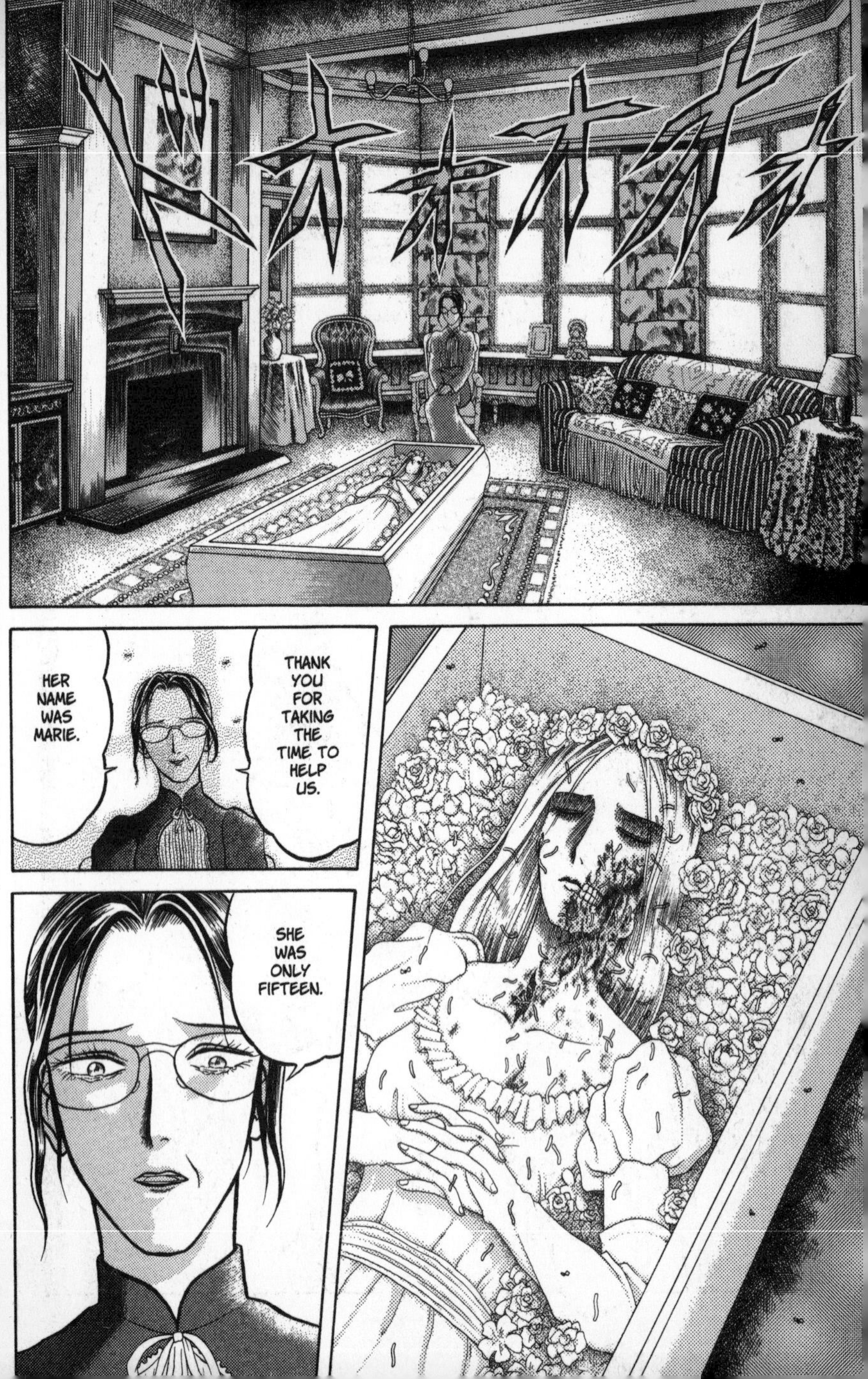
THANK YOU FOR TAKING THE TIME TO HELP US.
HER NAME WAS MARIE.
SHE WAS ONLY FIFTEEN.

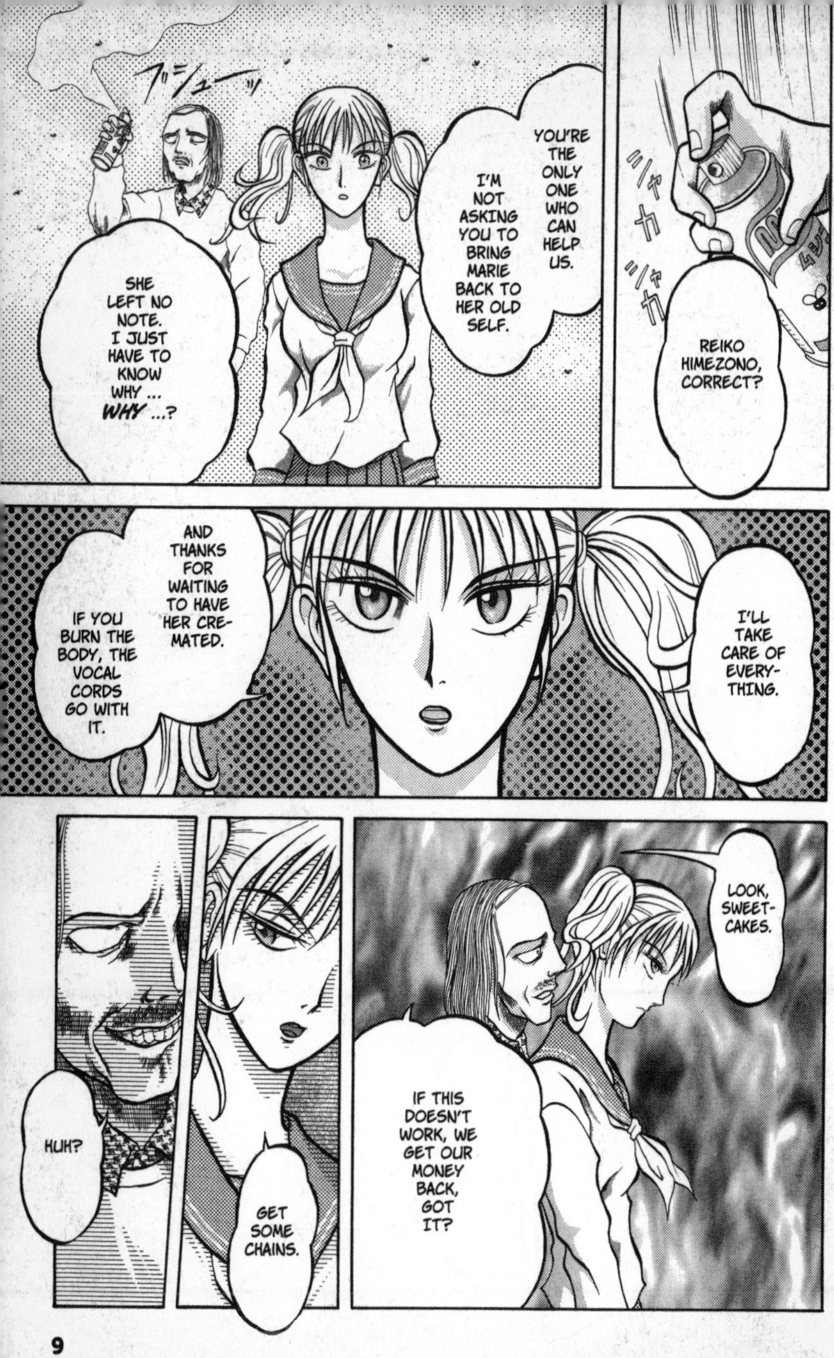
シャカ
シャカ
REIKO HIMEZONO, CORRECT?
ブシューッ
YOU'RE THE ONLY ONE WHO CAN HELP US.
I'M NOT ASKING YOU TO BRING MARIE BACK TO HER OLD SELF.
SHE LEFT NO NOTE. I JUST HAVE TO KNOW WHY ... *WHY* ...?
I'LL TAKE CARE OF EVERY-THING.
AND THANKS FOR WAITING TO HAVE HER CRE-MATED.
IF YOU BURN THE BODY, THE VOCAL CORDS GO WITH IT.
LOOK, SWEET-CAKES.
IF THIS DOESN'T WORK, WE GET OUR MONEY BACK, GOT IT?
GET SOME CHAINS.
HUH?

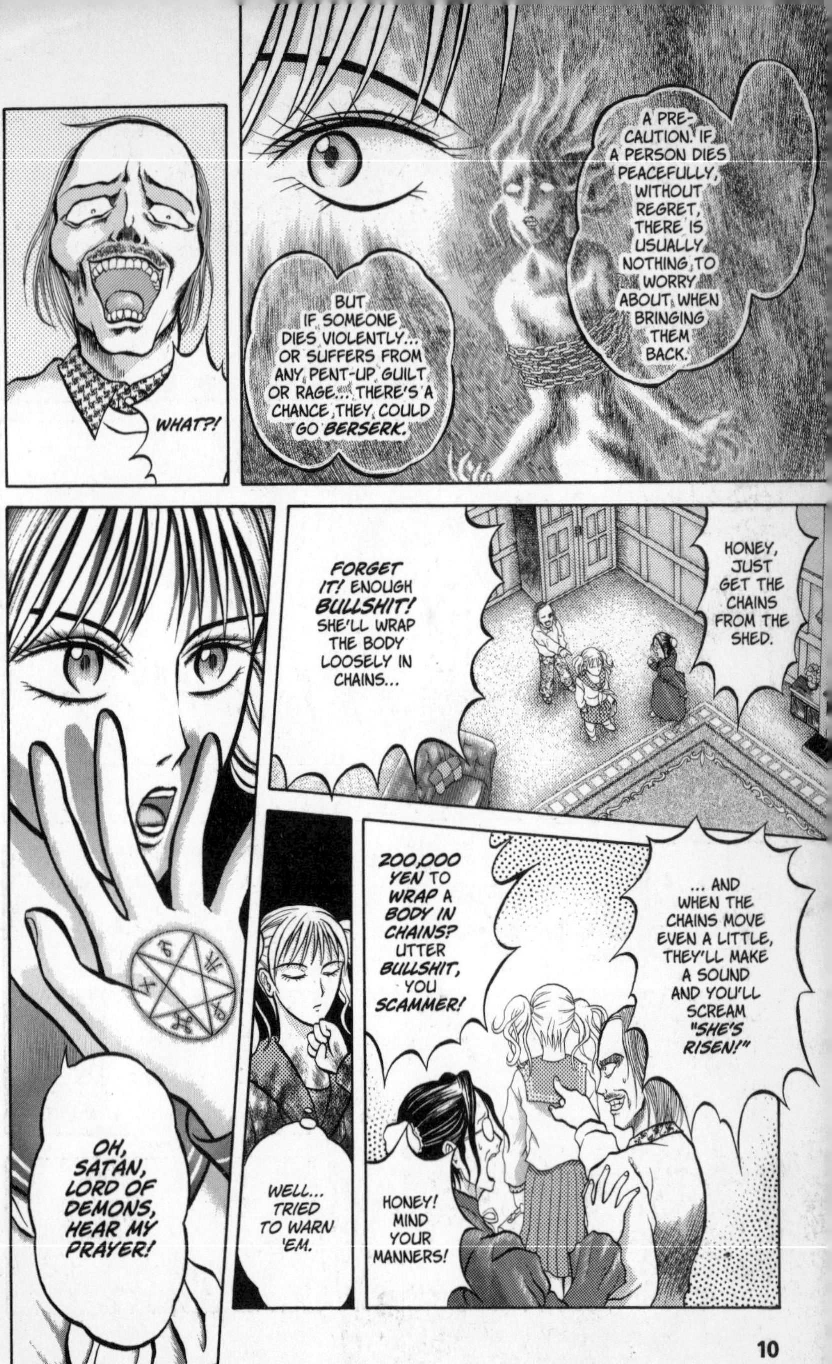
A PRE-CAUTION. IF A PERSON DIES PEACEFULLY, WITHOUT REGRET, THERE IS USUALLY NOTHING TO WORRY ABOUT WHEN BRINGING THEM BACK.
BUT IF SOMEONE DIES VIOLENTLY... OR SUFFERS FROM ANY PENT-UP GUILT OR RAGE... THERE'S A CHANCE THEY COULD GO BERSERK.
WHAT?!
HONEY, JUST GET THE CHAINS FROM THE SHED.
FORGET IT! ENOUGH BULLSHIT! SHE'LL WRAP THE BODY LOOSELY IN CHAINS...
... AND WHEN THE CHAINS MOVE EVEN A LITTLE, THEY'LL MAKE A SOUND AND YOU'LL SCREAM "SHE'S RISEN!"
200,000 YEN TO WRAP A BODY IN CHAINS? UTTER BULLSHIT, YOU SCAMMER!
HONEY! MIND YOUR MANNERS!
WELL... TRIED TO WARN 'EM.
OH, SATAN, LORD OF DEMONS, HEAR MY PRAYER!

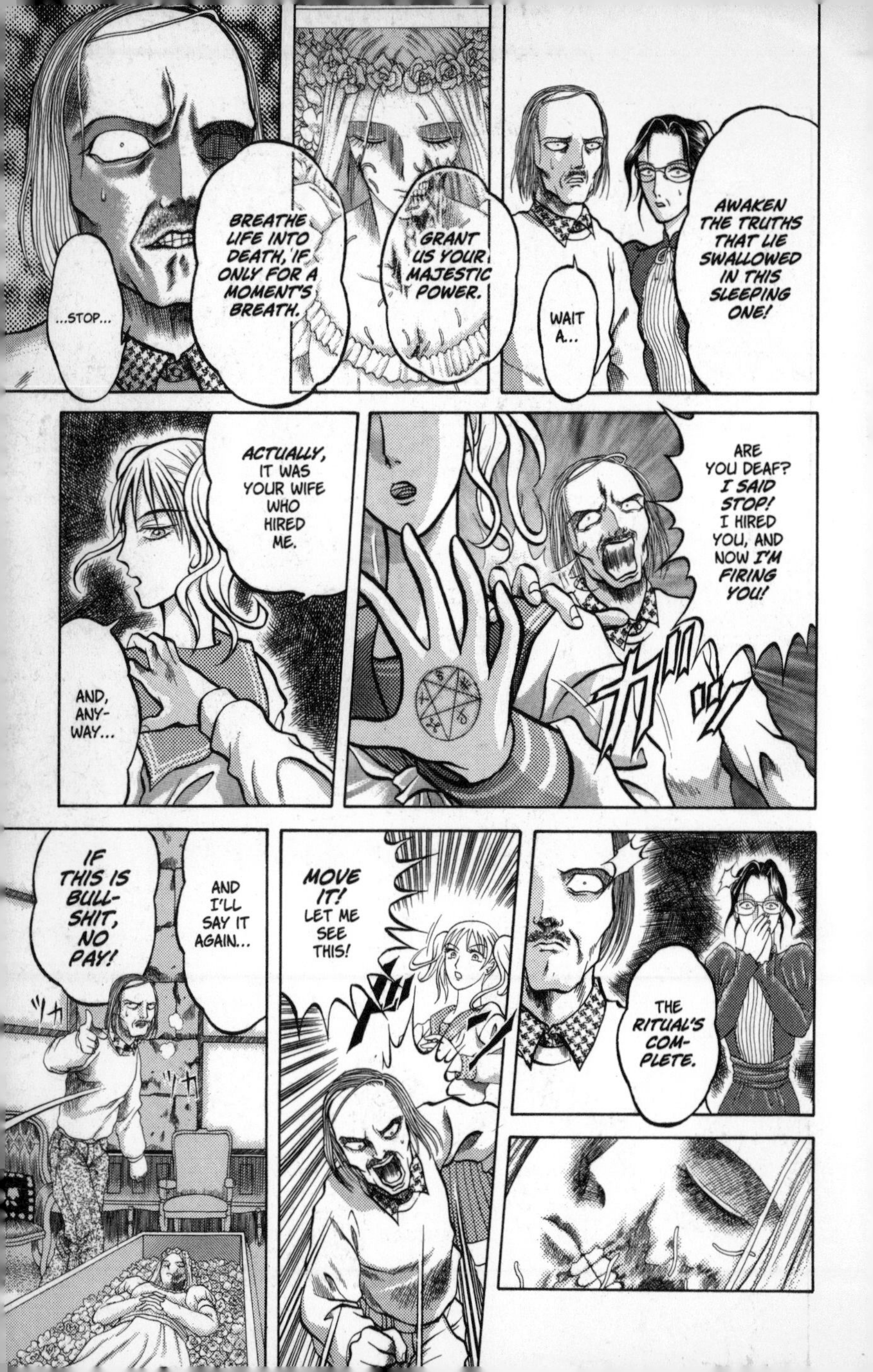
AWAKEN THE TRUTHS THAT LIE SWALLOWED IN THIS SLEEPING ONE!
WAIT A...
GRANT US YOUR MAJESTIC POWER.
BREATHE LIFE INTO DEATH, IF ONLY FOR A MOMENT'S BREATH.
...STOP...
ARE YOU DEAF? I SAID STOP! I HIRED YOU, AND NOW I'M FIRING YOU!
ACTUALLY, IT WAS YOUR WIFE WHO HIRED ME.
AND, ANY-WAY...
THE RITUAL'S COM-PLETE.
MOVE IT! LET ME SEE THIS!
AND I'LL SAY IT AGAIN...
IF THIS IS BULL-SHIT, NO PAY!

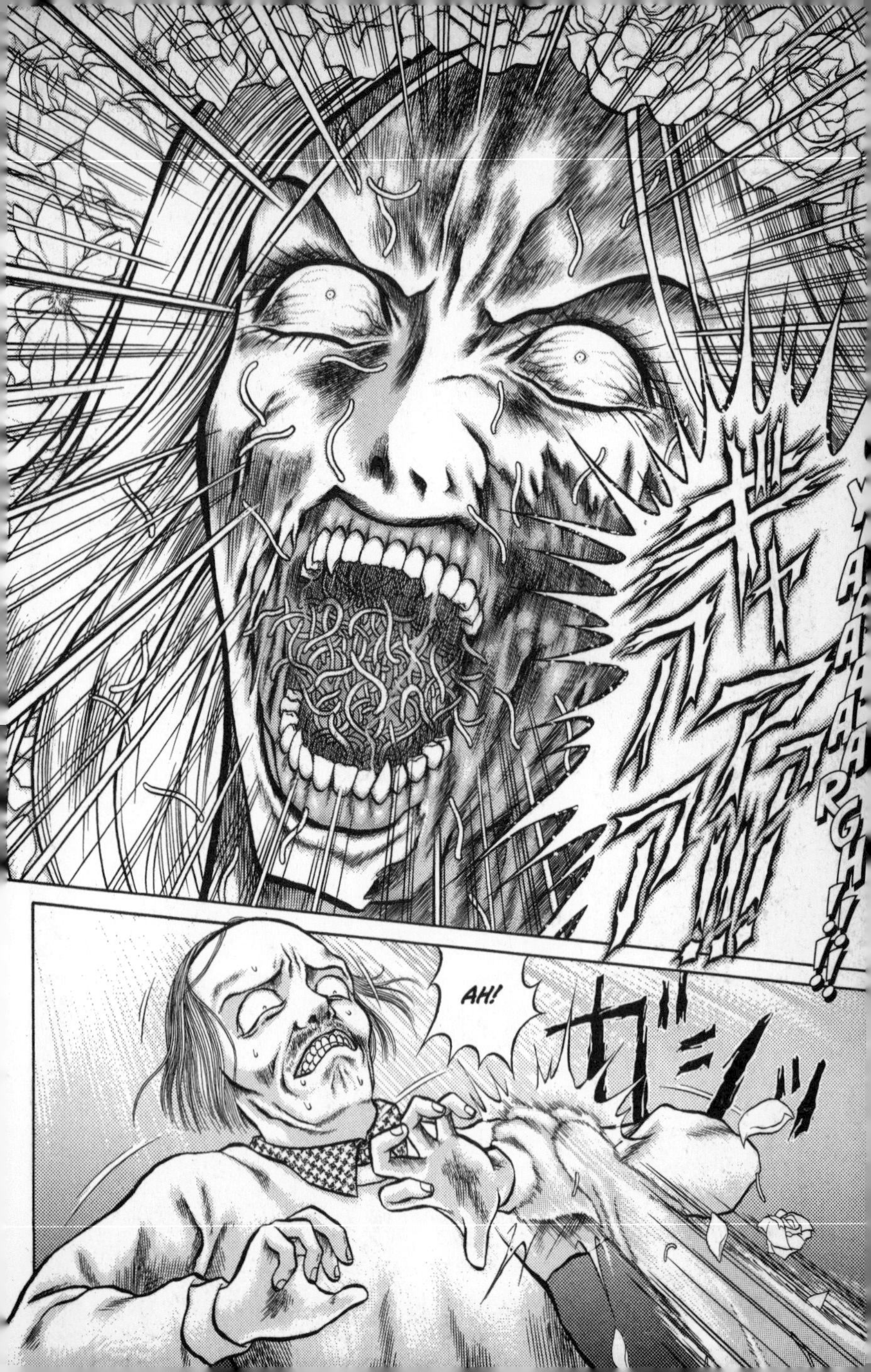
YAAAAAAARGH!!!!
AH!

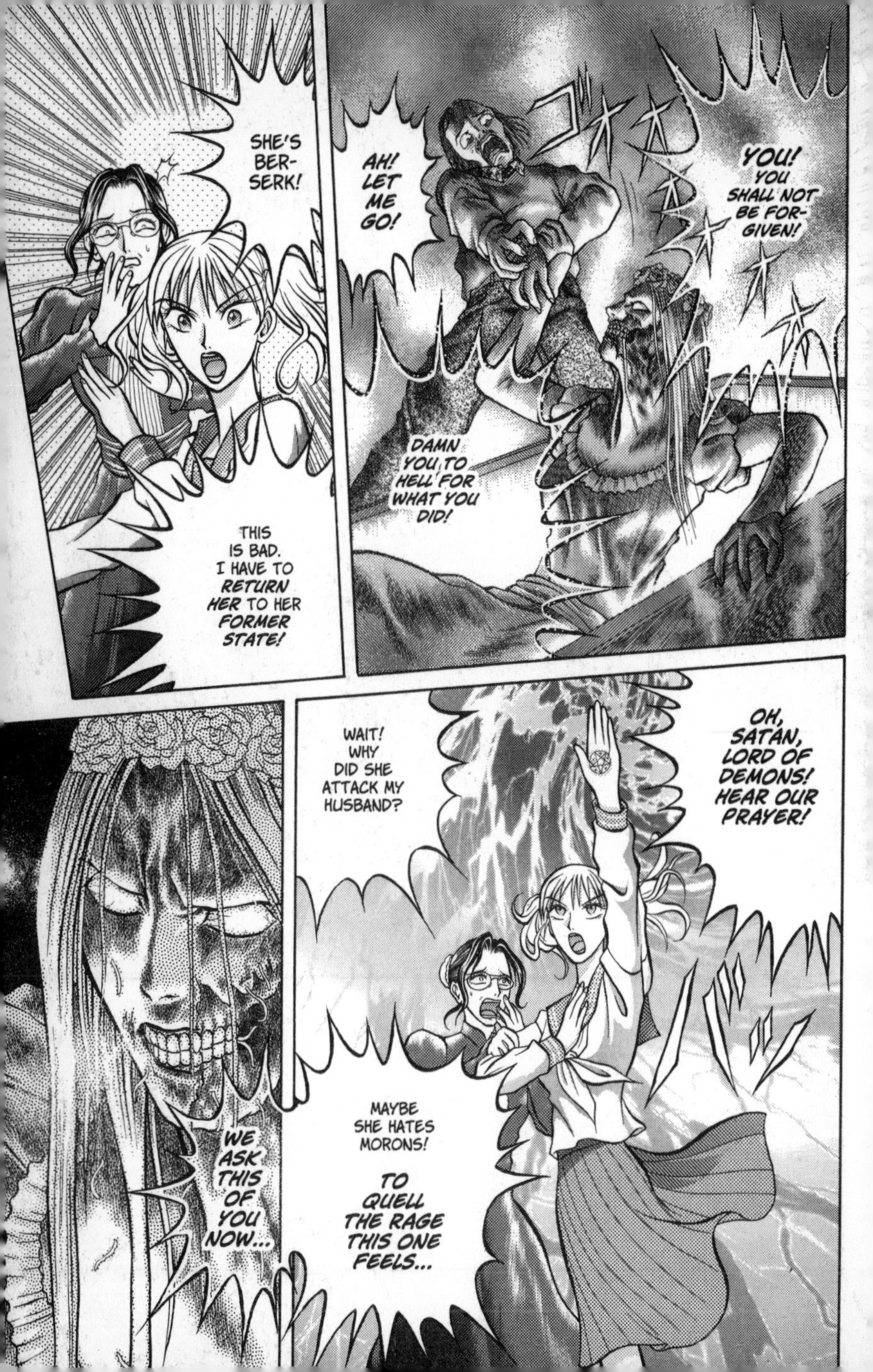
YOU! YOU SHALL NOT BE FORGIVEN!
AH! LET ME GO!
DAMN YOU TO HELL FOR WHAT YOU DID!
SHE'S BERSERK!
THIS IS BAD. I HAVE TO RETURN HER TO HER FORMER STATE!
OH, SATAN, LORD OF DEMONS! HEAR OUR PRAYER!
WAIT! WHY DID SHE ATTACK MY HUSBAND?
MAYBE SHE HATES MORONS!
TO QUELL THE RAGE THIS ONE FEELS...
WE ASK THIS OF YOU NOW...

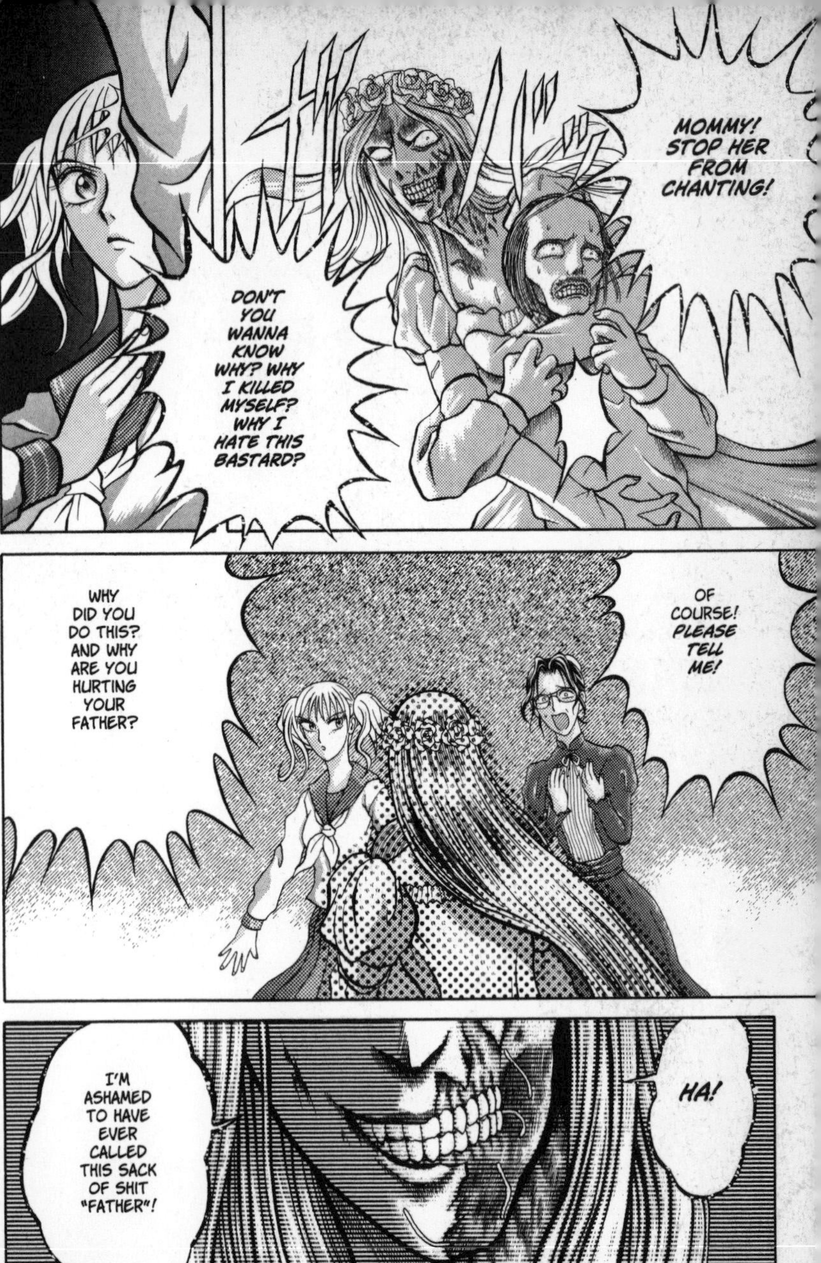
MOMMY! STOP HER FROM CHANTING!
DON'T YOU WANNA KNOW WHY? WHY I KILLED MYSELF? WHY I HATE THIS BASTARD?
OF COURSE! PLEASE TELL ME!
WHY DID YOU DO THIS? AND WHY ARE YOU HURTING YOUR FATHER?
HA!
I'M ASHAMED TO HAVE EVER CALLED THIS SACK OF SHIT "FATHER"!

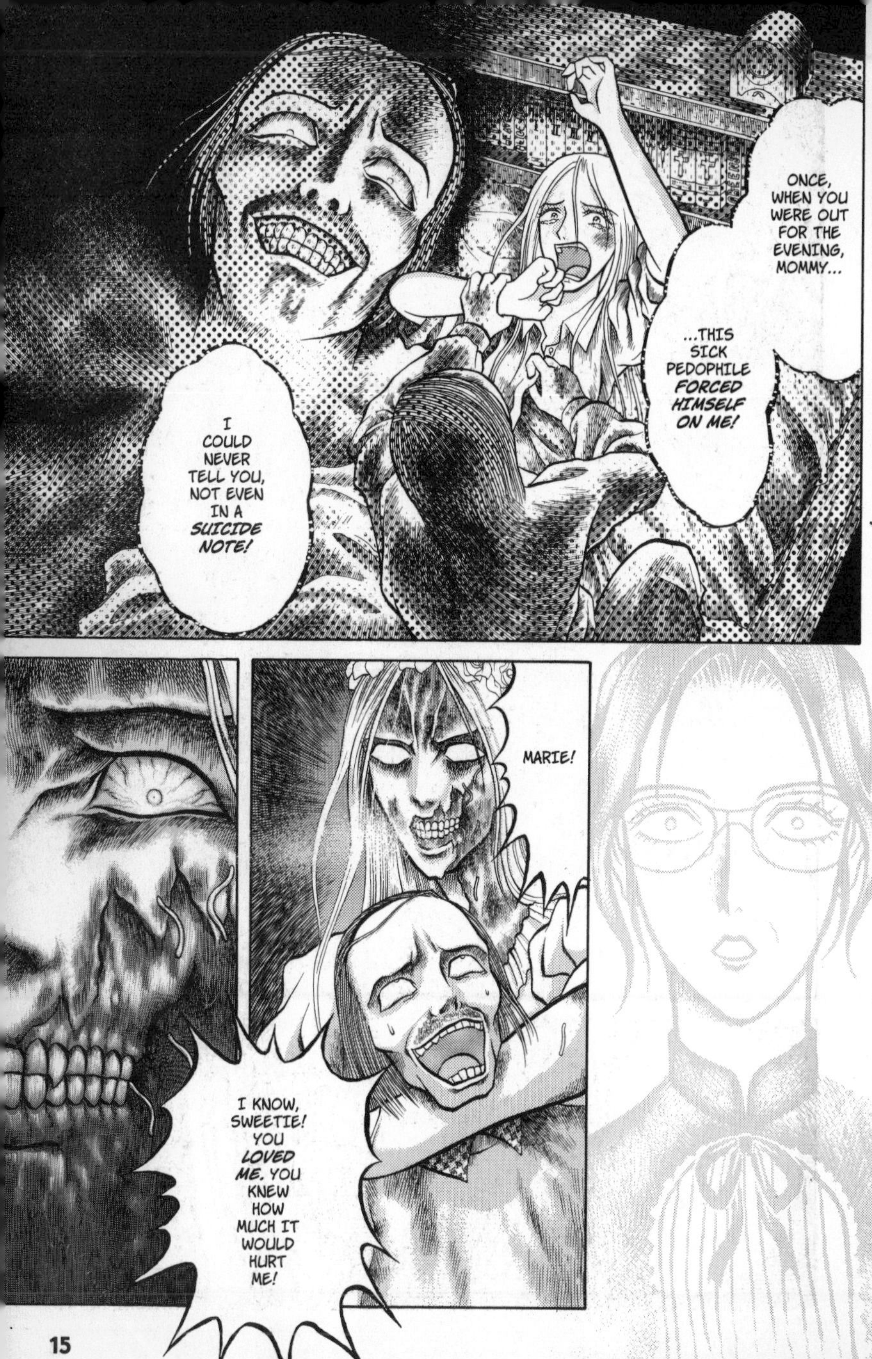
ONCE, WHEN YOU WERE OUT FOR THE EVENING, MOMMY...
...THIS SICK PEDOPHILE *FORCED HIMSELF ON ME!*
I COULD NEVER TELL YOU, NOT EVEN IN A *SUICIDE NOTE!*
MARIE!
I KNOW, SWEETIE! YOU *LOVED ME.* YOU KNEW HOW MUCH IT WOULD HURT ME!

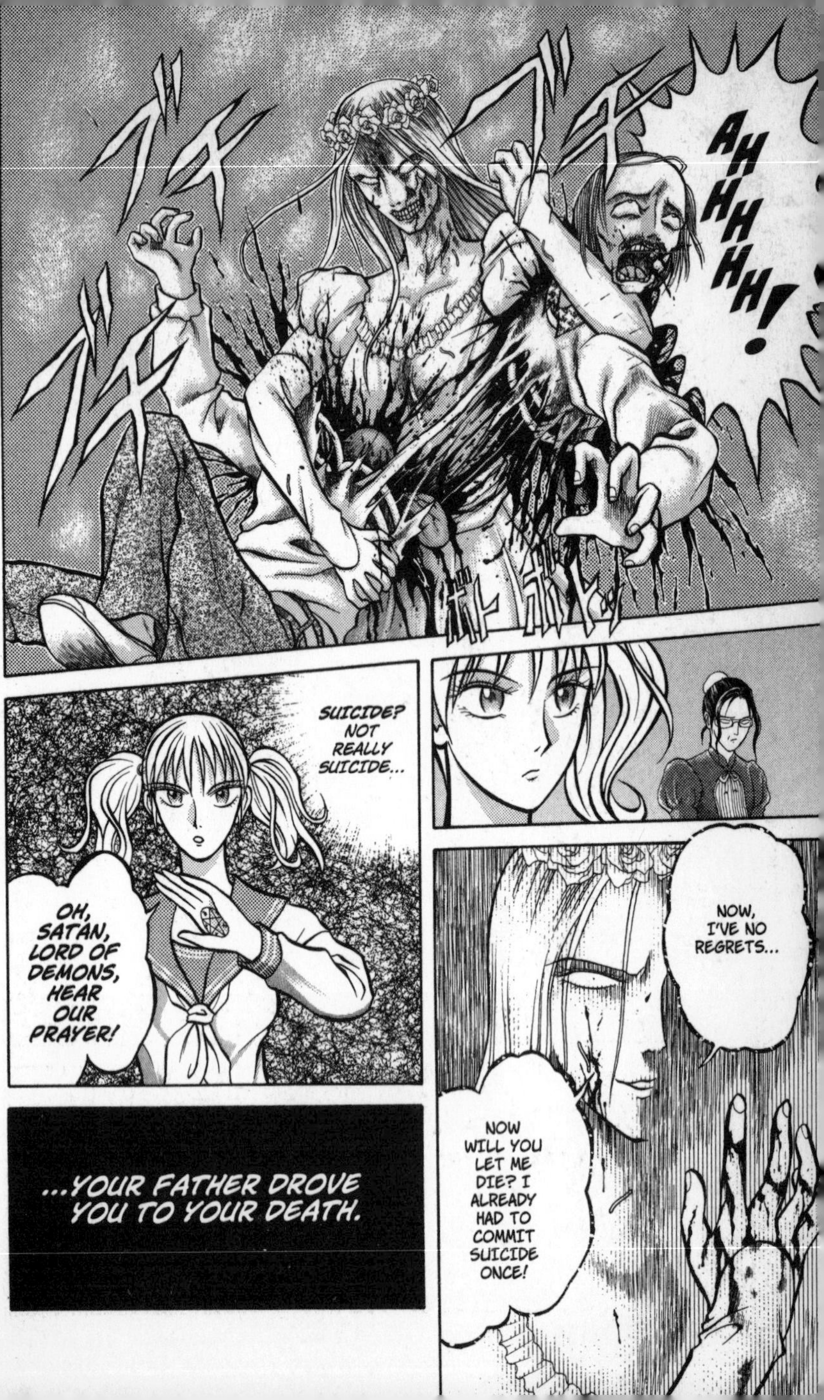
AHHHHHH!
NOW, I'VE NO REGRETS...
NOW WILL YOU LET ME DIE? I ALREADY HAD TO COMMIT SUICIDE ONCE!
SUICIDE? NOT REALLY SUICIDE...
OH, SATAN, LORD OF DEMONS, HEAR OUR PRAYER!
...YOUR FATHER DROVE YOU TO YOUR DEATH.

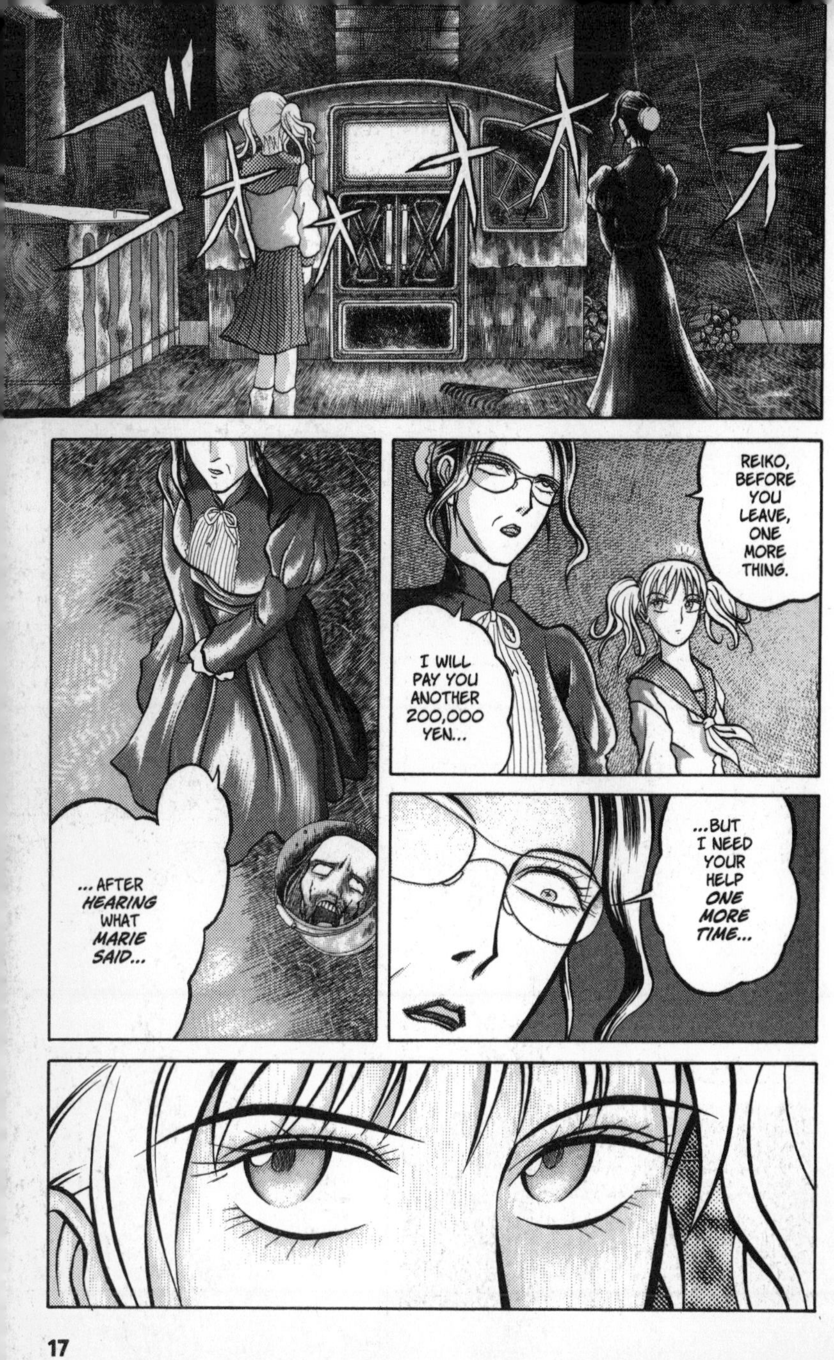
REIKO, BEFORE YOU LEAVE, ONE MORE THING.
I WILL PAY YOU ANOTHER 200,000 YEN...
...BUT I NEED YOUR HELP *ONE MORE TIME...*
...AFTER *HEARING* WHAT *MARIE SAID...*

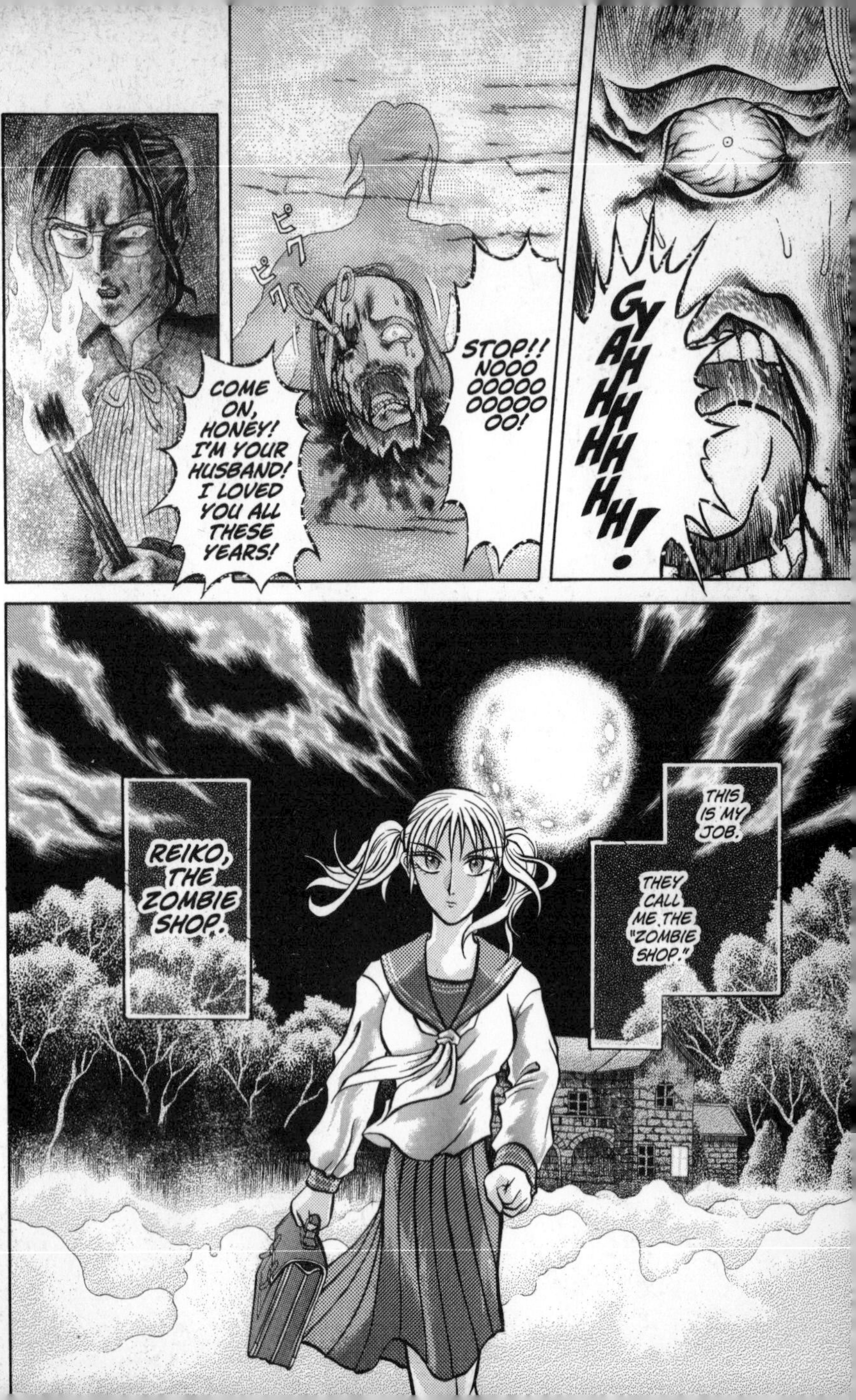
GYAHHHHHHH!
STOP!! NOOOOOOOOOOOOOOO!
ピクピク
COME ON, HONEY! I'M YOUR HUSBAND! I LOVED YOU ALL THESE YEARS!
THIS IS MY JOB.
THEY CALL ME THE "ZOMBIE SHOP."
REIKO, THE ZOMBIE SHOP.

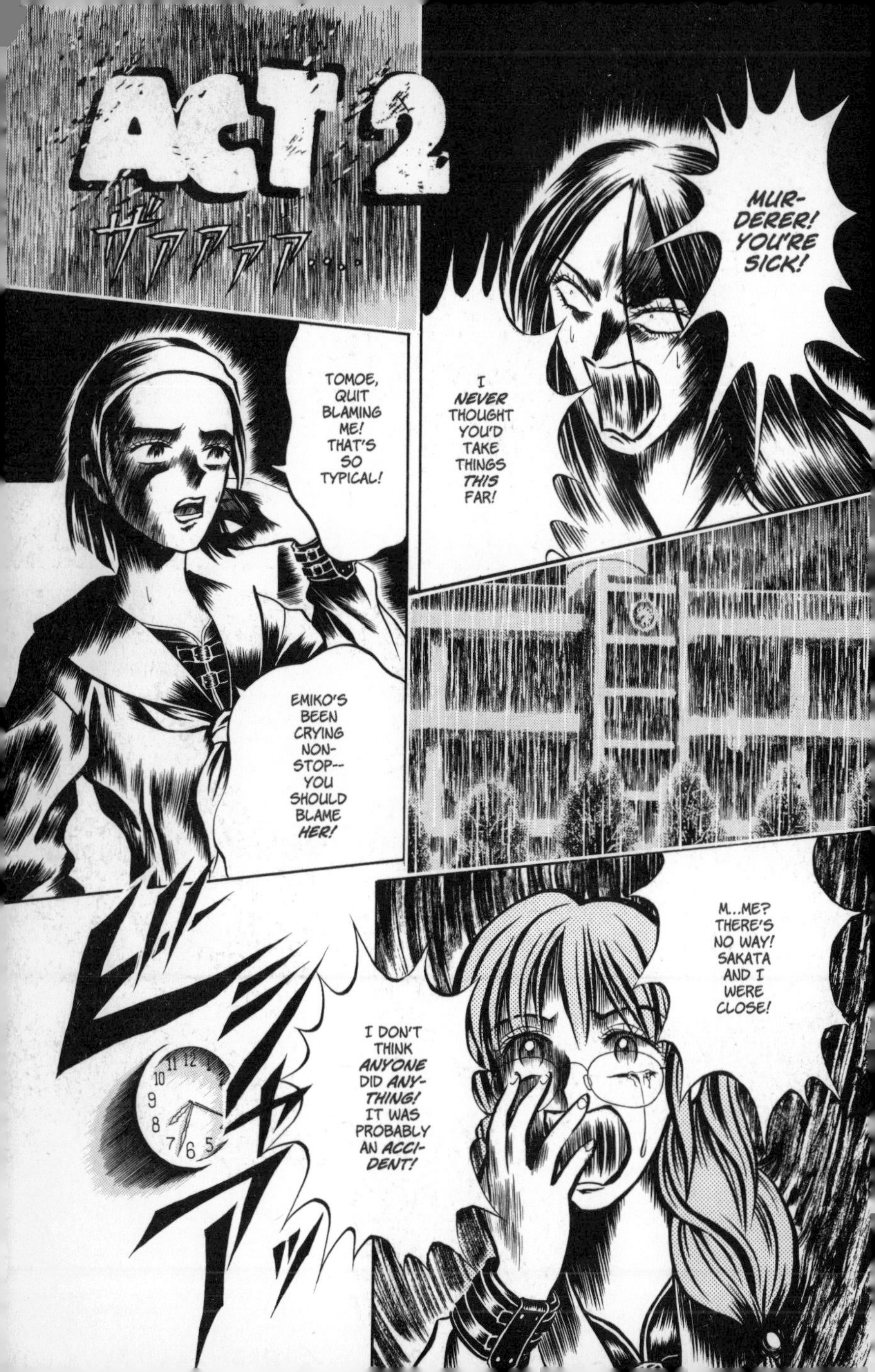
MUR-DERER! YOU'RE SICK!
I NEVER THOUGHT YOU'D TAKE THINGS THIS FAR!
ACT 2
ザァァァァ....
TOMOE, QUIT BLAMING ME! THAT'S SO TYPICAL!
EMIKO'S BEEN CRYING NON-STOP-- YOU SHOULD BLAME HER!
M...ME? THERE'S NO WAY! SAKATA AND I WERE CLOSE!
I DON'T THINK ANYONE DID ANY-THING! IT WAS PROBABLY AN ACCI-DENT!

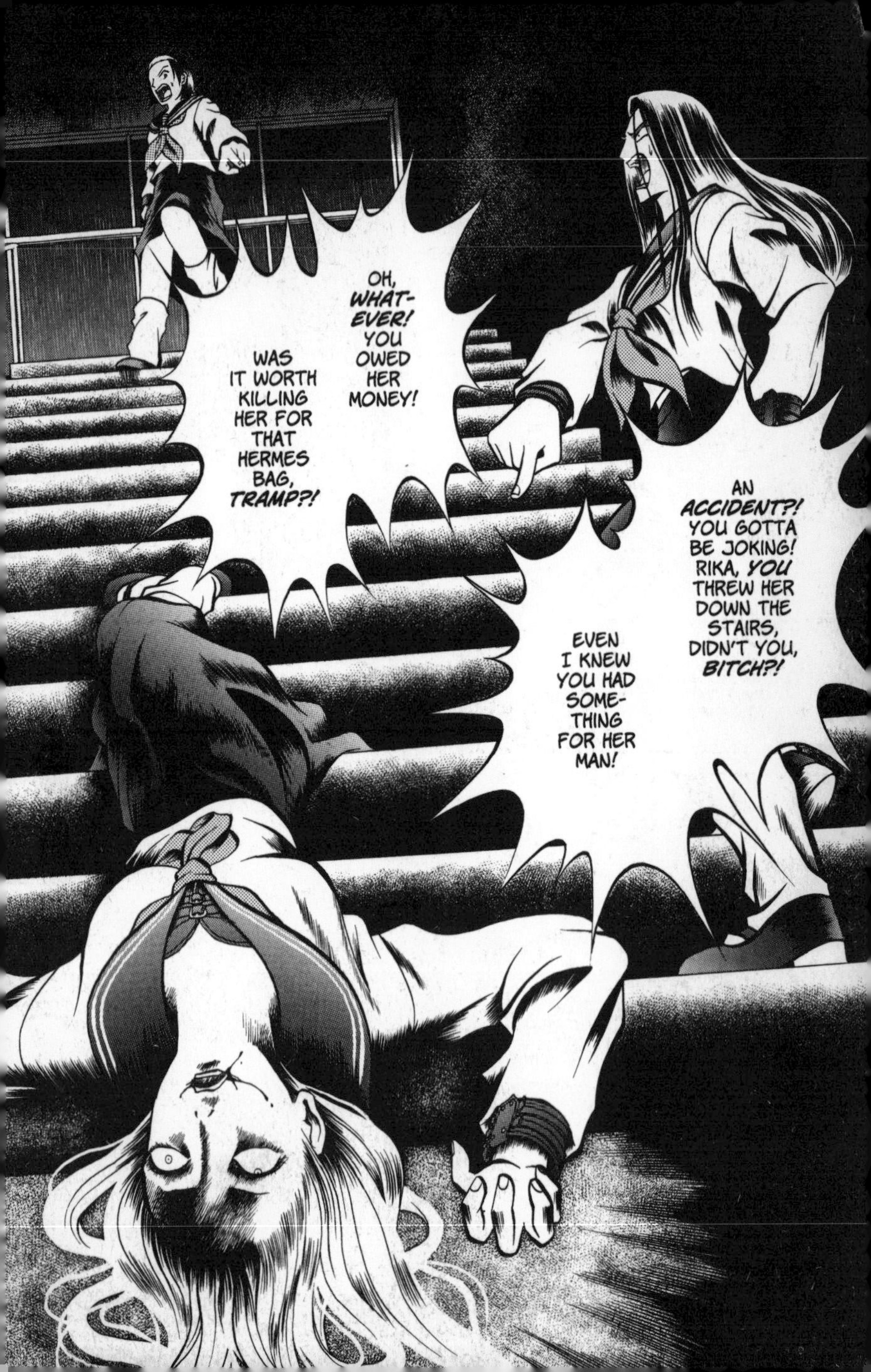
AN ACCIDENT?! YOU GOTTA BE JOKING! RIKA, YOU THREW HER DOWN THE STAIRS, DIDN'T YOU, BITCH?!
EVEN I KNEW YOU HAD SOME-THING FOR HER MAN!
OH, WHAT-EVER! YOU OWED HER MONEY!
WAS IT WORTH KILLING HER FOR THAT HERMES BAG, TRAMP?!

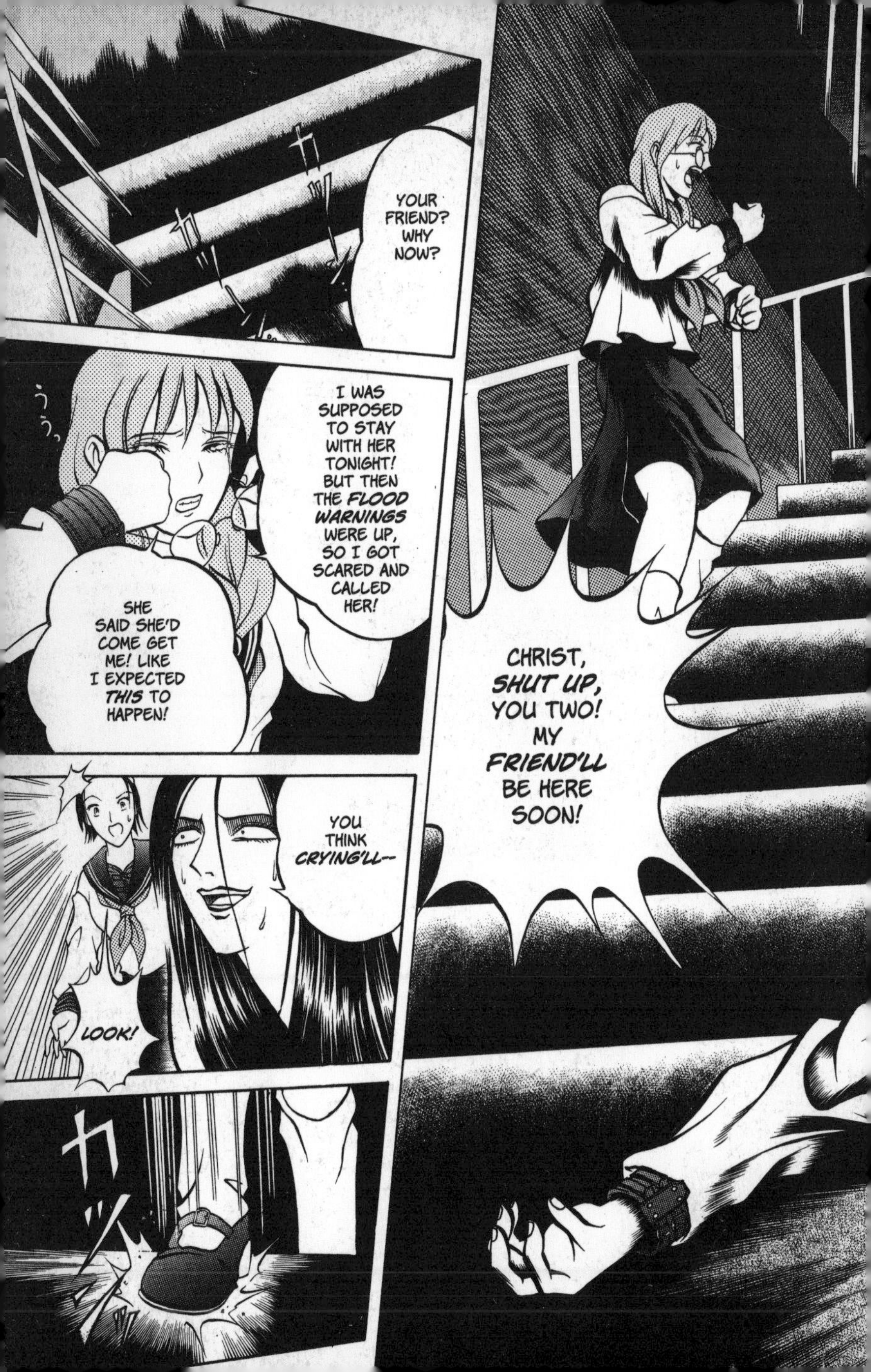
CHRIST, SHUT UP, YOU TWO! MY FRIEND'LL BE HERE SOON!
YOUR FRIEND? WHY NOW?
I WAS SUPPOSED TO STAY WITH HER TONIGHT! BUT THEN THE FLOOD WARNINGS WERE UP, SO I GOT SCARED AND CALLED HER!
SHE SAID SHE'D COME GET ME! LIKE I EXPECTED THIS TO HAPPEN!
YOU THINK CRYING'LL--
LOOK!

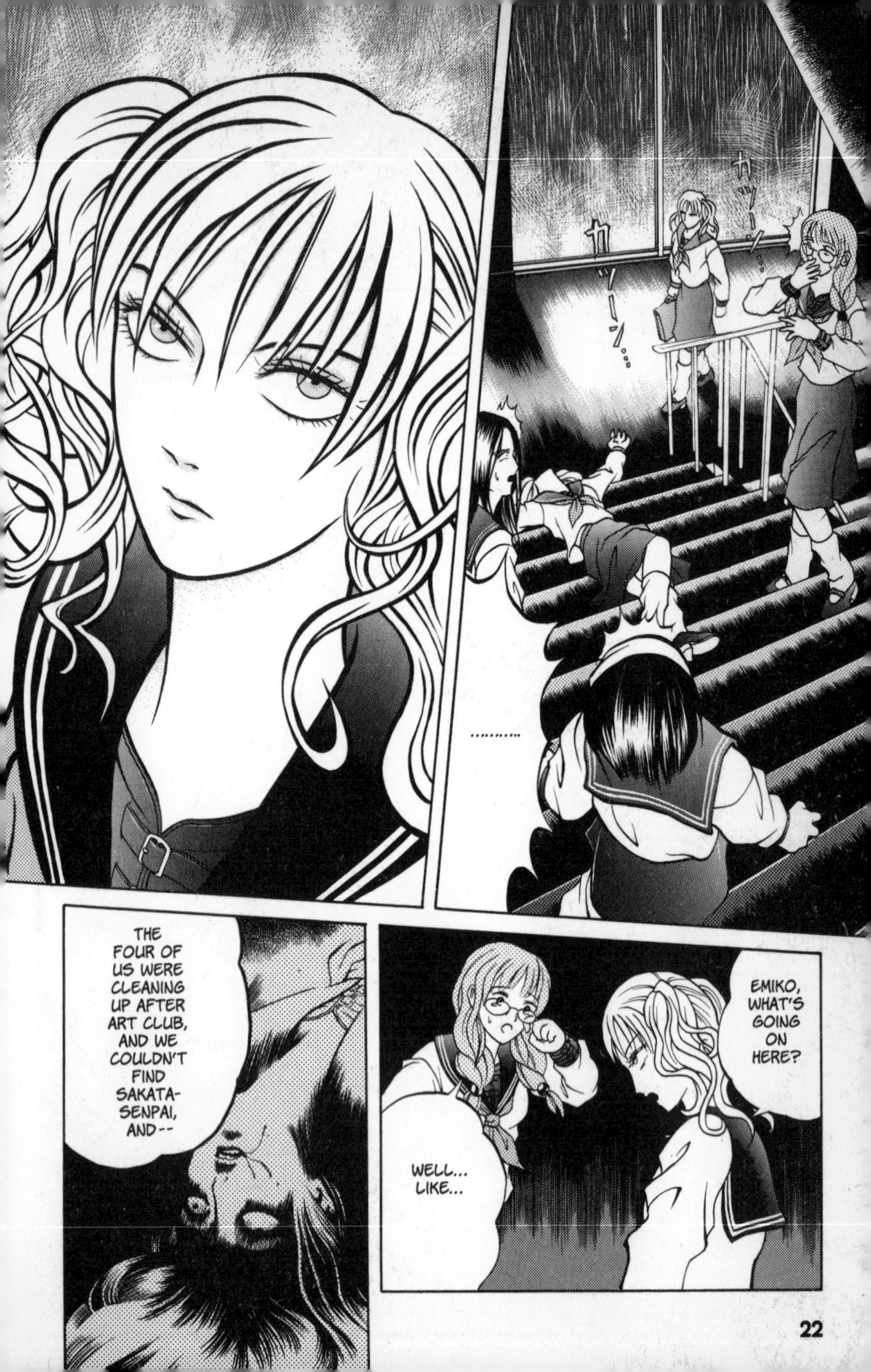

..........
EMIKO, WHAT'S GOING ON HERE?
WELL... LIKE...
THE FOUR OF US WERE CLEANING UP AFTER ART CLUB, AND WE COULDN'T FIND SAKATA-SENPAI, AND--

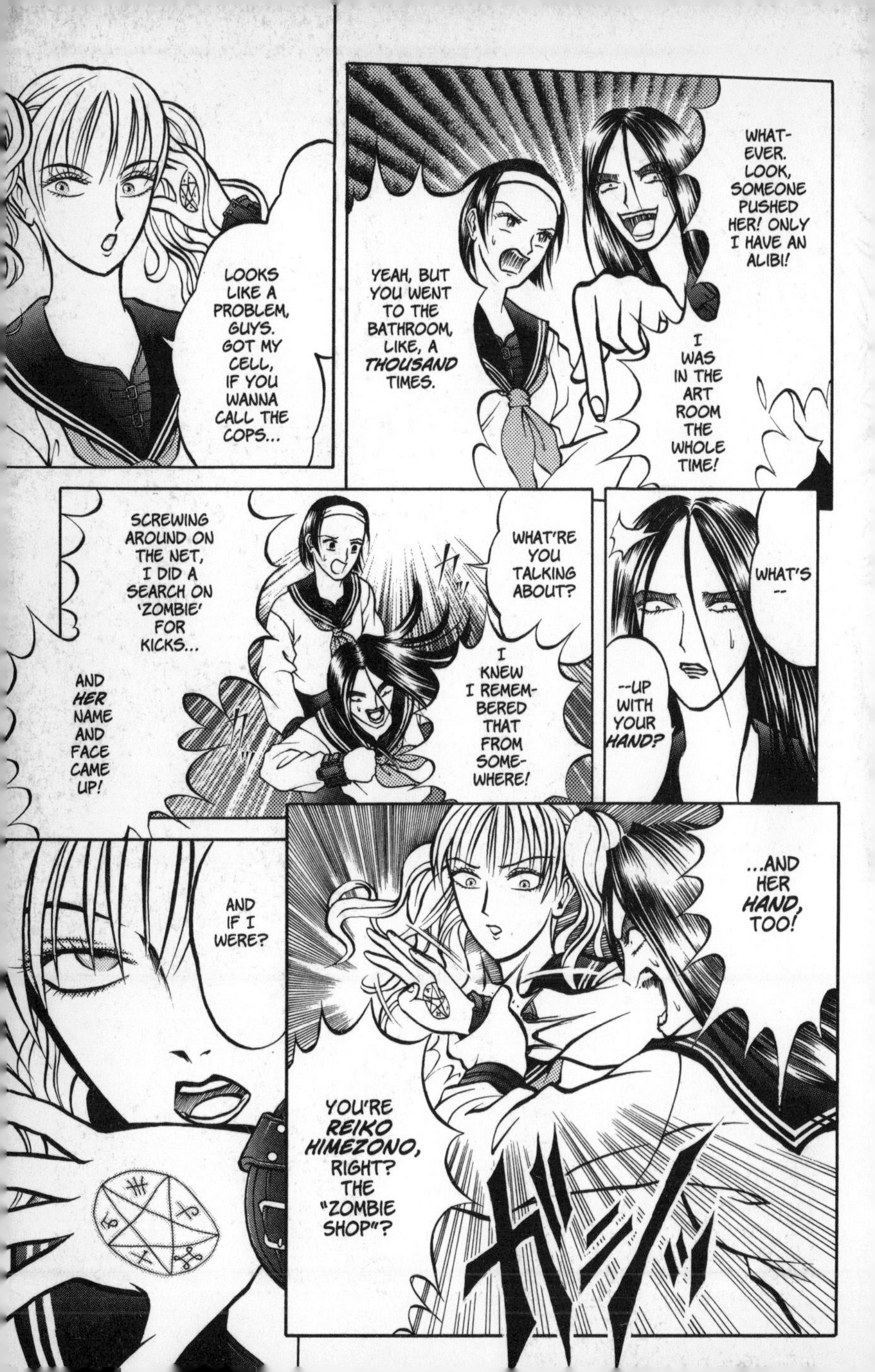
WHAT-EVER. LOOK, SOMEONE PUSHED HER! ONLY I HAVE AN ALIBI!
I WAS IN THE ART ROOM THE WHOLE TIME!
YEAH, BUT YOU WENT TO THE BATHROOM, LIKE, A *THOUSAND* TIMES.
LOOKS LIKE A PROBLEM, GUYS. GOT MY CELL, IF YOU WANNA CALL THE COPS...
WHAT'S --
--UP WITH YOUR *HAND?*
WHAT'RE YOU TALKING ABOUT?
I KNEW I REMEM-BERED THAT FROM SOME-WHERE!
SCREWING AROUND ON THE NET, I DID A SEARCH ON 'ZOMBIE' FOR KICKS...
AND *HER* NAME AND FACE CAME UP!
...AND HER *HAND,* TOO!
YOU'RE *REIKO HIMEZONO,* RIGHT? THE "ZOMBIE SHOP"?
AND IF I WERE?

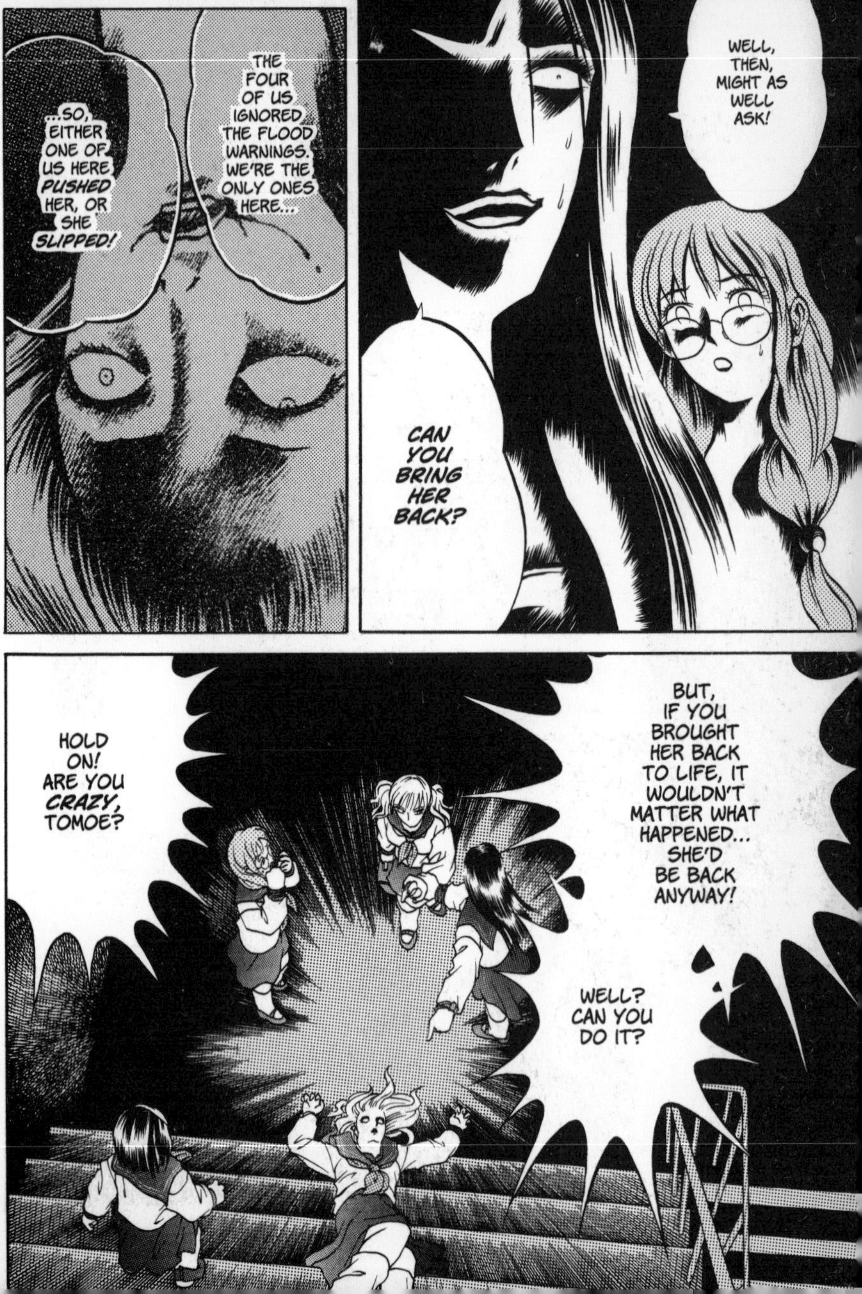
WELL, THEN, MIGHT AS WELL ASK!
CAN YOU BRING HER BACK?
THE FOUR OF US IGNORED THE FLOOD WARNINGS. WE'RE THE ONLY ONES HERE...
...SO, EITHER ONE OF US HERE *PUSHED* HER, OR SHE *SLIPPED!*
BUT, IF YOU BROUGHT HER BACK TO LIFE, IT WOULDN'T MATTER WHAT HAPPENED... SHE'D BE BACK ANYWAY!
HOLD ON! ARE YOU *CRAZY*, TOMOE?
WELL? CAN YOU DO IT?

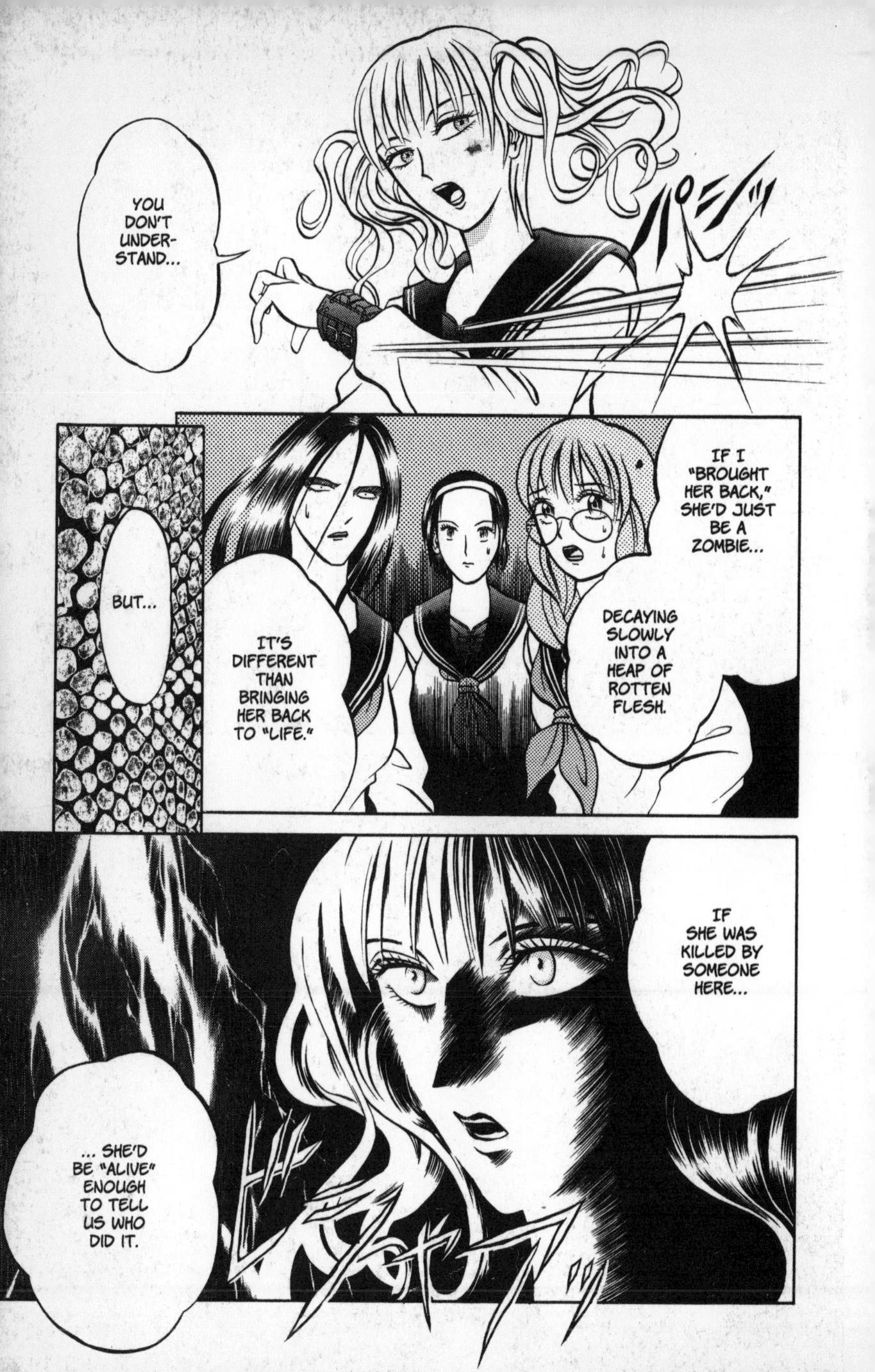
YOU DON'T UNDERSTAND...
IF I "BROUGHT HER BACK," SHE'D JUST BE A ZOMBIE...
DECAYING SLOWLY INTO A HEAP OF ROTTEN FLESH.
IT'S DIFFERENT THAN BRINGING HER BACK TO "LIFE."
BUT...
IF SHE WAS KILLED BY SOMEONE HERE...
... SHE'D BE "ALIVE" ENOUGH TO TELL US WHO DID IT.

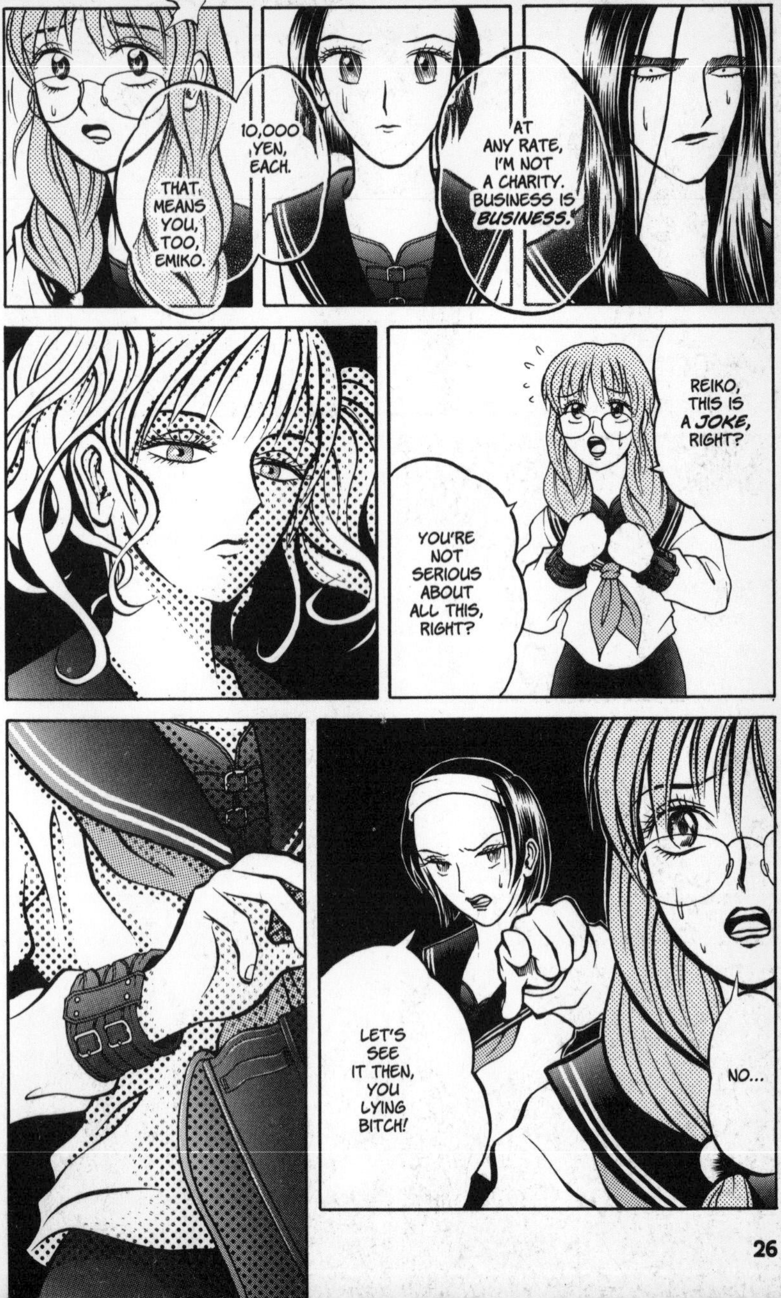
AT ANY RATE, I'M NOT A CHARITY. BUSINESS IS *BUSINESS.*
10,000 YEN, EACH.
THAT MEANS YOU, TOO, EMIKO.
REIKO, THIS IS A *JOKE,* RIGHT?
YOU'RE NOT SERIOUS ABOUT ALL THIS, RIGHT?
LET'S SEE IT THEN, YOU LYING BITCH!
NO...

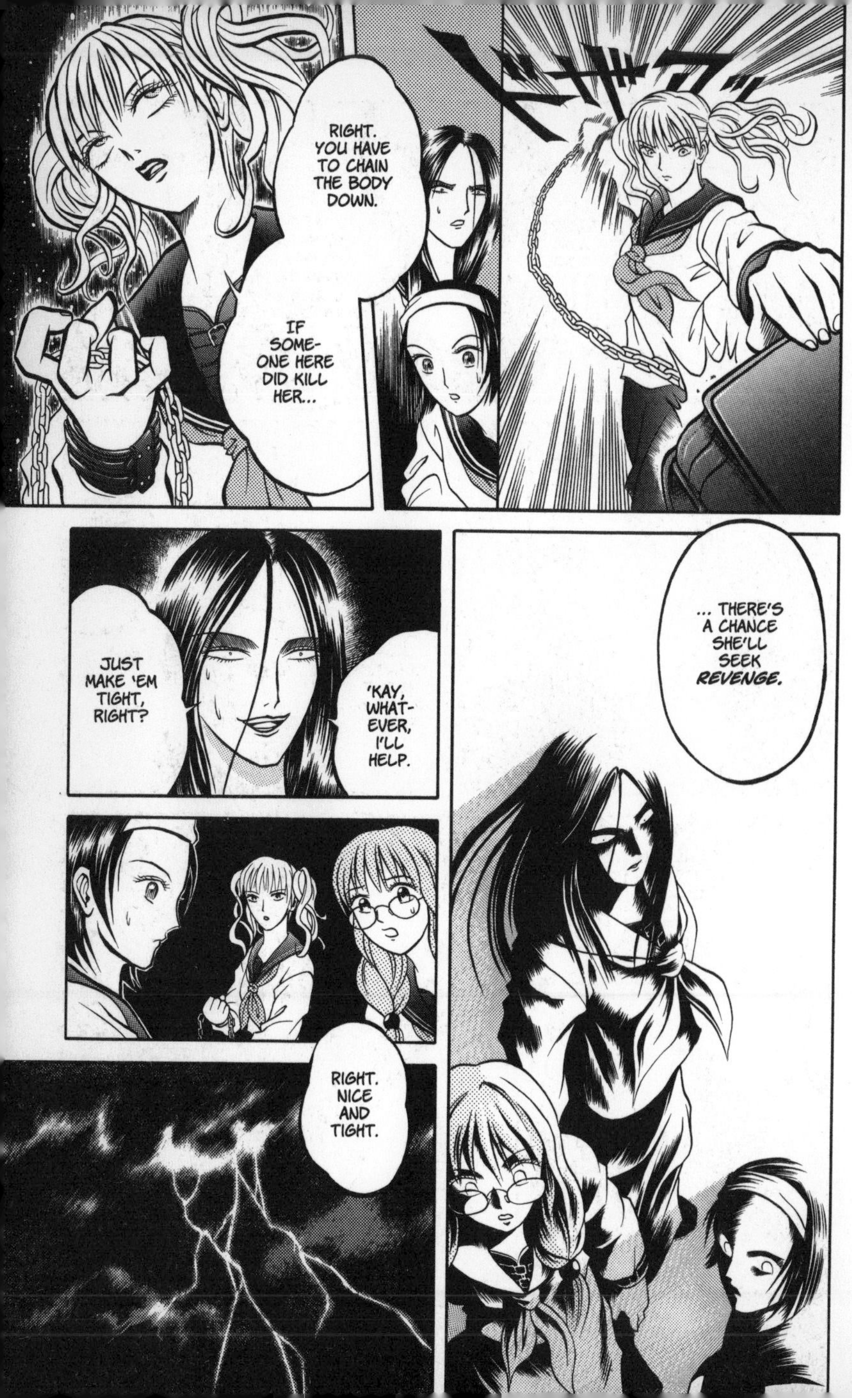
RIGHT. YOU HAVE TO CHAIN THE BODY DOWN.
IF SOME-ONE HERE DID KILL HER...
... THERE'S A CHANCE SHE'LL SEEK *REVENGE.*
'KAY, WHAT-EVER, I'LL HELP.
JUST MAKE 'EM TIGHT, RIGHT?
RIGHT. NICE AND TIGHT.

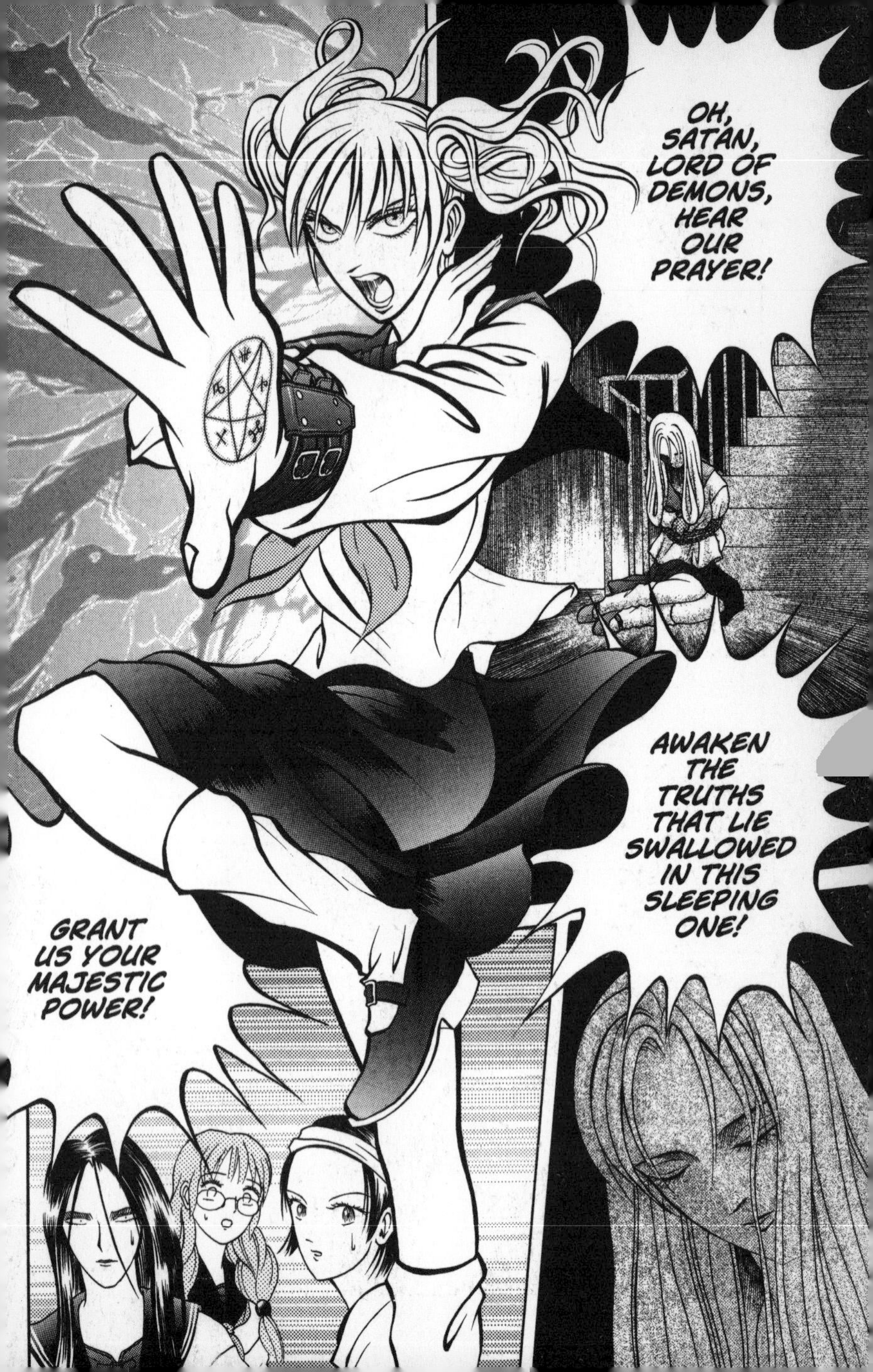
OH, SATAN, LORD OF DEMONS, HEAR OUR PRAYER!
AWAKEN THE TRUTHS THAT LIE SWALLOWED IN THIS SLEEPING ONE!
GRANT US YOUR MAJESTIC POWER!

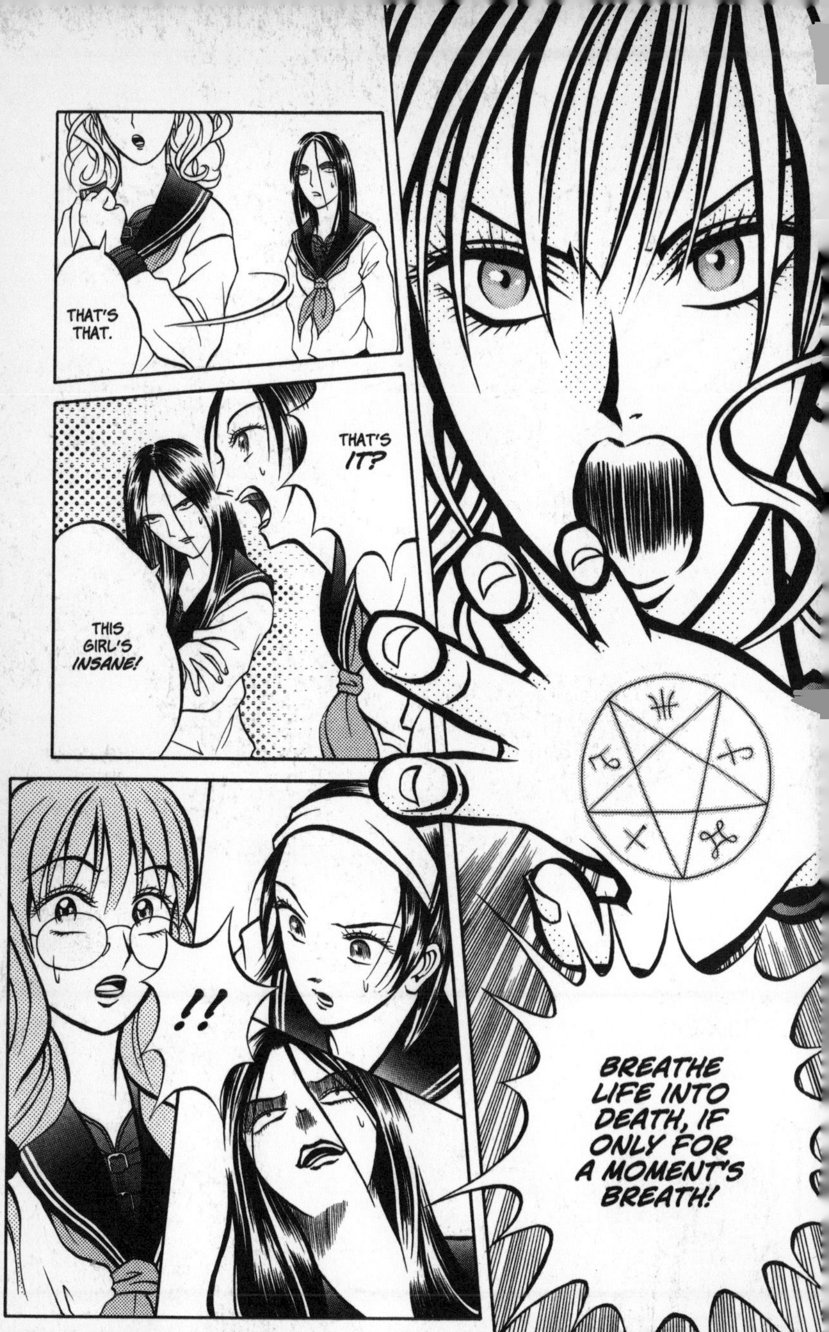
BREATHE LIFE INTO DEATH, IF ONLY FOR A MOMENT'S BREATH!
THAT'S THAT.
THAT'S *IT?*
THIS GIRL'S *INSANE!*
!!

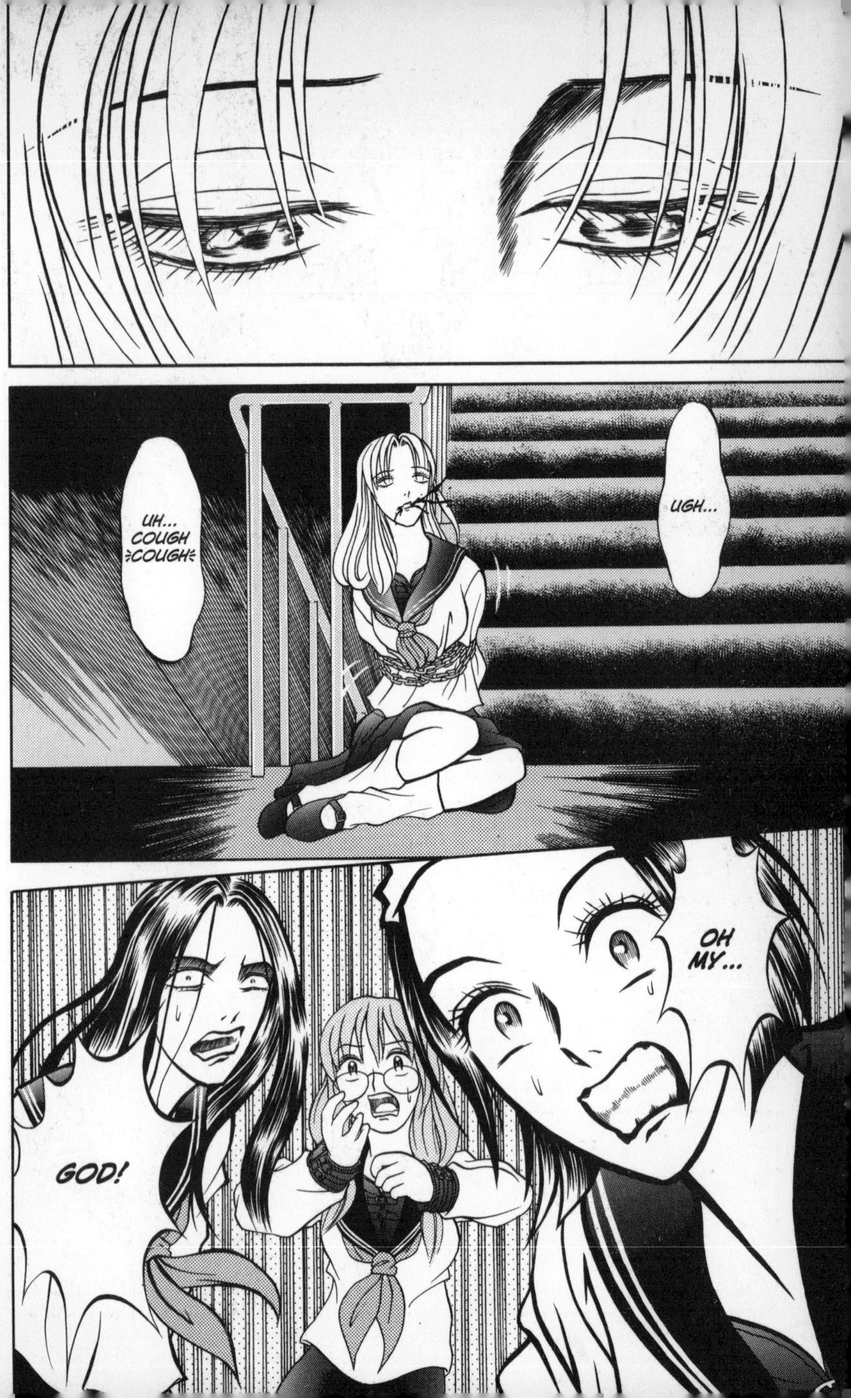
UGH...
UH... COUGH ≈COUGH≈
OH MY...
GOD!

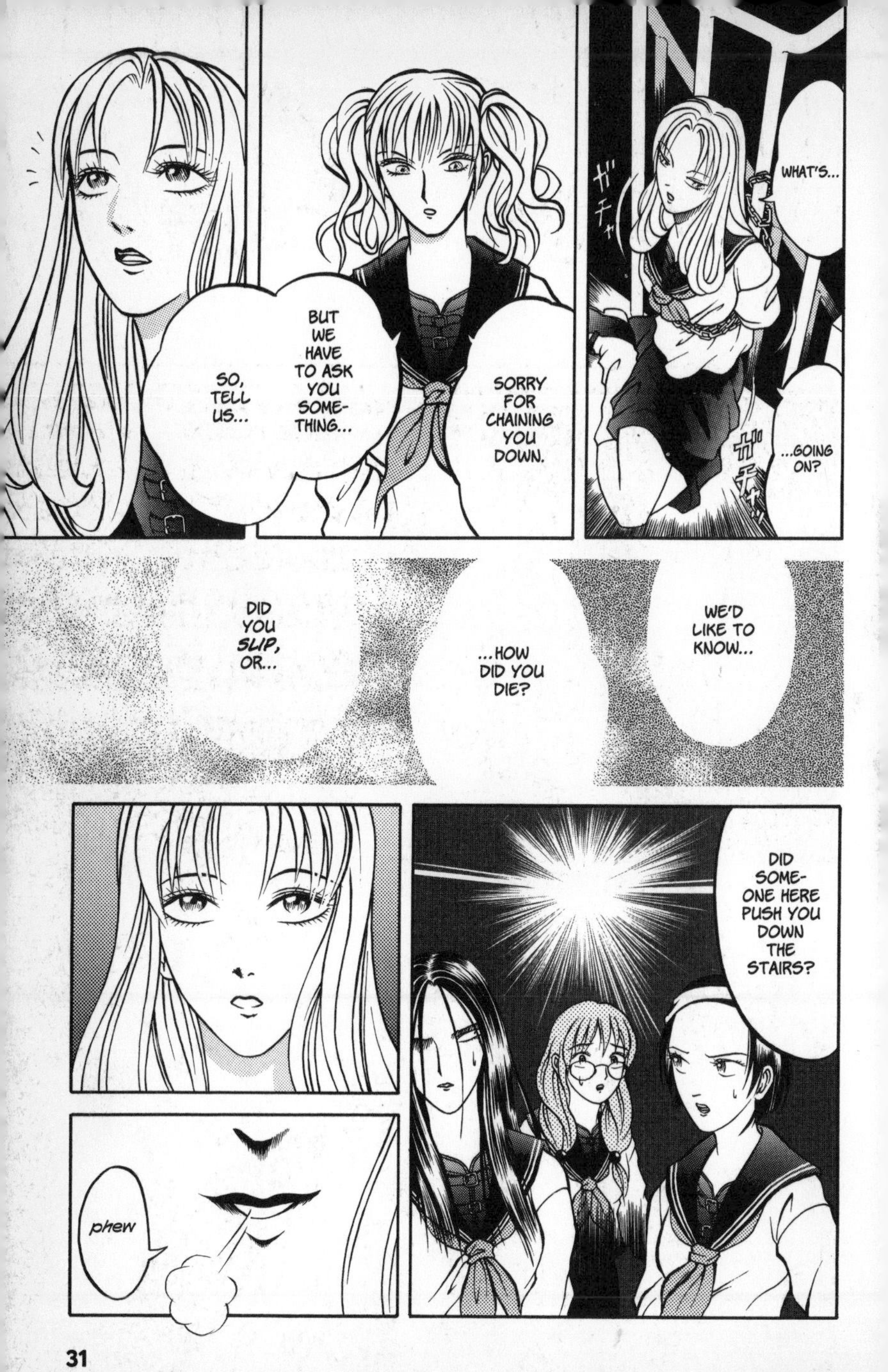
WHAT'S...
ガチャ
ガチャ
...GOING ON?
SORRY FOR CHAINING YOU DOWN.
BUT WE HAVE TO ASK YOU SOME-THING...
SO, TELL US...
WE'D LIKE TO KNOW...
...HOW DID YOU DIE?
DID YOU *SLIP*, OR...
DID SOME-ONE HERE PUSH YOU DOWN THE STAIRS?
*phew*

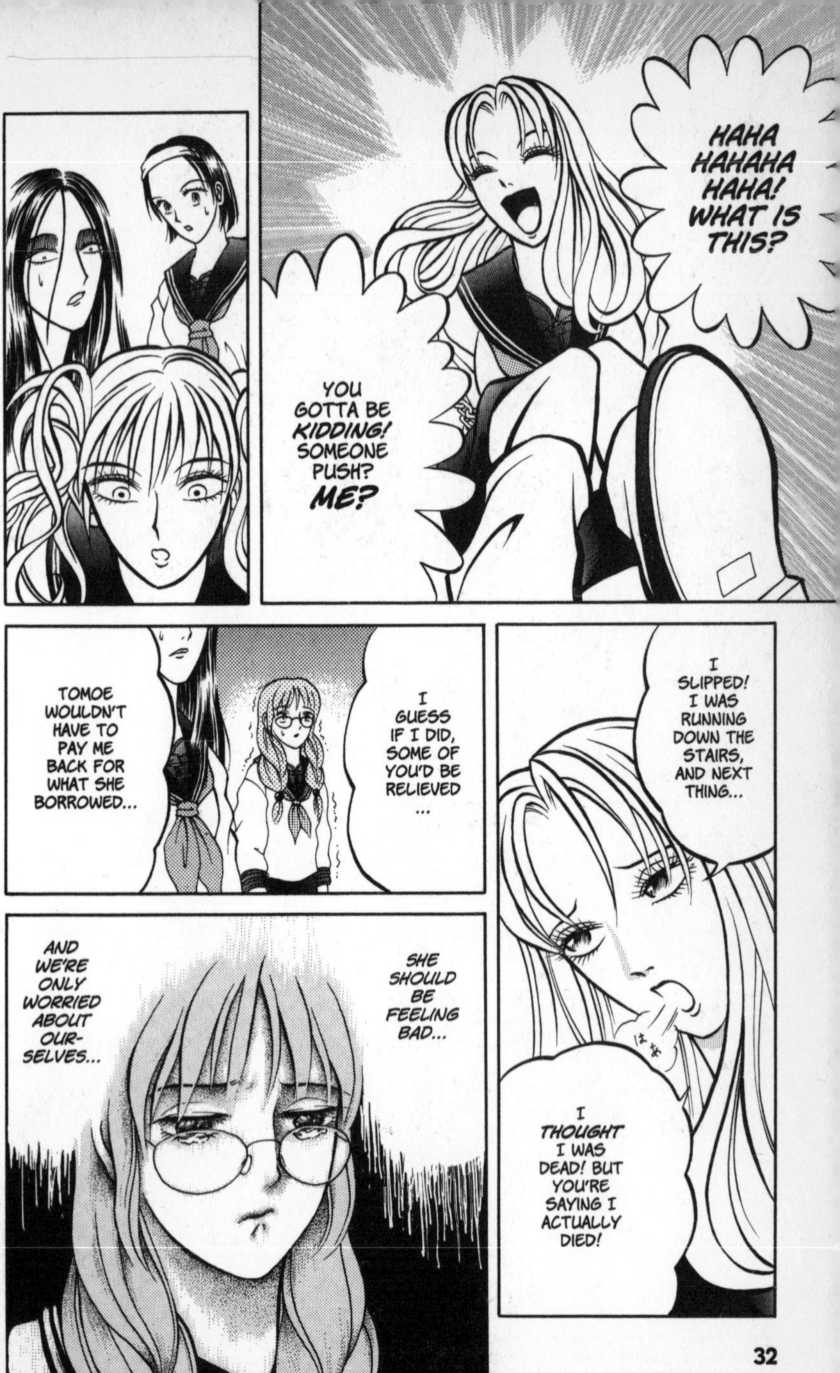
HAHA HAHAHA HAHA! WHAT IS THIS?
YOU GOTTA BE *KIDDING!* SOMEONE PUSH? ***ME?***
I SLIPPED! I WAS RUNNING DOWN THE STAIRS, AND NEXT THING...
I *THOUGHT* I WAS DEAD! BUT YOU'RE SAYING I ACTUALLY DIED!
I GUESS IF I DID, SOME OF YOU'D BE RELIEVED ...
TOMOE WOULDN'T HAVE TO PAY ME BACK FOR WHAT SHE BORROWED...
*SHE SHOULD BE FEELING BAD...*
*AND WE'RE ONLY WORRIED ABOUT OUR-SELVES...*

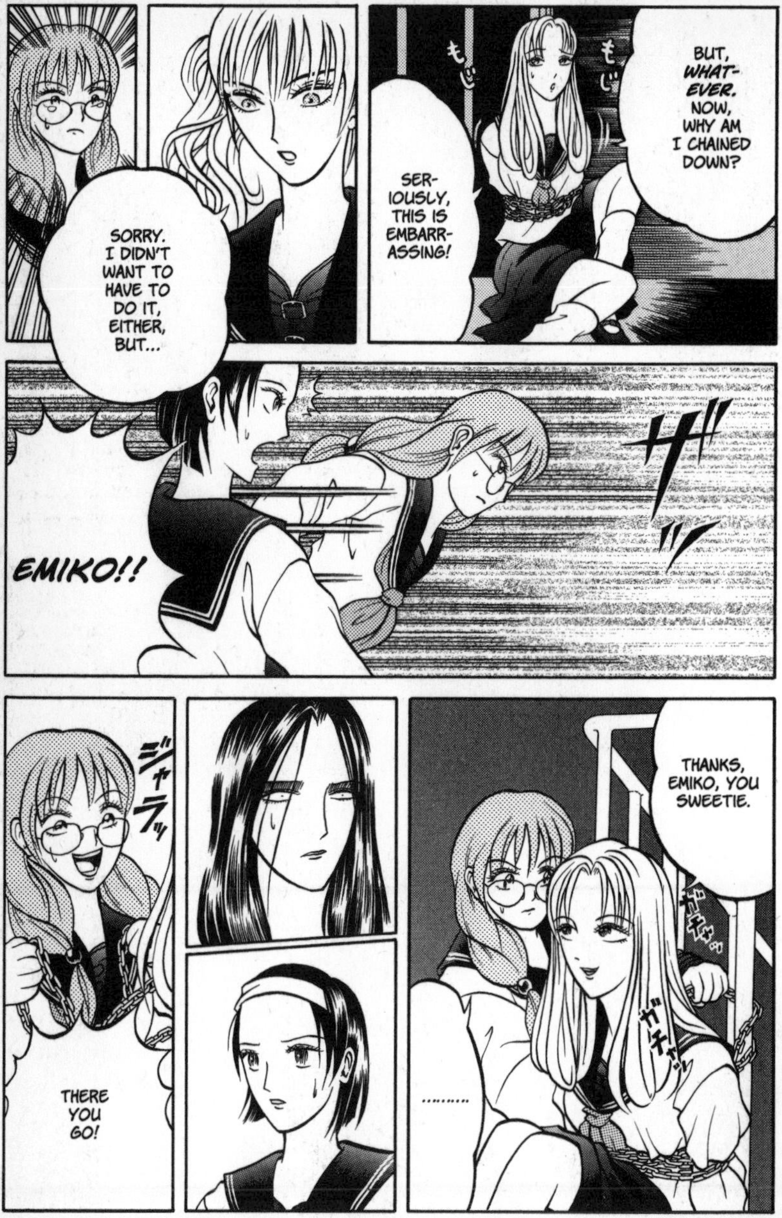
BUT, WHATEVER. NOW, WHY AM I CHAINED DOWN?
もじ
もじ
SERIOUSLY, THIS IS EMBARRASSING!
SORRY. I DIDN'T WANT TO HAVE TO DO IT, EITHER, BUT...
ザザッ
EMIKO!!
THANKS, EMIKO, YOU SWEETIE.
ガチャッ
.........
ジャラッ
THERE YOU GO!

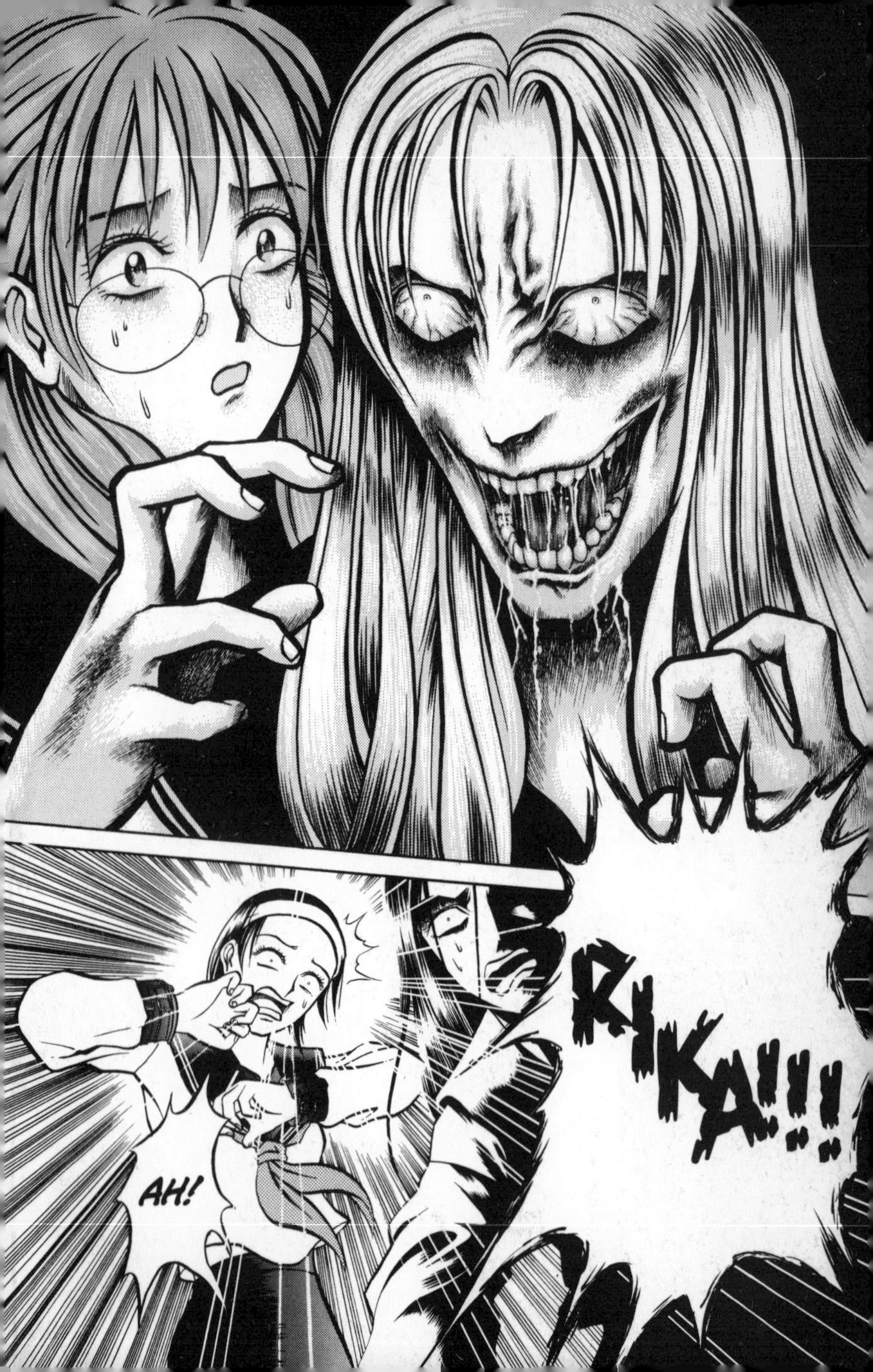
RIKA!!!
AH!

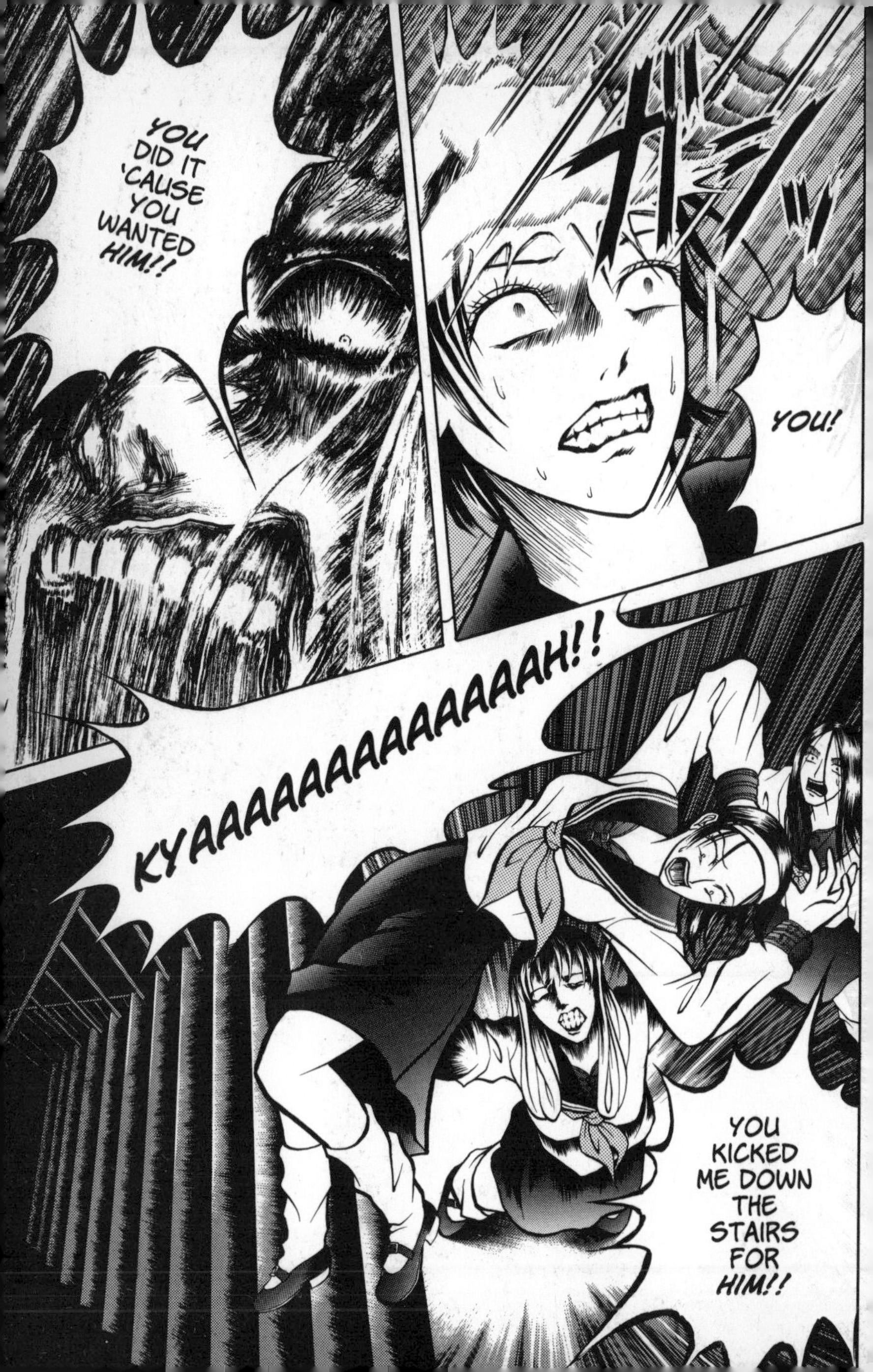
YOU!
YOU DID IT 'CAUSE YOU WANTED HIM!!
KYAAAAAAAAAAAAAH!!
YOU KICKED ME DOWN THE STAIRS FOR HIM!!

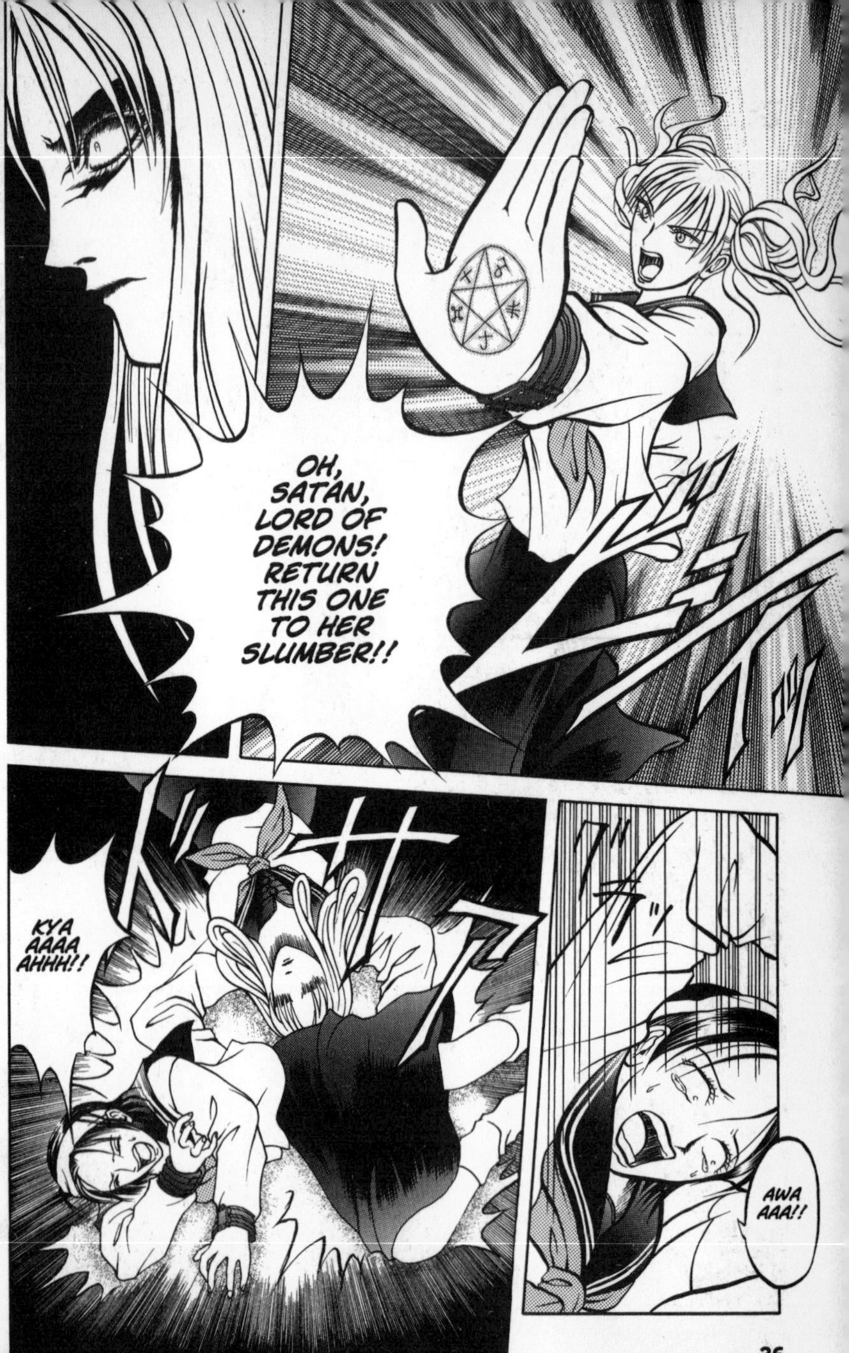
OH, SATAN, LORD OF DEMONS! RETURN THIS ONE TO HER SLUMBER!!
AWA AAA!!
KYA AAAA AHHH!!

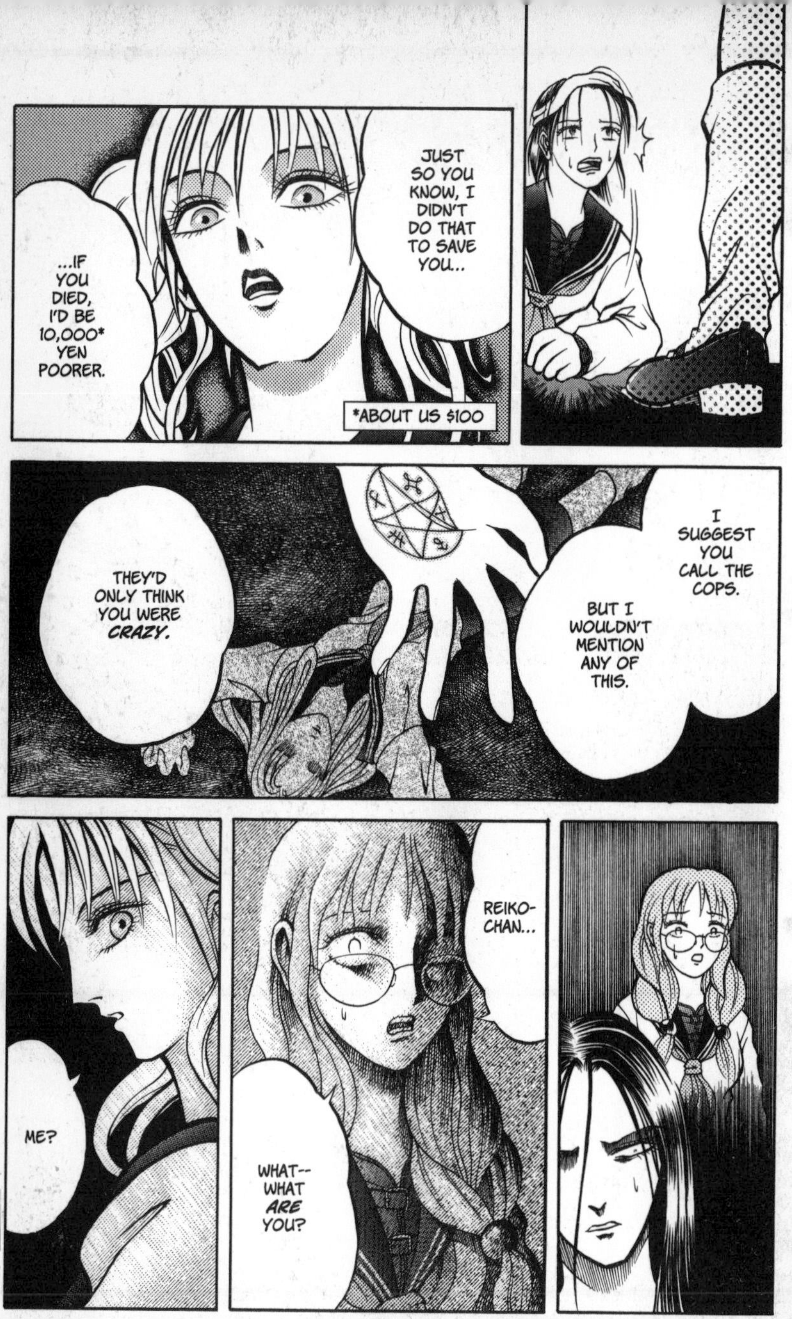
JUST SO YOU KNOW, I DIDN'T DO THAT TO SAVE YOU...
...IF YOU DIED, I'D BE 10,000* YEN POORER.
*ABOUT US $100
I SUGGEST YOU CALL THE COPS.
BUT I WOULDN'T MENTION ANY OF THIS.
THEY'D ONLY THINK YOU WERE *CRAZY.*
REIKO-CHAN...
WHAT--WHAT *ARE* YOU?
ME?

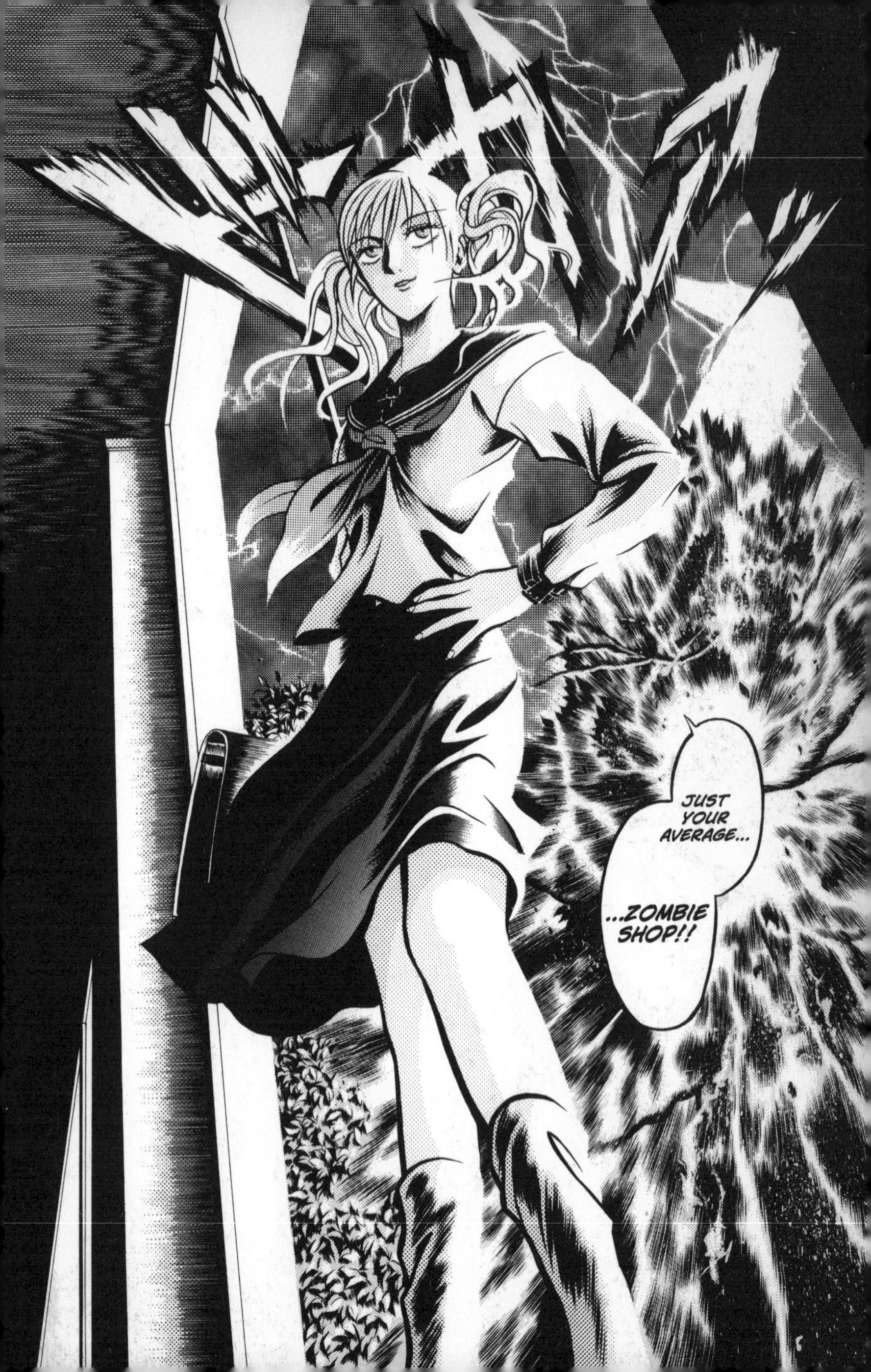
JUST YOUR AVERAGE...
...ZOMBIE SHOP!!

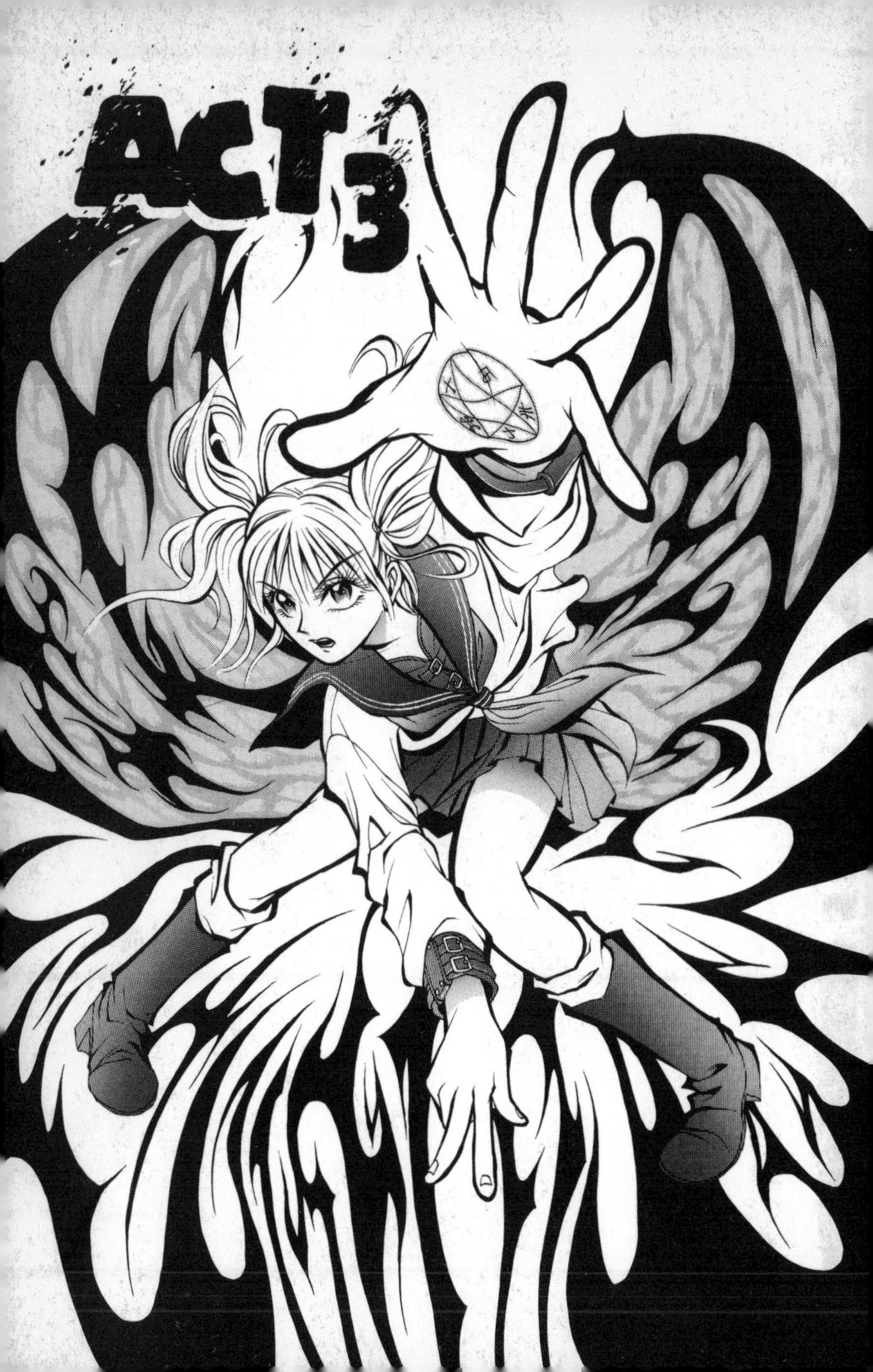
ACT 3

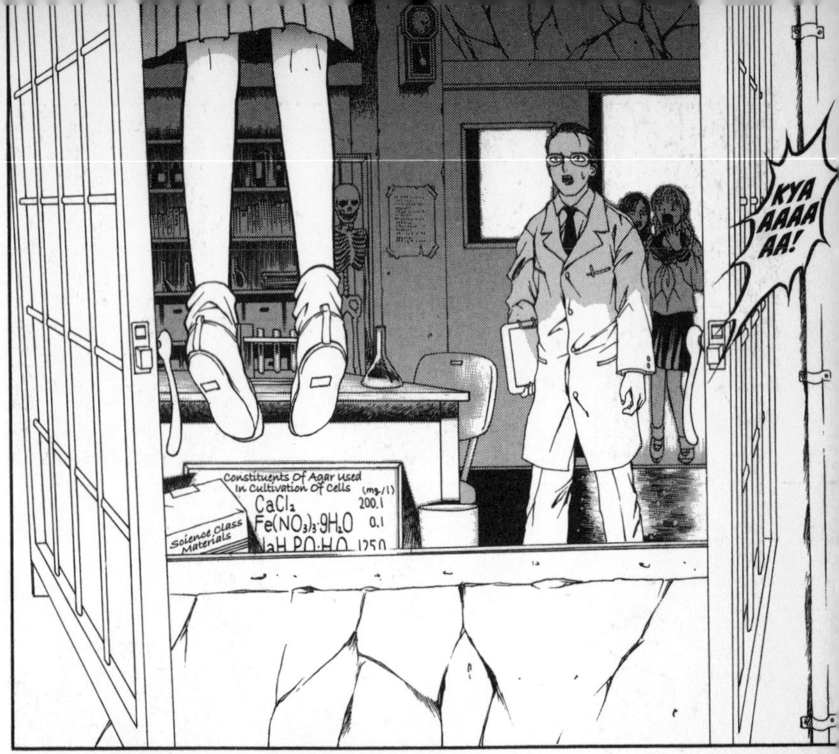
KYAAAAAAA!
Constituents Of Agar Used In Cultivation Of Cells (mg/l)
Science Class Materials

SHOWA ERA, YEAR 49

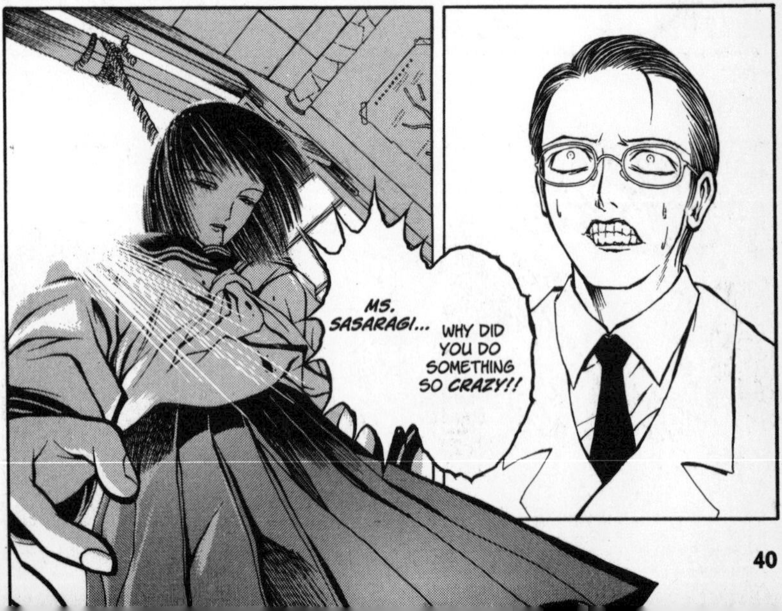
MS. SASARAGI... WHY DID YOU DO SOMETHING SO CRAZY!!

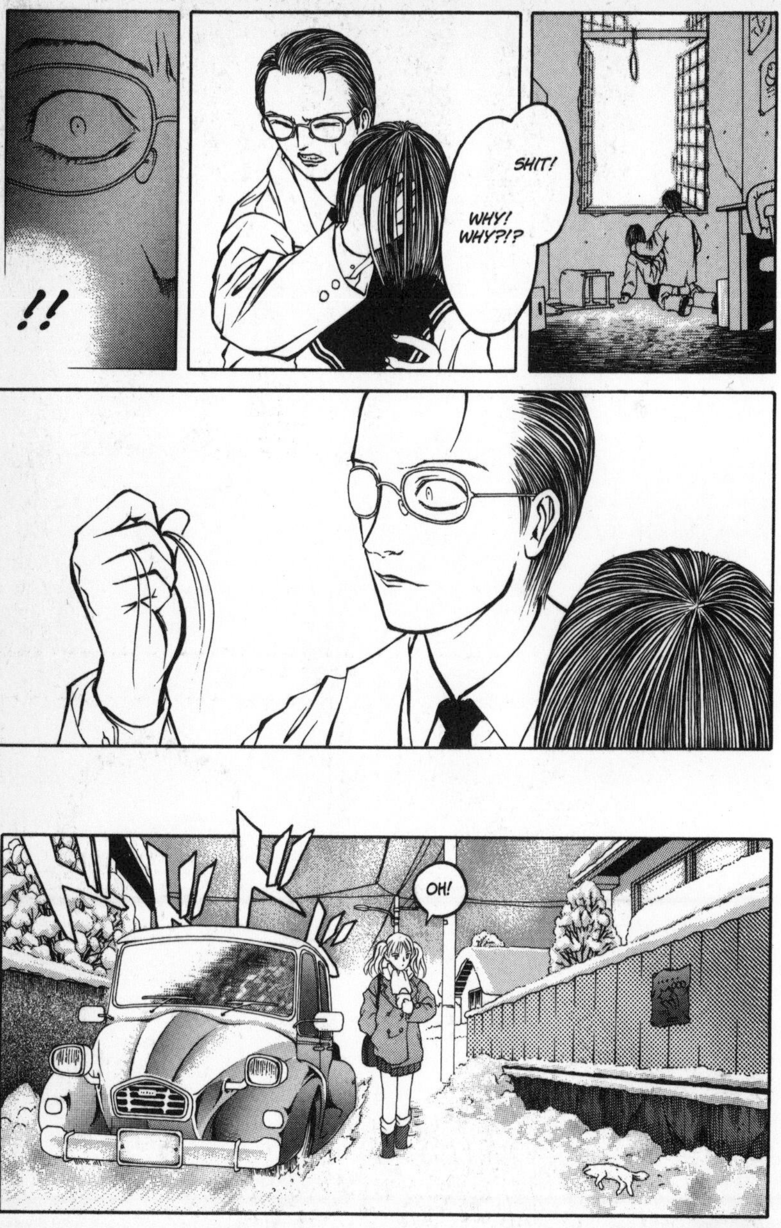
SHIT!
WHY! WHY?!?
!!
OH!

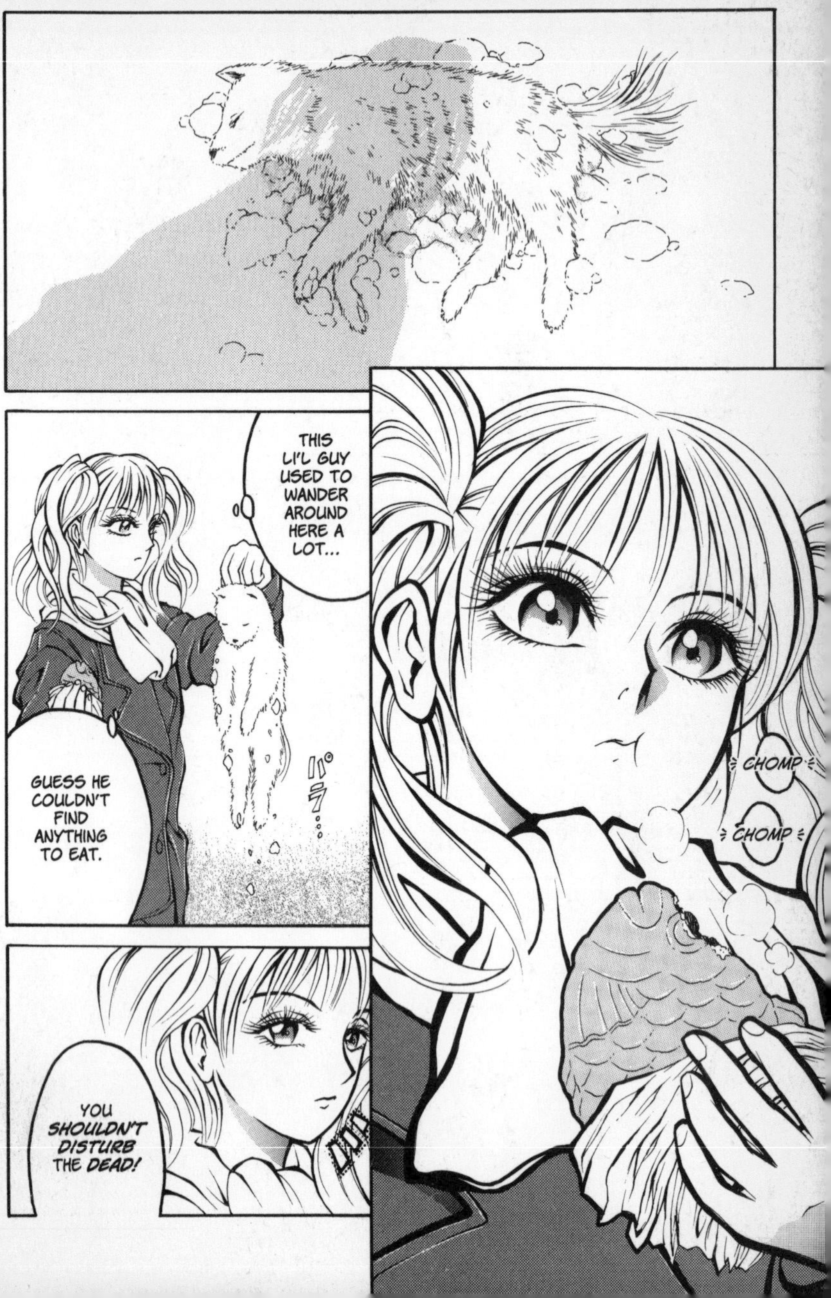
CHOMP
CHOMP
THIS LI'L GUY USED TO WANDER AROUND HERE A LOT...
GUESS HE COULDN'T FIND ANYTHING TO EAT.
YOU *SHOULDN'T DISTURB* THE *DEAD!*

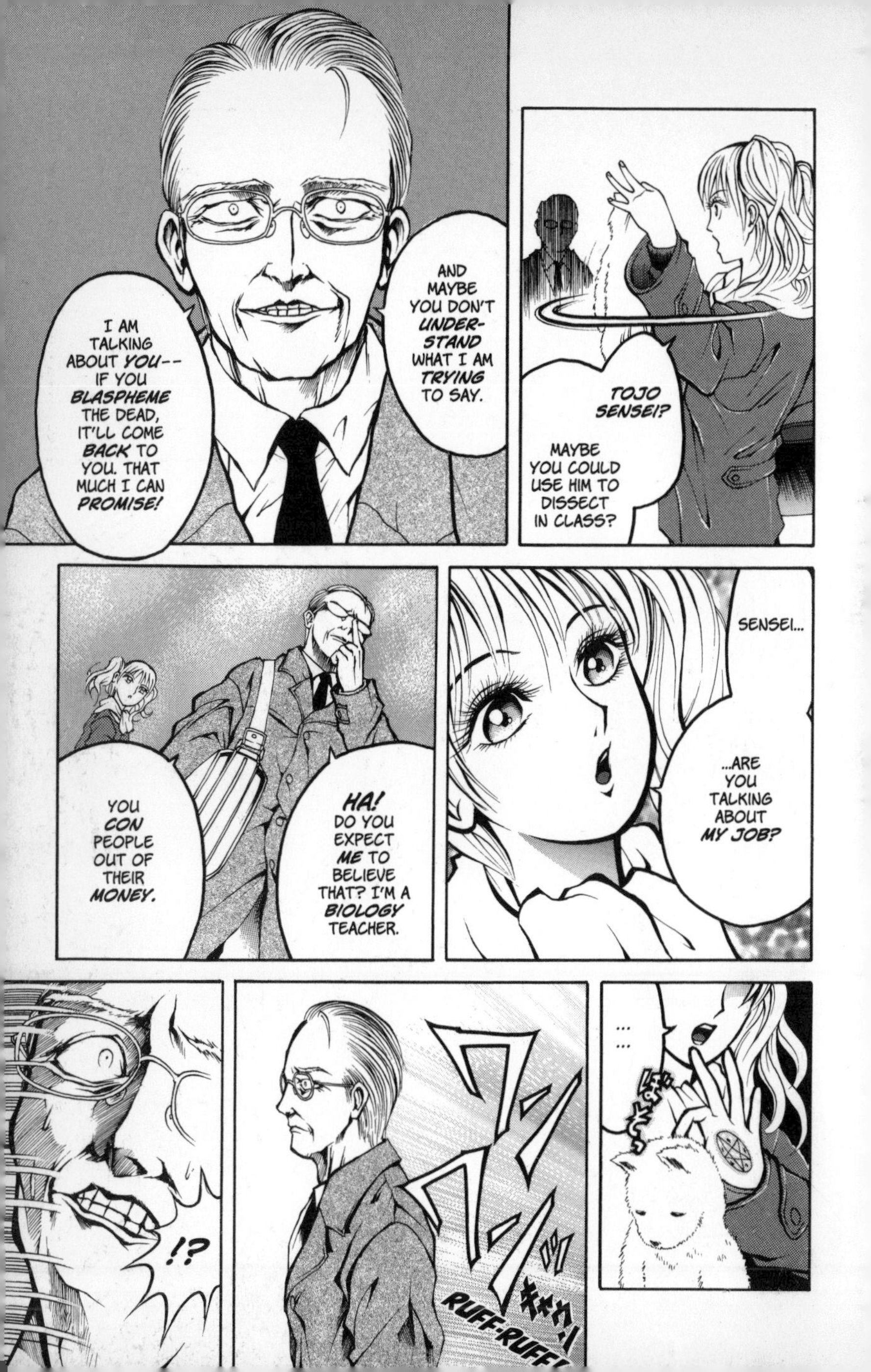
TOJO SENSEI?
MAYBE YOU COULD USE HIM TO DISSECT IN CLASS?
AND MAYBE YOU DON'T UNDERSTAND WHAT I AM TRYING TO SAY.
I AM TALKING ABOUT YOU-- IF YOU BLASPHEME THE DEAD, IT'LL COME BACK TO YOU. THAT MUCH I CAN PROMISE!
SENSEI...
...ARE YOU TALKING ABOUT MY JOB?
HA! DO YOU EXPECT ME TO BELIEVE THAT? I'M A BIOLOGY TEACHER.
YOU CON PEOPLE OUT OF THEIR MONEY.
...
...
RUFF-RUFF!
!?

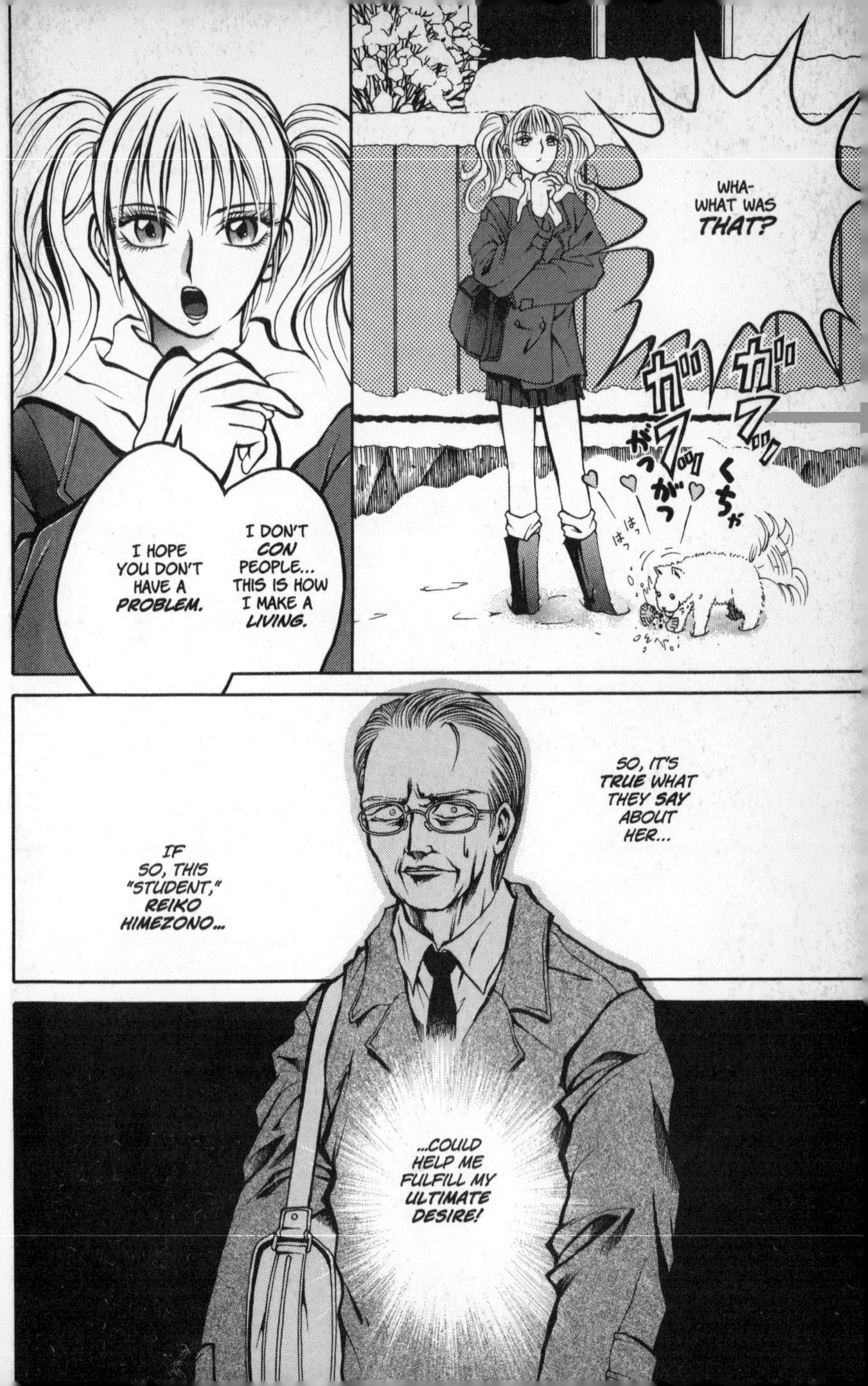
WHA- WHAT WAS THAT?
がっがっ
くちゃ
はっ はっ
I DON'T CON PEOPLE... THIS IS HOW I MAKE A LIVING.
I HOPE YOU DON'T HAVE A PROBLEM.
SO, IT'S TRUE WHAT THEY SAY ABOUT HER...
IF SO, THIS "STUDENT," REIKO HIMEZONO...
...COULD HELP ME FULFILL MY ULTIMATE DESIRE!

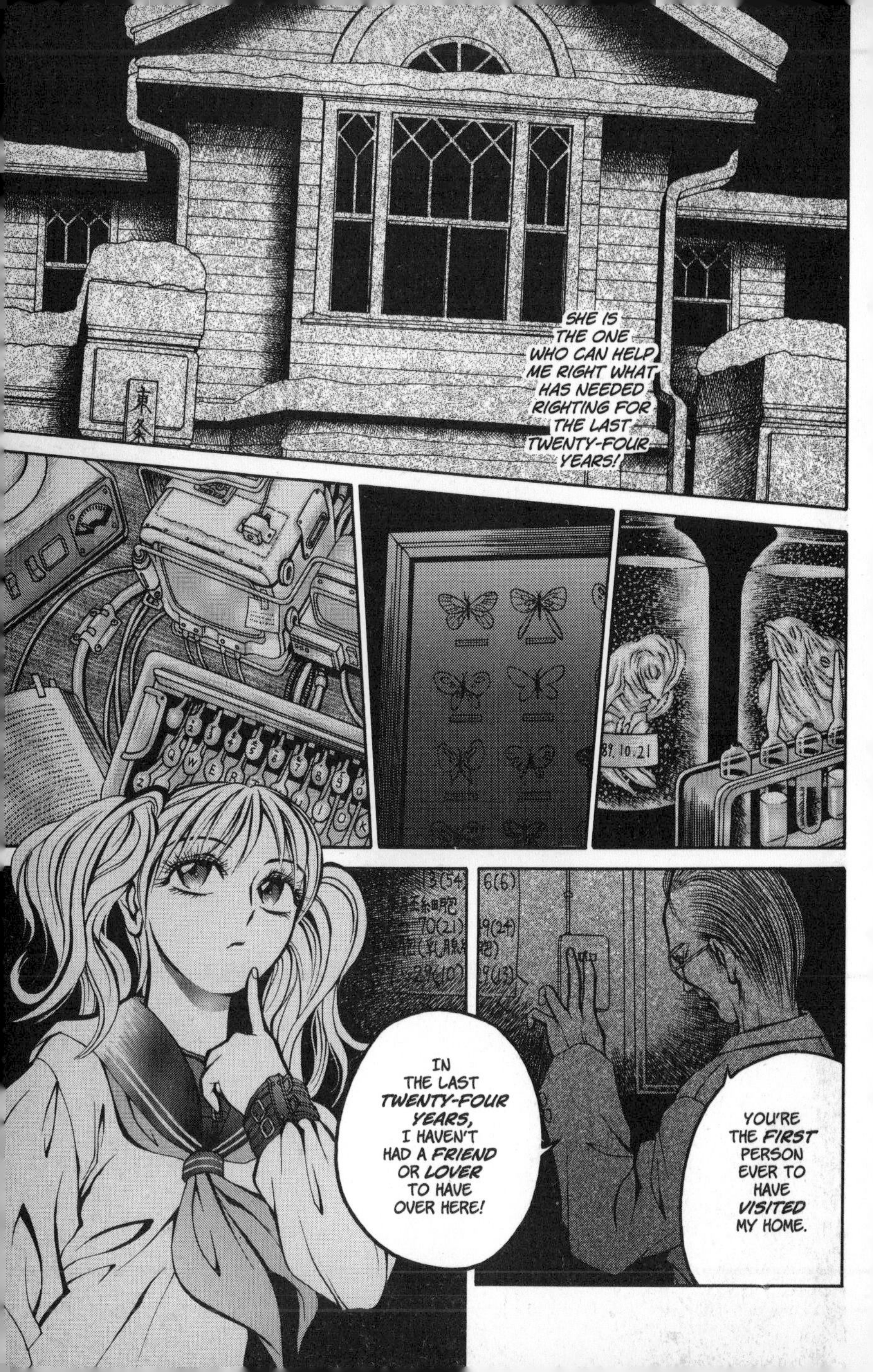
SHE IS THE ONE WHO CAN HELP ME RIGHT WHAT HAS NEEDED RIGHTING FOR THE LAST TWENTY-FOUR YEARS!
89.10.21
YOU'RE THE *FIRST* PERSON EVER TO HAVE *VISITED* MY HOME.
IN THE LAST *TWENTY-FOUR YEARS,* I HAVEN'T HAD A *FRIEND* OR *LOVER* TO HAVE OVER HERE!

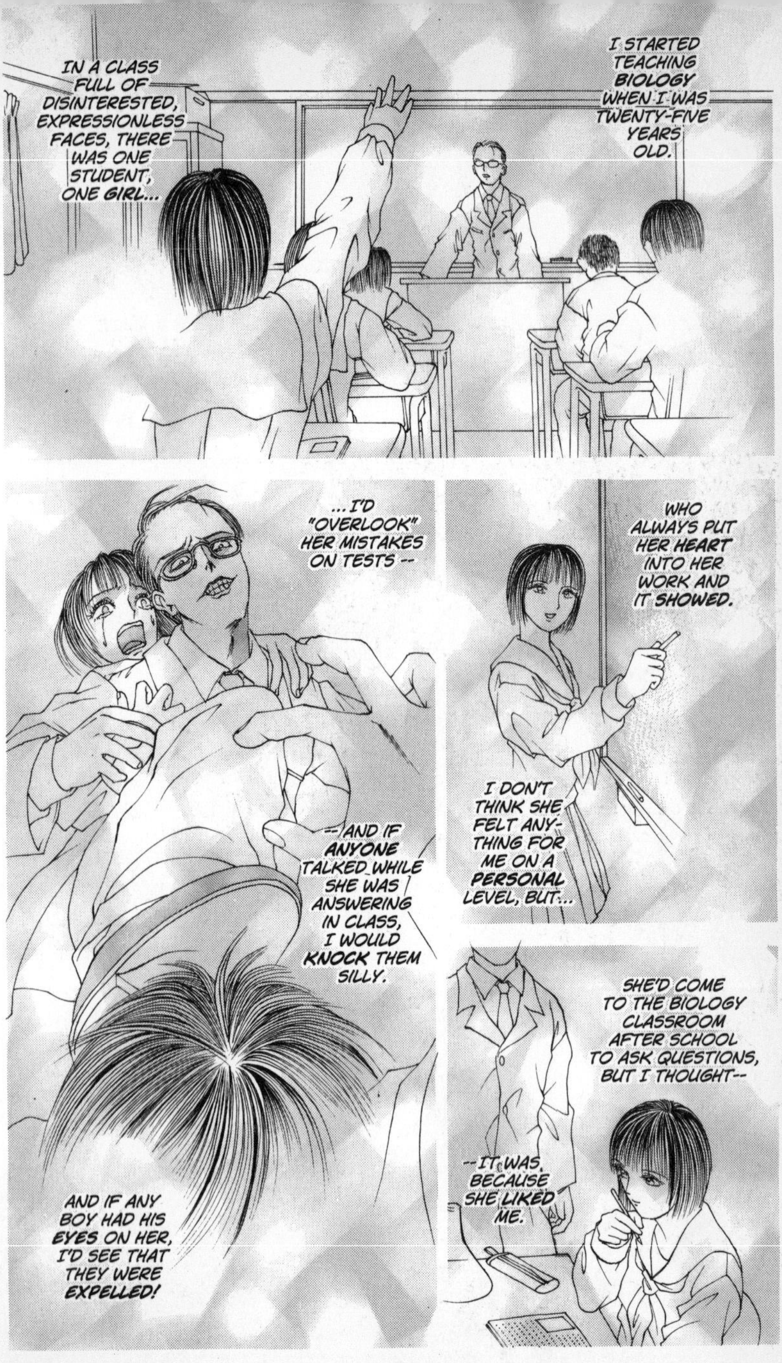
I STARTED TEACHING BIOLOGY WHEN I WAS TWENTY-FIVE YEARS OLD.
IN A CLASS FULL OF DISINTERESTED, EXPRESSIONLESS FACES, THERE WAS ONE STUDENT, ONE GIRL...
WHO ALWAYS PUT HER HEART INTO HER WORK AND IT SHOWED.
I DON'T THINK SHE FELT ANY-THING FOR ME ON A PERSONAL LEVEL, BUT...
SHE'D COME TO THE BIOLOGY CLASSROOM AFTER SCHOOL TO ASK QUESTIONS, BUT I THOUGHT--
--IT WAS BECAUSE SHE LIKED ME.
...I'D "OVERLOOK" HER MISTAKES ON TESTS --
-- AND IF ANYONE TALKED WHILE SHE WAS ANSWERING IN CLASS, I WOULD KNOCK THEM SILLY.
AND IF ANY BOY HAD HIS EYES ON HER, I'D SEE THAT THEY WERE EXPELLED!

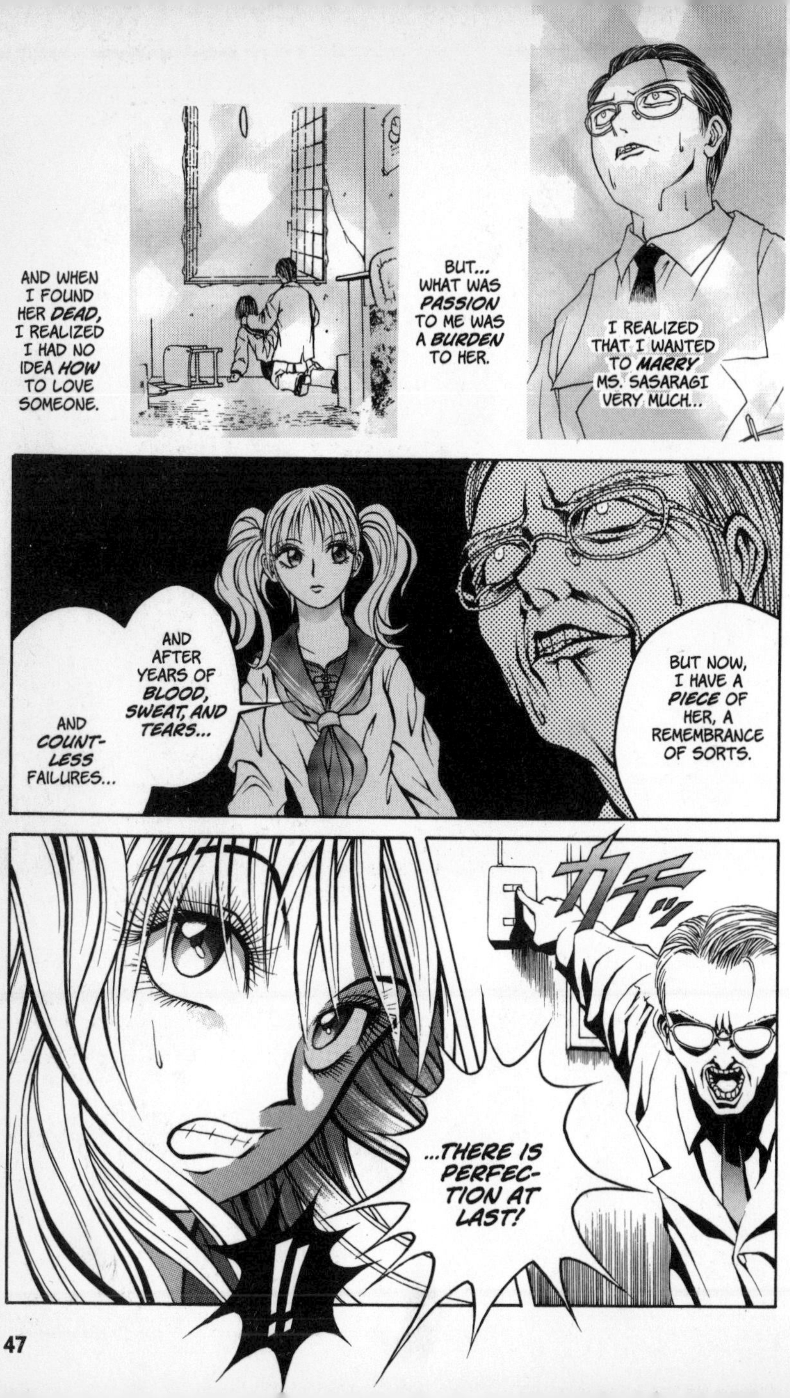
I REALIZED THAT I WANTED TO MARRY MS. SASARAGI VERY MUCH...
BUT... WHAT WAS PASSION TO ME WAS A BURDEN TO HER.
AND WHEN I FOUND HER DEAD, I REALIZED I HAD NO IDEA HOW TO LOVE SOMEONE.
BUT NOW, I HAVE A PIECE OF HER, A REMEMBRANCE OF SORTS.
AND AFTER YEARS OF BLOOD, SWEAT, AND TEARS...
AND COUNTLESS FAILURES...
カチッ
...THERE IS PERFECTION AT LAST!
!!

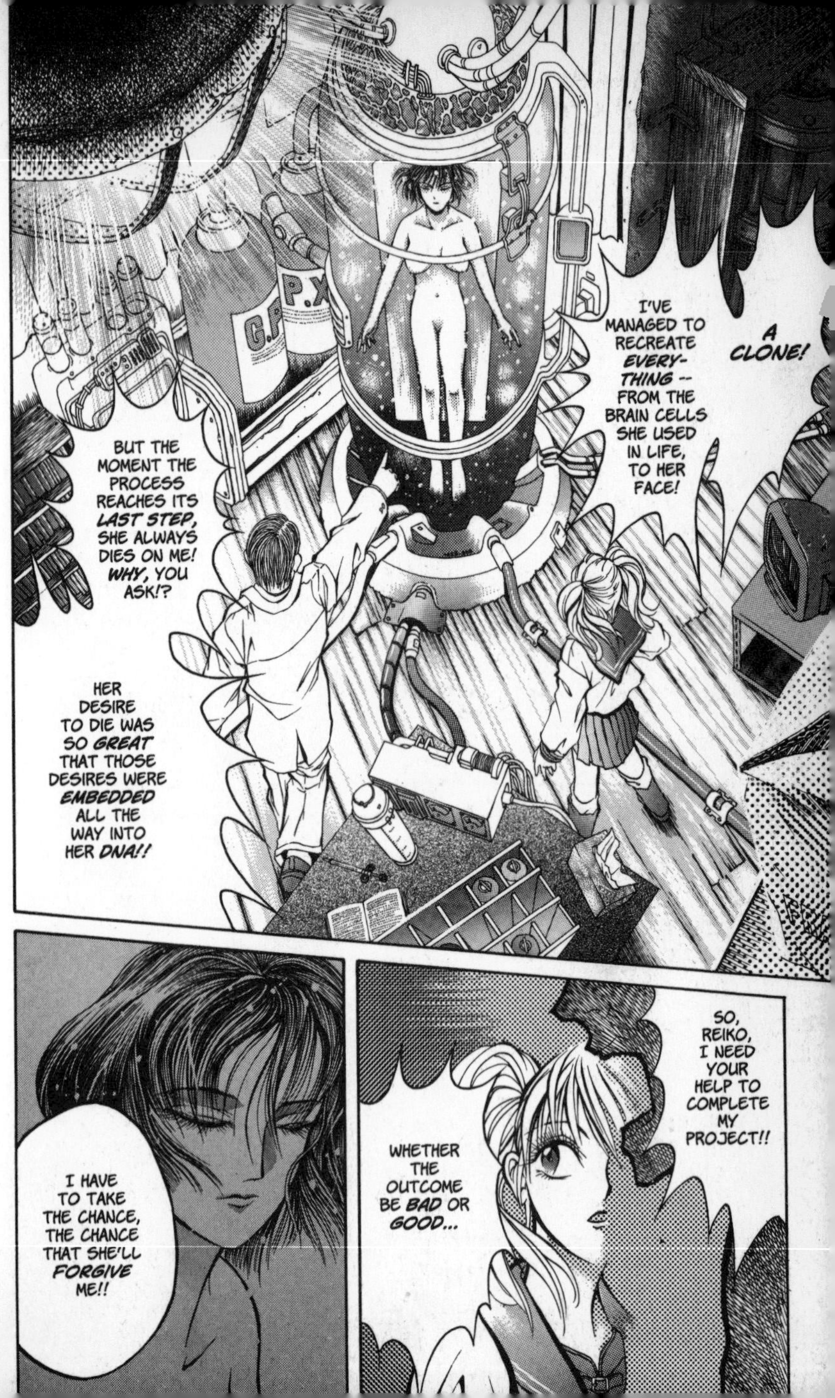
A CLONE!
I'VE MANAGED TO RECREATE EVERYTHING -- FROM THE BRAIN CELLS SHE USED IN LIFE, TO HER FACE!
BUT THE MOMENT THE PROCESS REACHES ITS LAST STEP, SHE ALWAYS DIES ON ME! WHY, YOU ASK!?
HER DESIRE TO DIE WAS SO GREAT THAT THOSE DESIRES WERE EMBEDDED ALL THE WAY INTO HER DNA!!
SO, REIKO, I NEED YOUR HELP TO COMPLETE MY PROJECT!!
WHETHER THE OUTCOME BE BAD OR GOOD...
I HAVE TO TAKE THE CHANCE, THE CHANCE THAT SHE'LL FORGIVE ME!!

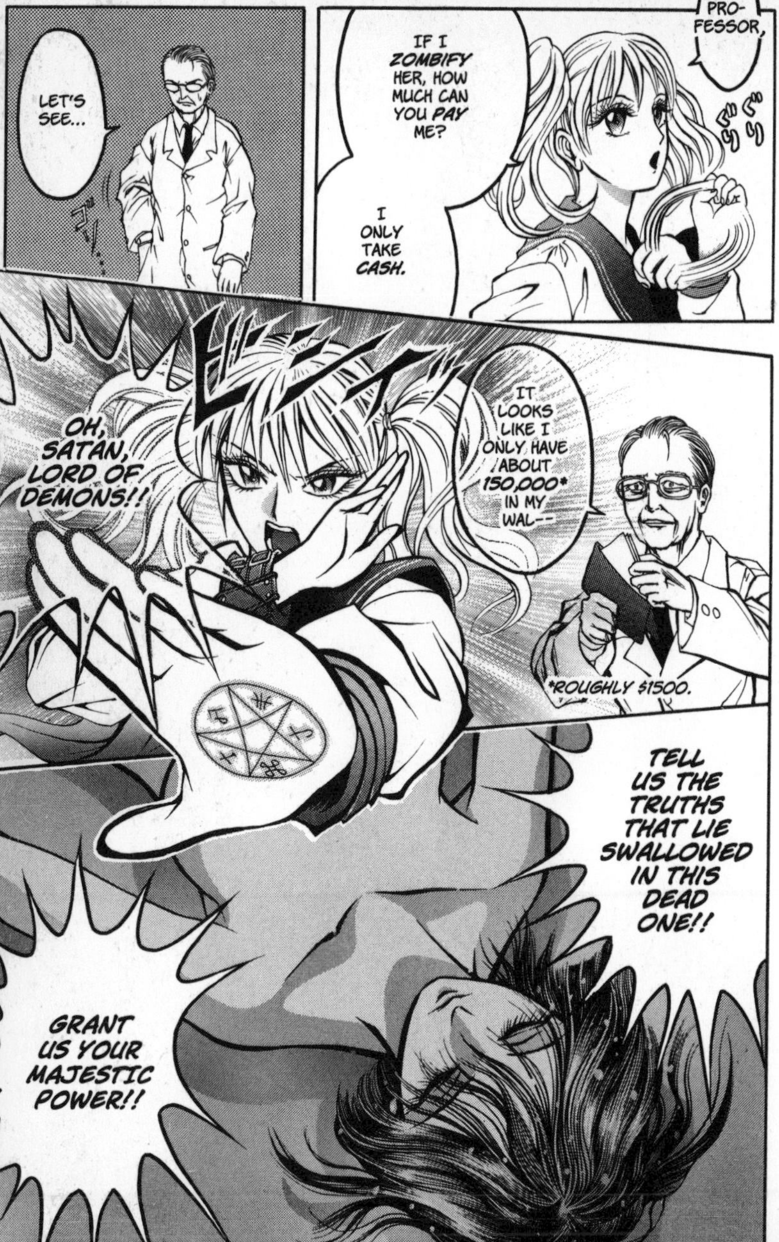
PRO-FESSOR,
IF I ZOMBIFY HER, HOW MUCH CAN YOU PAY ME?
I ONLY TAKE CASH.
LET'S SEE...
IT LOOKS LIKE I ONLY HAVE ABOUT 150,000* IN MY WAL--
*ROUGHLY $1500.
OH, SATAN, LORD OF DEMONS!!
TELL US THE TRUTHS THAT LIE SWALLOWED IN THIS DEAD ONE!!
GRANT US YOUR MAJESTIC POWER!!

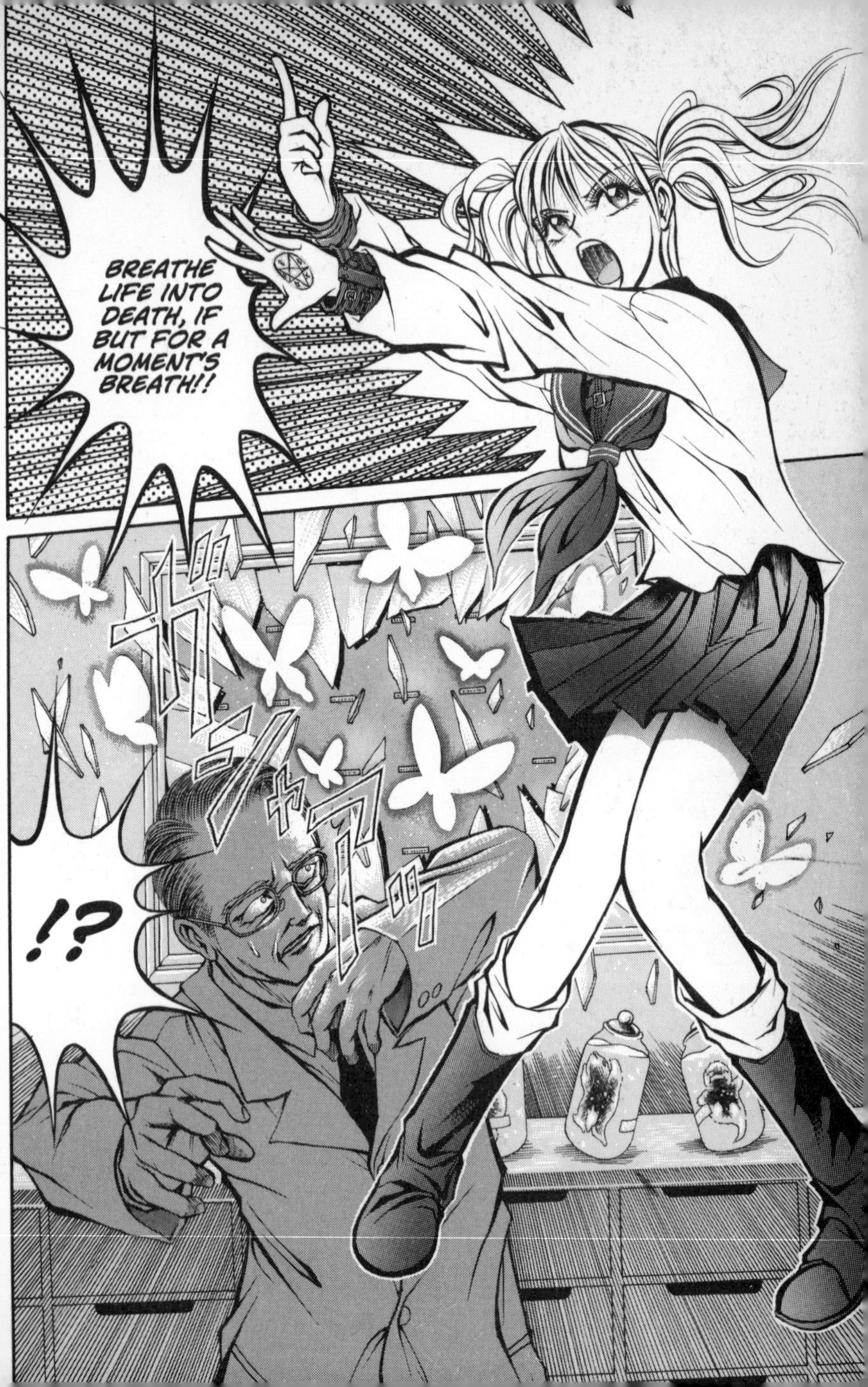
BREATHE LIFE INTO DEATH, IF BUT FOR A MOMENT'S BREATH!!
!?

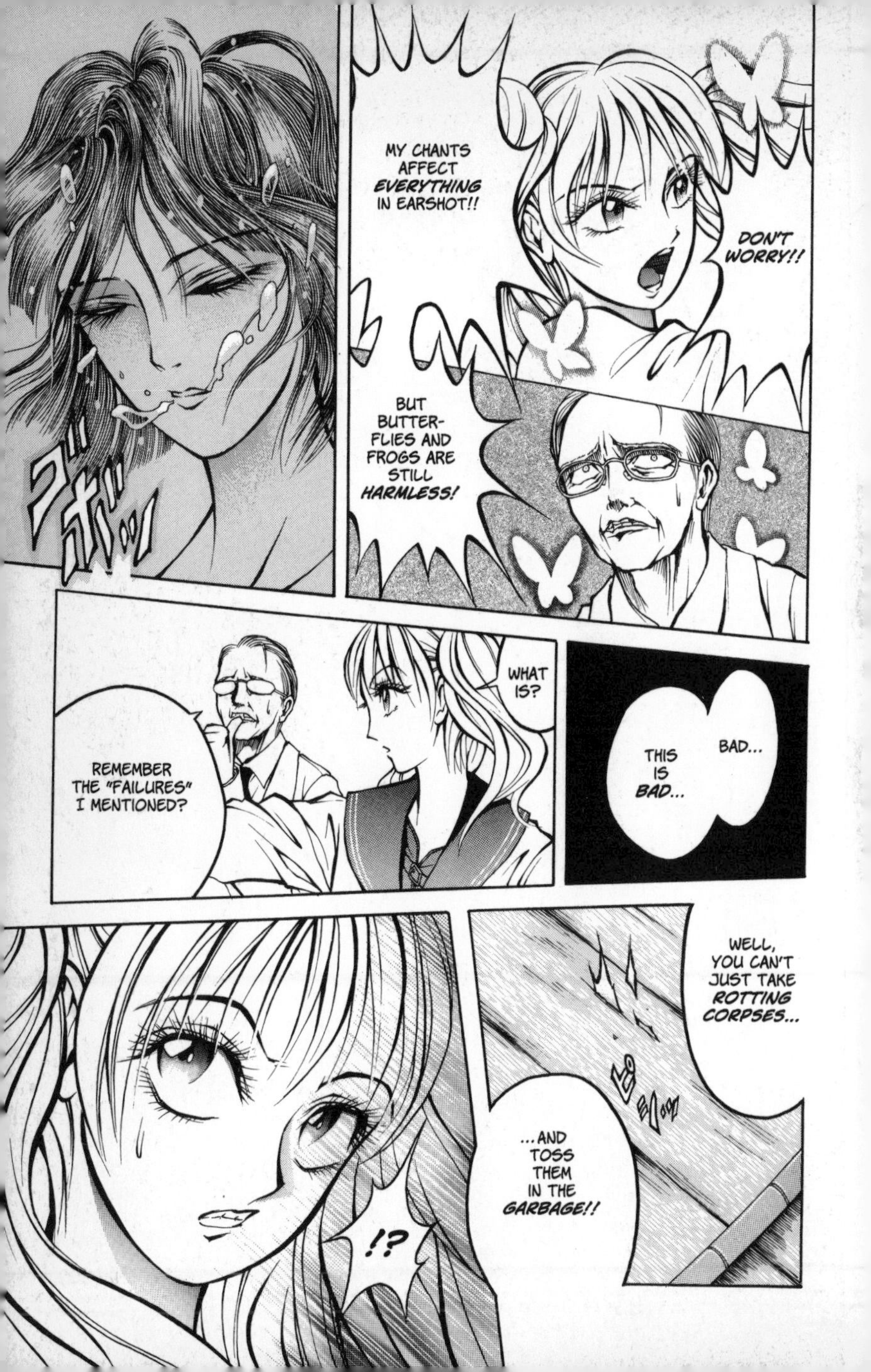
DON'T WORRY!!
MY CHANTS AFFECT EVERYTHING IN EARSHOT!!
BUT BUTTER-FLIES AND FROGS ARE STILL HARMLESS!
BAD...
THIS IS BAD...
WHAT IS?
REMEMBER THE "FAILURES" I MENTIONED?
WELL, YOU CAN'T JUST TAKE ROTTING CORPSES...
...AND TOSS THEM IN THE GARBAGE!!
!?

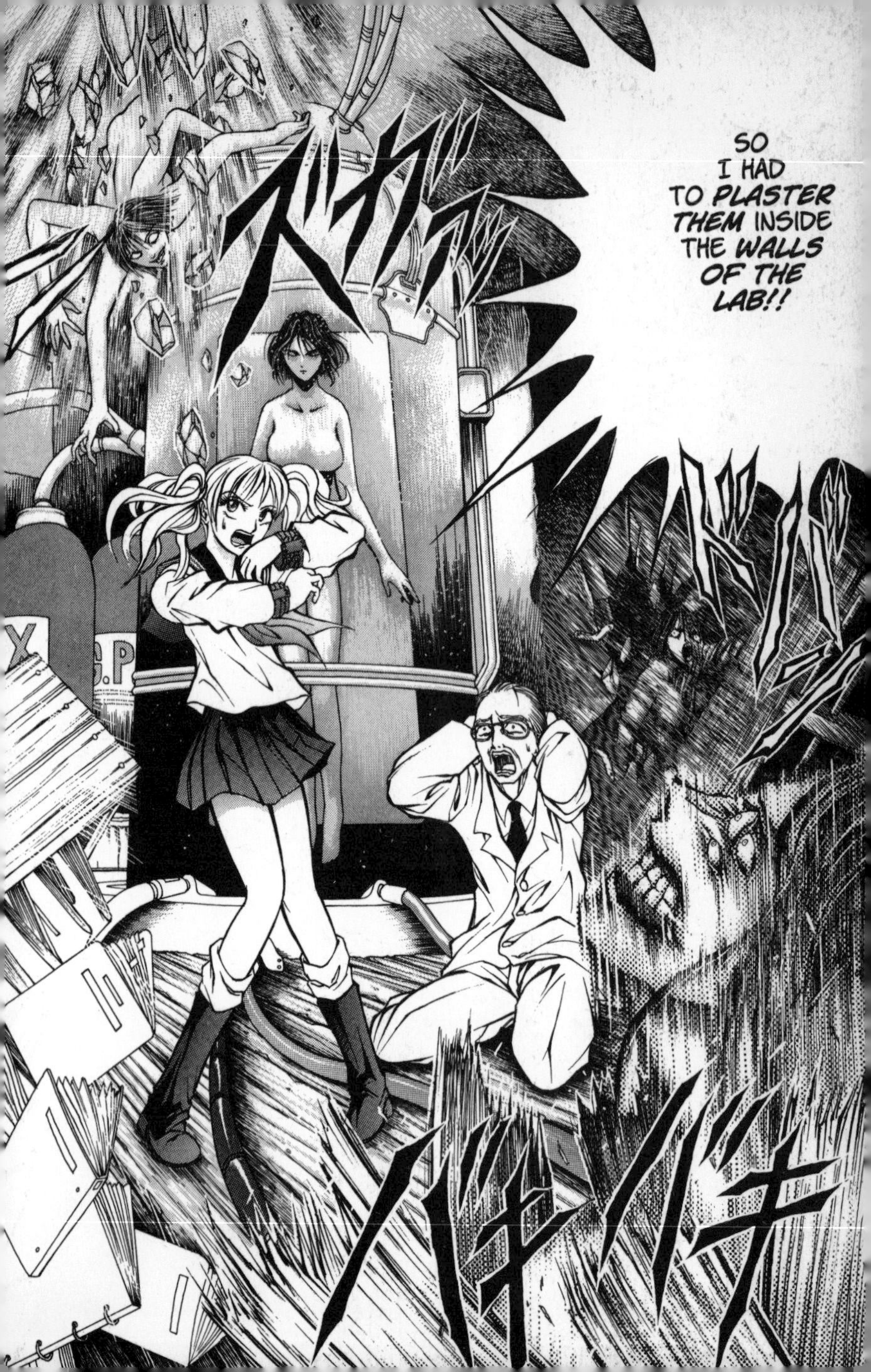
SO I HAD TO PLASTER THEM INSIDE THE WALLS OF THE LAB!!

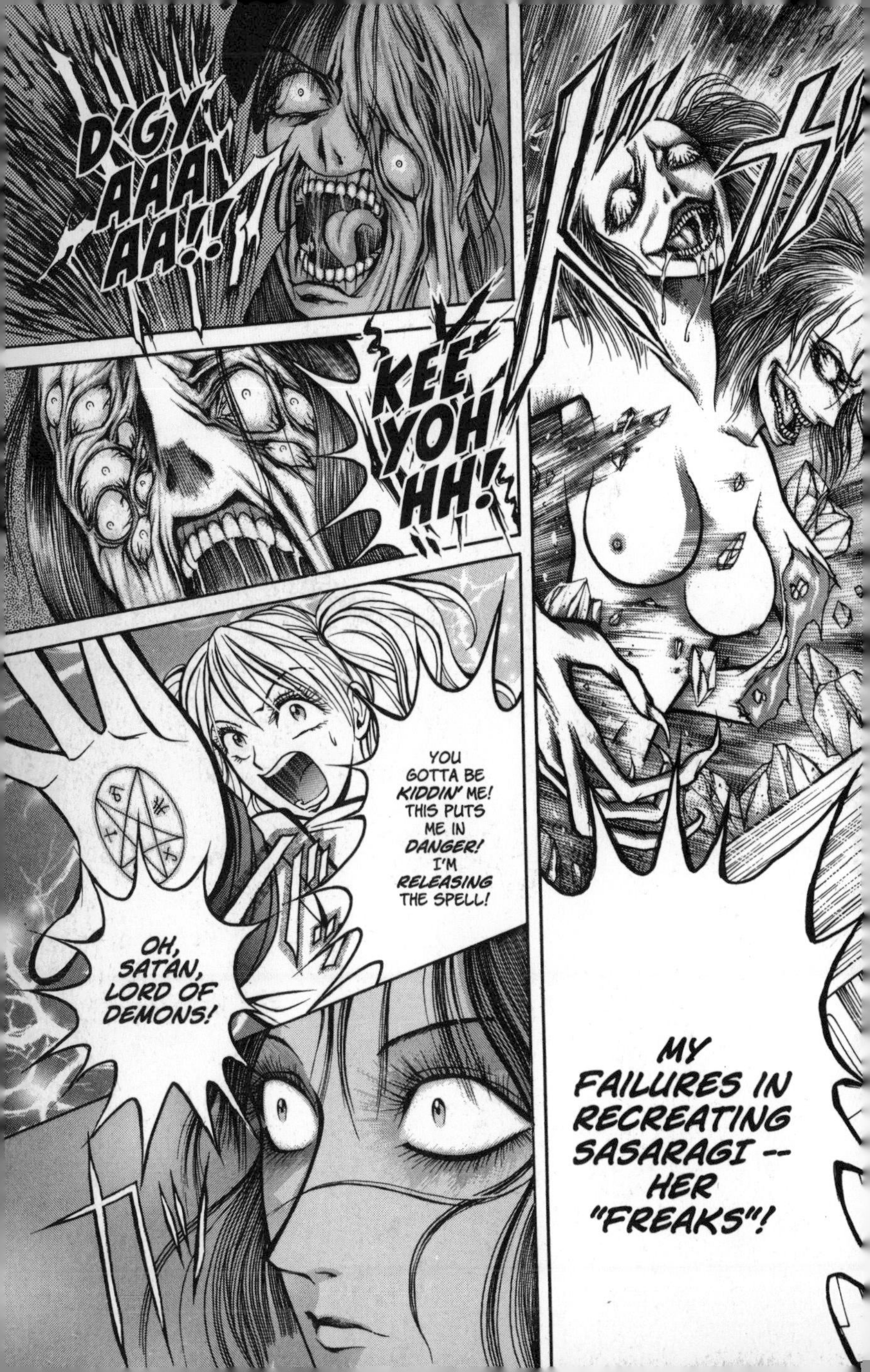
MY FAILURES IN RECREATING SASARAGI -- HER "FREAKS"!
D-GYAAAAA!!
KEEYOHHH!
YOU GOTTA BE KIDDIN' ME! THIS PUTS ME IN DANGER! I'M RELEASING THE SPELL!
OH, SATAN, LORD OF DEMONS!

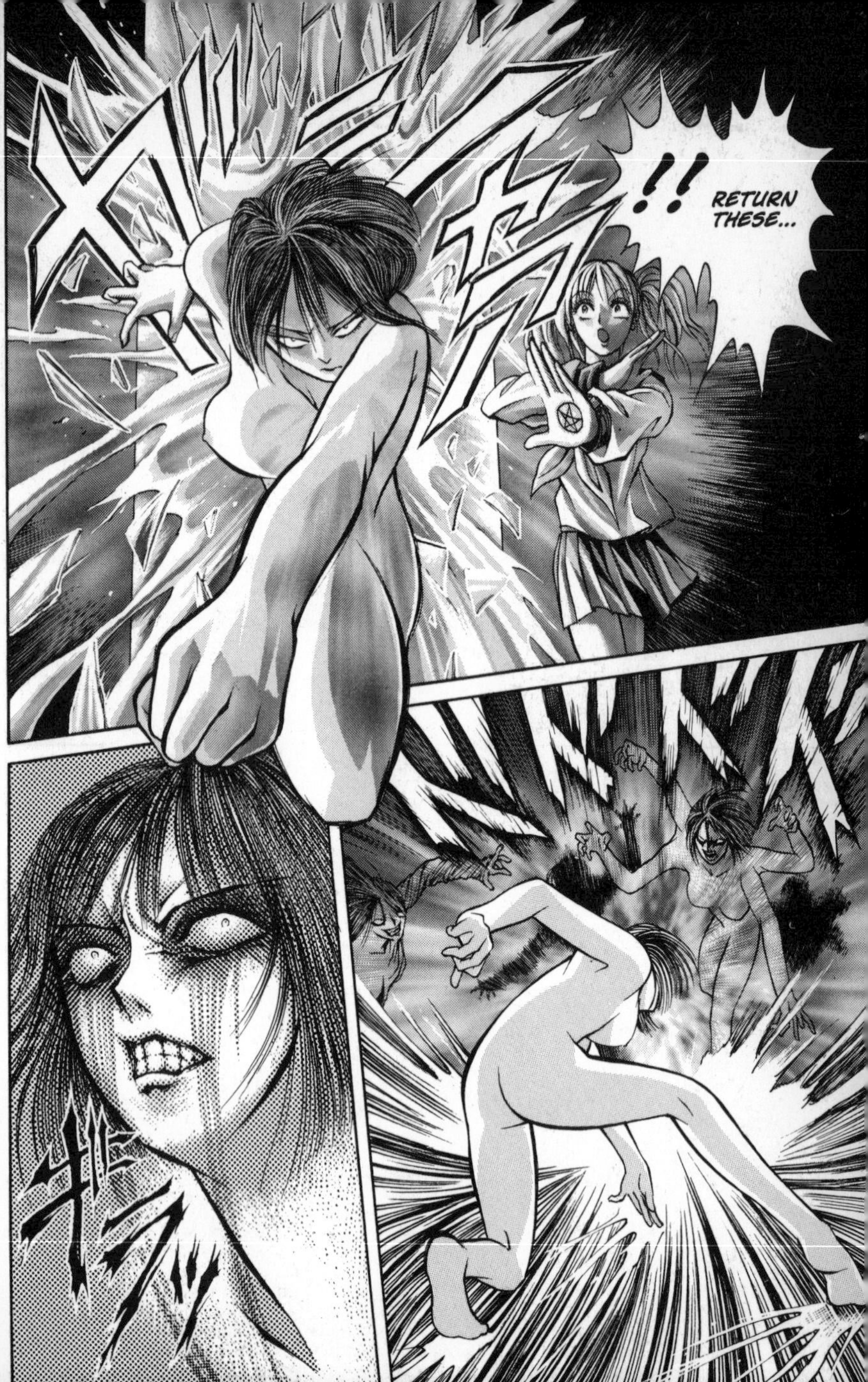
!!
RETURN THESE...

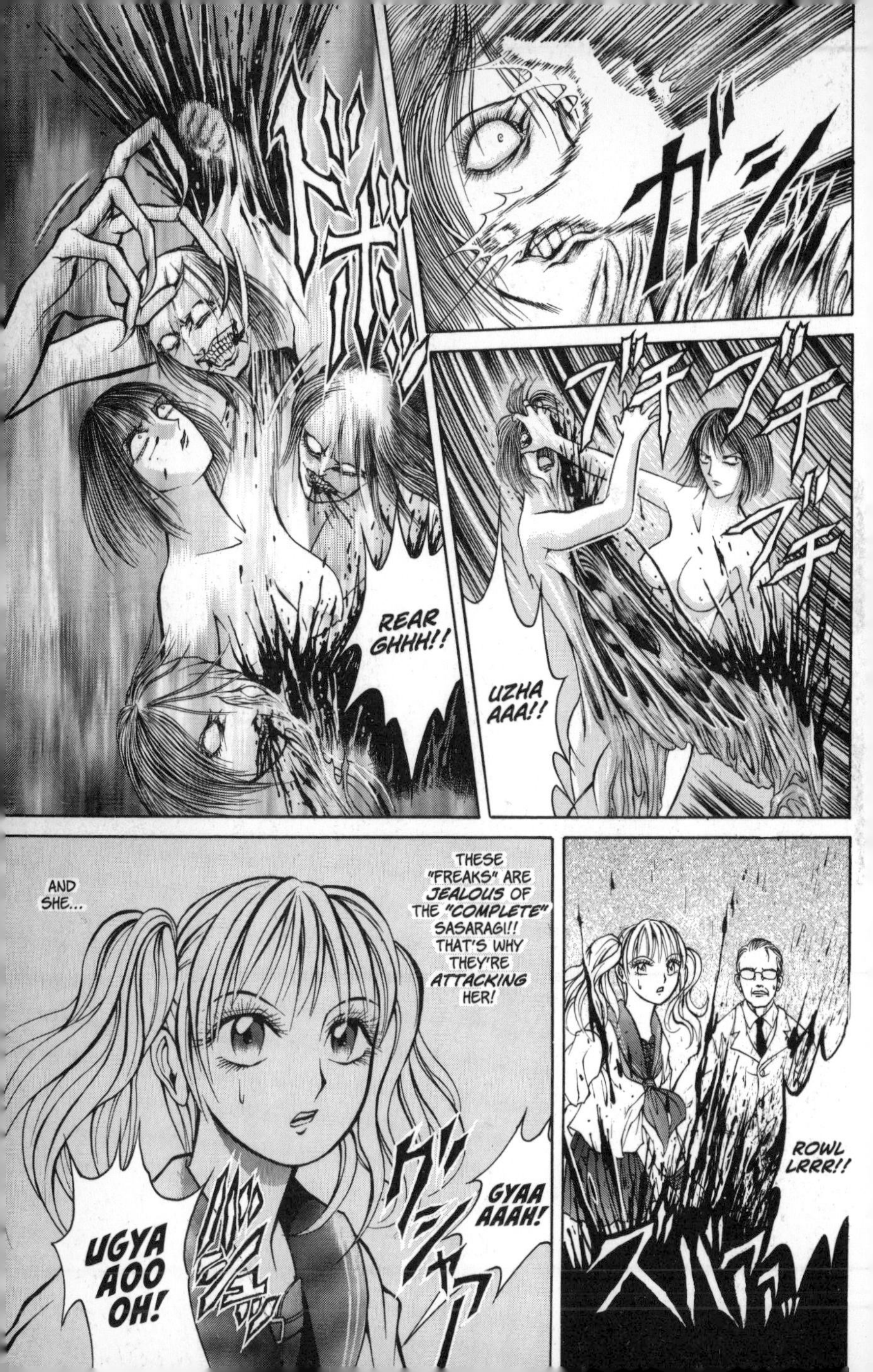
UZHA AAA!!
REAR GHHH!!
ROWL LRRR!!
AND SHE...
THESE "FREAKS" ARE JEALOUS OF THE "COMPLETE" SASARAGI!! THAT'S WHY THEY'RE ATTACKING HER!
GYAA AAAH!
UGYA AOO OH!

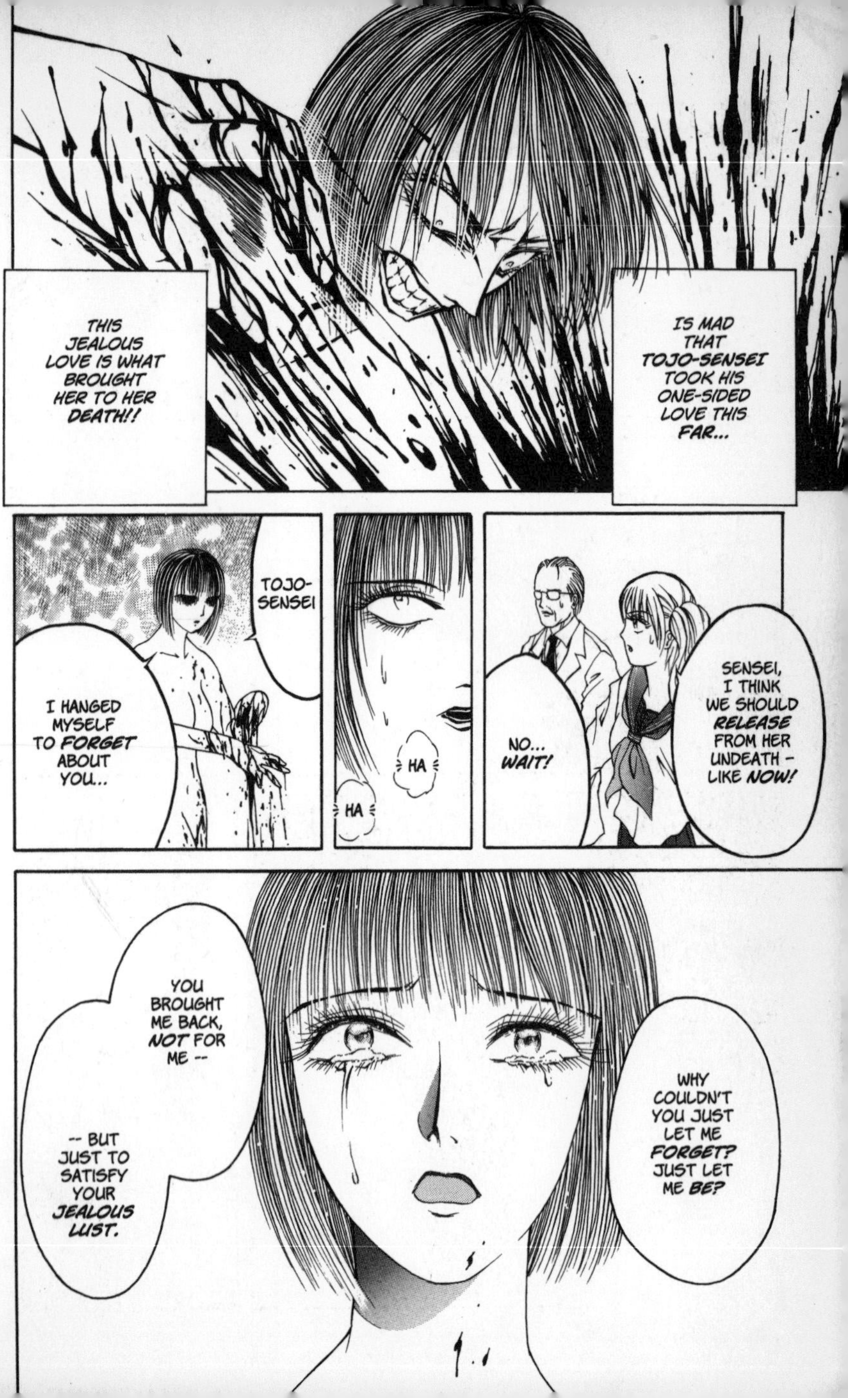
IS MAD THAT TOJO-SENSEI TOOK HIS ONE-SIDED LOVE THIS FAR...
THIS JEALOUS LOVE IS WHAT BROUGHT HER TO HER DEATH!!
SENSEI, I THINK WE SHOULD RELEASE FROM HER UNDEATH – LIKE NOW!
NO... WAIT!
HA
HA
TOJO-SENSEI
I HANGED MYSELF TO FORGET ABOUT YOU...
WHY COULDN'T YOU JUST LET ME FORGET? JUST LET ME BE?
YOU BROUGHT ME BACK, NOT FOR ME --
-- BUT JUST TO SATISFY YOUR JEALOUS LUST.

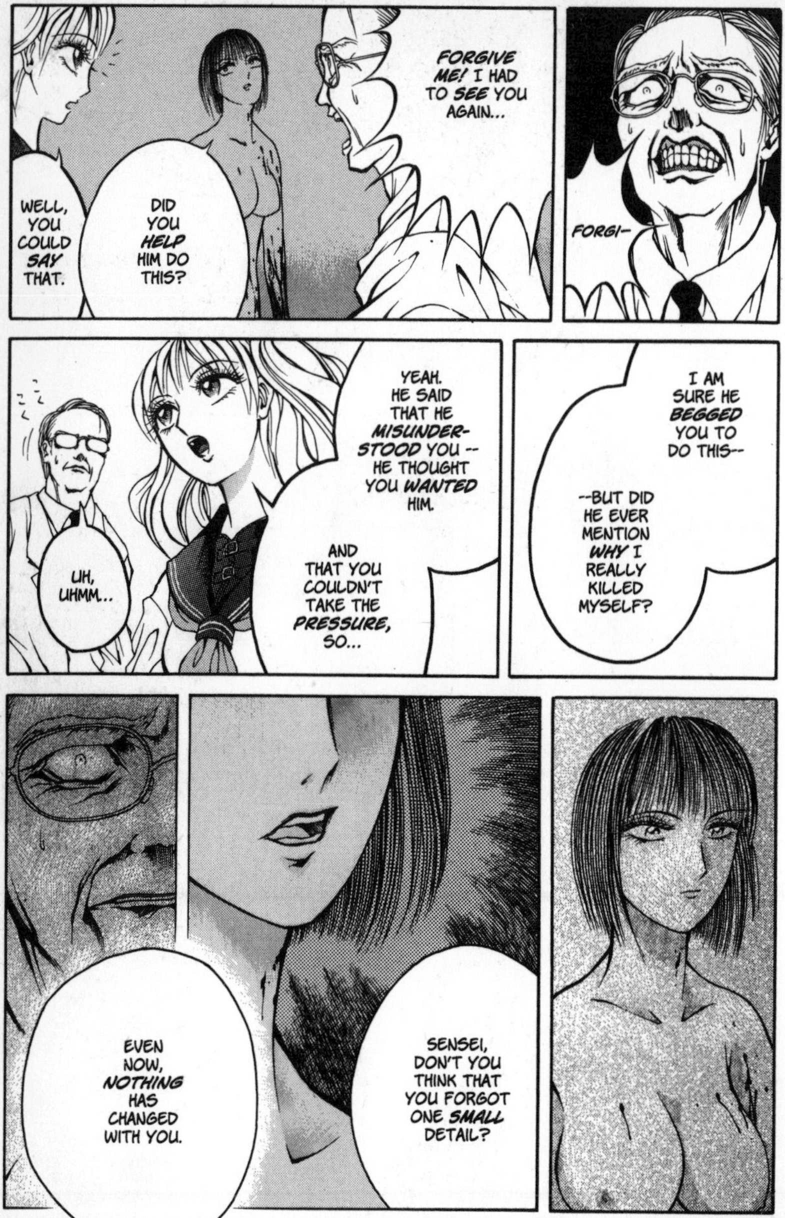
FORGI—
FORGIVE ME! I HAD TO SEE YOU AGAIN...
DID YOU HELP HIM DO THIS?
WELL, YOU COULD SAY THAT.
I AM SURE HE BEGGED YOU TO DO THIS--
--BUT DID HE EVER MENTION WHY I REALLY KILLED MYSELF?
YEAH. HE SAID THAT HE MISUNDERSTOOD YOU -- HE THOUGHT YOU WANTED HIM.
AND THAT YOU COULDN'T TAKE THE PRESSURE, SO...
UH, UHMM...
SENSEI, DON'T YOU THINK THAT YOU FORGOT ONE SMALL DETAIL?
EVEN NOW, NOTHING HAS CHANGED WITH YOU.

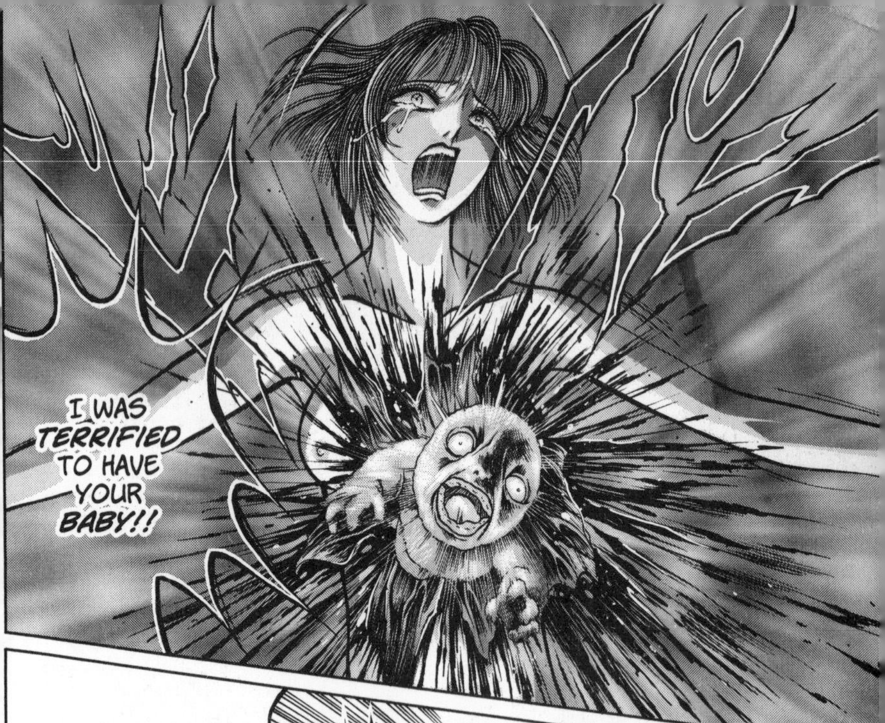
I WAS TERRIFIED TO HAVE YOUR BABY!!

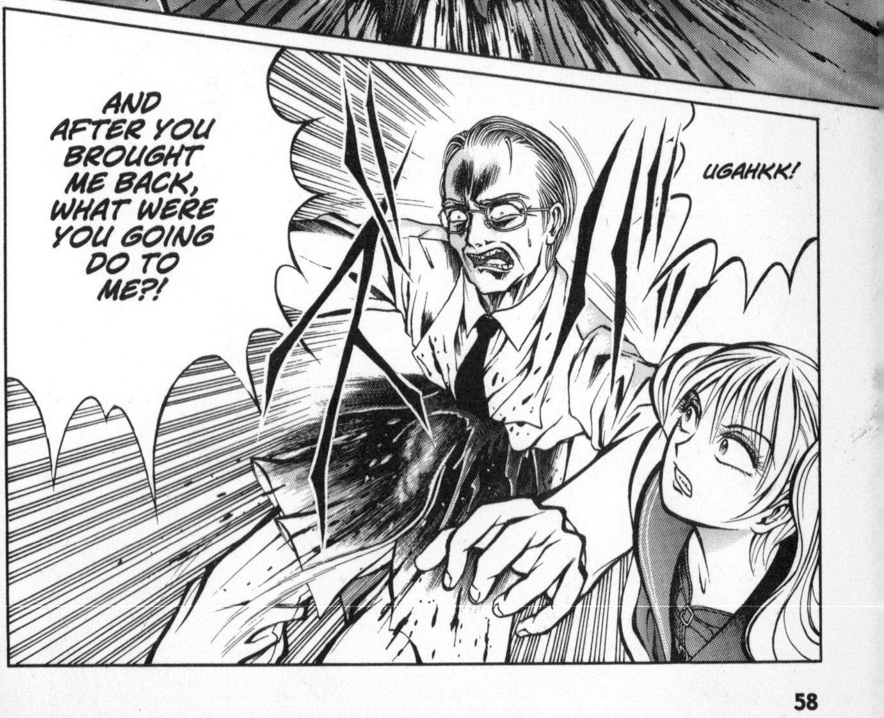
UGAHKK!
AND AFTER YOU BROUGHT ME BACK, WHAT WERE YOU GOING DO TO ME?!

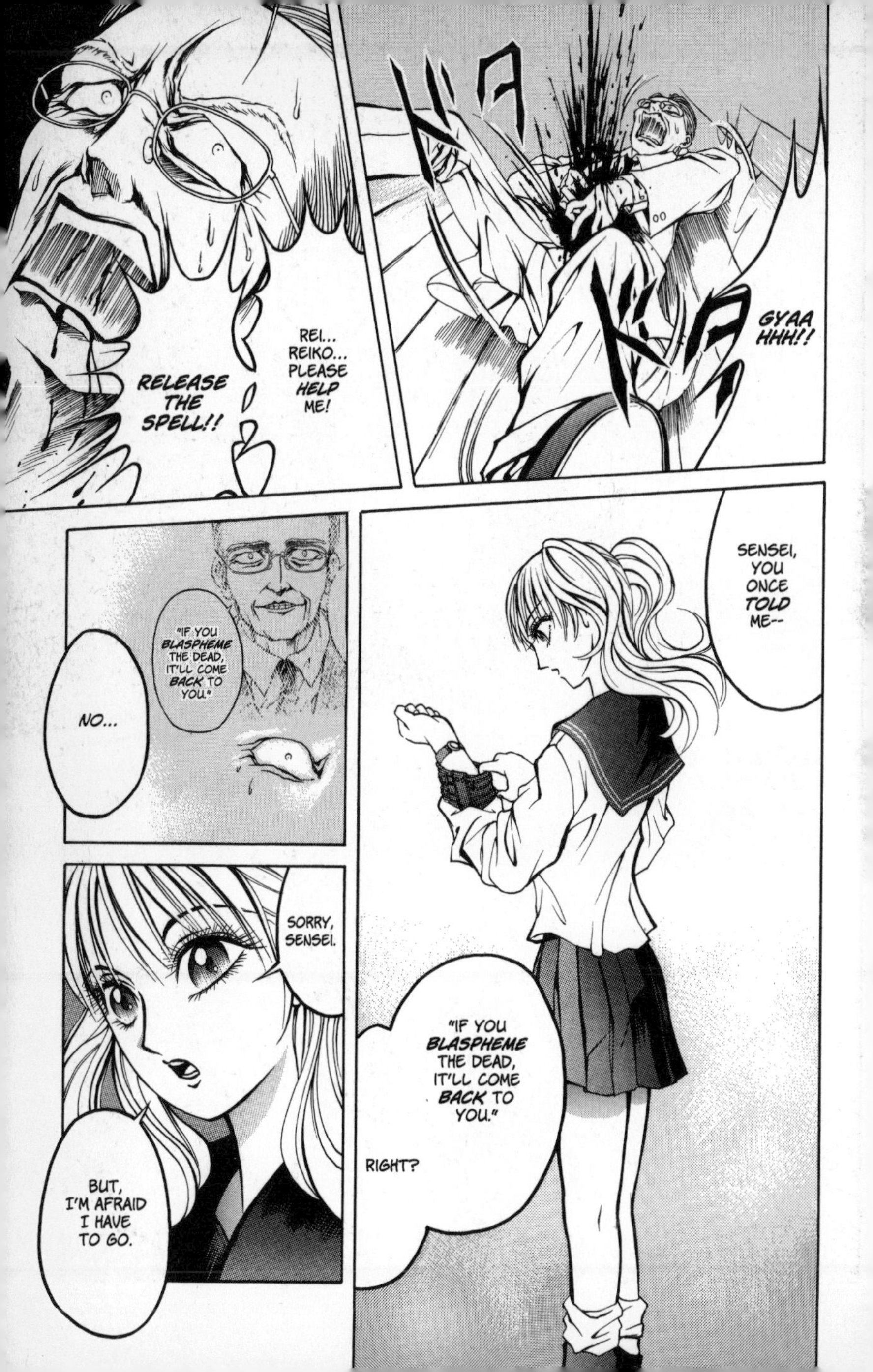
GYAA HHH!!
REI... REIKO... PLEASE HELP ME!
RELEASE THE SPELL!!
SENSEI, YOU ONCE TOLD ME--
"IF YOU BLASPHEME THE DEAD, IT'LL COME BACK TO YOU."
RIGHT?
"IF YOU BLASPHEME THE DEAD, IT'LL COME BACK TO YOU."
NO...
SORRY, SENSEI.
BUT, I'M AFRAID I HAVE TO GO.

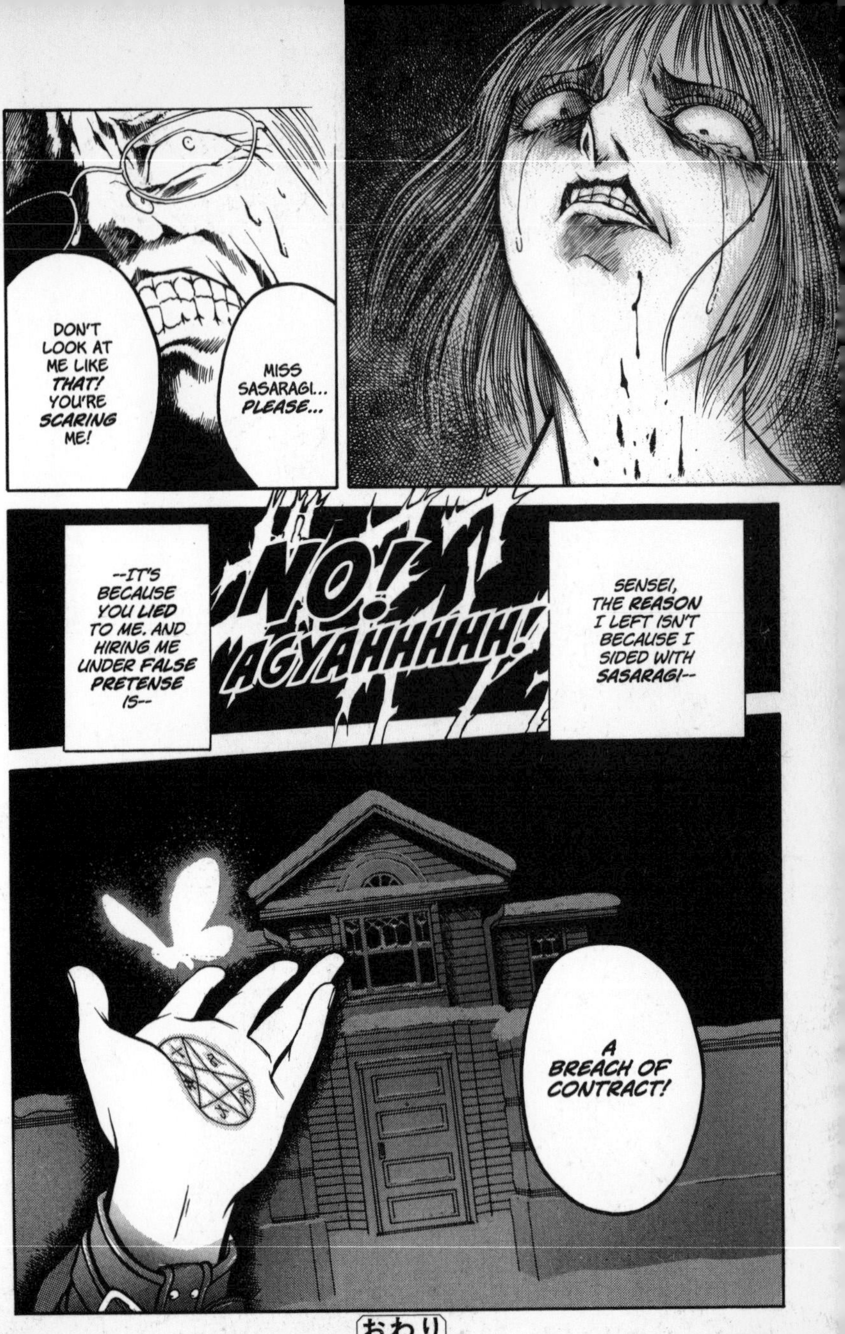
MISS SASARAGI... PLEASE...
DON'T LOOK AT ME LIKE THAT! YOU'RE SCARING ME!
SENSEI, THE REASON I LEFT ISN'T BECAUSE I SIDED WITH SASARAGI--
NO! AGYAHHHHHH!
--IT'S BECAUSE YOU LIED TO ME. AND HIRING ME UNDER FALSE PRETENSE IS--
A BREACH OF CONTRACT!

おわり

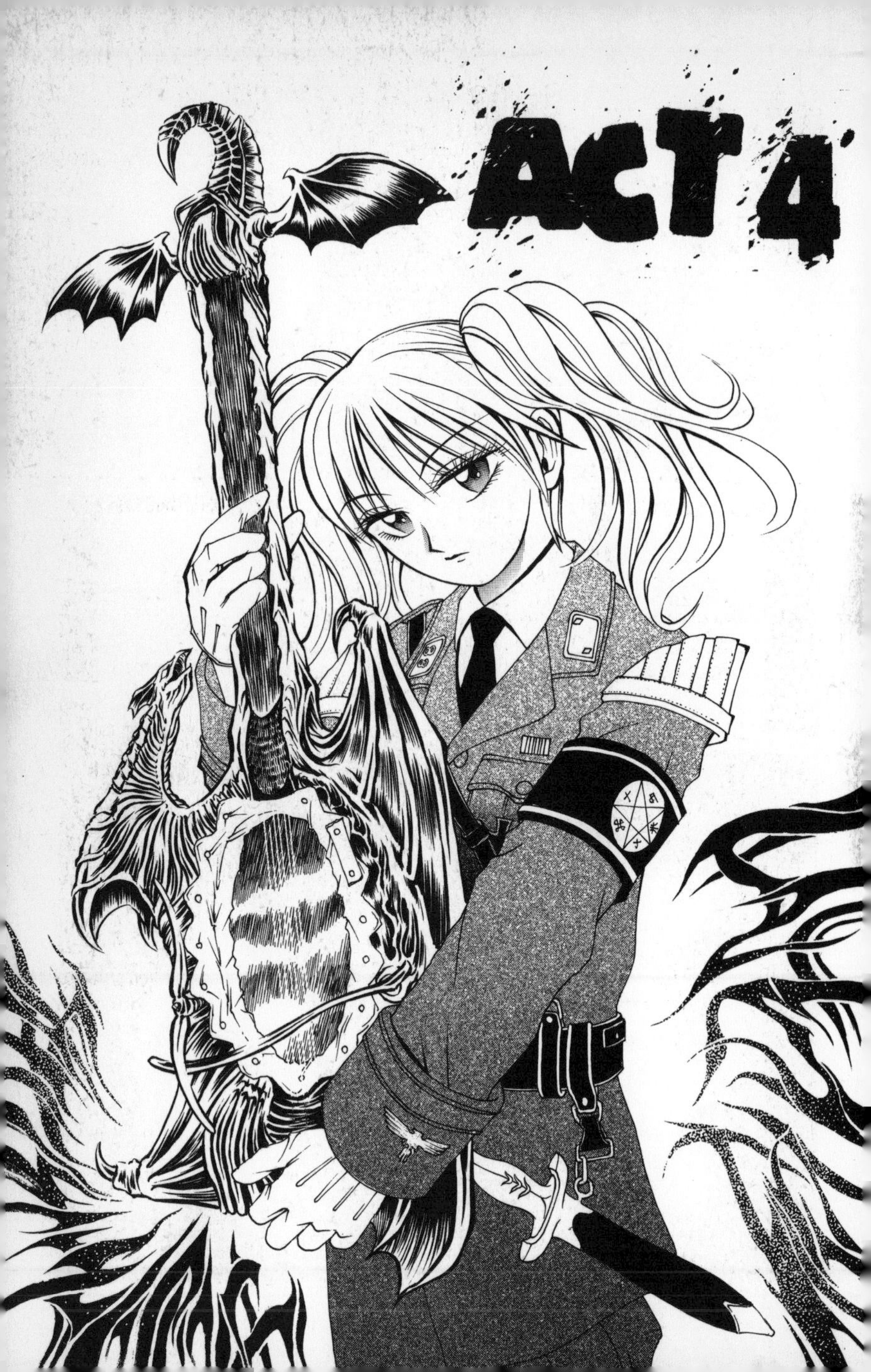
ACT 4

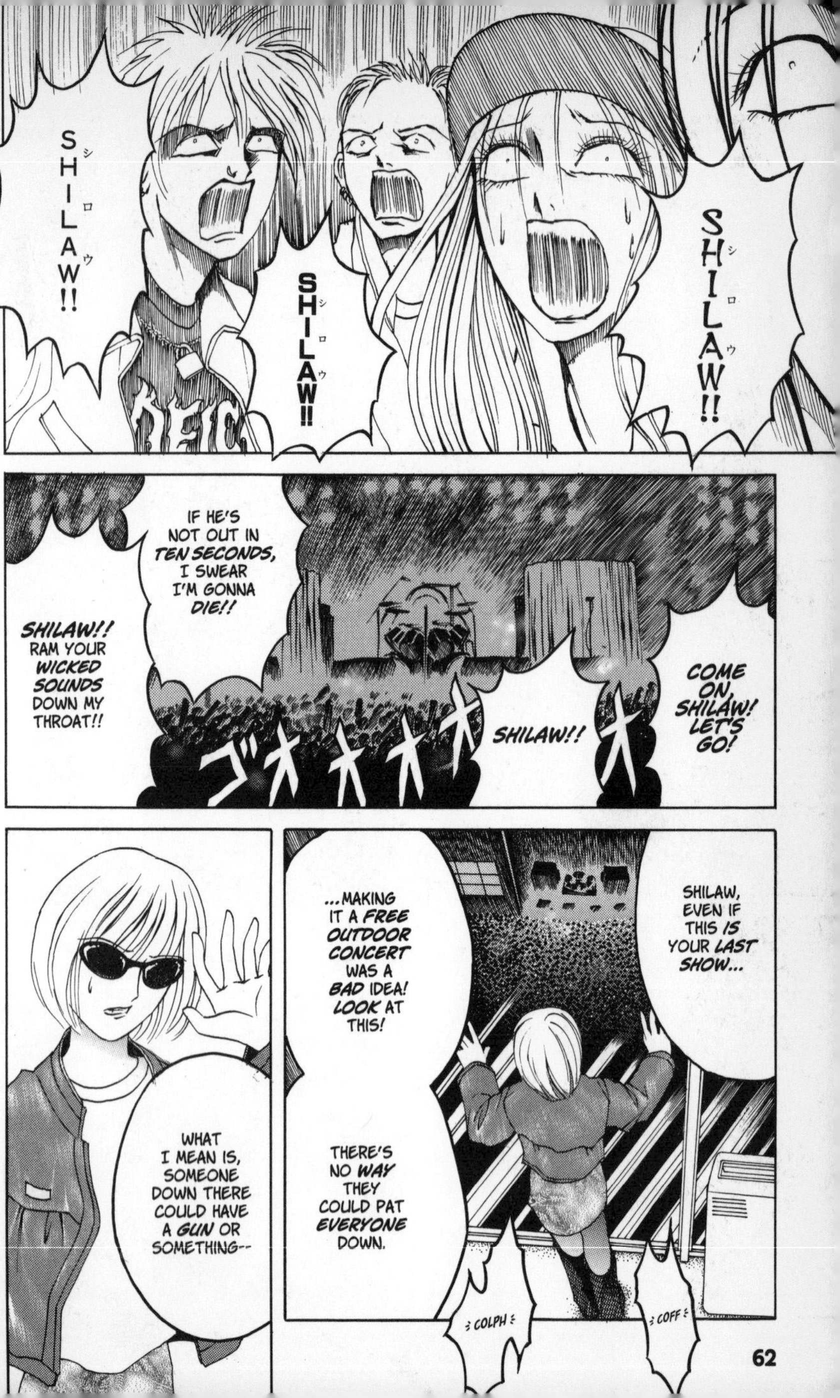
SHILAW!!
SHILAW!!
SHILAW!!
COME ON, SHILAW! LET'S GO!
SHILAW!!
ゴオオオオオ
IF HE'S NOT OUT IN TEN SECONDS, I SWEAR I'M GONNA DIE!!
SHILAW!! RAM YOUR WICKED SOUNDS DOWN MY THROAT!!
SHILAW, EVEN IF THIS IS YOUR LAST SHOW...
...MAKING IT A FREE OUTDOOR CONCERT WAS A BAD IDEA! LOOK AT THIS!
THERE'S NO WAY THEY COULD PAT EVERYONE DOWN.
COFF
COLPH
WHAT I MEAN IS, SOMEONE DOWN THERE COULD HAVE A GUN OR SOMETHING--

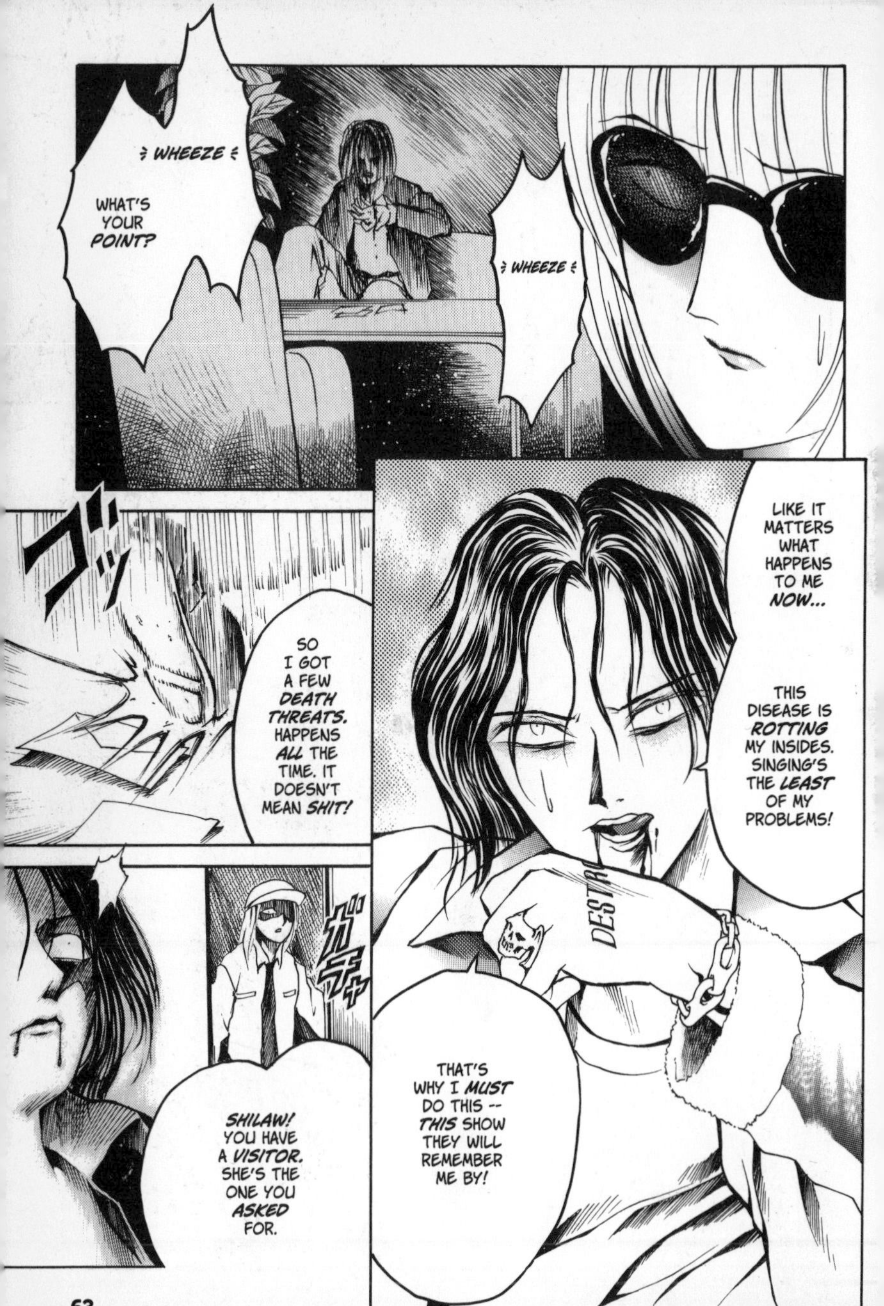
WHEEZE
WHEEZE
WHAT'S YOUR POINT?
LIKE IT MATTERS WHAT HAPPENS TO ME NOW...
THIS DISEASE IS ROTTING MY INSIDES. SINGING'S THE LEAST OF MY PROBLEMS!
THAT'S WHY I MUST DO THIS -- THIS SHOW THEY WILL REMEMBER ME BY!
ゴッ
SO I GOT A FEW DEATH THREATS. HAPPENS ALL THE TIME. IT DOESN'T MEAN SHIT!
ガチャ
SHILAW! YOU HAVE A VISITOR. SHE'S THE ONE YOU ASKED FOR.

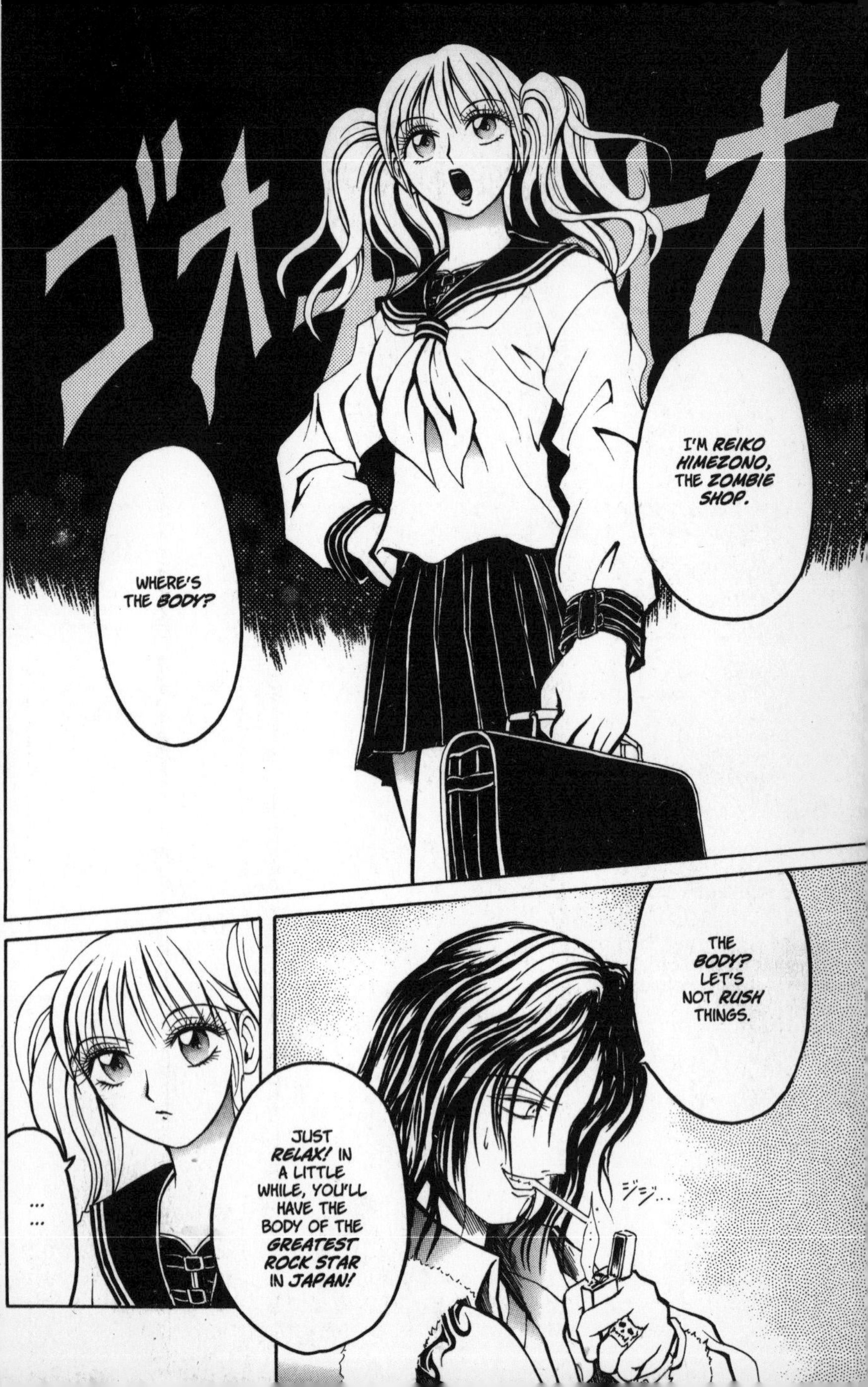
I'M REIKO HIMEZONO, THE ZOMBIE SHOP.
WHERE'S THE BODY?
THE BODY? LET'S NOT RUSH THINGS.
JUST RELAX! IN A LITTLE WHILE, YOU'LL HAVE THE BODY OF THE GREATEST ROCK STAR IN JAPAN!
ジジ...
...
...

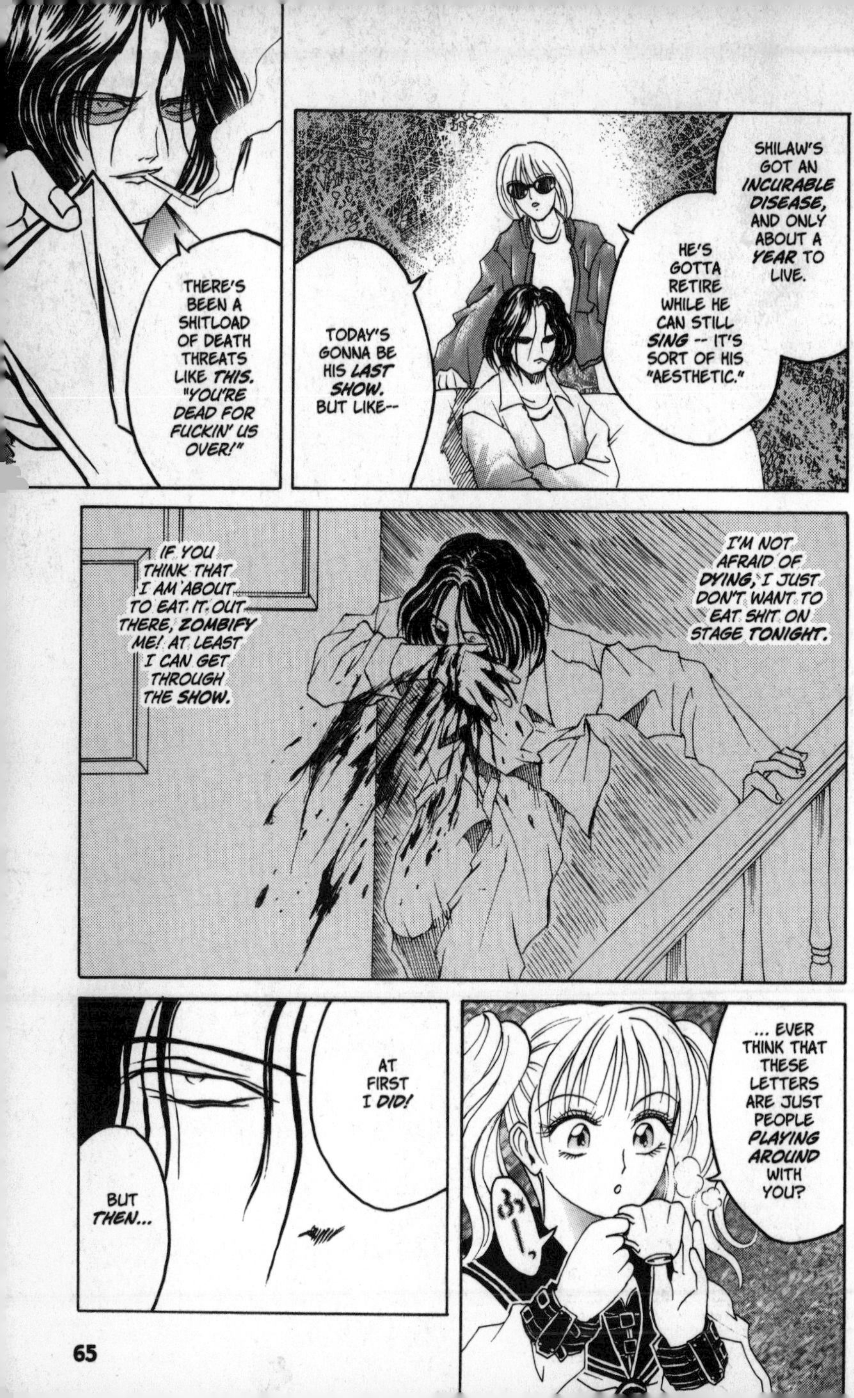
SHILAW'S GOT AN *INCURABLE DISEASE,* AND ONLY ABOUT A *YEAR* TO LIVE.
HE'S GOTTA RETIRE WHILE HE CAN STILL *SING* -- IT'S SORT OF HIS "AESTHETIC."
TODAY'S GONNA BE HIS *LAST SHOW.* BUT LIKE--
THERE'S BEEN A SHITLOAD OF DEATH THREATS LIKE *THIS.* *"YOU'RE DEAD FOR FUCKIN' US OVER!"*
*I'M NOT AFRAID OF DYING, I JUST DON'T WANT TO EAT SHIT ON STAGE TONIGHT.*
*IF YOU THINK THAT I AM ABOUT TO EAT IT OUT THERE, ZOMBIFY ME! AT LEAST I CAN GET THROUGH THE SHOW.*
... EVER THINK THAT THESE LETTERS ARE JUST PEOPLE *PLAYING AROUND* WITH YOU?
AT FIRST I *DID!*
BUT *THEN...*

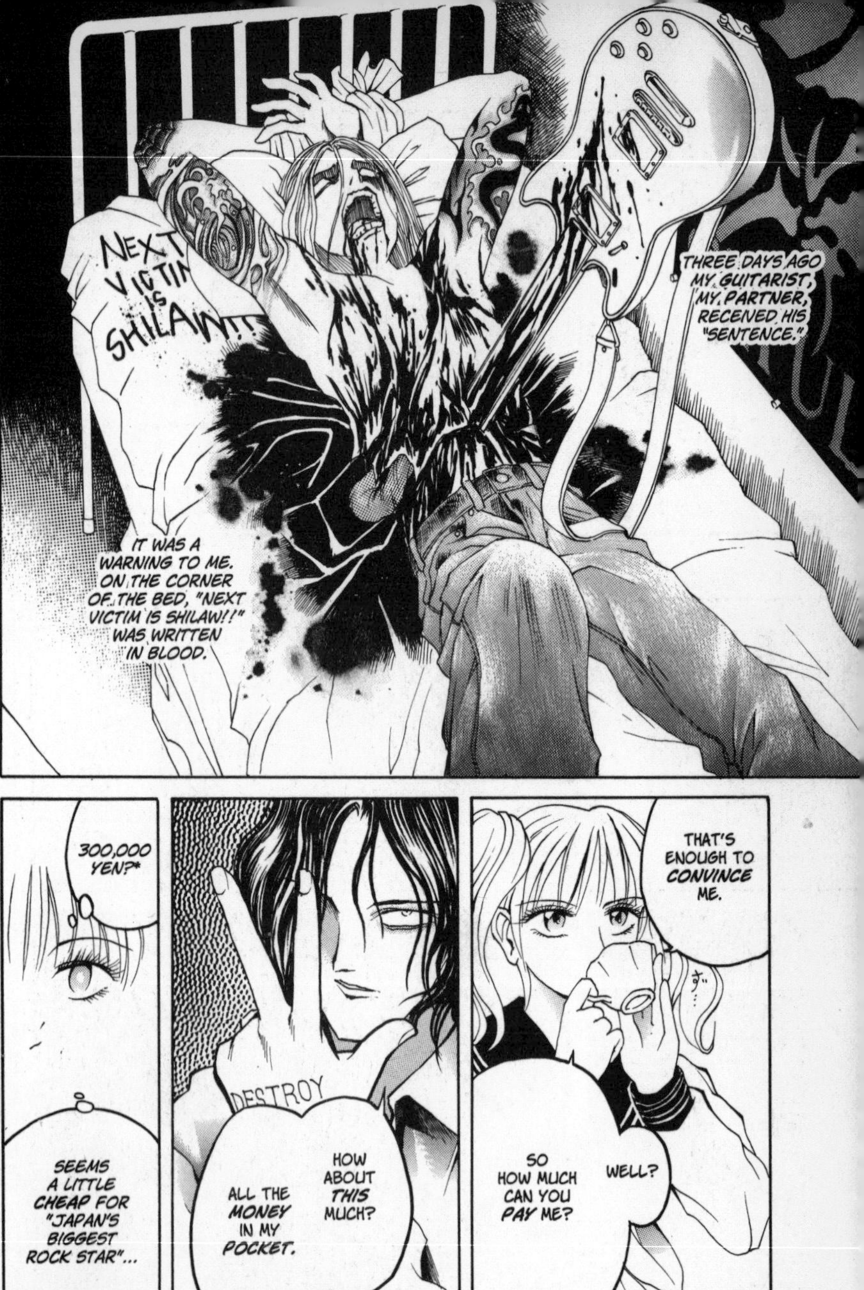

THREE DAYS AGO MY GUITARIST, MY PARTNER, RECEIVED HIS "SENTENCE."
NEXT VICTIM IS SHILAW!!
IT WAS A WARNING TO ME. ON THE CORNER OF THE BED, "NEXT VICTIM IS SHILAW!!" WAS WRITTEN IN BLOOD.
THAT'S ENOUGH TO CONVINCE ME.
WELL?
SO HOW MUCH CAN YOU PAY ME?
HOW ABOUT THIS MUCH?
DESTROY
ALL THE MONEY IN MY POCKET.
300,000 YEN?*
SEEMS A LITTLE CHEAP FOR "JAPAN'S BIGGEST ROCK STAR"...


*ABOUT $3,000.

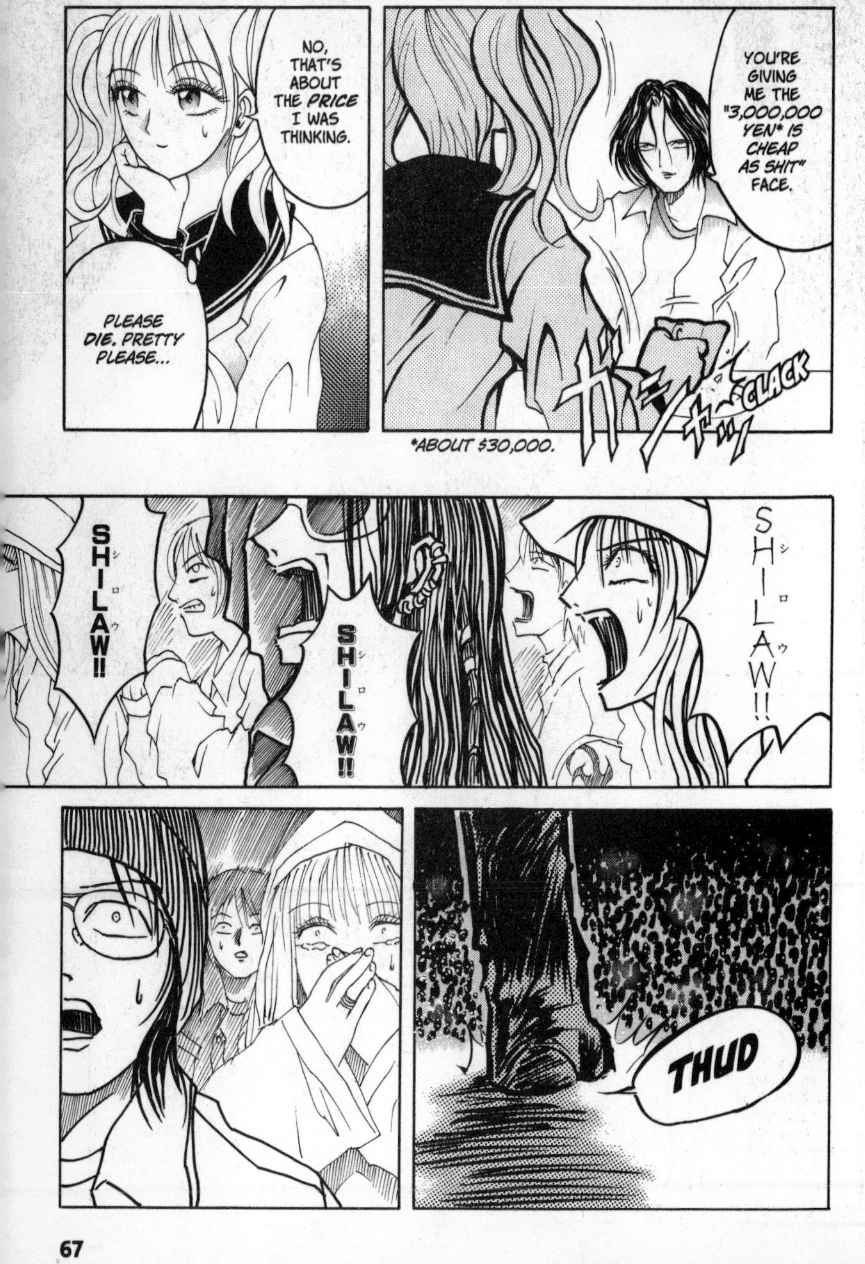
YOU'RE GIVING ME THE "3,000,000 YEN* IS CHEAP AS SHIT" FACE.
CLACK
NO, THAT'S ABOUT THE *PRICE* I WAS THINKING.
PLEASE DIE. PRETTY PLEASE...
SHILAW!!
SHILAW!!
SHILAW!!
THUD
*ABOUT $30,000.

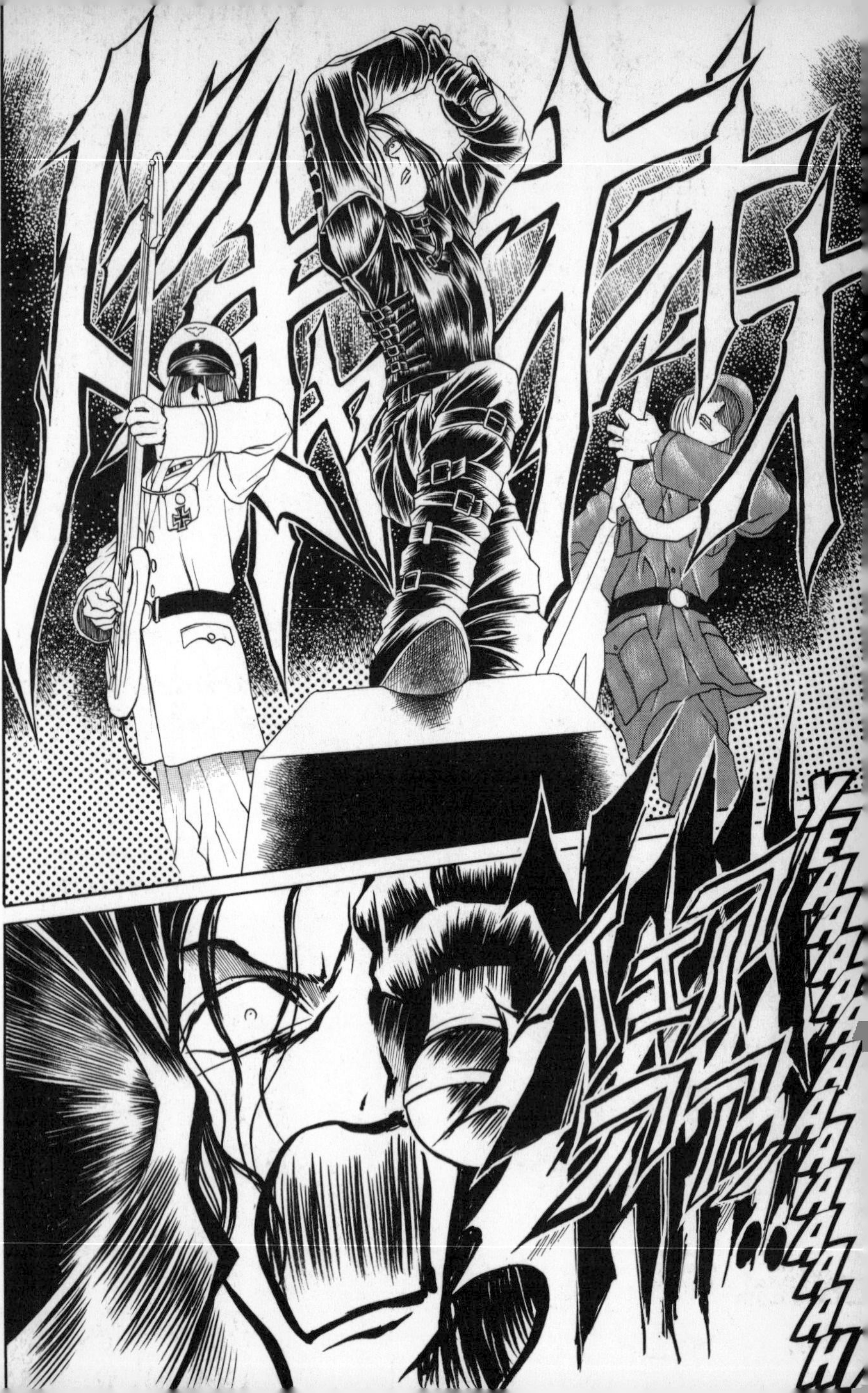
YEAAAAAAAAAAAAAH!

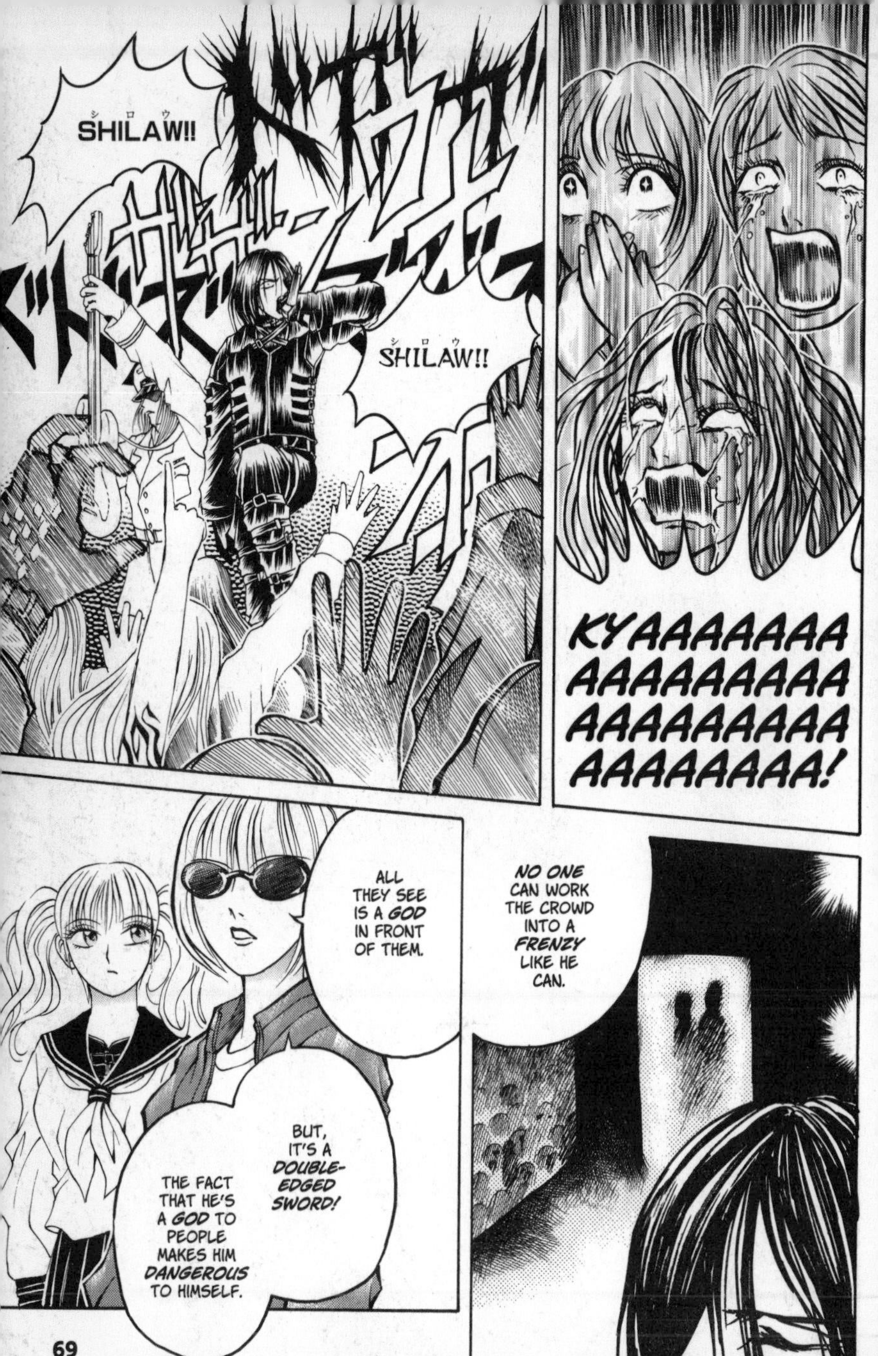

KYAAAAAAAAAAAAAAAAAAAAAAAAAAAAAAAAAAA!
SHILAW!!
SHILAW!!
NO ONE CAN WORK THE CROWD INTO A FRENZY LIKE HE CAN.
ALL THEY SEE IS A GOD IN FRONT OF THEM.
BUT, IT'S A DOUBLE-EDGED SWORD!
THE FACT THAT HE'S A GOD TO PEOPLE MAKES HIM DANGEROUS TO HIMSELF.

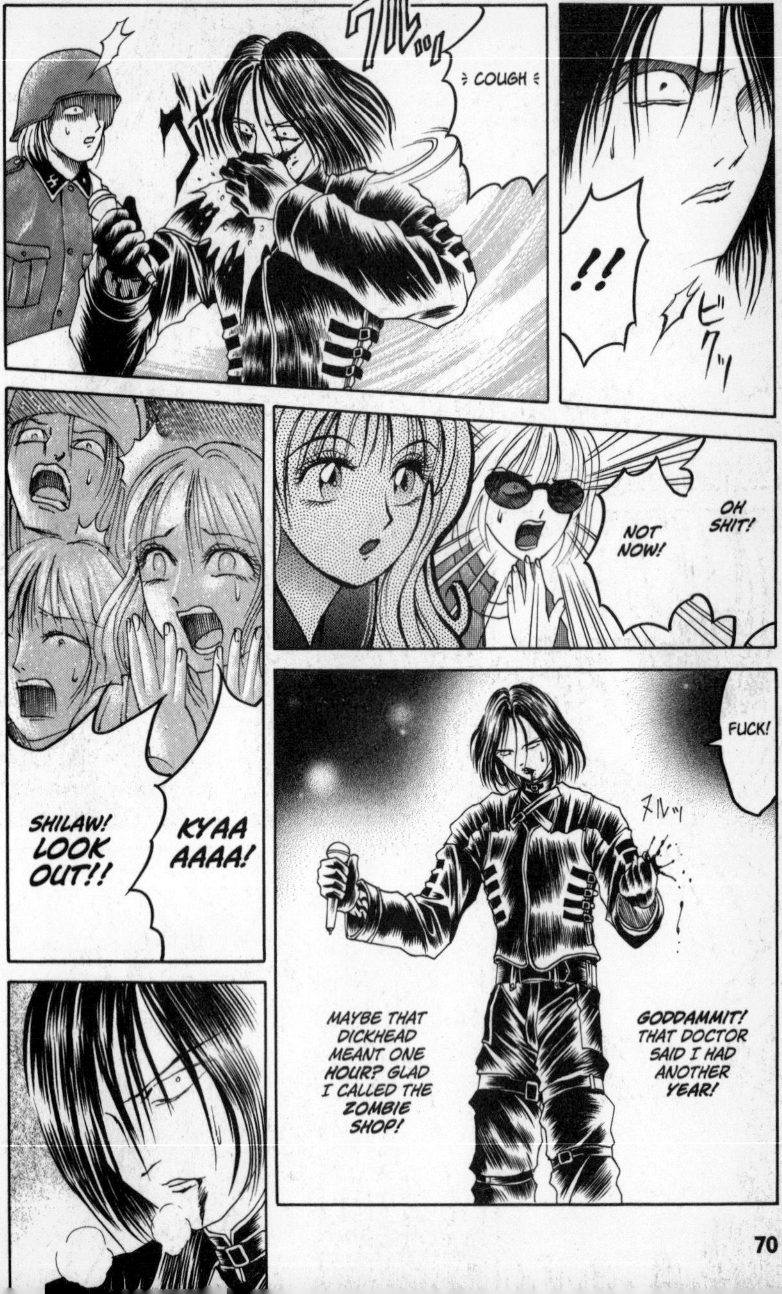

!!
ビクッ
COUGH
OH SHIT!
NOT NOW!
KYAA AAAA!
SHILAW! LOOK OUT!!
FUCK!
ヌルッ
GODDAMMIT! THAT DOCTOR SAID I HAD ANOTHER YEAR!
MAYBE THAT DICKHEAD MEANT ONE HOUR? GLAD I CALLED THE ZOMBIE SHOP!

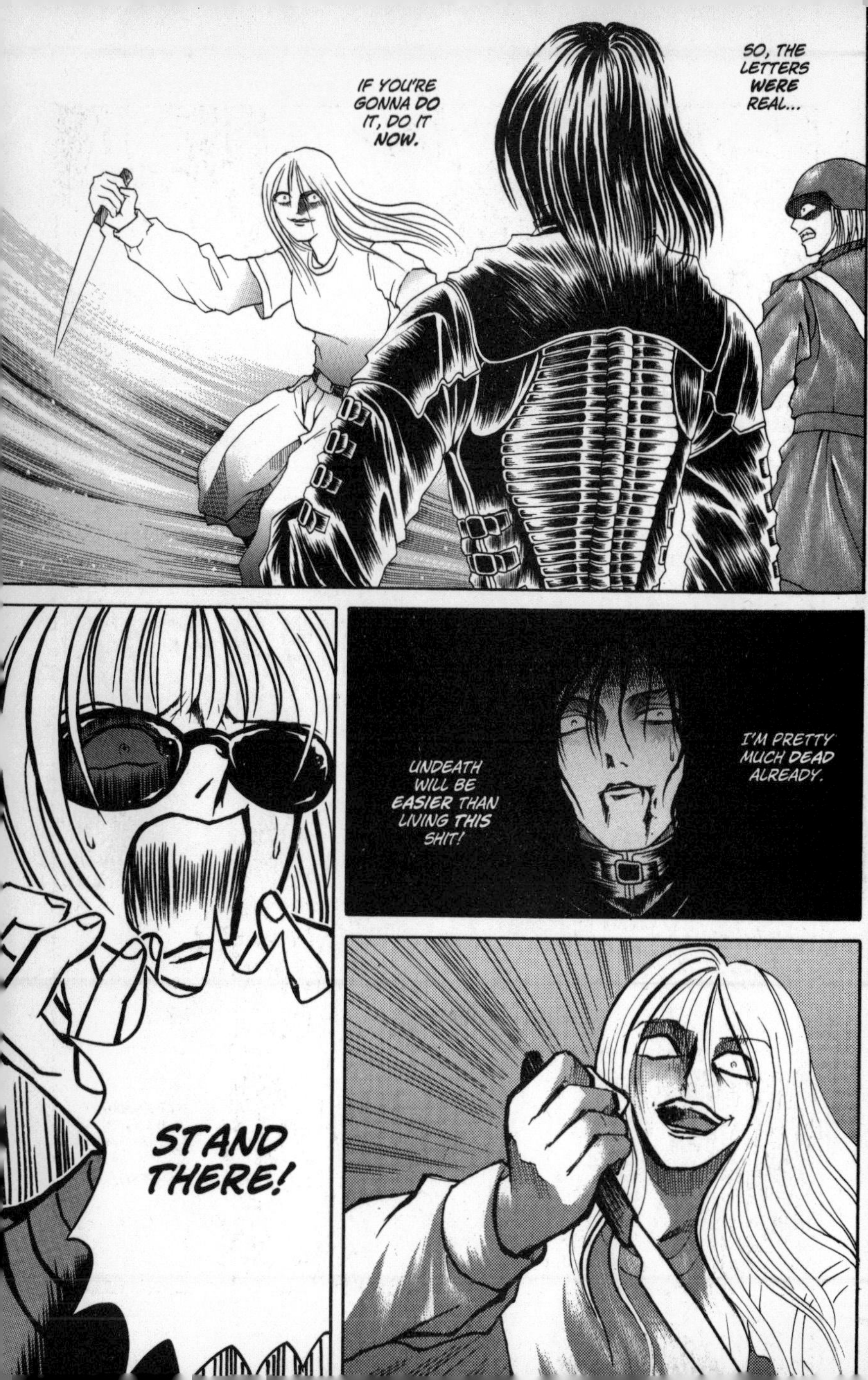
SO, THE LETTERS WERE REAL...
IF YOU'RE GONNA DO IT, DO IT NOW.
I'M PRETTY MUCH DEAD ALREADY.
UNDEATH WILL BE EASIER THAN LIVING THIS SHIT!
STAND THERE!

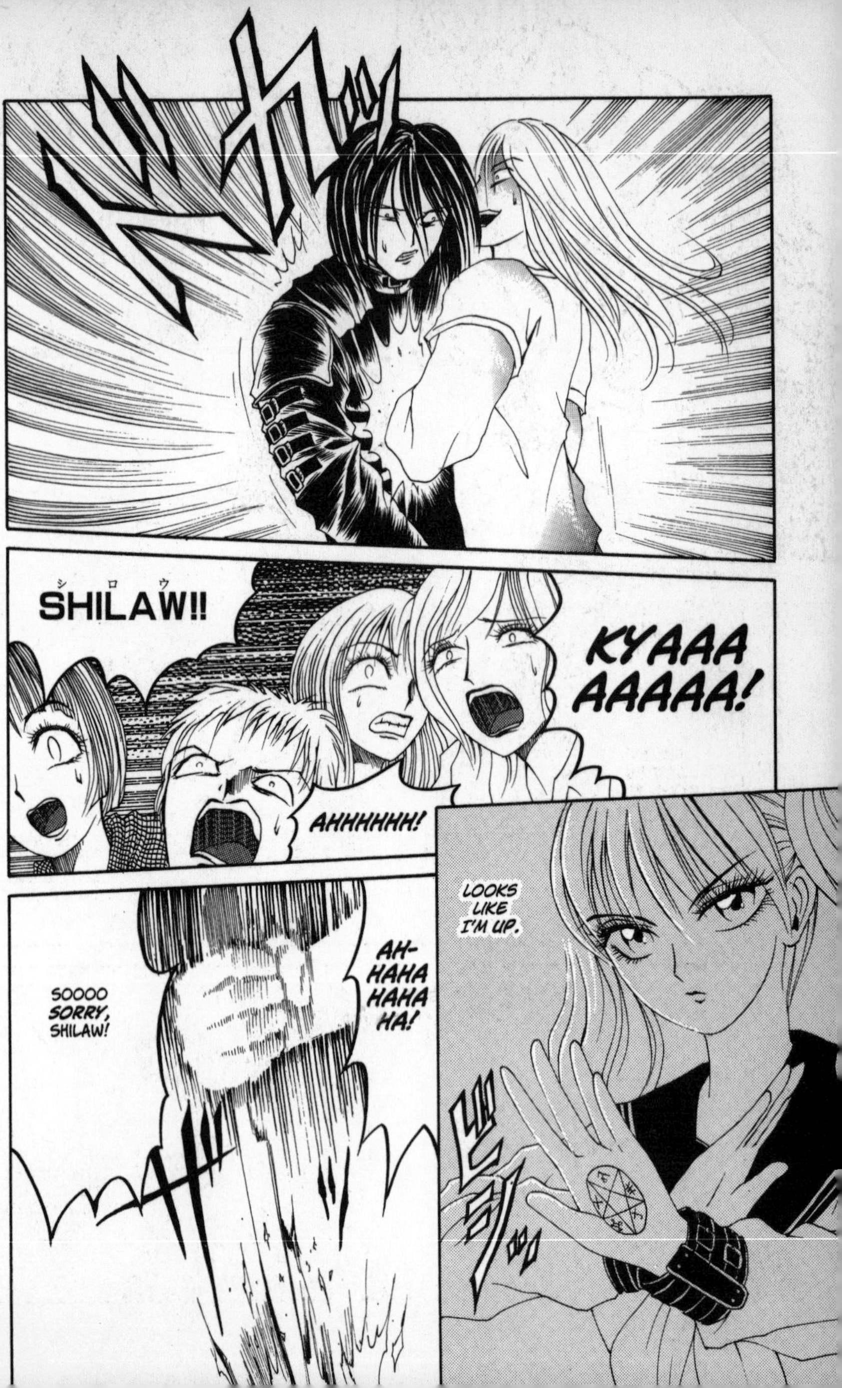
KYAAA AAAAA!
シロウ
SHILAW!!
AHHHHHH!
LOOKS LIKE I'M UP.
AH-HAHA HAHAHA HA!
SOOOO SORRY, SHILAW!

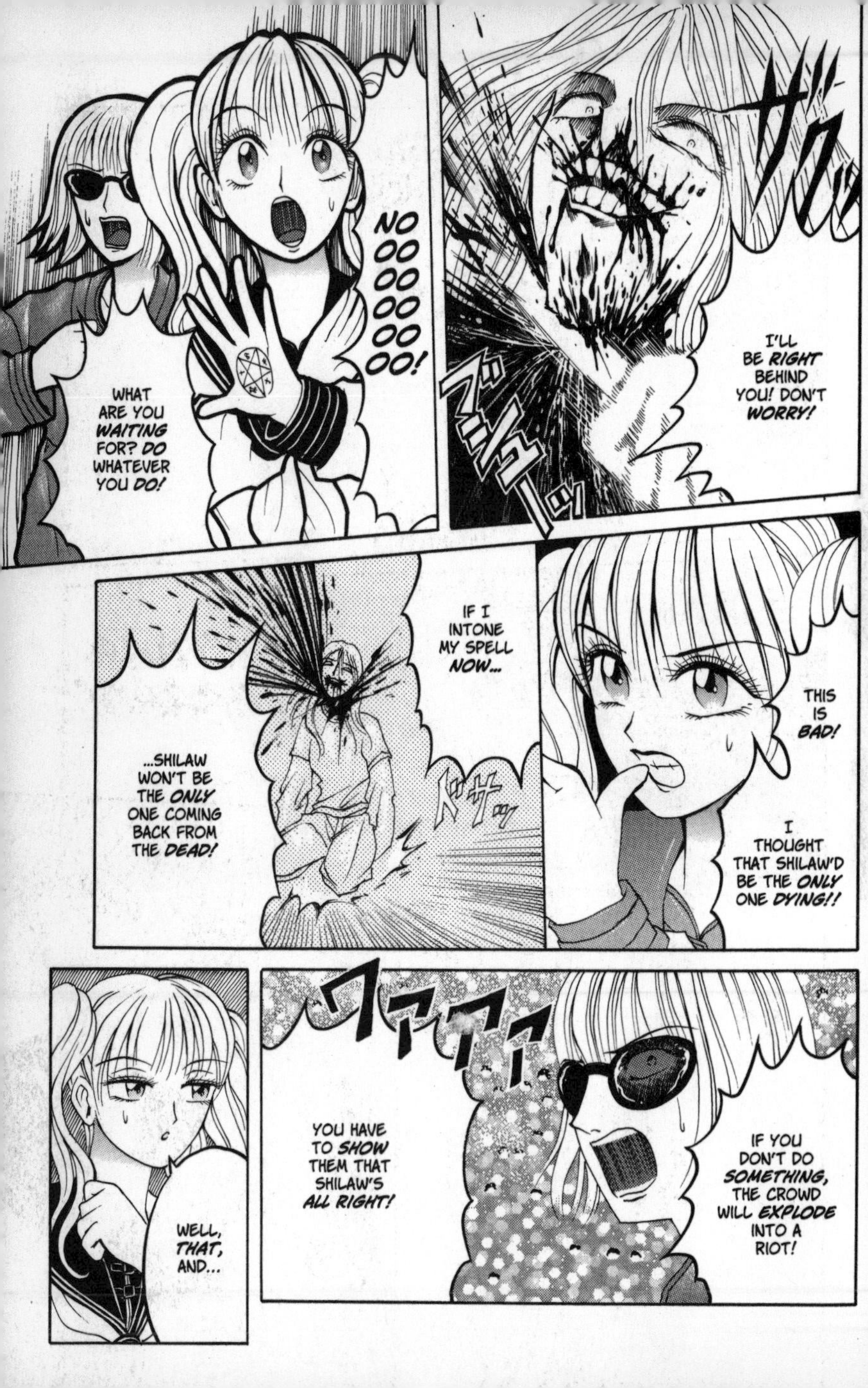
I'LL BE RIGHT BEHIND YOU! DON'T WORRY!
NOOOOOOOOOOOOOOO!
WHAT ARE YOU WAITING FOR? DO WHATEVER YOU DO!
THIS IS BAD!
I THOUGHT THAT SHILAW'D BE THE ONLY ONE DYING!!
IF I INTONE MY SPELL NOW...
...SHILAW WON'T BE THE ONLY ONE COMING BACK FROM THE DEAD!
IF YOU DON'T DO SOMETHING, THE CROWD WILL EXPLODE INTO A RIOT!
YOU HAVE TO SHOW THEM THAT SHILAW'S ALL RIGHT!
WELL, THAT, AND...

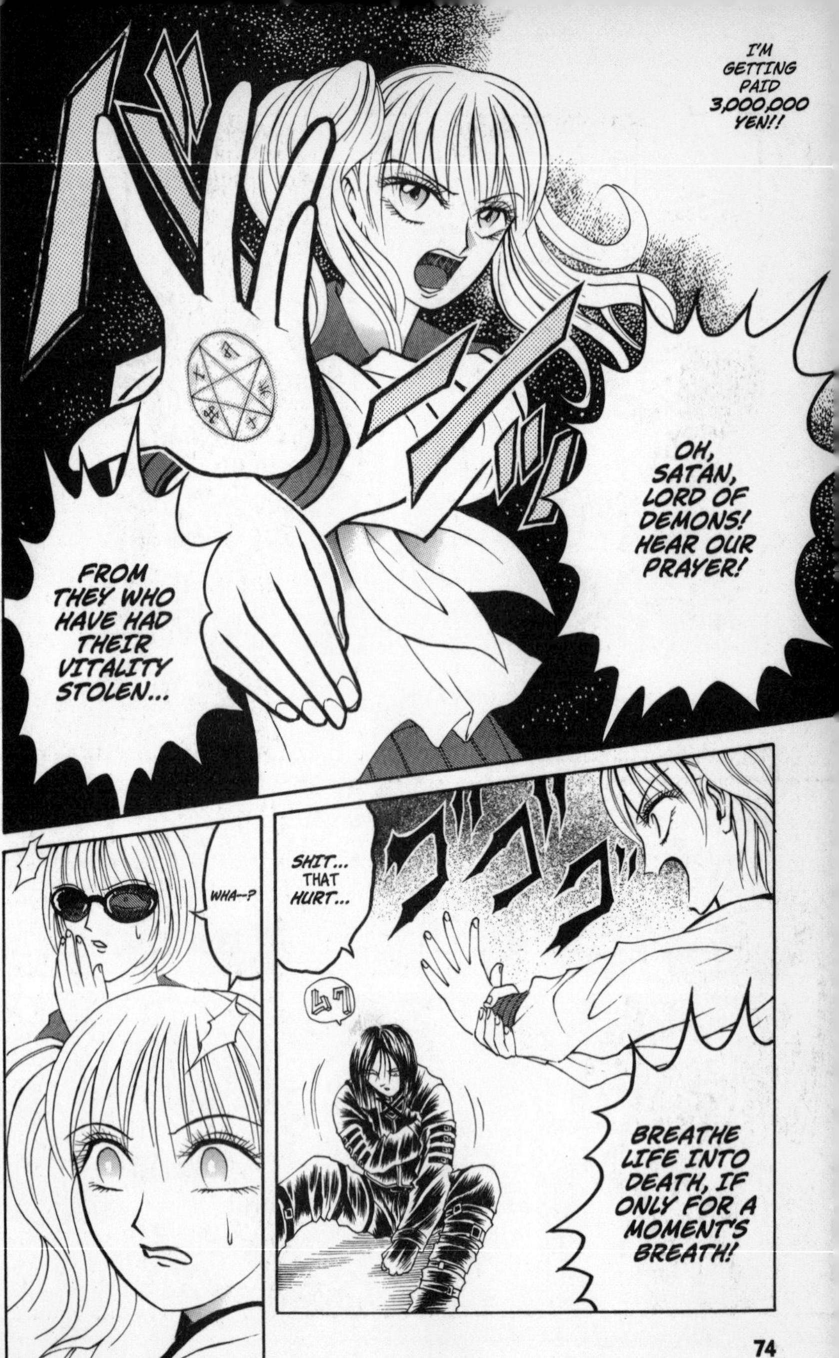
I'M GETTING PAID 3,000,000 YEN!!
OH, SATAN, LORD OF DEMONS! HEAR OUR PRAYER!
FROM THEY WHO HAVE HAD THEIR VITALITY STOLEN...
SHIT... THAT HURT...
BREATHE LIFE INTO DEATH, IF ONLY FOR A MOMENT'S BREATH!
WHA--?

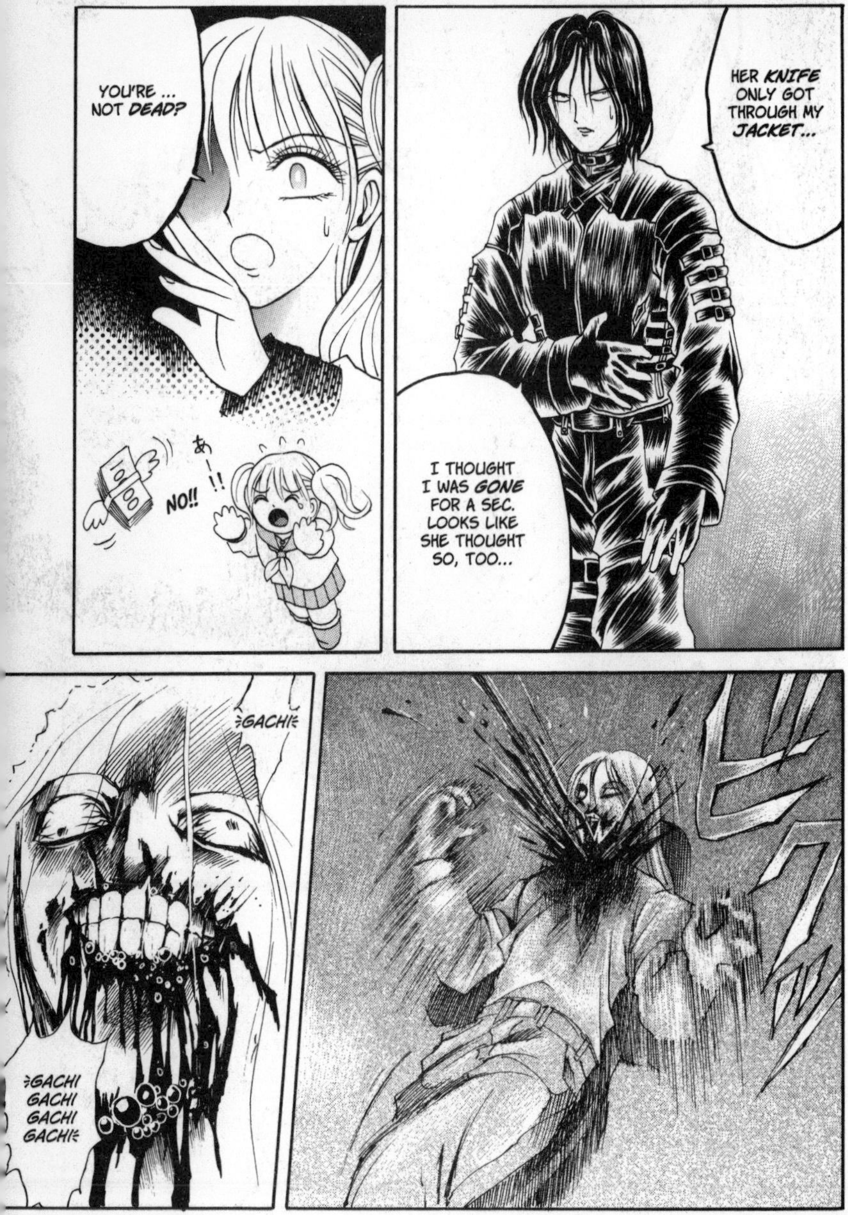
HER *KNIFE* ONLY GOT THROUGH MY *JACKET*...
I THOUGHT I WAS *GONE* FOR A SEC. LOOKS LIKE SHE THOUGHT SO, TOO...
YOU'RE ... NOT *DEAD?*
あー!!
NO!!
GACHI
GACHI GACHI GACHI GACHI

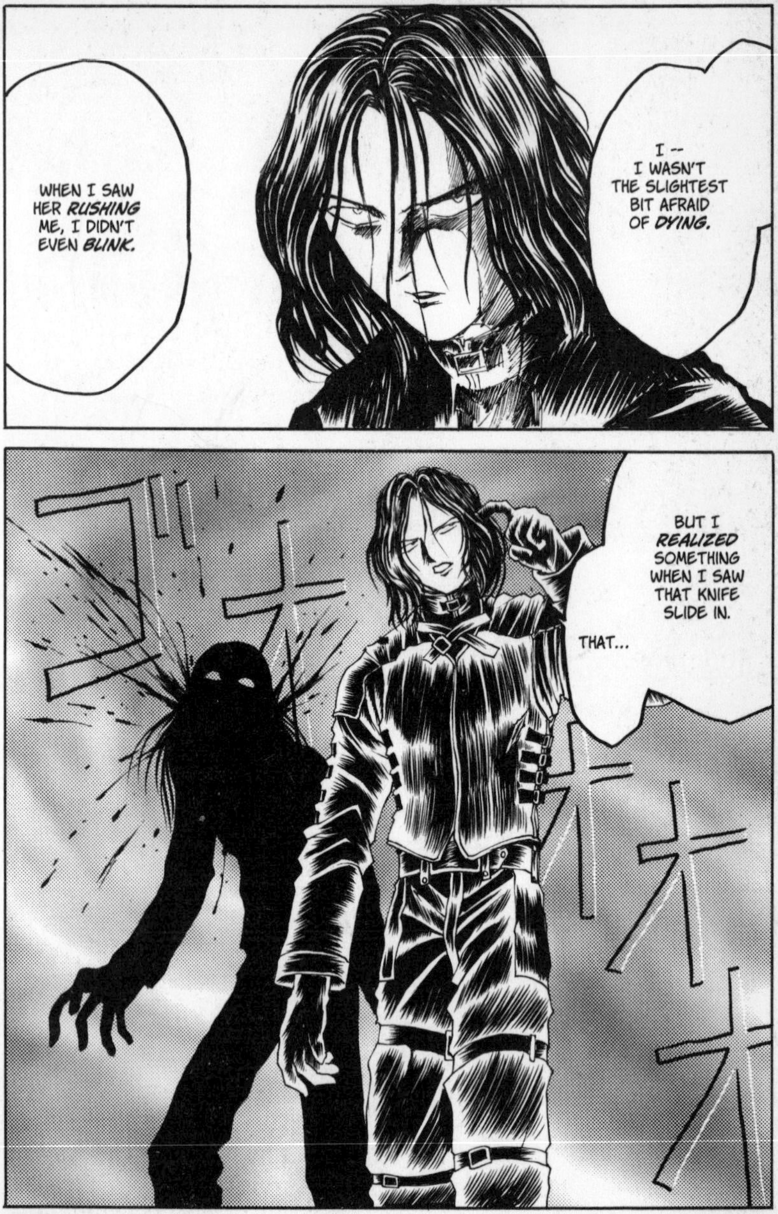
I -- I WASN'T THE SLIGHTEST BIT AFRAID OF *DYING.*
WHEN I SAW HER *RUSHING* ME, I DIDN'T EVEN *BLINK.*
BUT I *REALIZED* SOMETHING WHEN I SAW THAT KNIFE SLIDE IN.
THAT...

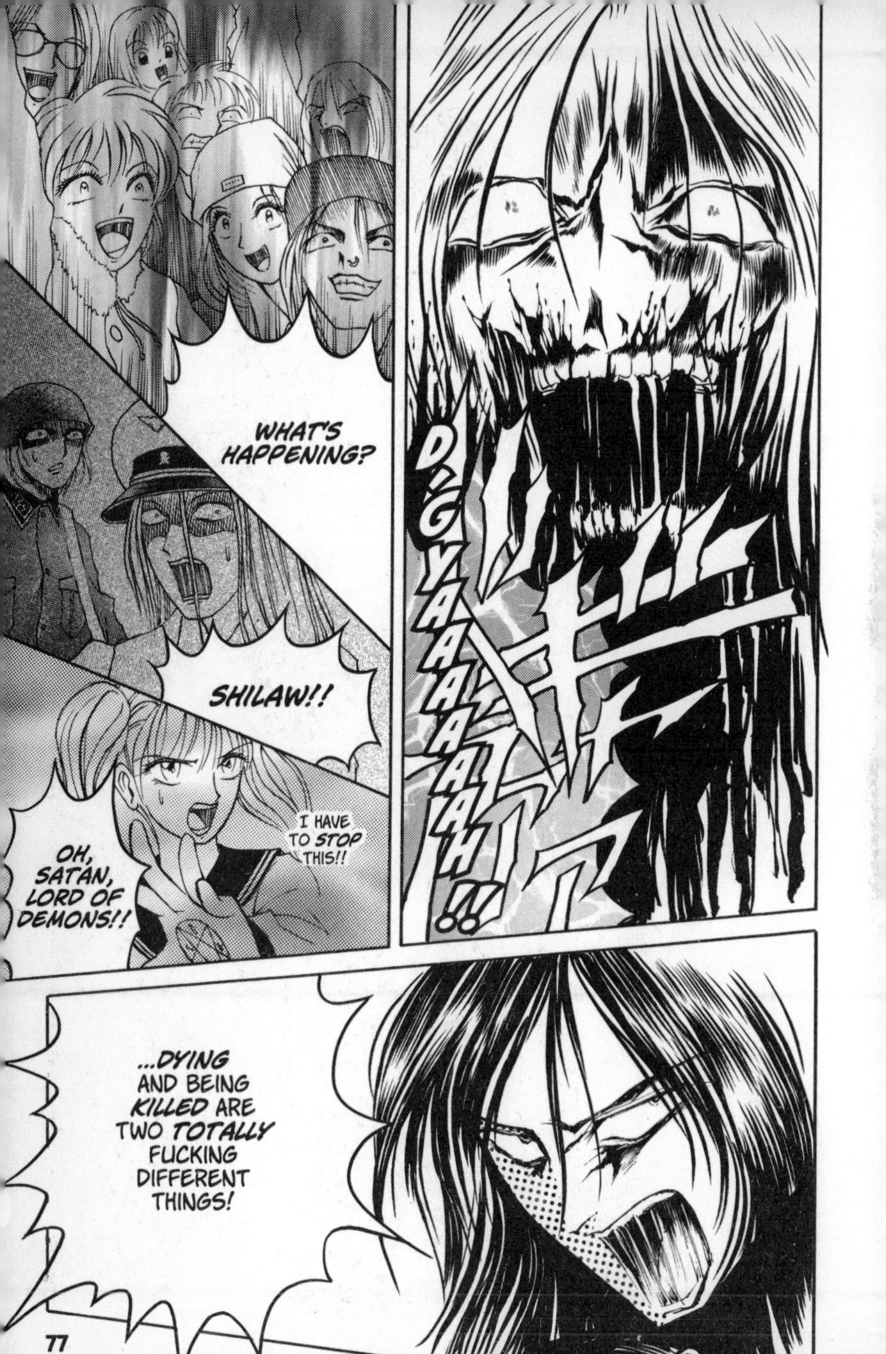
DGYAAAAAAAAH!!
WHAT'S HAPPENING?
SHILAW!!
I HAVE TO STOP THIS!!
OH, SATAN, LORD OF DEMONS!!
...DYING AND BEING KILLED ARE TWO TOTALLY FUCKING DIFFERENT THINGS!

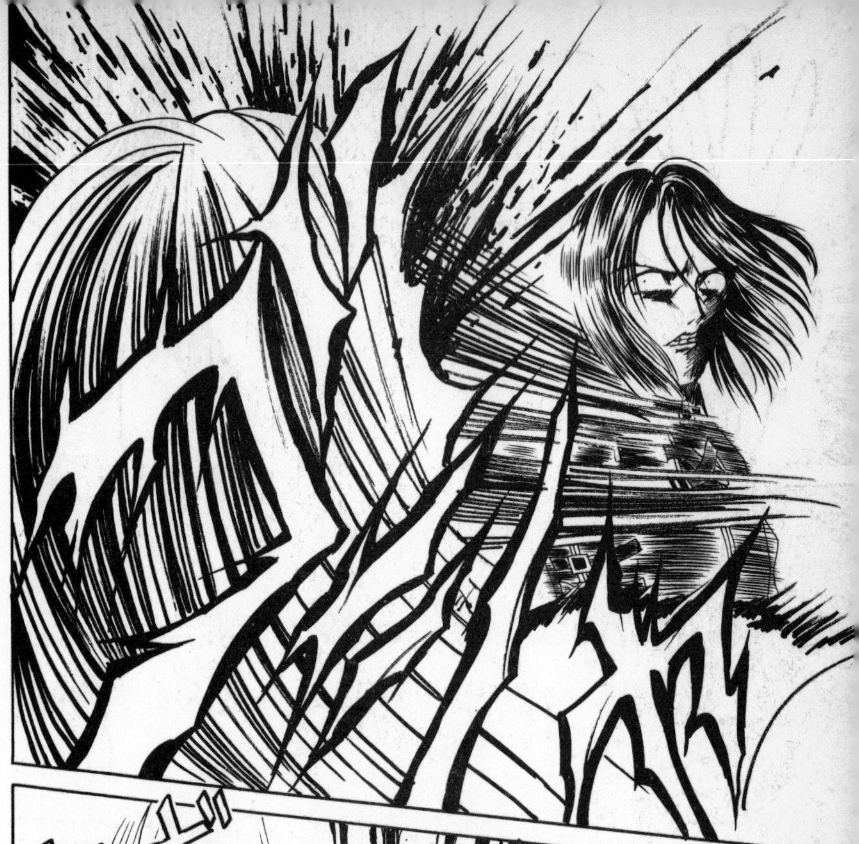

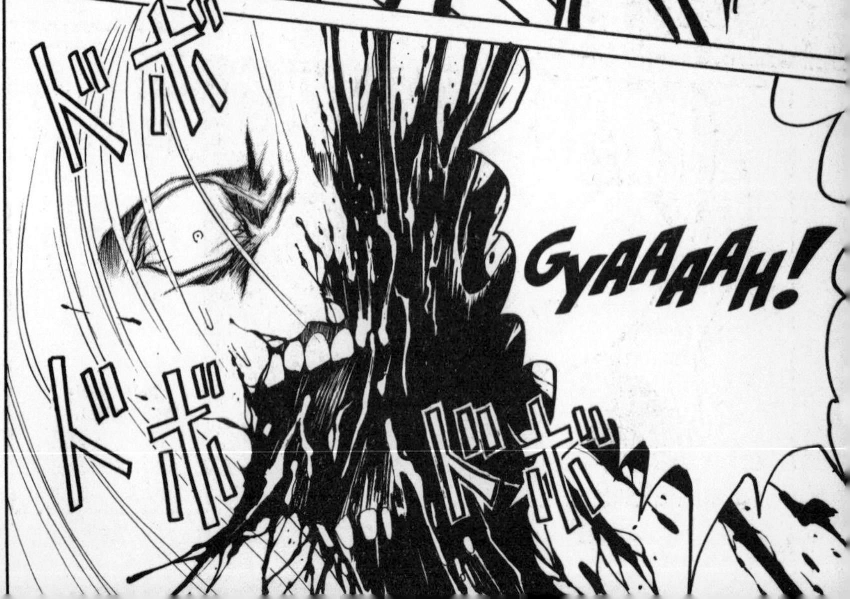
ドボ
GYAAAAH!
ドボ
ドボ

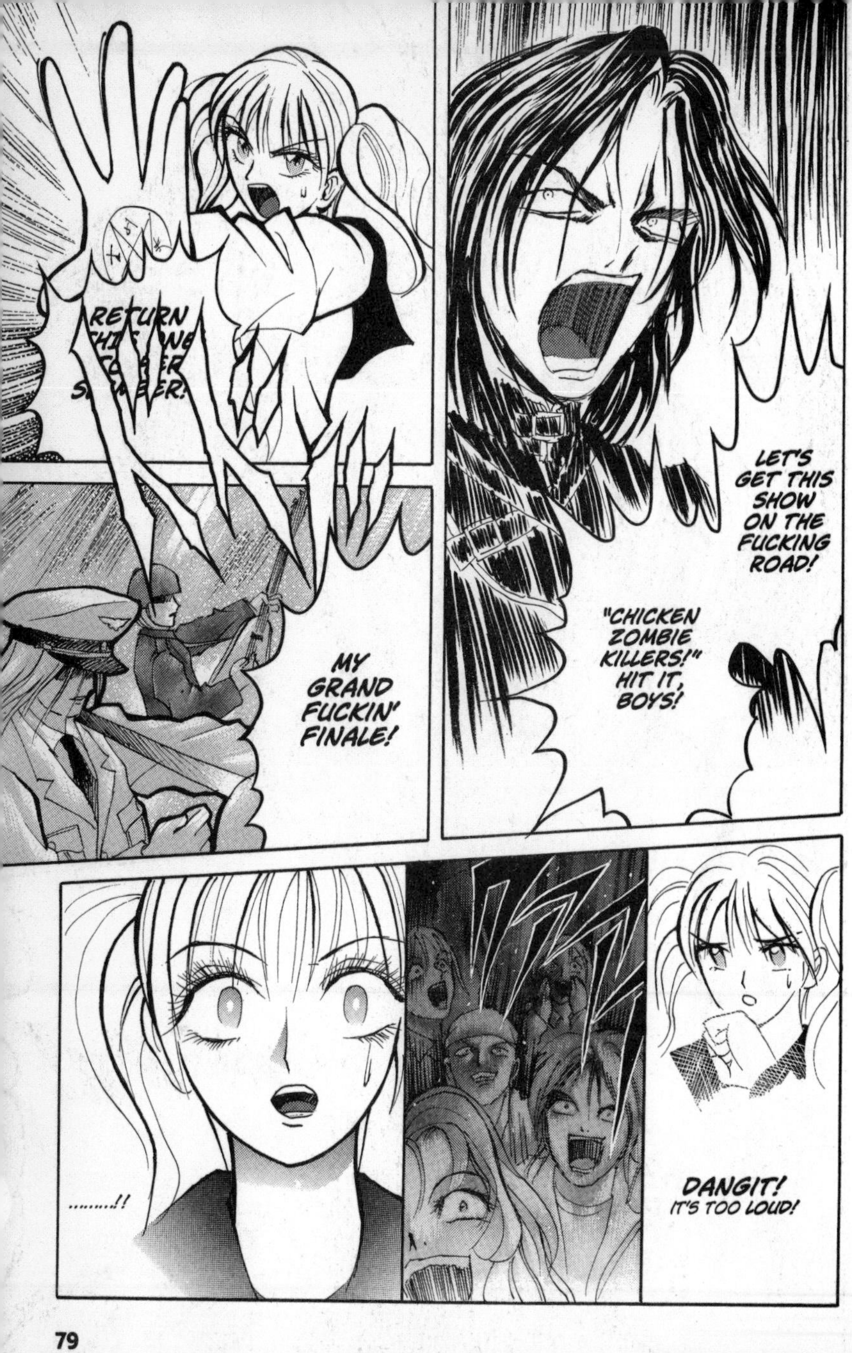
LET'S GET THIS SHOW ON THE FUCKING ROAD!
"CHICKEN ZOMBIE KILLERS!" HIT IT, BOYS!
RETURN
MY GRAND FUCKIN' FINALE!
DANGIT! IT'S TOO LOUD!
........!!

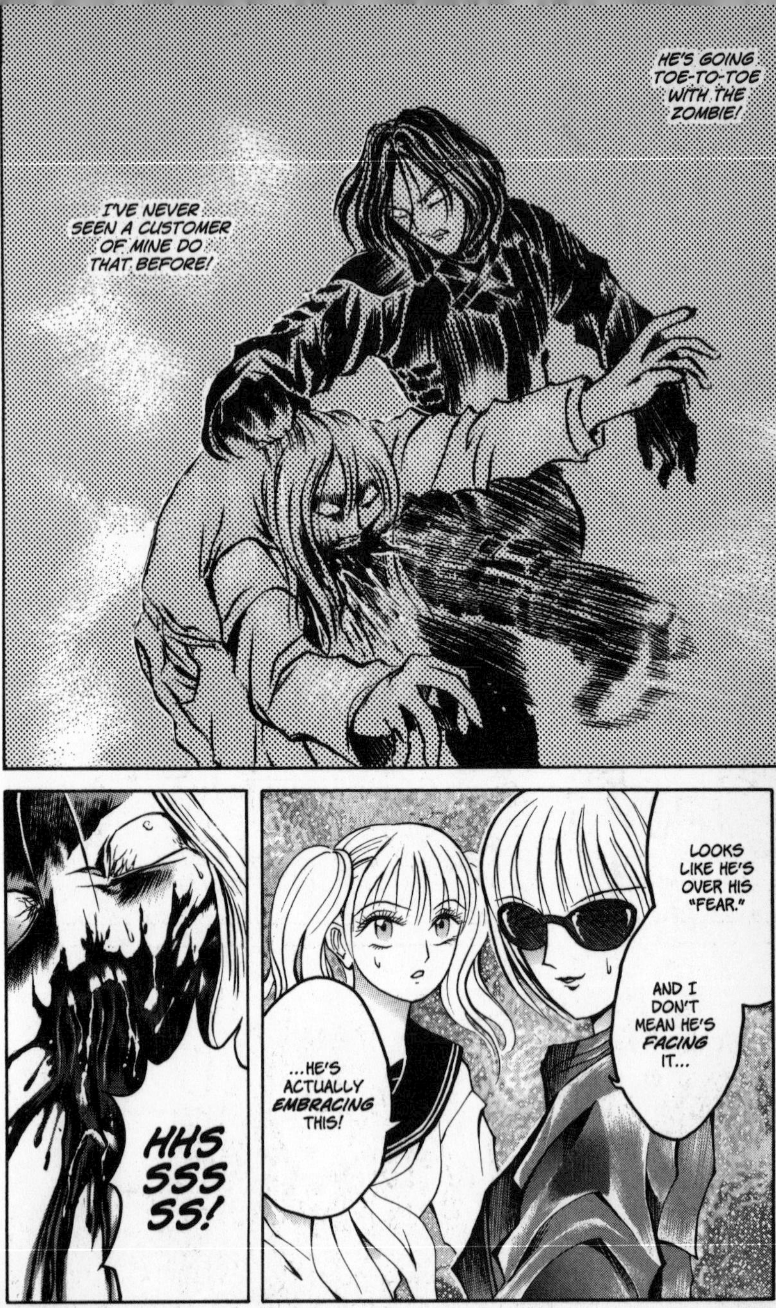
HE'S GOING TOE-TO-TOE WITH THE ZOMBIE!
I'VE NEVER SEEN A CUSTOMER OF MINE DO THAT BEFORE!
LOOKS LIKE HE'S OVER HIS "FEAR."
AND I DON'T MEAN HE'S *FACING* IT...
...HE'S ACTUALLY *EMBRACING* THIS!
HHSSSSSSS!

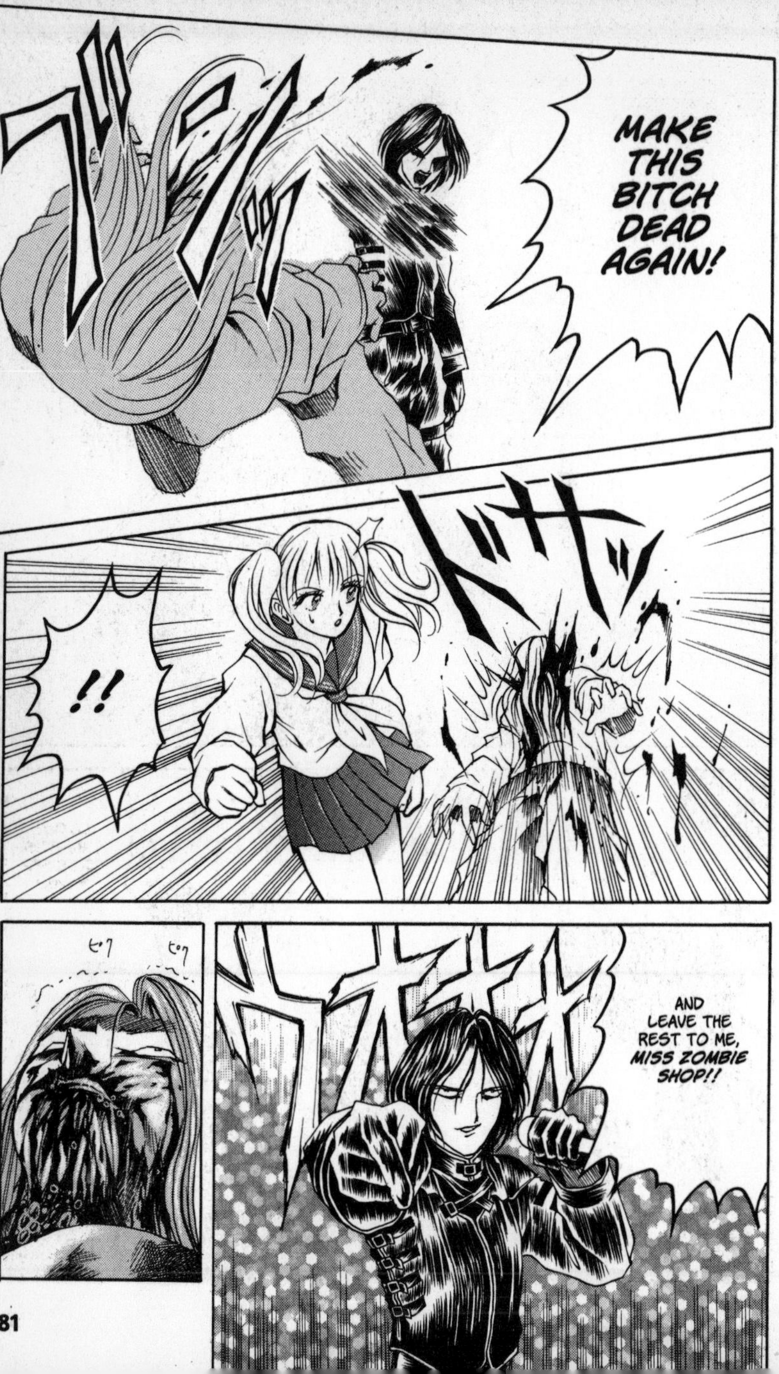
MAKE THIS BITCH DEAD AGAIN!
!!
AND LEAVE THE REST TO ME, MISS ZOMBIE SHOP!!
ピク
ピク

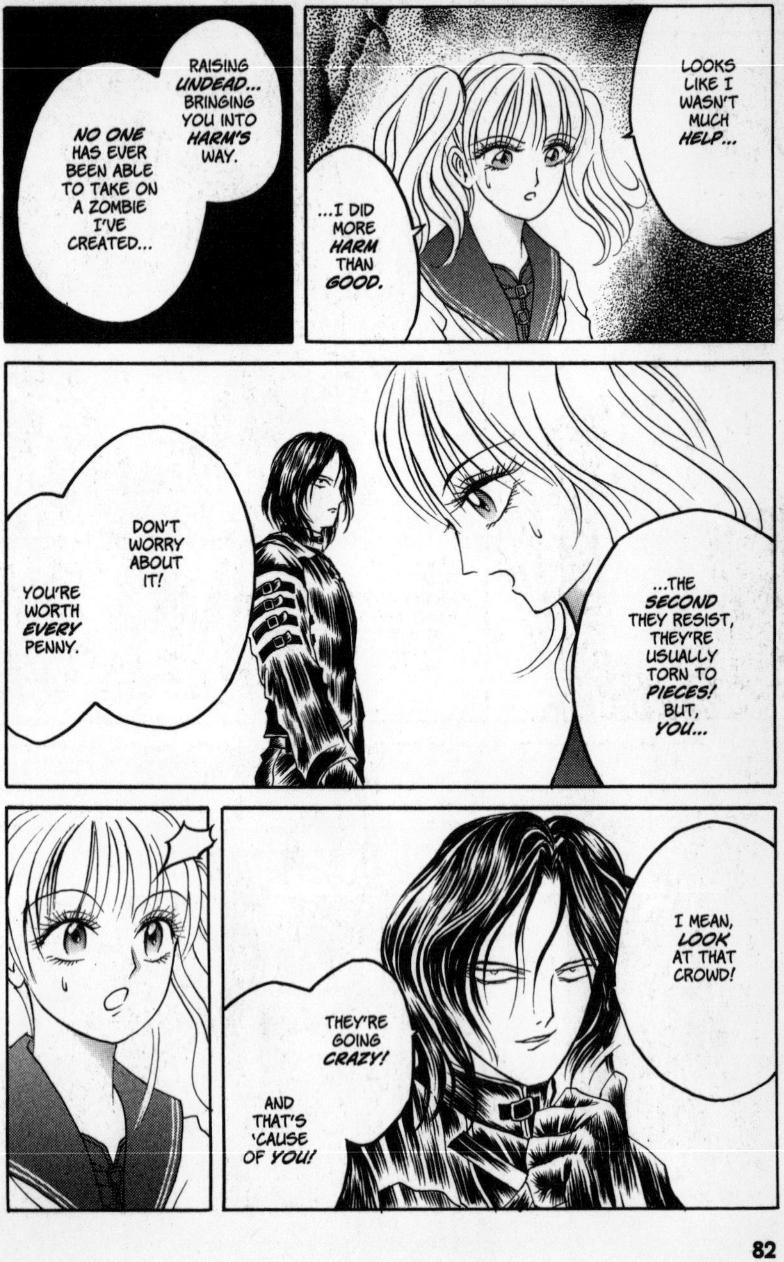

LOOKS LIKE I WASN'T MUCH HELP...
...I DID MORE HARM THAN GOOD.
RAISING UNDEAD... BRINGING YOU INTO HARM'S WAY.
NO ONE HAS EVER BEEN ABLE TO TAKE ON A ZOMBIE I'VE CREATED...
...THE SECOND THEY RESIST, THEY'RE USUALLY TORN TO PIECES! BUT, YOU...
DON'T WORRY ABOUT IT!
YOU'RE WORTH EVERY PENNY.
I MEAN, LOOK AT THAT CROWD!
THEY'RE GOING CRAZY!
AND THAT'S 'CAUSE OF YOU!

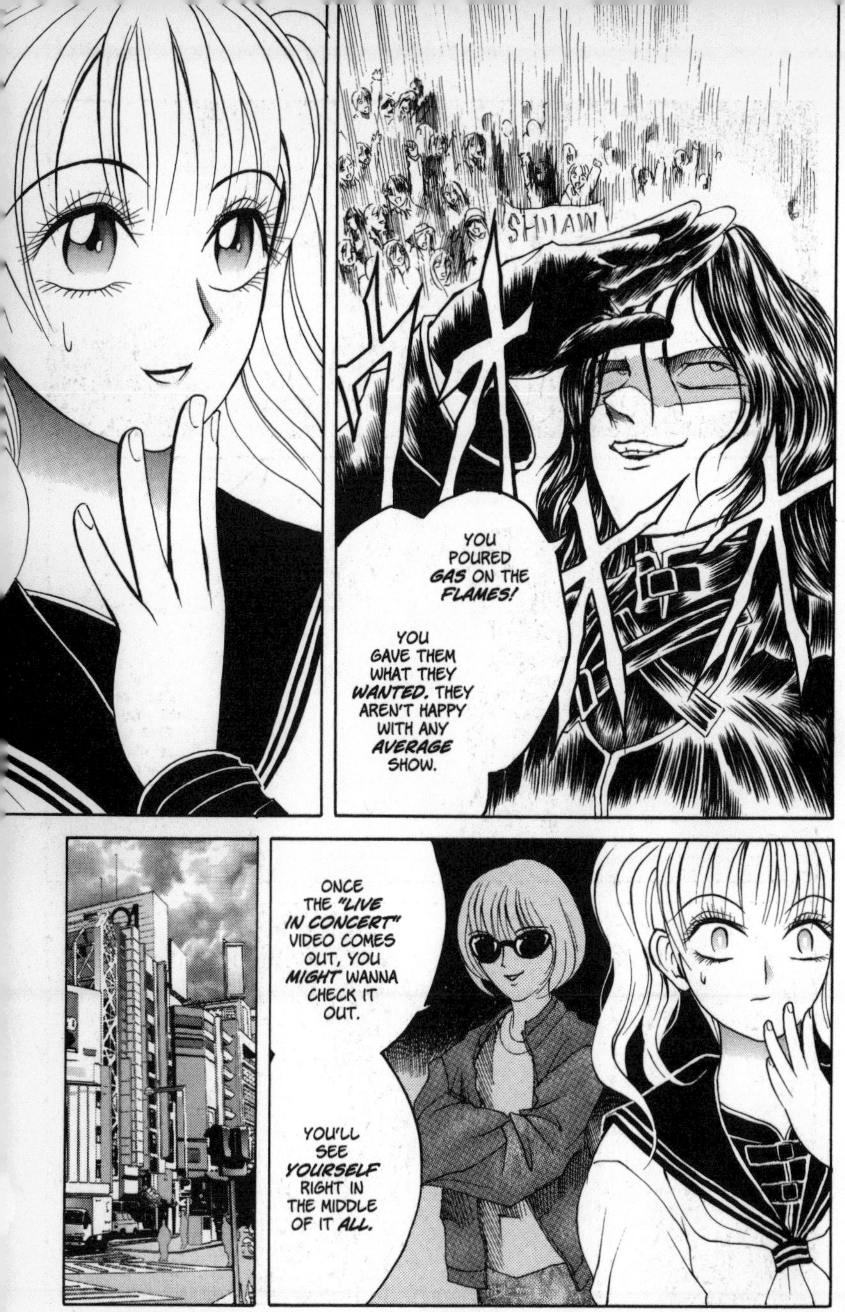
YOU POURED *GAS* ON THE *FLAMES!*
YOU GAVE THEM WHAT THEY *WANTED.* THEY AREN'T HAPPY WITH ANY *AVERAGE* SHOW.
ONCE THE *"LIVE IN CONCERT"* VIDEO COMES OUT, YOU *MIGHT* WANNA CHECK IT OUT.
YOU'LL SEE *YOURSELF* RIGHT IN THE MIDDLE OF IT *ALL.*

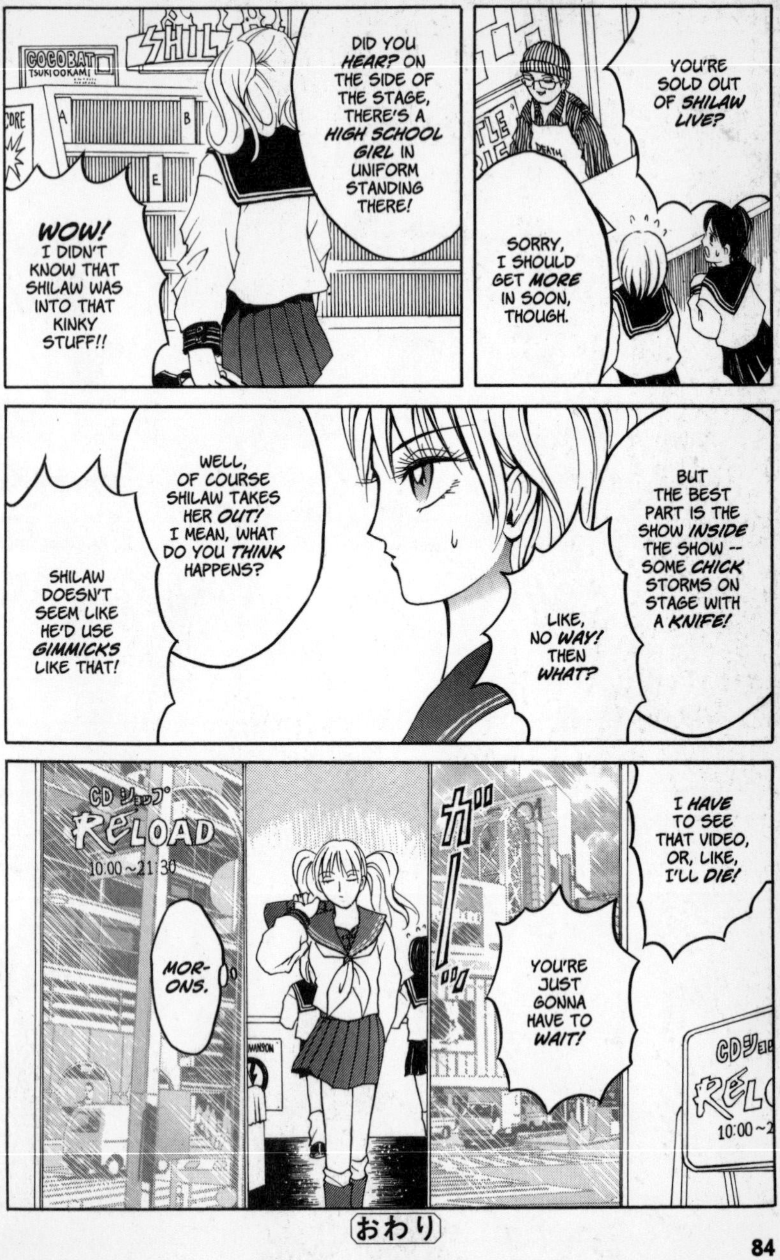
YOU'RE SOLD OUT OF SHILAW LIVE?
SORRY, I SHOULD GET MORE IN SOON, THOUGH.
DEATH
COCOBAT
TSUKIOOKAMI
DID YOU HEAR? ON THE SIDE OF THE STAGE, THERE'S A HIGH SCHOOL GIRL IN UNIFORM STANDING THERE!
WOW! I DIDN'T KNOW THAT SHILAW WAS INTO THAT KINKY STUFF!!
BUT THE BEST PART IS THE SHOW INSIDE THE SHOW -- SOME CHICK STORMS ON STAGE WITH A KNIFE!
LIKE, NO WAY! THEN WHAT?
WELL, OF COURSE SHILAW TAKES HER OUT! I MEAN, WHAT DO YOU THINK HAPPENS?
SHILAW DOESN'T SEEM LIKE HE'D USE GIMMICKS LIKE THAT!
I HAVE TO SEE THAT VIDEO, OR, LIKE, I'LL DIE!
YOU'RE JUST GONNA HAVE TO WAIT!
ガーー
CD ショップ
RELOAD
10:00~21:30
MOR-ONS.

おわり

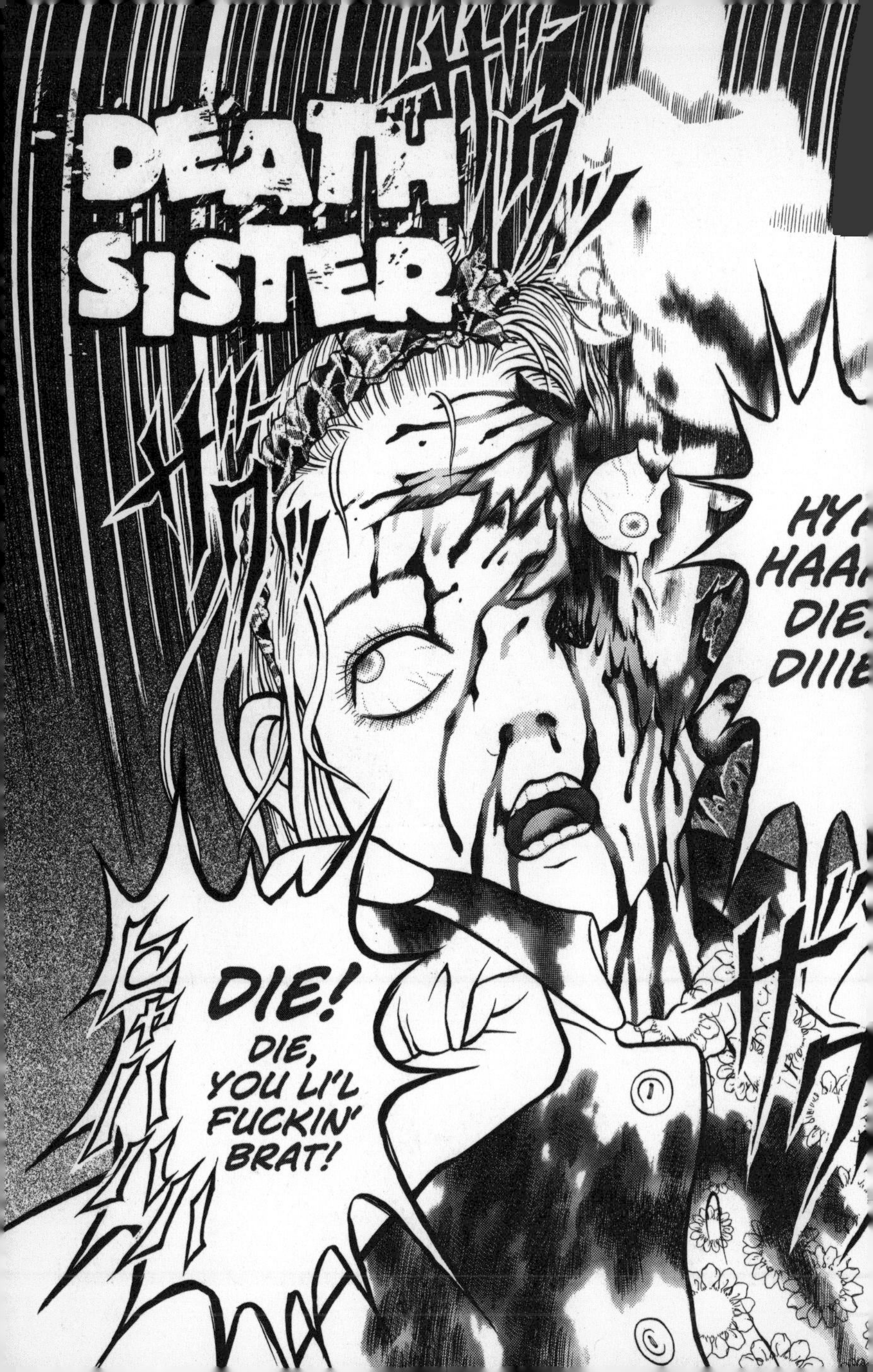
DEATH SISTER
HY HAA DIE, DIIIE
DIE! DIE, YOU LI'L FUCKIN' BRAT!

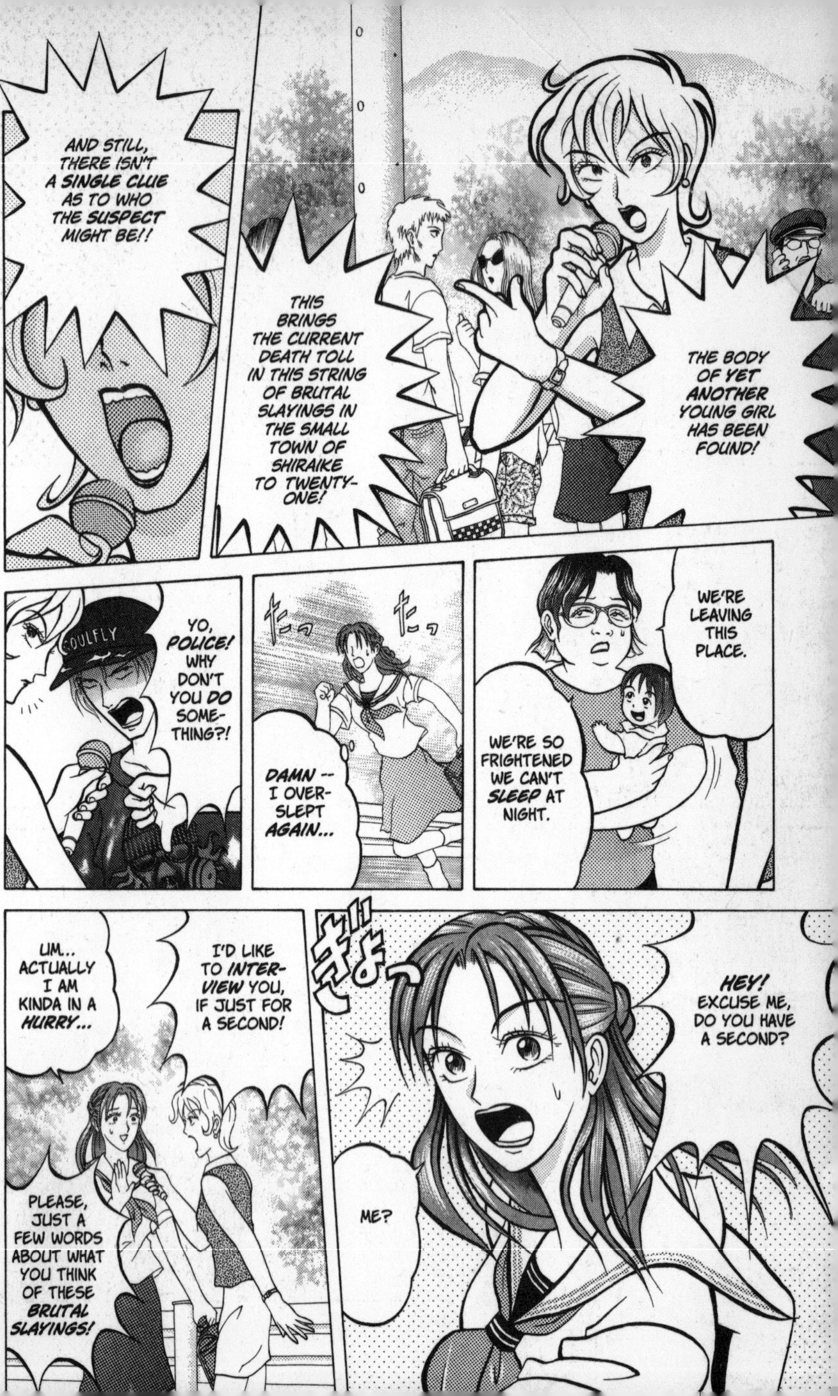
THE BODY OF YET ANOTHER YOUNG GIRL HAS BEEN FOUND!
THIS BRINGS THE CURRENT DEATH TOLL IN THIS STRING OF BRUTAL SLAYINGS IN THE SMALL TOWN OF SHIRAIKE TO TWENTY-ONE!
AND STILL, THERE ISN'T A SINGLE CLUE AS TO WHO THE SUSPECT MIGHT BE!!
WE'RE LEAVING THIS PLACE.
WE'RE SO FRIGHTENED WE CAN'T SLEEP AT NIGHT.
たっ
たっ
DAMN -- I OVERSLEPT AGAIN...
SOULFLY
YO, POLICE! WHY DON'T YOU DO SOMETHING?!
ぎょっ
HEY! EXCUSE ME, DO YOU HAVE A SECOND?
ME?
I'D LIKE TO INTERVIEW YOU, IF JUST FOR A SECOND!
UM... ACTUALLY I AM KINDA IN A HURRY...
PLEASE, JUST A FEW WORDS ABOUT WHAT YOU THINK OF THESE BRUTAL SLAYINGS!

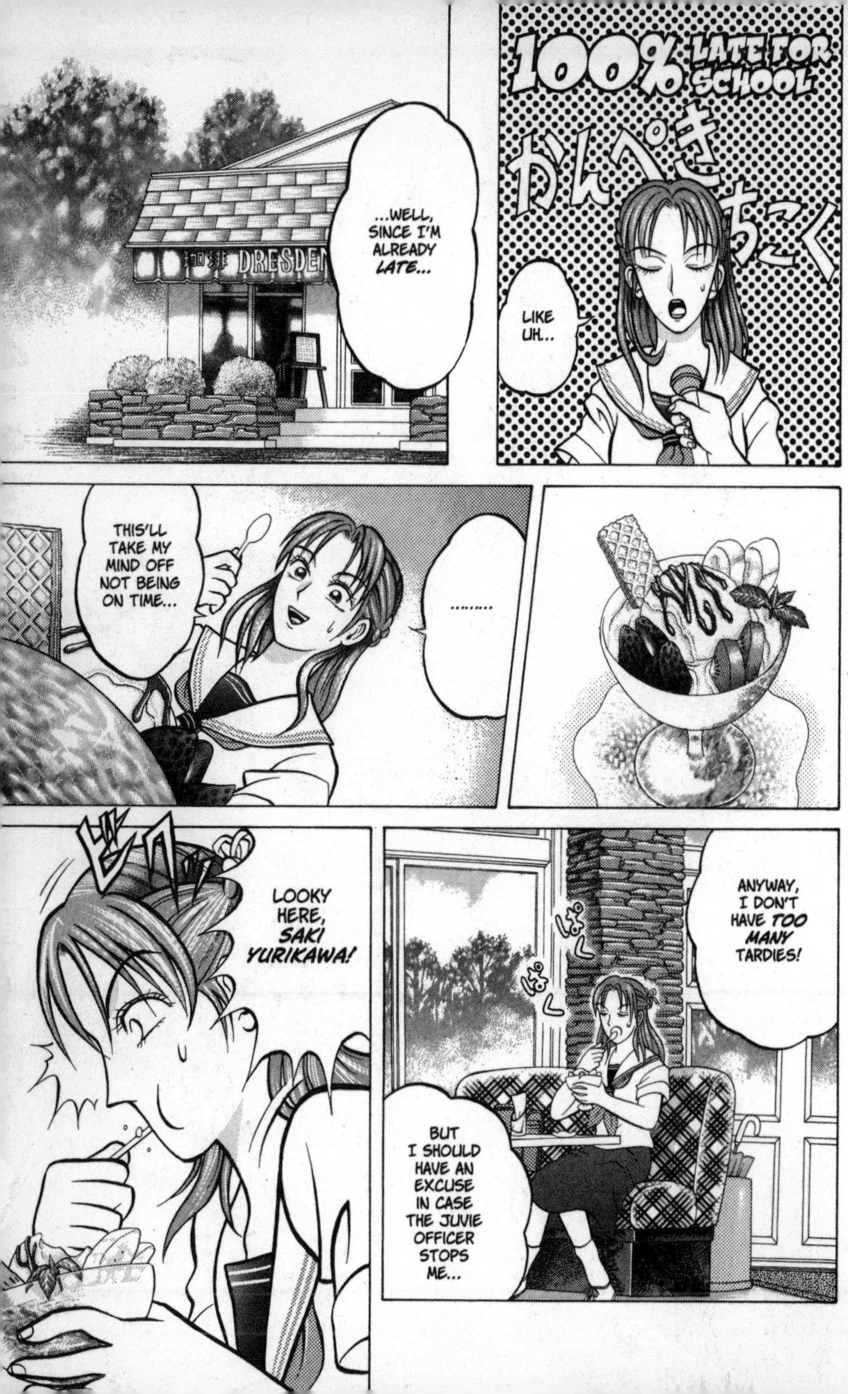
100% LATE FOR SCHOOL
かんぺきちこく
LIKE UH...
...WELL, SINCE I'M ALREADY *LATE*...
........
THIS'LL TAKE MY MIND OFF NOT BEING ON TIME...
ANYWAY, I DON'T HAVE *TOO MANY* TARDIES!
ぱくぱく
BUT I SHOULD HAVE AN EXCUSE IN CASE THE JUVIE OFFICER STOPS ME...
LOOKY HERE, *SAKI YURIKAWA!*

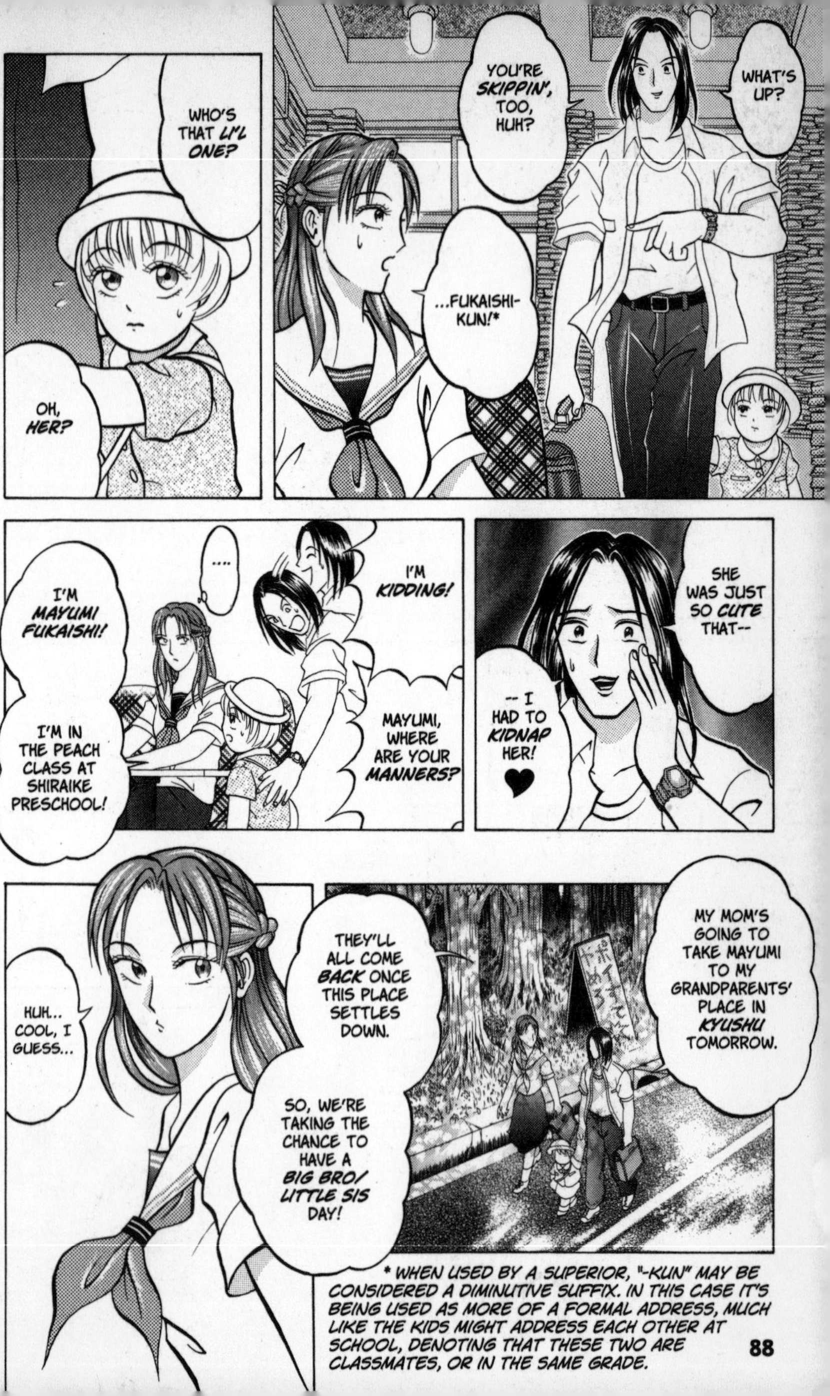
WHAT'S UP?
YOU'RE SKIPPIN', TOO, HUH?
...FUKAISHI-KUN!*
WHO'S THAT LI'L ONE?
OH, HER?
SHE WAS JUST SO CUTE THAT--
-- I HAD TO KIDNAP HER! ♥
I'M KIDDING!
....
MAYUMI, WHERE ARE YOUR MANNERS?
I'M MAYUMI FUKAISHI!
I'M IN THE PEACH CLASS AT SHIRAIKE PRESCHOOL!
MY MOM'S GOING TO TAKE MAYUMI TO MY GRANDPARENTS' PLACE IN KYUSHU TOMORROW.
THEY'LL ALL COME BACK ONCE THIS PLACE SETTLES DOWN.
SO, WE'RE TAKING THE CHANCE TO HAVE A BIG BRO/ LITTLE SIS DAY!
HUH... COOL, I GUESS...

* WHEN USED BY A SUPERIOR, "-KUN" MAY BE CONSIDERED A DIMINUTIVE SUFFIX. IN THIS CASE IT'S BEING USED AS MORE OF A FORMAL ADDRESS, MUCH LIKE THE KIDS MIGHT ADDRESS EACH OTHER AT SCHOOL, DENOTING THAT THESE TWO ARE CLASSMATES, OR IN THE SAME GRADE.

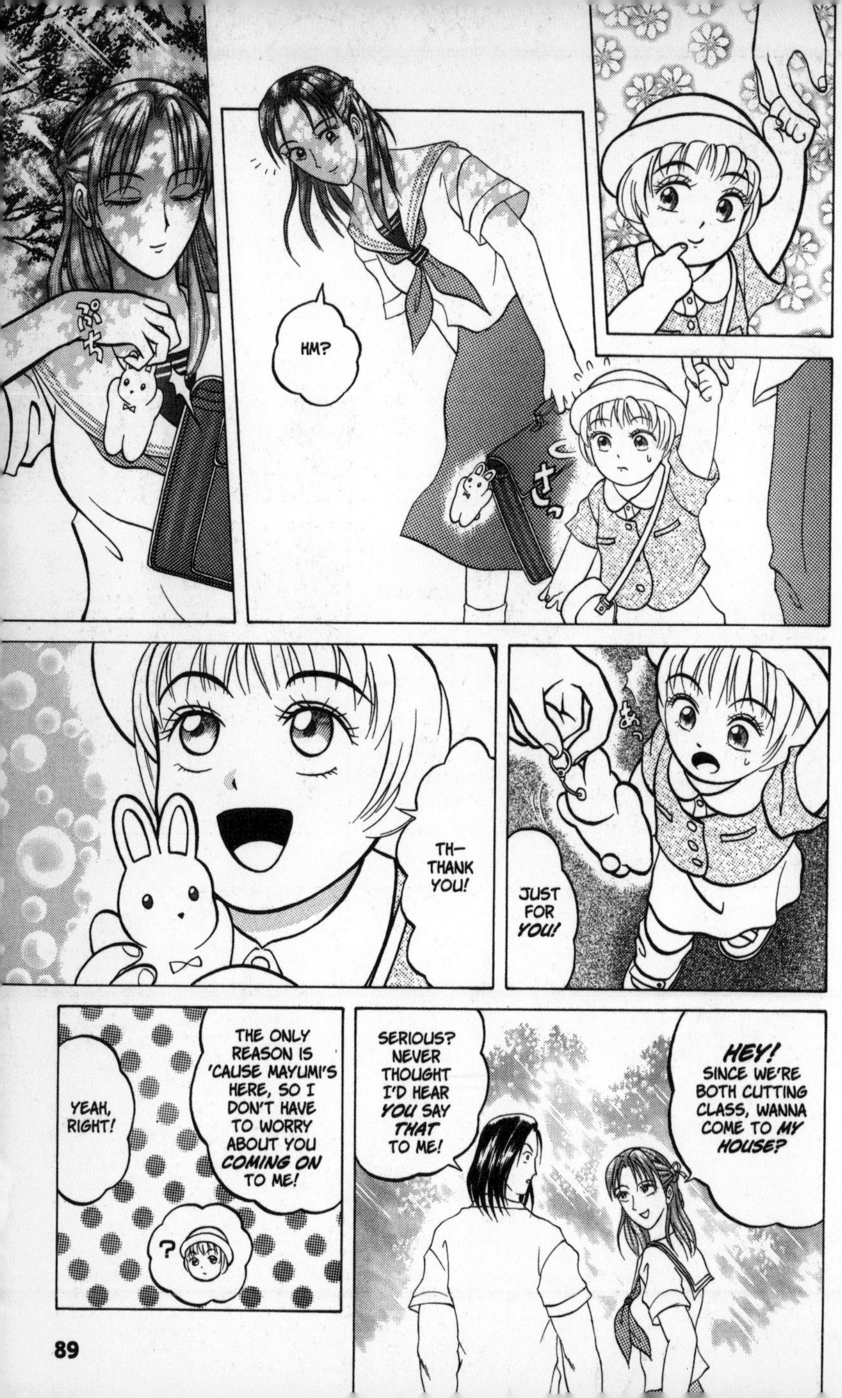
HM?
JUST FOR YOU!
TH— THANK YOU!
HEY! SINCE WE'RE BOTH CUTTING CLASS, WANNA COME TO MY HOUSE?
SERIOUS? NEVER THOUGHT I'D HEAR YOU SAY THAT TO ME!
THE ONLY REASON IS 'CAUSE MAYUMI'S HERE, SO I DON'T HAVE TO WORRY ABOUT YOU COMING ON TO ME!
YEAH, RIGHT!
?

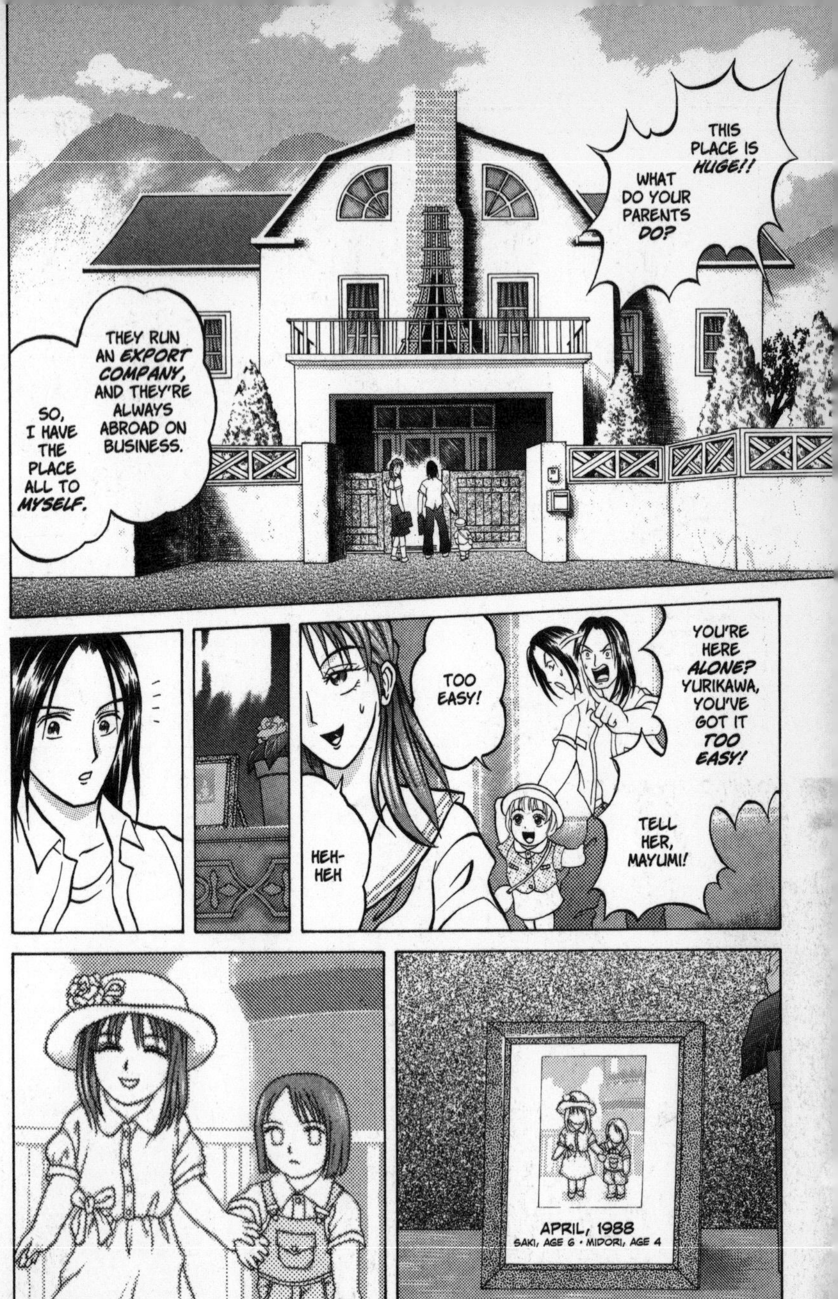
THIS PLACE IS HUGE!!
WHAT DO YOUR PARENTS DO?
THEY RUN AN EXPORT COMPANY, AND THEY'RE ALWAYS ABROAD ON BUSINESS.
SO, I HAVE THE PLACE ALL TO MYSELF.
YOU'RE HERE ALONE? YURIKAWA, YOU'VE GOT IT TOO EASY!
TELL HER, MAYUMI!
TOO EASY!
HEH-HEH
APRIL, 1988
SAKI, AGE 6 • MIDORI, AGE 4

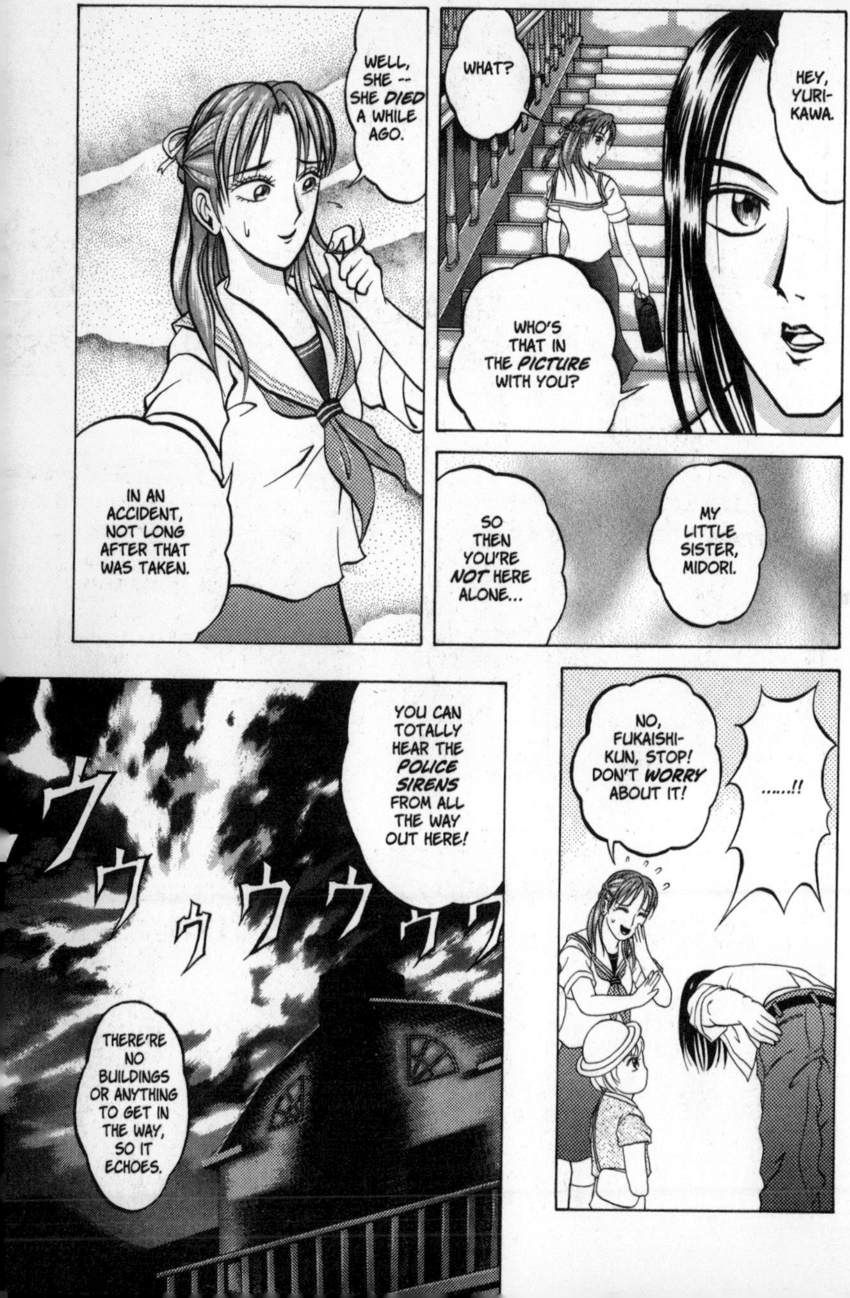
HEY, YURI-KAWA.
WHAT?
WHO'S THAT IN THE *PICTURE* WITH YOU?
MY LITTLE SISTER, MIDORI.
SO THEN YOU'RE *NOT* HERE ALONE...
WELL, SHE -- SHE *DIED* A WHILE AGO.
IN AN ACCIDENT, NOT LONG AFTER THAT WAS TAKEN.
......!!
NO, FUKAISHI-KUN, STOP! DON'T *WORRY* ABOUT IT!
YOU CAN TOTALLY HEAR THE *POLICE SIRENS* FROM ALL THE WAY OUT HERE!
ウウゥウウゥウ
THERE'RE NO BUILDINGS OR ANYTHING TO GET IN THE WAY, SO IT ECHOES.

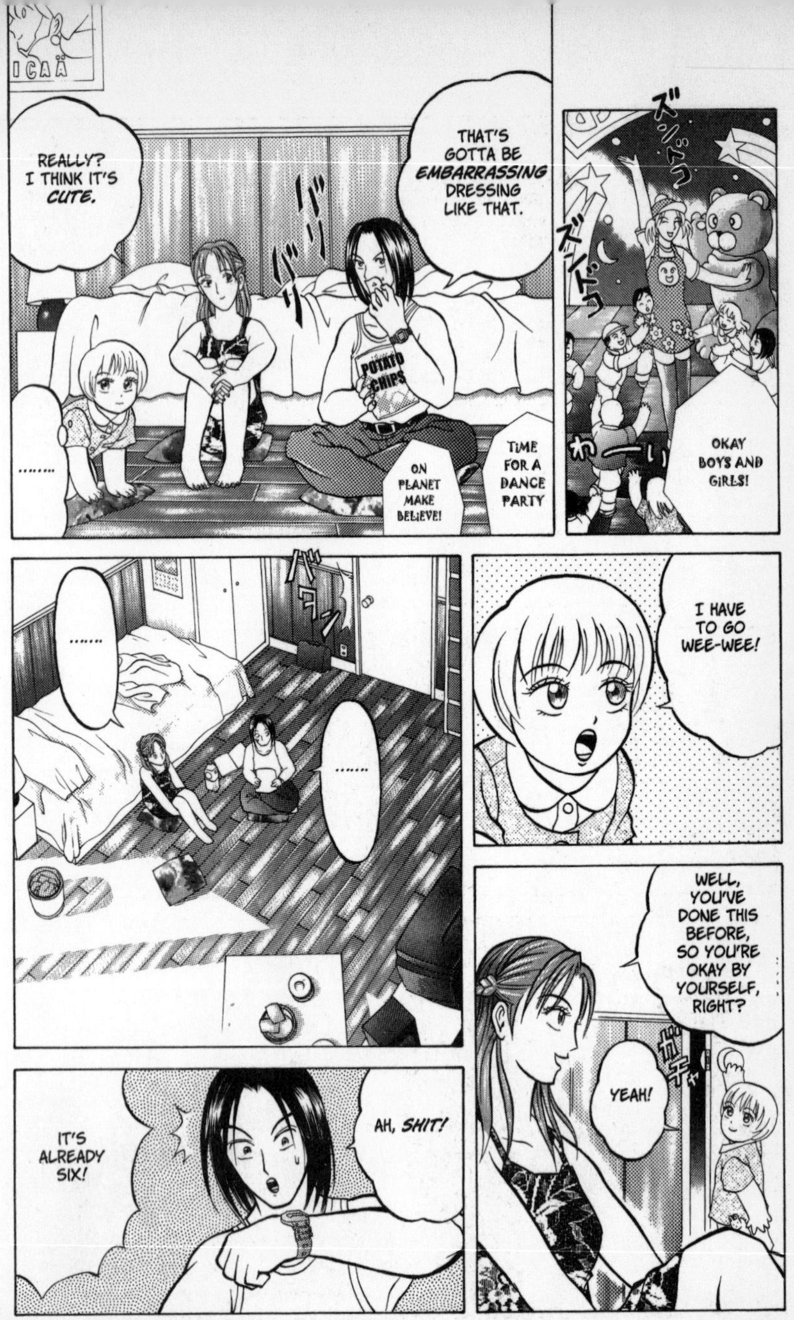
OKAY BOYS AND GIRLS!
わーい
TIME FOR A DANCE PARTY
ON PLANET MAKE BELIEVE!
THAT'S GOTTA BE *EMBARRASSING* DRESSING LIKE THAT.
REALLY? I THINK IT'S *CUTE.*
........
I HAVE TO GO WEE-WEE!
.......
.......
WELL, YOU'VE DONE THIS BEFORE, SO YOU'RE OKAY BY YOURSELF, RIGHT?
YEAH!
AH, *SHIT!*
IT'S ALREADY SIX!

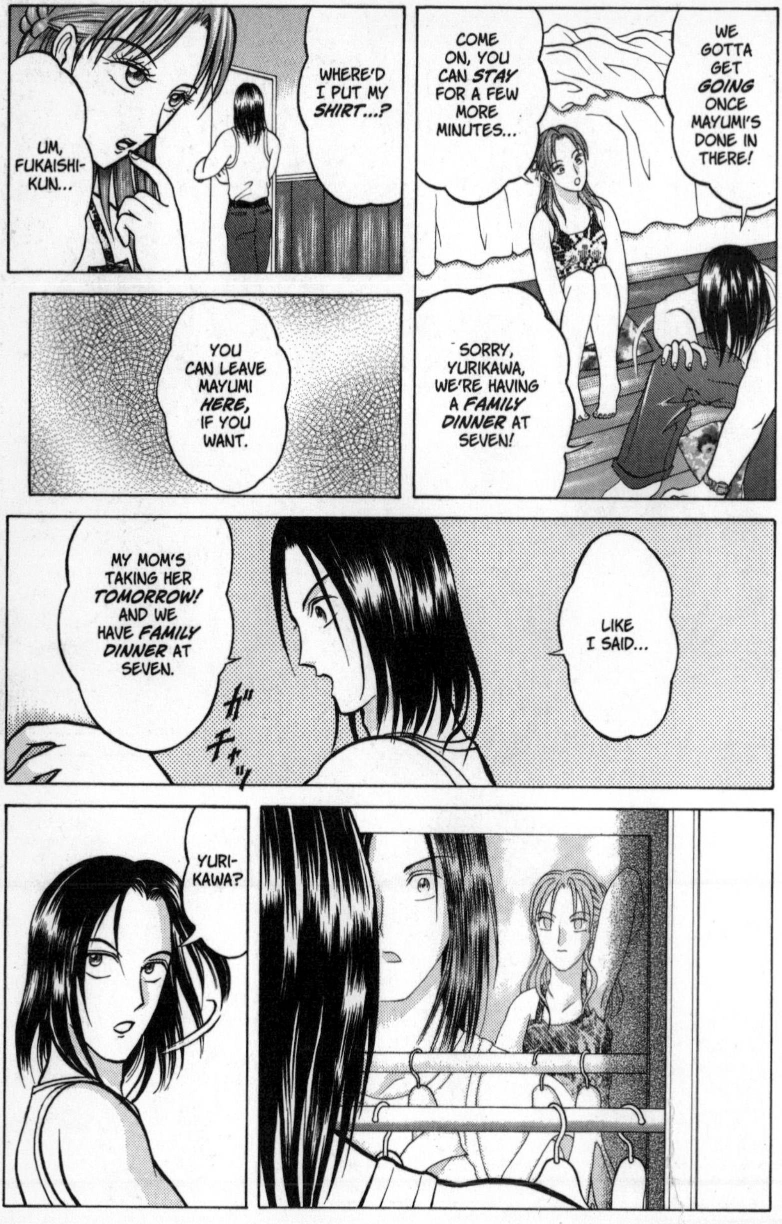
WE GOTTA GET GOING ONCE MAYUMI'S DONE IN THERE!
COME ON, YOU CAN STAY FOR A FEW MORE MINUTES...
SORRY, YURIKAWA, WE'RE HAVING A FAMILY DINNER AT SEVEN!
WHERE'D I PUT MY SHIRT...?
UM, FUKAISHI-KUN...
YOU CAN LEAVE MAYUMI HERE, IF YOU WANT.
LIKE I SAID...
MY MOM'S TAKING HER TOMORROW! AND WE HAVE FAMILY DINNER AT SEVEN.
YURI-KAWA?

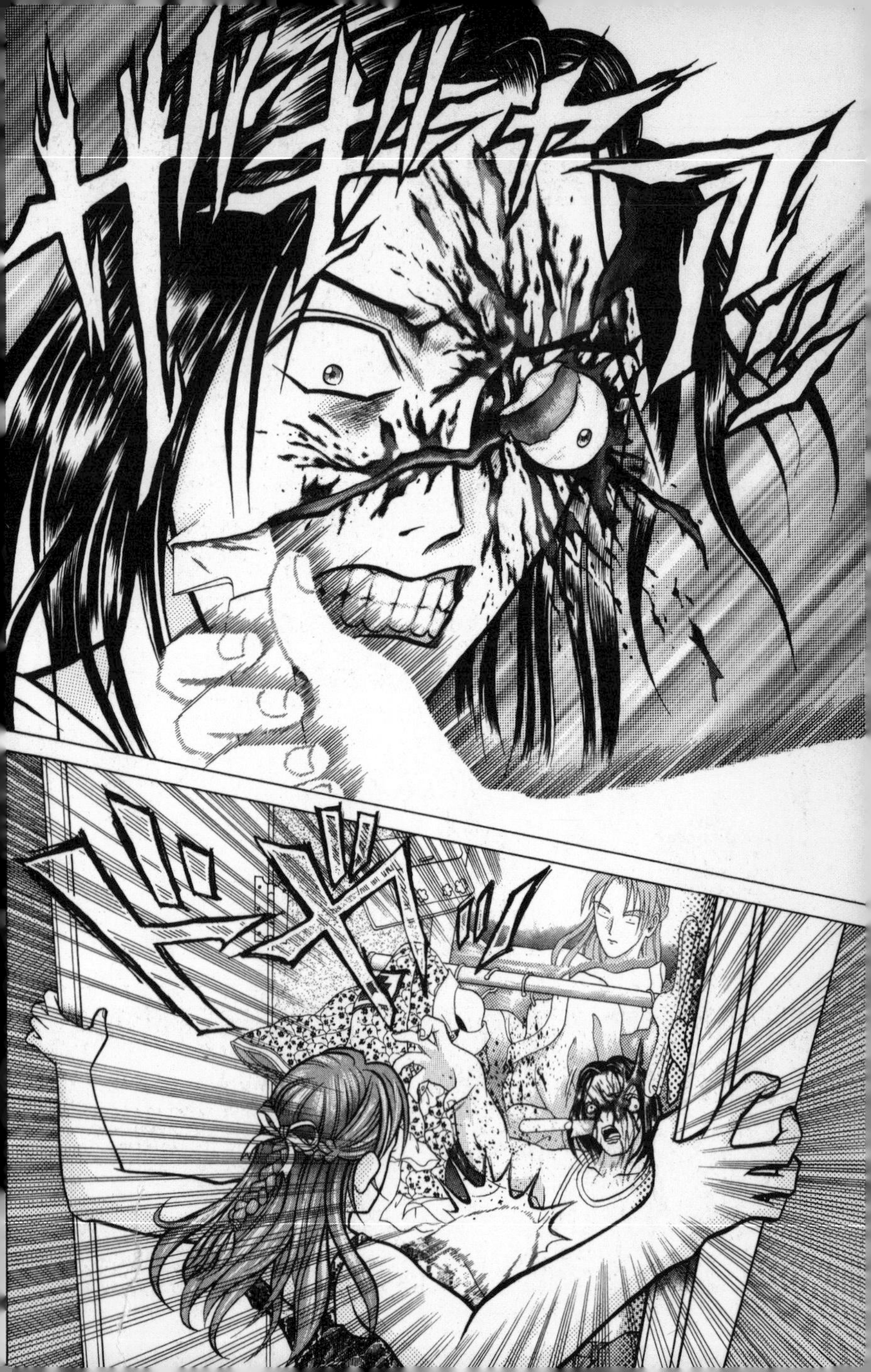

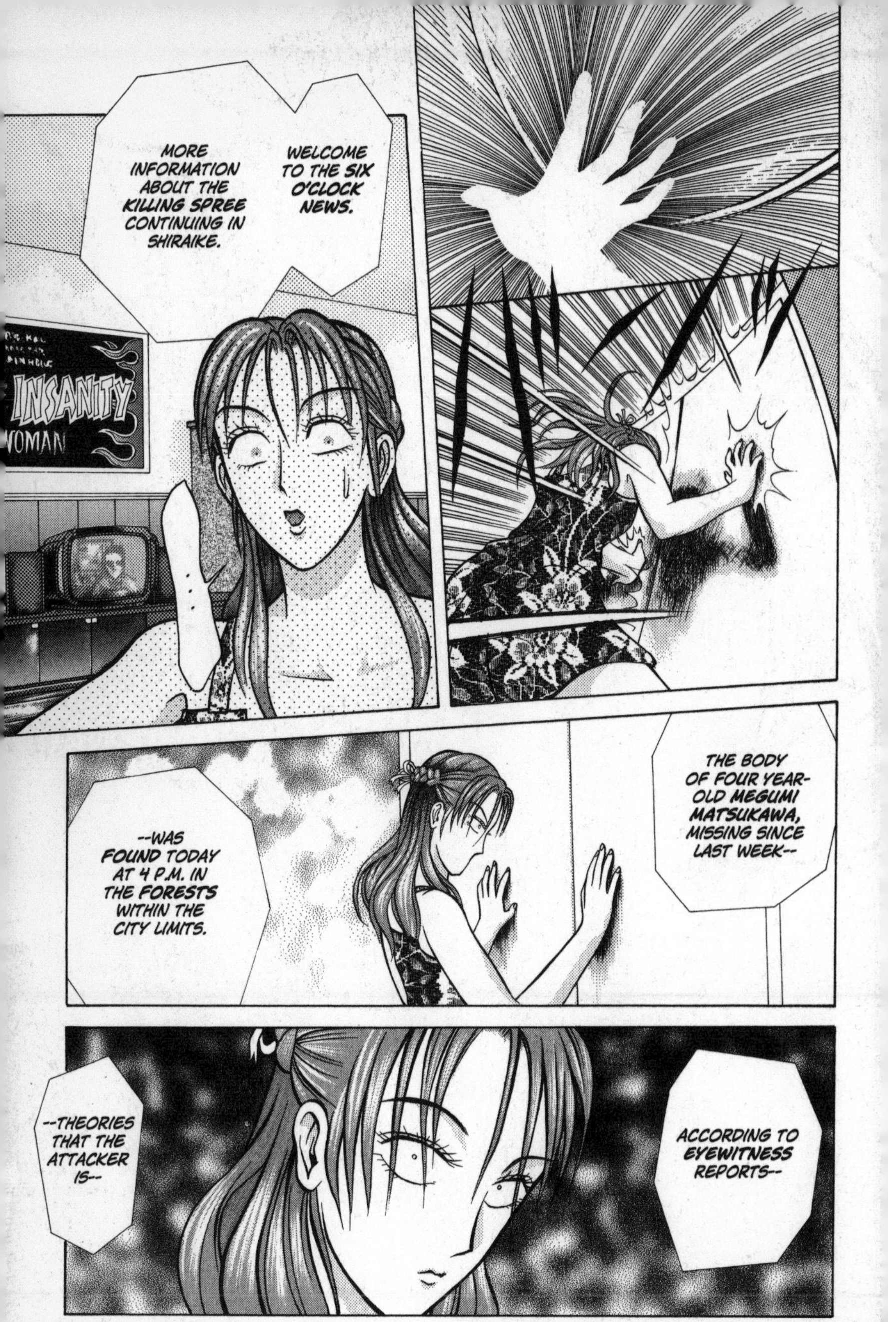
WELCOME TO THE SIX O'CLOCK NEWS.
MORE INFORMATION ABOUT THE KILLING SPREE CONTINUING IN SHIRAIKE.
INSANITY
THE BODY OF FOUR YEAR-OLD MEGUMI MATSUKAWA, MISSING SINCE LAST WEEK--
--WAS FOUND TODAY AT 4 P.M. IN THE FORESTS WITHIN THE CITY LIMITS.
ACCORDING TO EYEWITNESS REPORTS--
--THEORIES THAT THE ATTACKER IS--

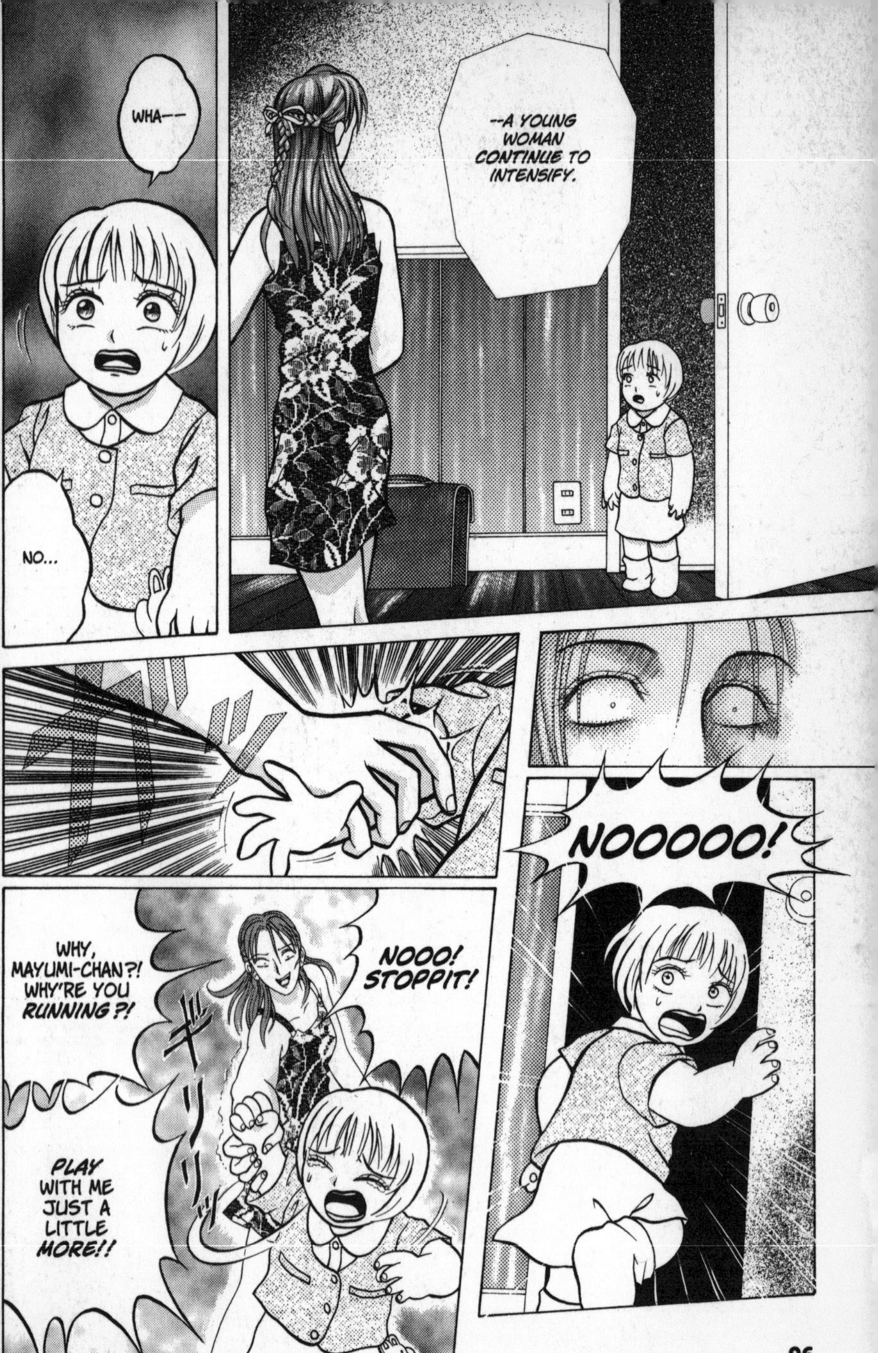
--A YOUNG WOMAN CONTINUE TO INTENSIFY.
WHA---
NO...
NOOOOO!
NOOO! STOPPIT!
WHY, MAYUMI-CHAN?! WHY'RE YOU RUNNING?!
PLAY WITH ME JUST A LITTLE MORE!!

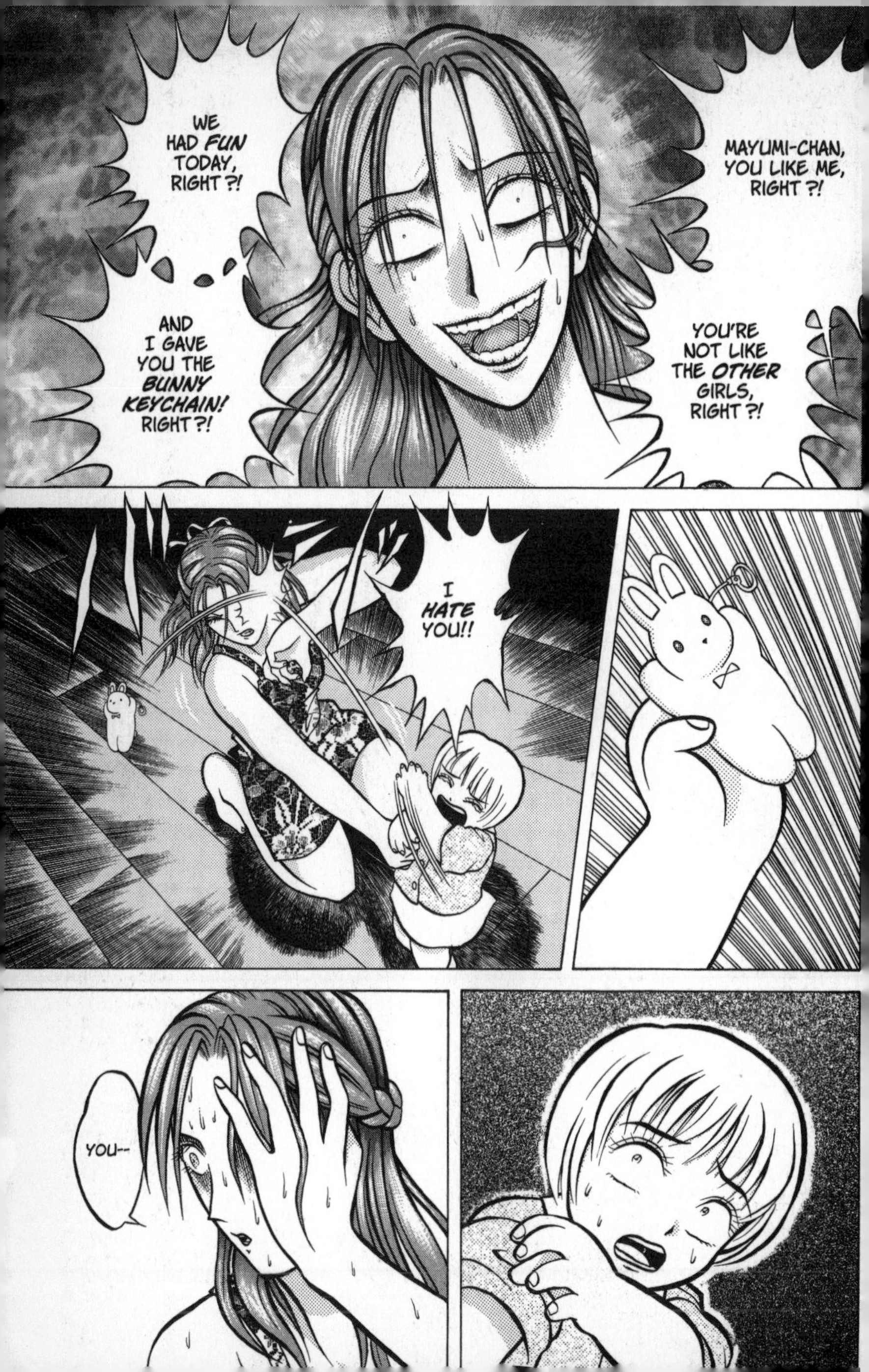
MAYUMI-CHAN, YOU LIKE ME, RIGHT?!
WE HAD FUN TODAY, RIGHT?!
YOU'RE NOT LIKE THE OTHER GIRLS, RIGHT?!
AND I GAVE YOU THE BUNNY KEYCHAIN! RIGHT?!
I HATE YOU!!
YOU--

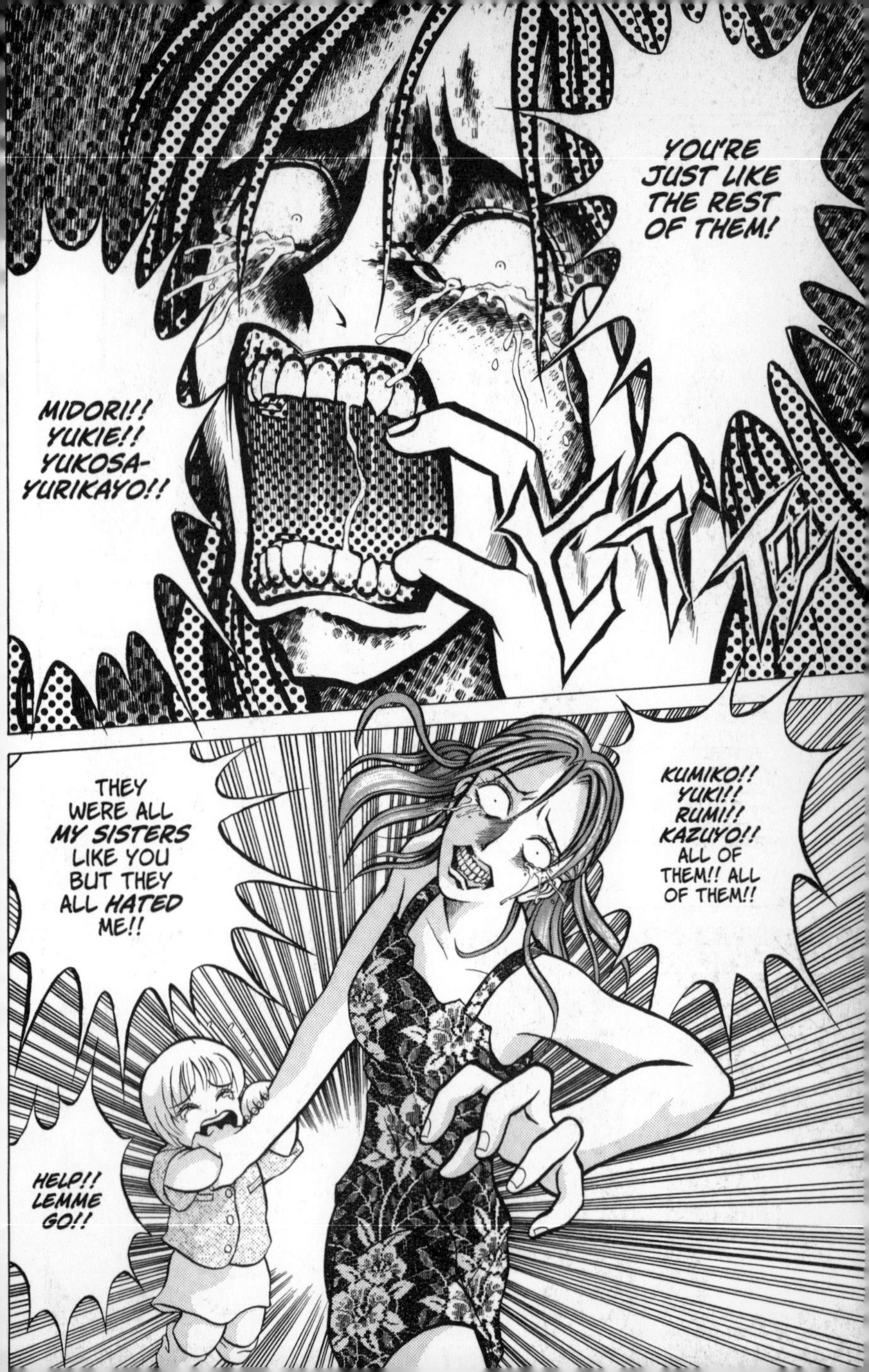
YOU'RE JUST LIKE THE REST OF THEM!
MIDORI!! YUKIE!! YUKOSA-YURIKAYO!!
KUMIKO!! YUKI!! RUMI!! KAZUYO!! ALL OF THEM!! ALL OF THEM!!
THEY WERE ALL MY SISTERS LIKE YOU BUT THEY ALL HATED ME!!
HELP!! LEMME GO!!

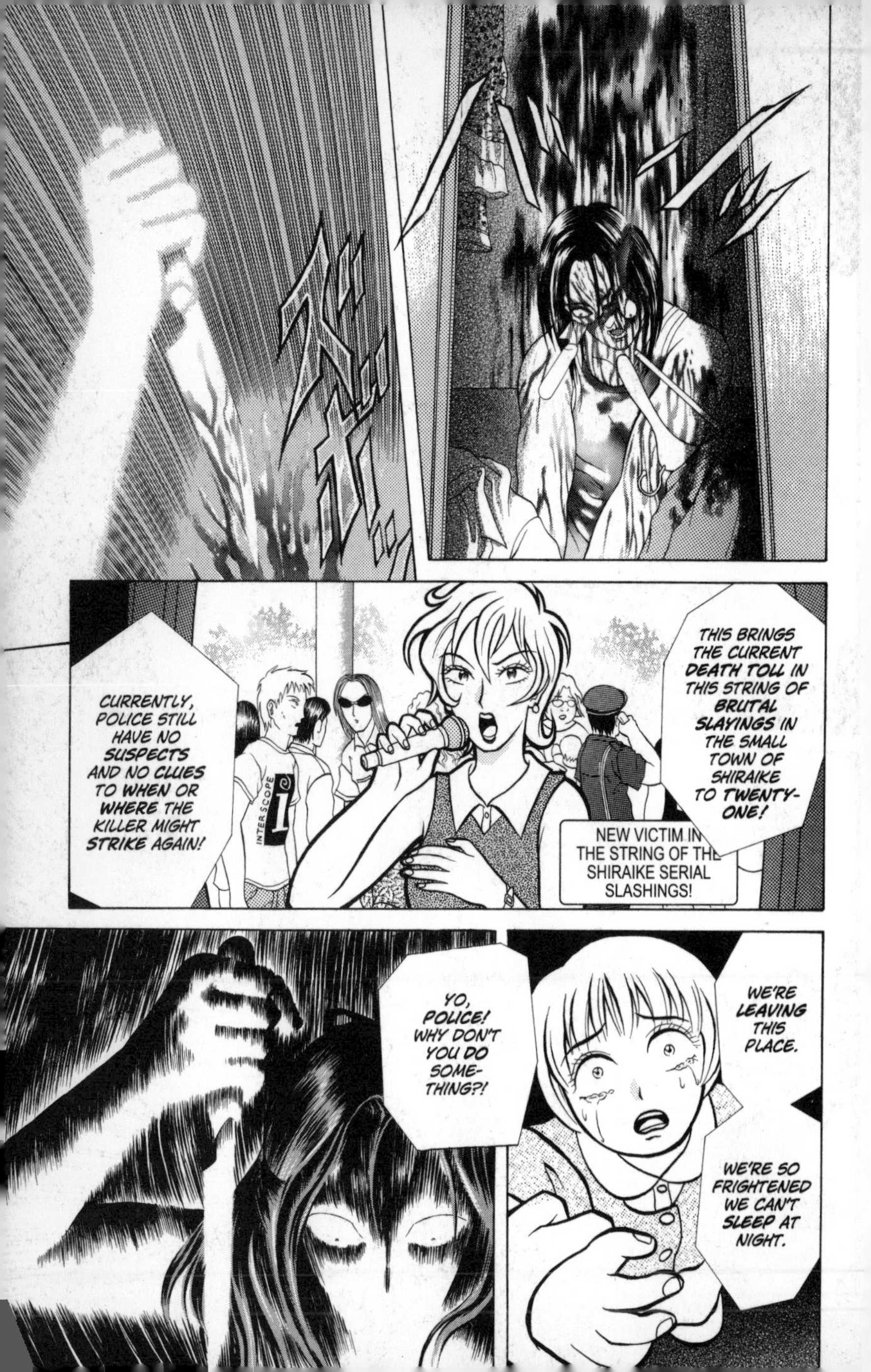
THIS BRINGS THE CURRENT DEATH TOLL IN THIS STRING OF BRUTAL SLAYINGS IN THE SMALL TOWN OF SHIRAIKE TO TWENTY-ONE!
NEW VICTIM IN THE STRING OF THE SHIRAIKE SERIAL SLASHINGS!
CURRENTLY, POLICE STILL HAVE NO SUSPECTS AND NO CLUES TO WHEN OR WHERE THE KILLER MIGHT STRIKE AGAIN!
INTERSCOPE
WE'RE LEAVING THIS PLACE.
WE'RE SO FRIGHTENED WE CAN'T SLEEP AT NIGHT.
YO, POLICE! WHY DON'T YOU DO SOME-THING?!

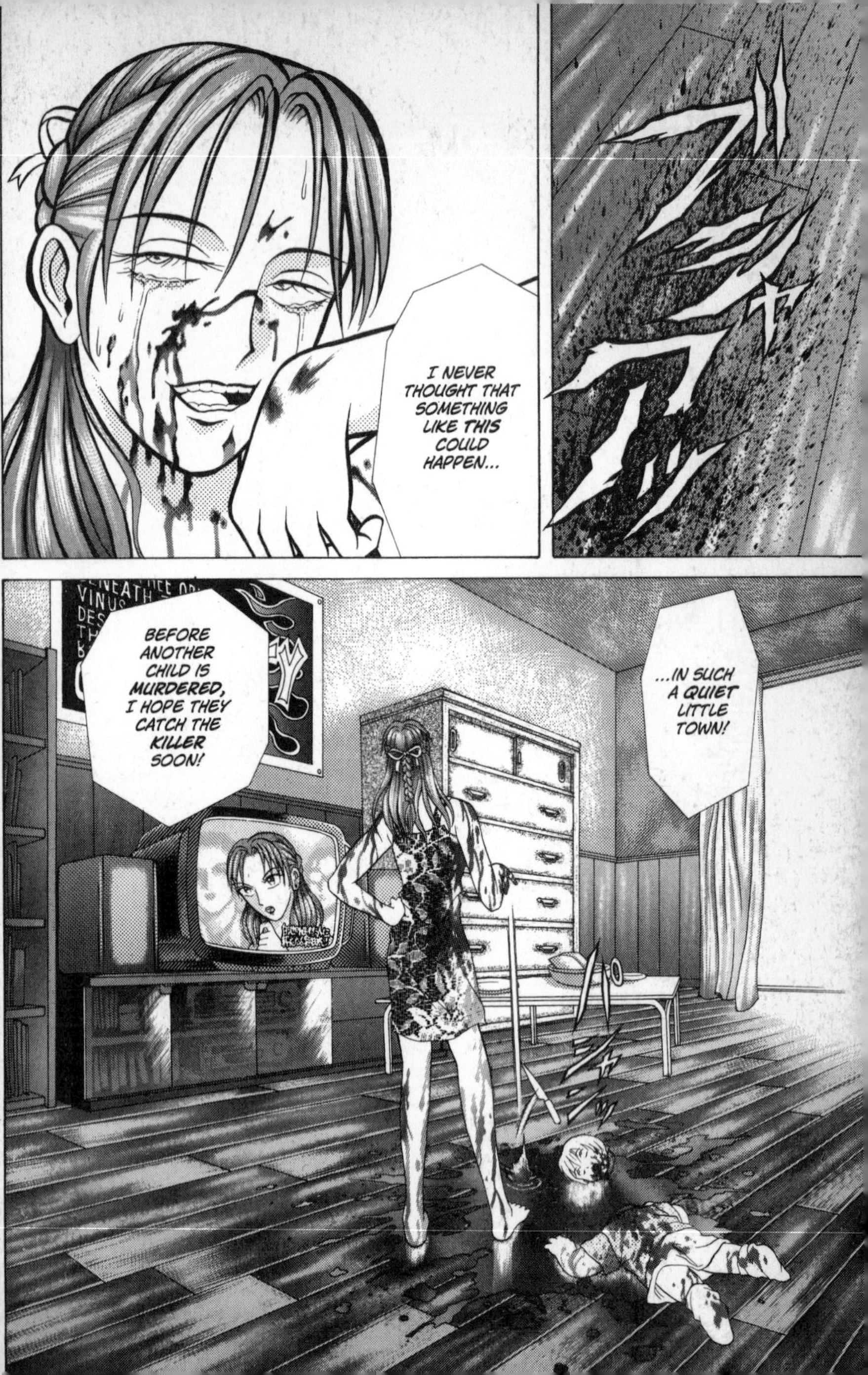
I NEVER THOUGHT THAT SOMETHING LIKE THIS COULD HAPPEN...
...IN SUCH A QUIET LITTLE TOWN!
BEFORE ANOTHER CHILD IS MURDERED, I HOPE THEY CATCH THE KILLER SOON!

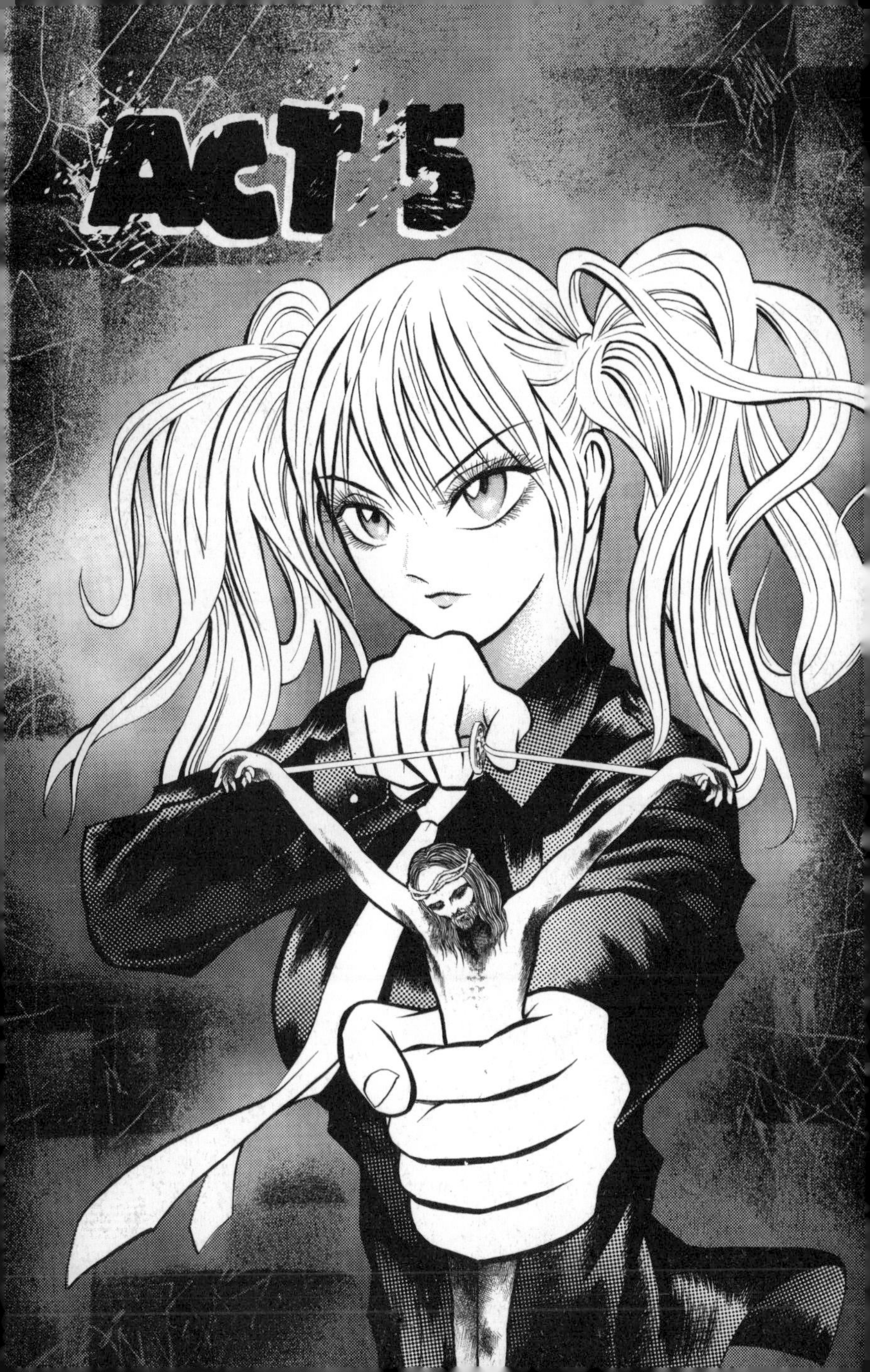
ACT 5

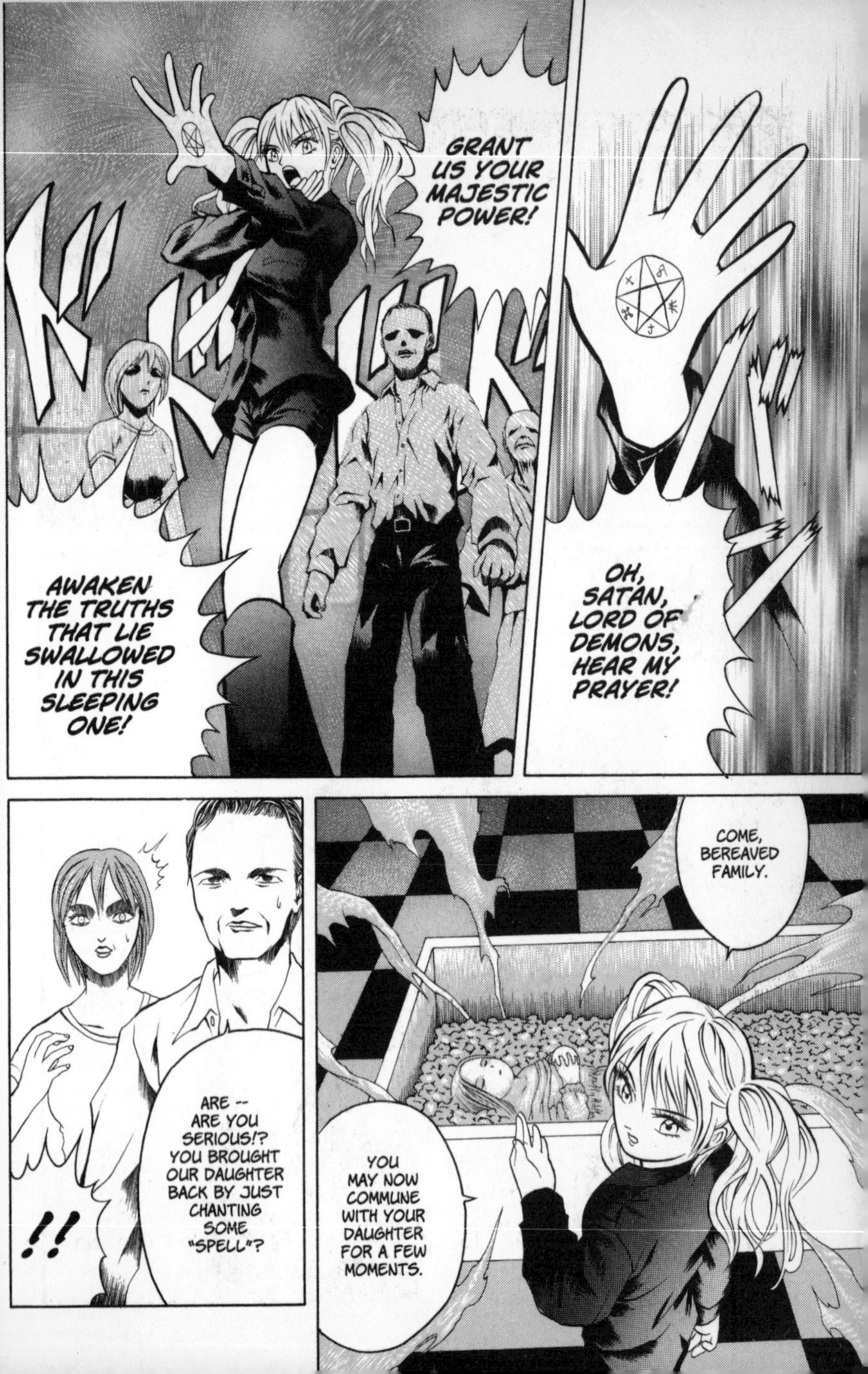
OH, SATAN, LORD OF DEMONS, HEAR MY PRAYER!
GRANT US YOUR MAJESTIC POWER!
AWAKEN THE TRUTHS THAT LIE SWALLOWED IN THIS SLEEPING ONE!
COME, BEREAVED FAMILY.
YOU MAY NOW COMMUNE WITH YOUR DAUGHTER FOR A FEW MOMENTS.
ARE -- ARE YOU SERIOUS!? YOU BROUGHT OUR DAUGHTER BACK BY JUST CHANTING SOME "SPELL"?
!!

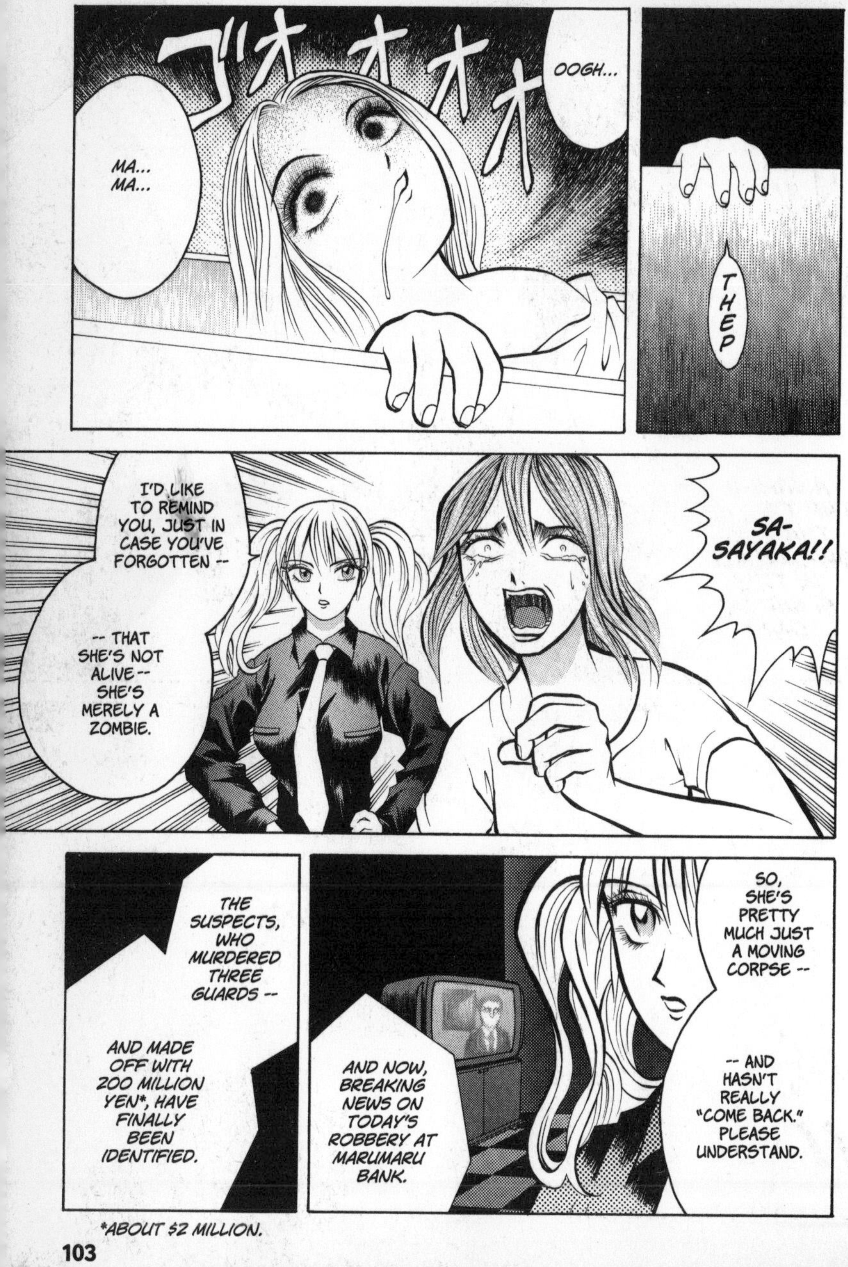
THEP
OOGH...
MA... MA...
ゴオオオオ
SA-SAYAKA!!
I'D LIKE TO REMIND YOU, JUST IN CASE YOU'VE FORGOTTEN --
-- THAT SHE'S NOT ALIVE -- SHE'S MERELY A ZOMBIE.
SO, SHE'S PRETTY MUCH JUST A MOVING CORPSE --
-- AND HASN'T REALLY "COME BACK." PLEASE UNDERSTAND.
AND NOW, BREAKING NEWS ON TODAY'S ROBBERY AT MARUMARU BANK.
THE SUSPECTS, WHO MURDERED THREE GUARDS --
AND MADE OFF WITH 200 MILLION YEN*, HAVE FINALLY BEEN IDENTIFIED.

*ABOUT $2 MILLION.

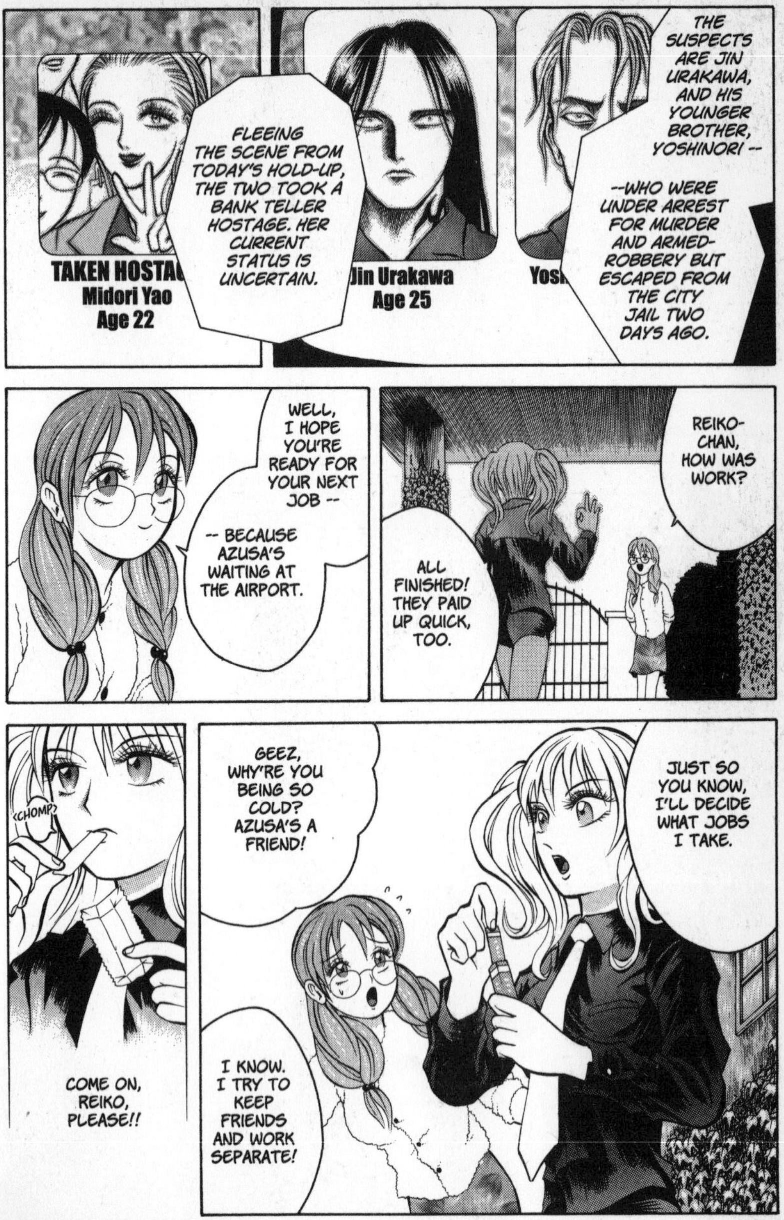
THE SUSPECTS ARE JIN URAKAWA, AND HIS YOUNGER BROTHER, YOSHINORI --
--WHO WERE UNDER ARREST FOR MURDER AND ARMED-ROBBERY BUT ESCAPED FROM THE CITY JAIL TWO DAYS AGO.
Yosh
Jin Urakawa
Age 25
FLEEING THE SCENE FROM TODAY'S HOLD-UP, THE TWO TOOK A BANK TELLER HOSTAGE. HER CURRENT STATUS IS UNCERTAIN.
TAKEN HOSTAG
Midori Yao
Age 22
REIKO-CHAN, HOW WAS WORK?
ALL FINISHED! THEY PAID UP QUICK, TOO.
WELL, I HOPE YOU'RE READY FOR YOUR NEXT JOB --
-- BECAUSE AZUSA'S WAITING AT THE AIRPORT.
JUST SO YOU KNOW, I'LL DECIDE WHAT JOBS I TAKE.
GEEZ, WHY'RE YOU BEING SO COLD? AZUSA'S A FRIEND!
I KNOW. I TRY TO KEEP FRIENDS AND WORK SEPARATE!
<CHOMP>
COME ON, REIKO, PLEASE!!

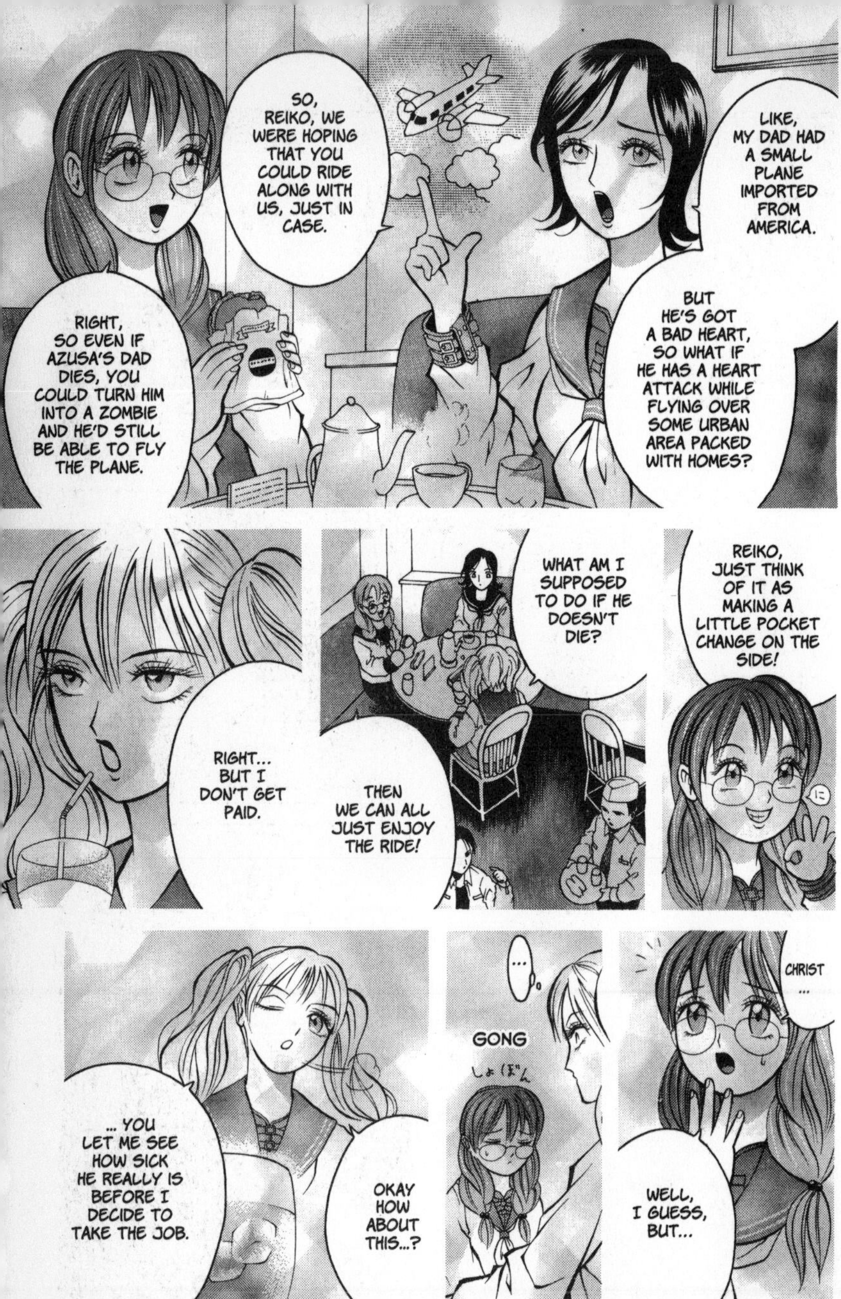
LIKE, MY DAD HAD A SMALL PLANE IMPORTED FROM AMERICA.
BUT HE'S GOT A BAD HEART, SO WHAT IF HE HAS A HEART ATTACK WHILE FLYING OVER SOME URBAN AREA PACKED WITH HOMES?
SO, REIKO, WE WERE HOPING THAT YOU COULD RIDE ALONG WITH US, JUST IN CASE.
RIGHT, SO EVEN IF AZUSA'S DAD DIES, YOU COULD TURN HIM INTO A ZOMBIE AND HE'D STILL BE ABLE TO FLY THE PLANE.
REIKO, JUST THINK OF IT AS MAKING A LITTLE POCKET CHANGE ON THE SIDE!
に
WHAT AM I SUPPOSED TO DO IF HE DOESN'T DIE?
THEN WE CAN ALL JUST ENJOY THE RIDE!
RIGHT... BUT I DON'T GET PAID.
CHRIST ...
WELL, I GUESS, BUT...
...
GONG
しょぼん
OKAY HOW ABOUT THIS...?
... YOU LET ME SEE HOW SICK HE REALLY IS BEFORE I DECIDE TO TAKE THE JOB.

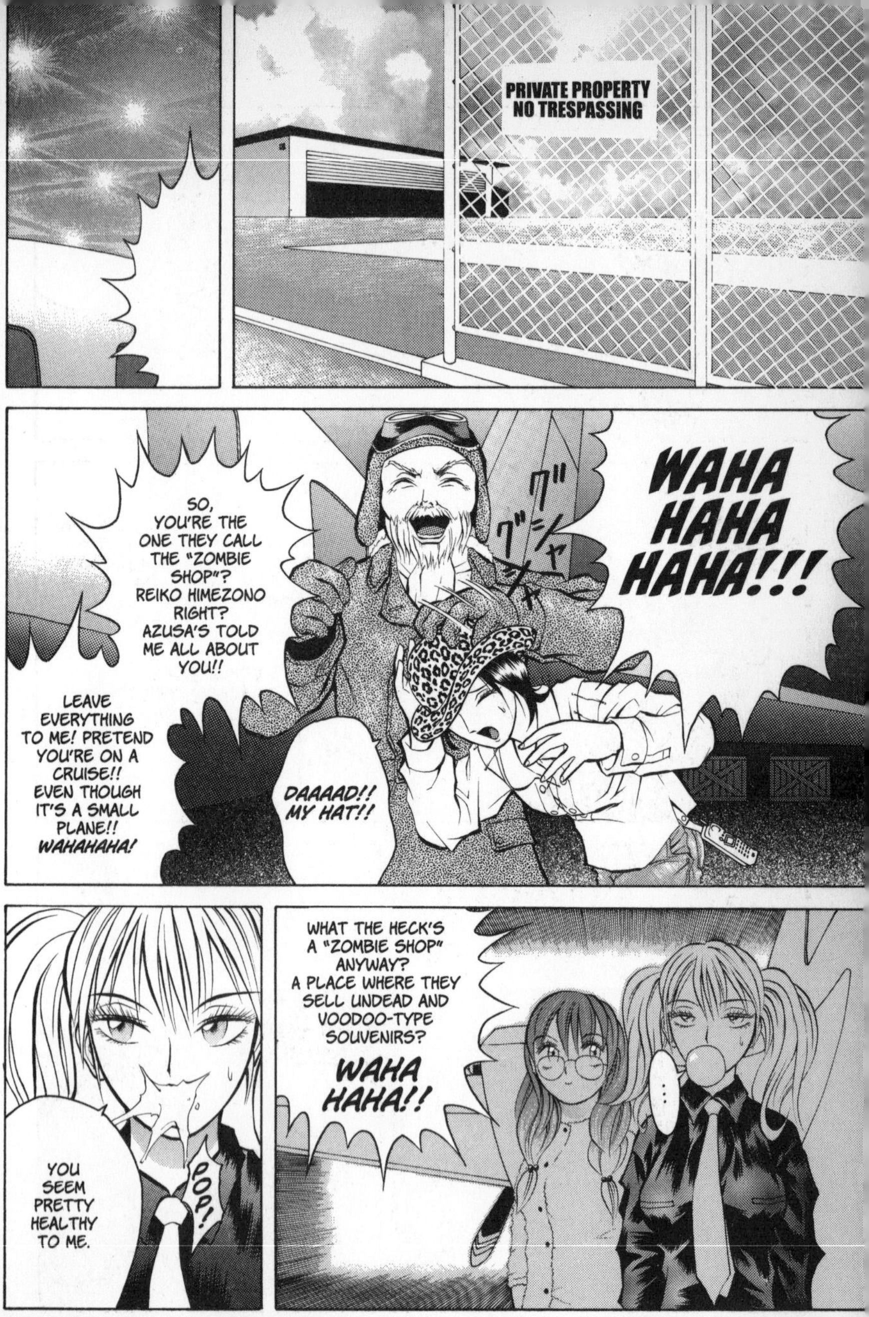

PRIVATE PROPERTY NO TRESPASSING
WAHA HAHA HAHA!!!
SO, YOU'RE THE ONE THEY CALL THE "ZOMBIE SHOP"? REIKO HIMEZONO RIGHT? AZUSA'S TOLD ME ALL ABOUT YOU!!
LEAVE EVERYTHING TO ME! PRETEND YOU'RE ON A CRUISE!! EVEN THOUGH IT'S A SMALL PLANE!! WAHAHAHA!
DAAAAD!! MY HAT!!
WHAT THE HECK'S A "ZOMBIE SHOP" ANYWAY? A PLACE WHERE THEY SELL UNDEAD AND VOODOO-TYPE SOUVENIRS?
WAHA HAHA!!
...
POP!
YOU SEEM PRETTY HEALTHY TO ME.

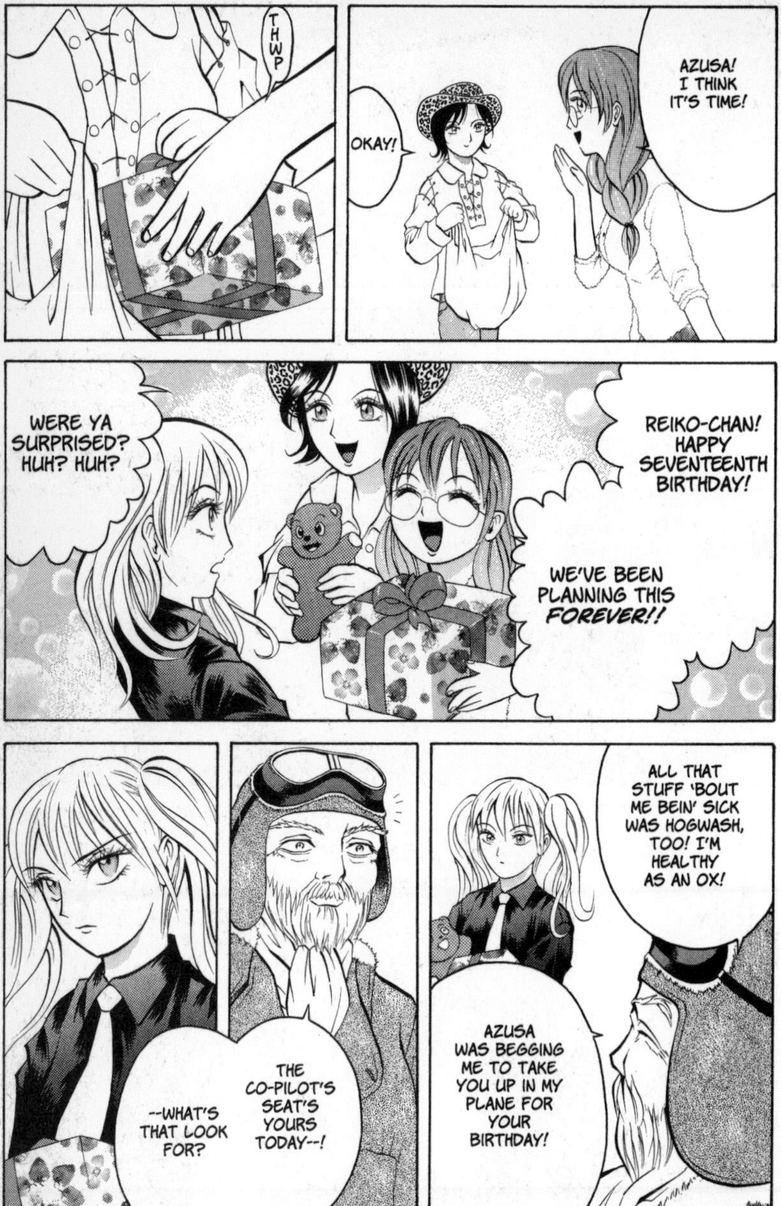
AZUSA! I THINK IT'S TIME!
OKAY!
THWP
REIKO-CHAN! HAPPY SEVENTEENTH BIRTHDAY!
WE'VE BEEN PLANNING THIS *FOREVER!!*
WERE YA SURPRISED? HUH? HUH?
ALL THAT STUFF 'BOUT ME BEIN' SICK WAS HOGWASH, TOO! I'M HEALTHY AS AN OX!
AZUSA WAS BEGGING ME TO TAKE YOU UP IN MY PLANE FOR YOUR BIRTHDAY!
THE CO-PILOT'S SEAT'S YOURS TODAY--!
--WHAT'S THAT LOOK FOR?

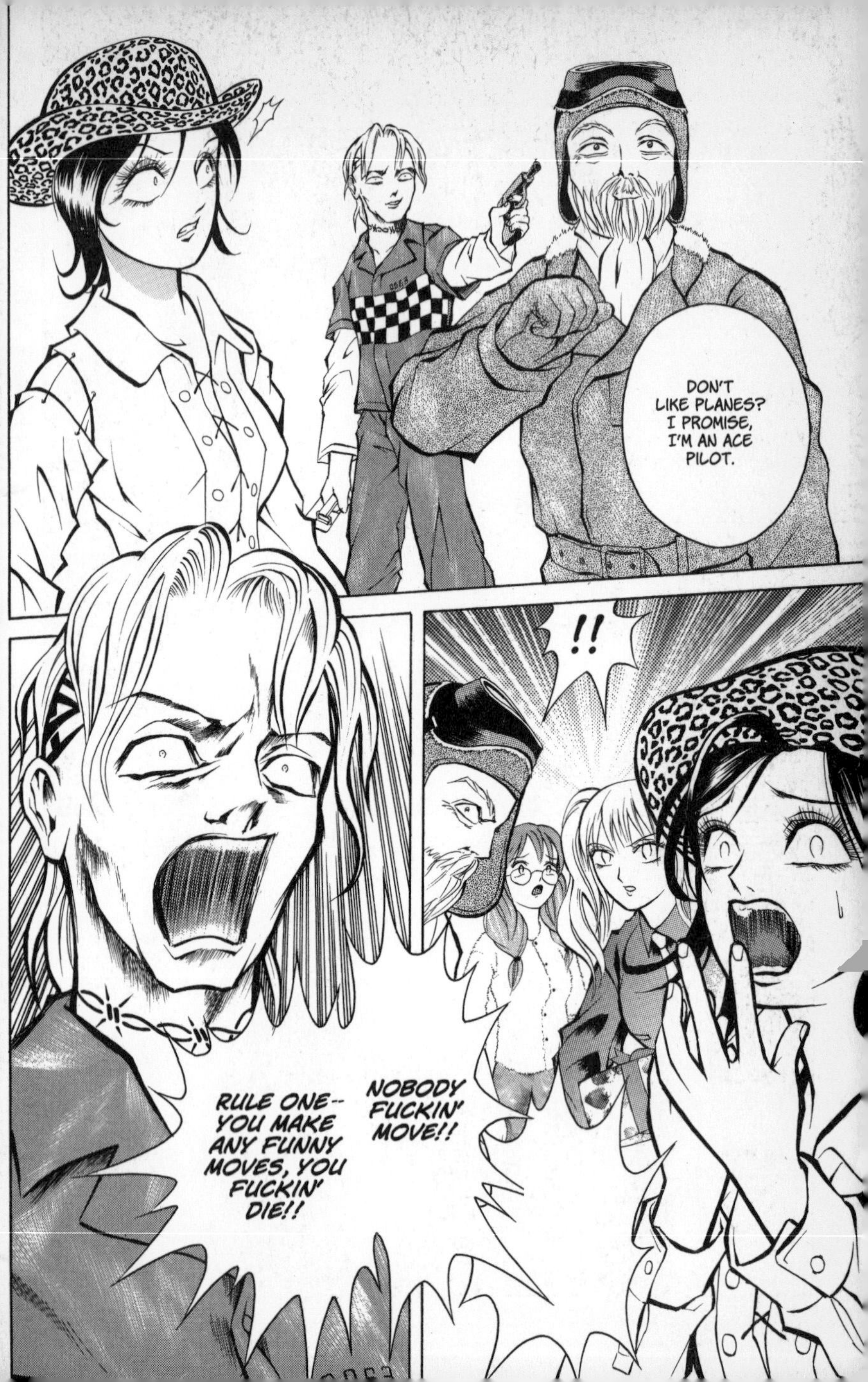
DON'T LIKE PLANES? I PROMISE, I'M AN ACE PILOT.
!!
NOBODY FUCKIN' MOVE!!
RULE ONE-- YOU MAKE ANY FUNNY MOVES, YOU FUCKIN' DIE!!

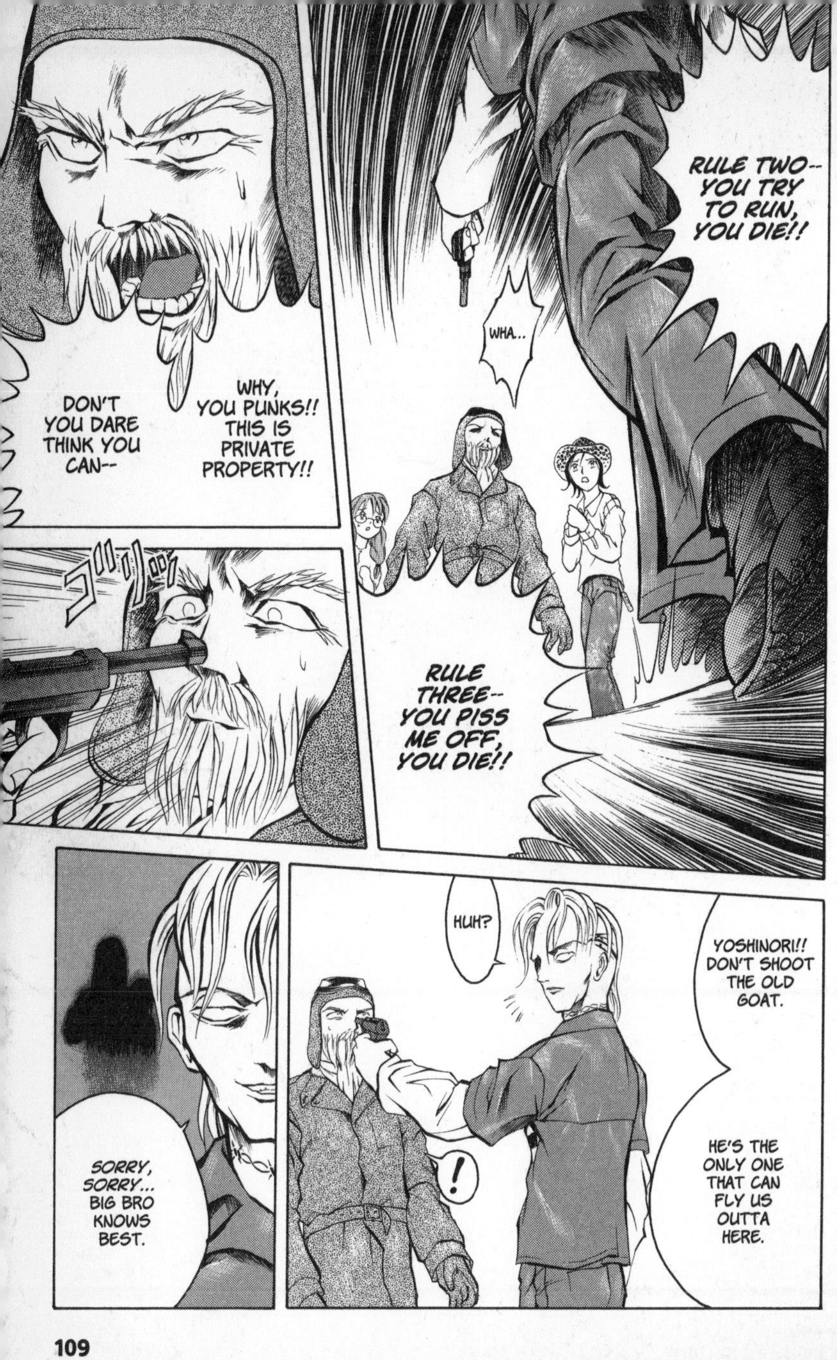
RULE TWO-- YOU TRY TO RUN, YOU DIE!!
WHA..
RULE THREE-- YOU PISS ME OFF, YOU DIE!!
WHY, YOU PUNKS!! THIS IS PRIVATE PROPERTY!!
DON'T YOU DARE THINK YOU CAN--
YOSHINORI!! DON'T SHOOT THE OLD GOAT.
HUH?
HE'S THE ONLY ONE THAT CAN FLY US OUTTA HERE.
!
SORRY, SORRY... BIG BRO KNOWS BEST.

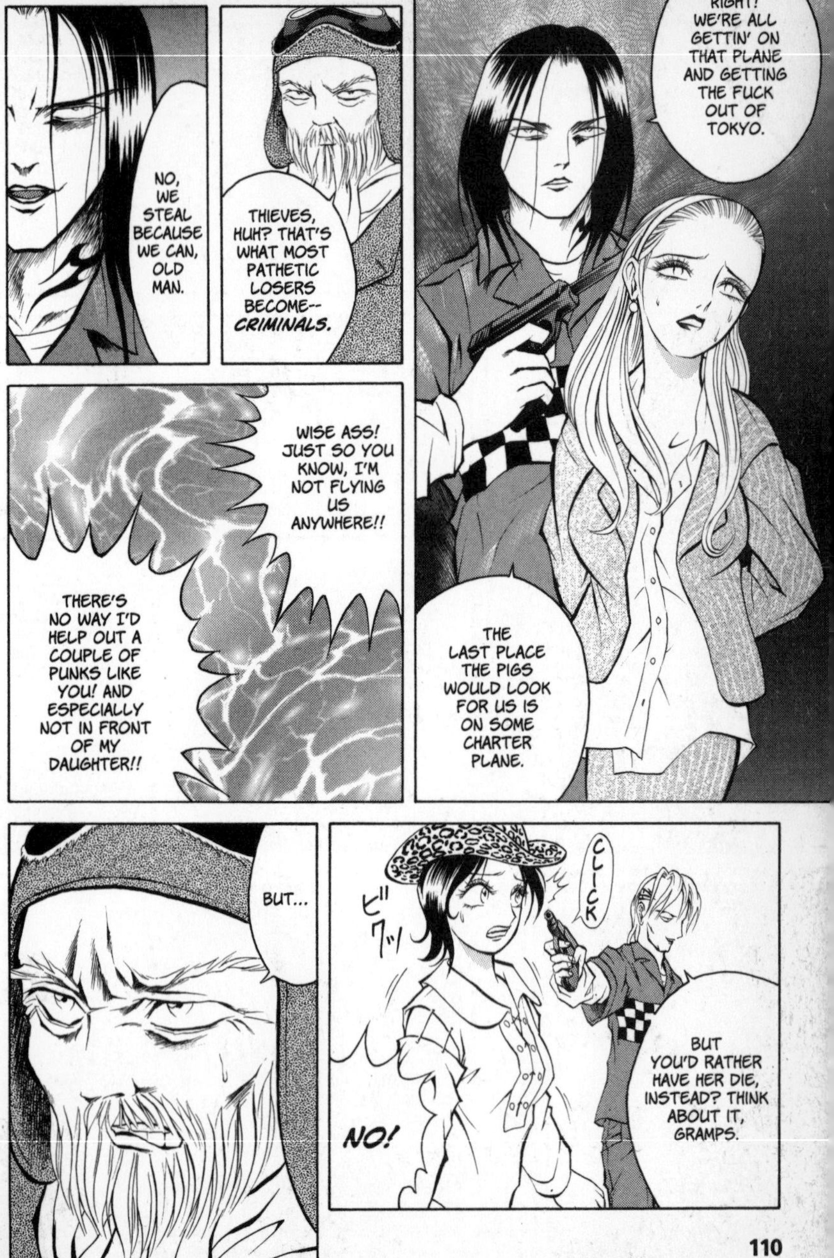
RIGHT! WE'RE ALL GETTIN' ON THAT PLANE AND GETTING THE FUCK OUT OF TOKYO.
THE LAST PLACE THE PIGS WOULD LOOK FOR US IS ON SOME CHARTER PLANE.
THIEVES, HUH? THAT'S WHAT MOST PATHETIC LOSERS BECOME--CRIMINALS.
NO, WE STEAL BECAUSE WE CAN, OLD MAN.
WISE ASS! JUST SO YOU KNOW, I'M NOT FLYING US ANYWHERE!!
THERE'S NO WAY I'D HELP OUT A COUPLE OF PUNKS LIKE YOU! AND ESPECIALLY NOT IN FRONT OF MY DAUGHTER!!
CLICK
ビクッ
BUT YOU'D RATHER HAVE HER DIE, INSTEAD? THINK ABOUT IT, GRAMPS.
NO!
BUT...

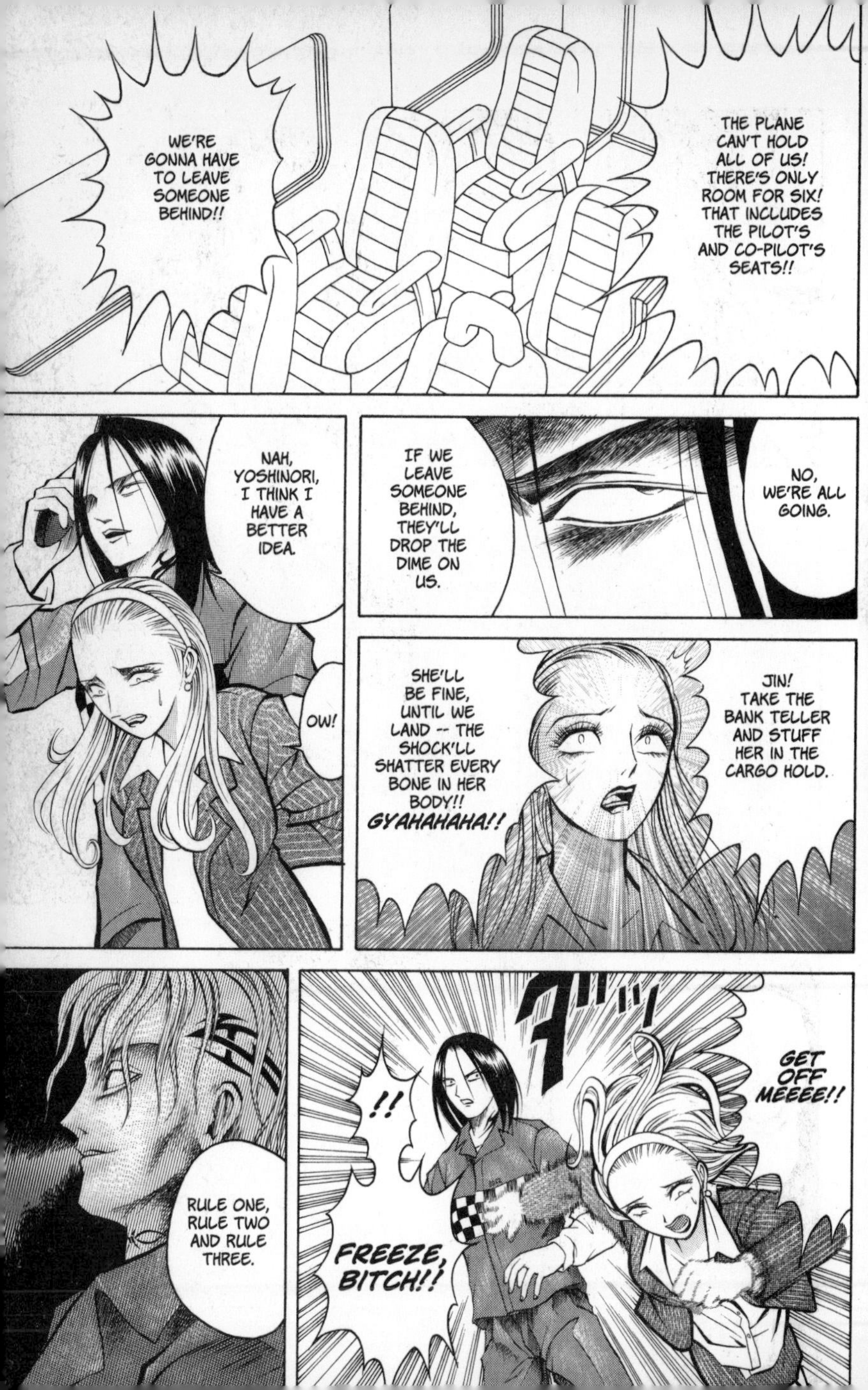
THE PLANE CAN'T HOLD ALL OF US! THERE'S ONLY ROOM FOR SIX! THAT INCLUDES THE PILOT'S AND CO-PILOT'S SEATS!!
WE'RE GONNA HAVE TO LEAVE SOMEONE BEHIND!!
NO, WE'RE ALL GOING.
IF WE LEAVE SOMEONE BEHIND, THEY'LL DROP THE DIME ON US.
JIN! TAKE THE BANK TELLER AND STUFF HER IN THE CARGO HOLD.
SHE'LL BE FINE, UNTIL WE LAND -- THE SHOCK'LL SHATTER EVERY BONE IN HER BODY!! GYAHAHAHA!!
NAH, YOSHINORI, I THINK I HAVE A BETTER IDEA.
OW!
GET OFF MEEEE!!
!!
FREEZE, BITCH!!
RULE ONE, RULE TWO AND RULE THREE.

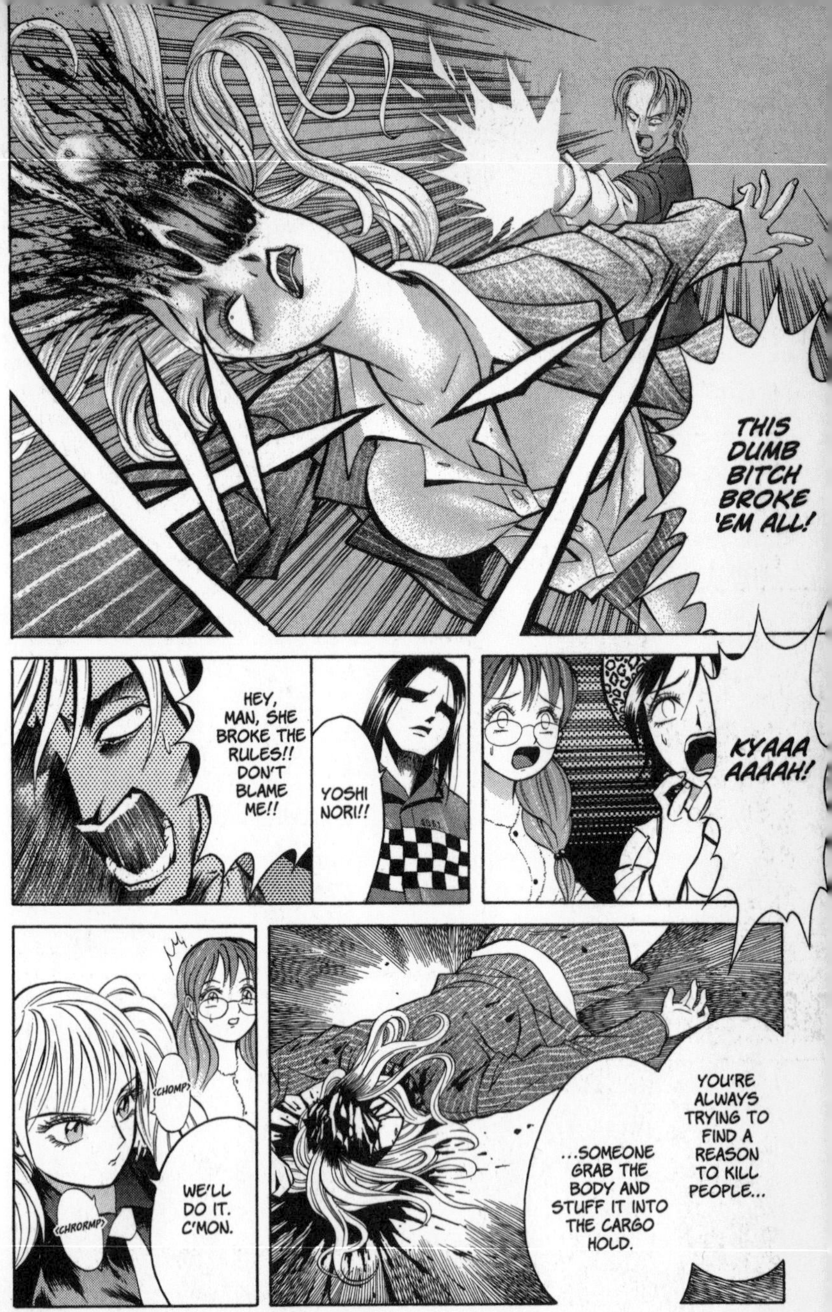
THIS DUMB BITCH BROKE 'EM ALL!
KYAAA AAAAH!
YOSHI NORI!!
HEY, MAN, SHE BROKE THE RULES!! DON'T BLAME ME!!
YOU'RE ALWAYS TRYING TO FIND A REASON TO KILL PEOPLE...
...SOMEONE GRAB THE BODY AND STUFF IT INTO THE CARGO HOLD.
<CHOMP>
WE'LL DO IT. C'MON.
<CHRORMP>

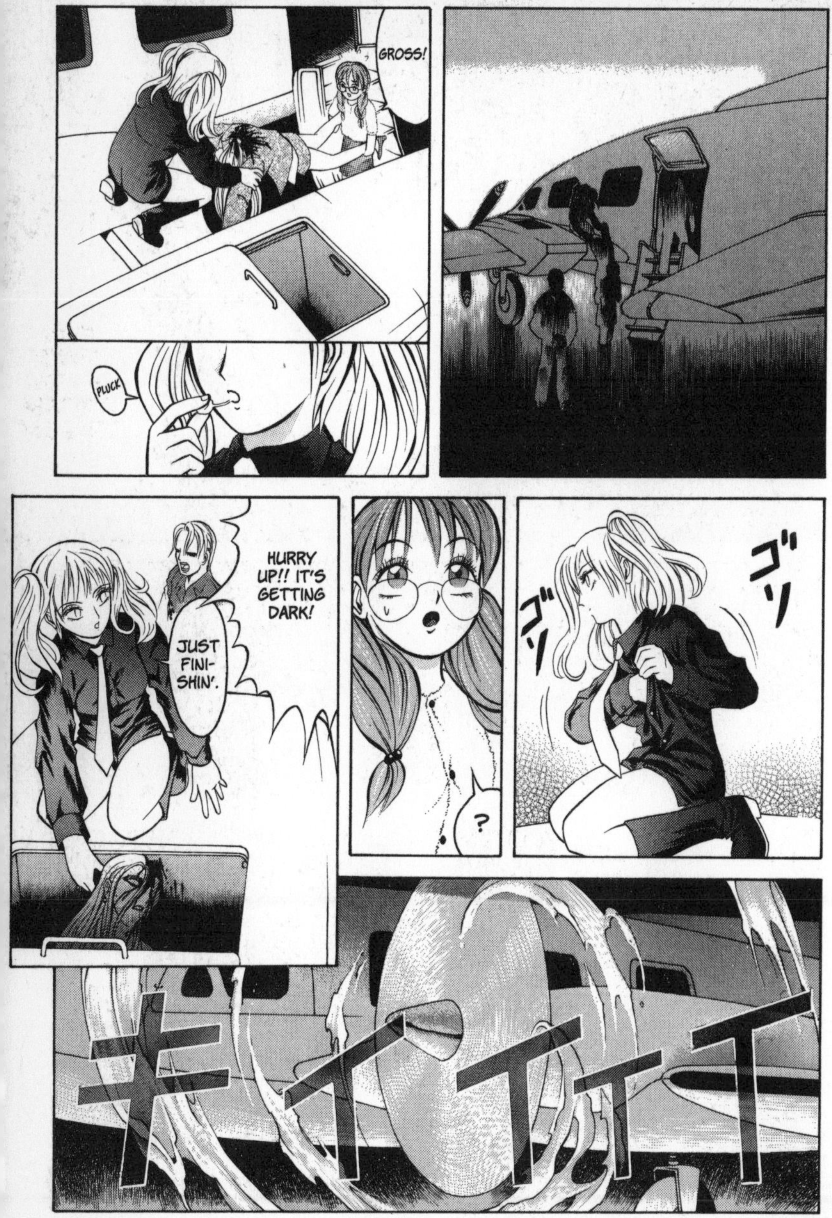
GROSS!
PLUCK
ゴソ
ゴソ
?
HURRY UP!! IT'S GETTING DARK!
JUST FINI-SHIN'.
キイイイイ

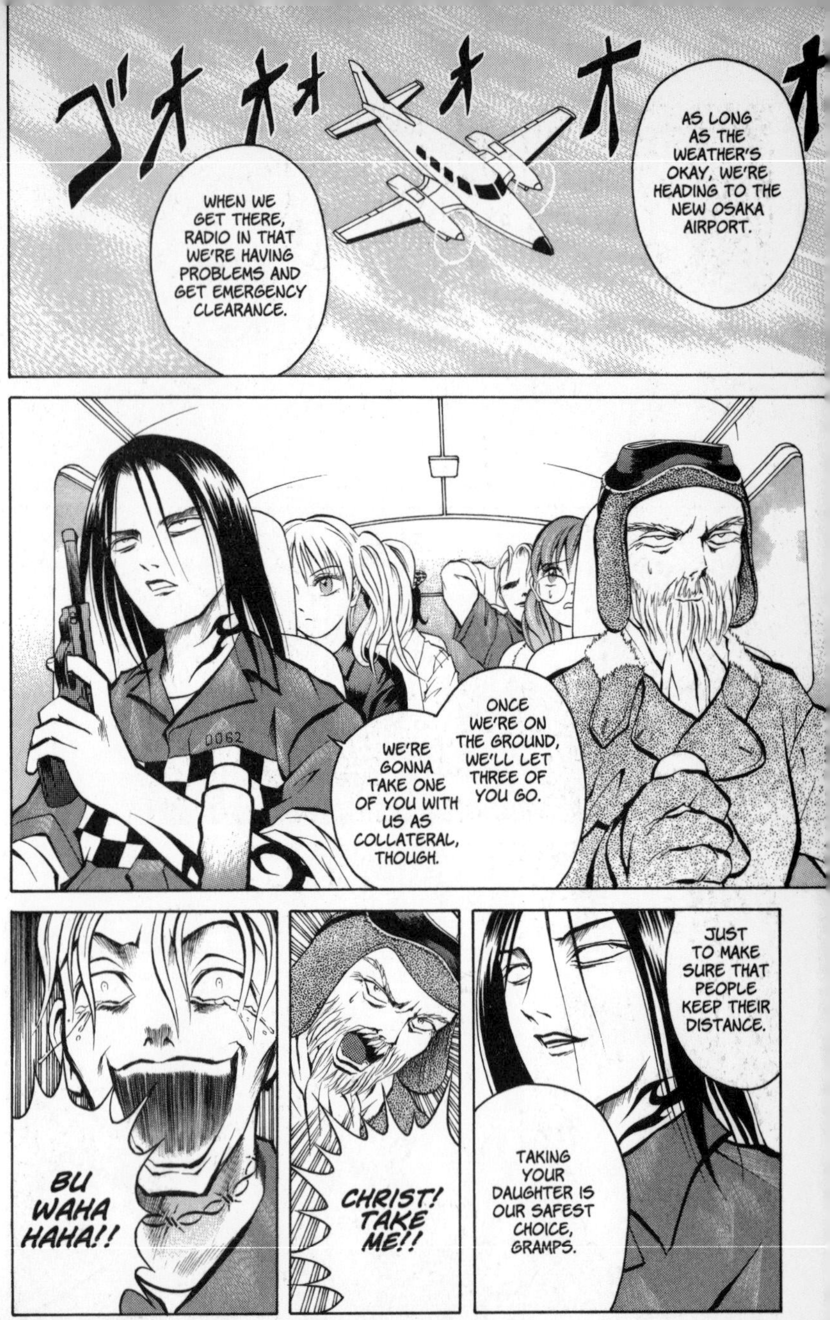
ゴオ オォーオ オ
AS LONG AS THE WEATHER'S OKAY, WE'RE HEADING TO THE NEW OSAKA AIRPORT.
WHEN WE GET THERE, RADIO IN THAT WE'RE HAVING PROBLEMS AND GET EMERGENCY CLEARANCE.
ONCE WE'RE ON THE GROUND, WE'LL LET THREE OF YOU GO.
WE'RE GONNA TAKE ONE OF YOU WITH US AS COLLATERAL, THOUGH.
JUST TO MAKE SURE THAT PEOPLE KEEP THEIR DISTANCE.
TAKING YOUR DAUGHTER IS OUR SAFEST CHOICE, GRAMPS.
CHRIST! TAKE ME!!
BU WAHA HAHA!!

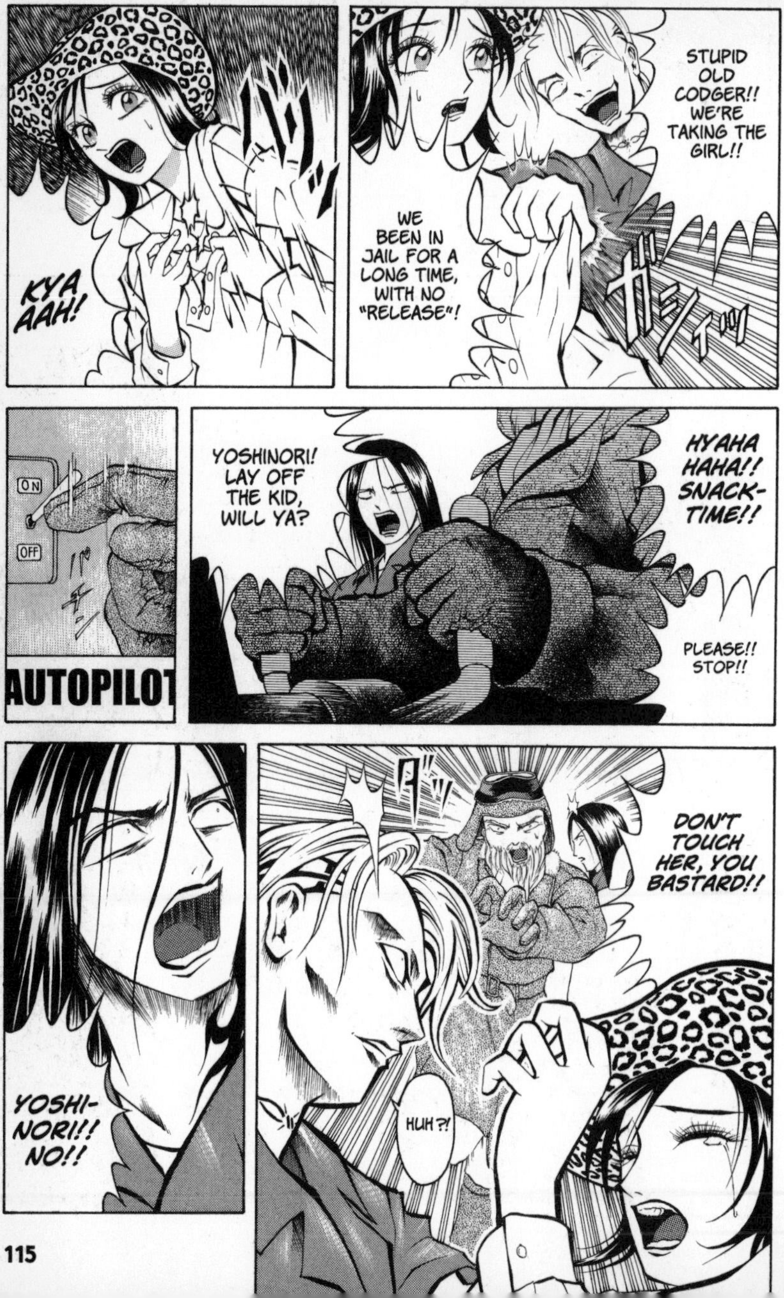

STUPID OLD CODGER!! WE'RE TAKING THE GIRL!!
WE BEEN IN JAIL FOR A LONG TIME, WITH NO "RELEASE"!
KYAAAH!
HYAHA HAHA!! SNACK-TIME!!
YOSHINORI! LAY OFF THE KID, WILL YA?
PLEASE!! STOP!!
ON
OFF
AUTOPILOT
DON'T TOUCH HER, YOU BASTARD!!
HUH?!
YOSHINORI!! NO!!

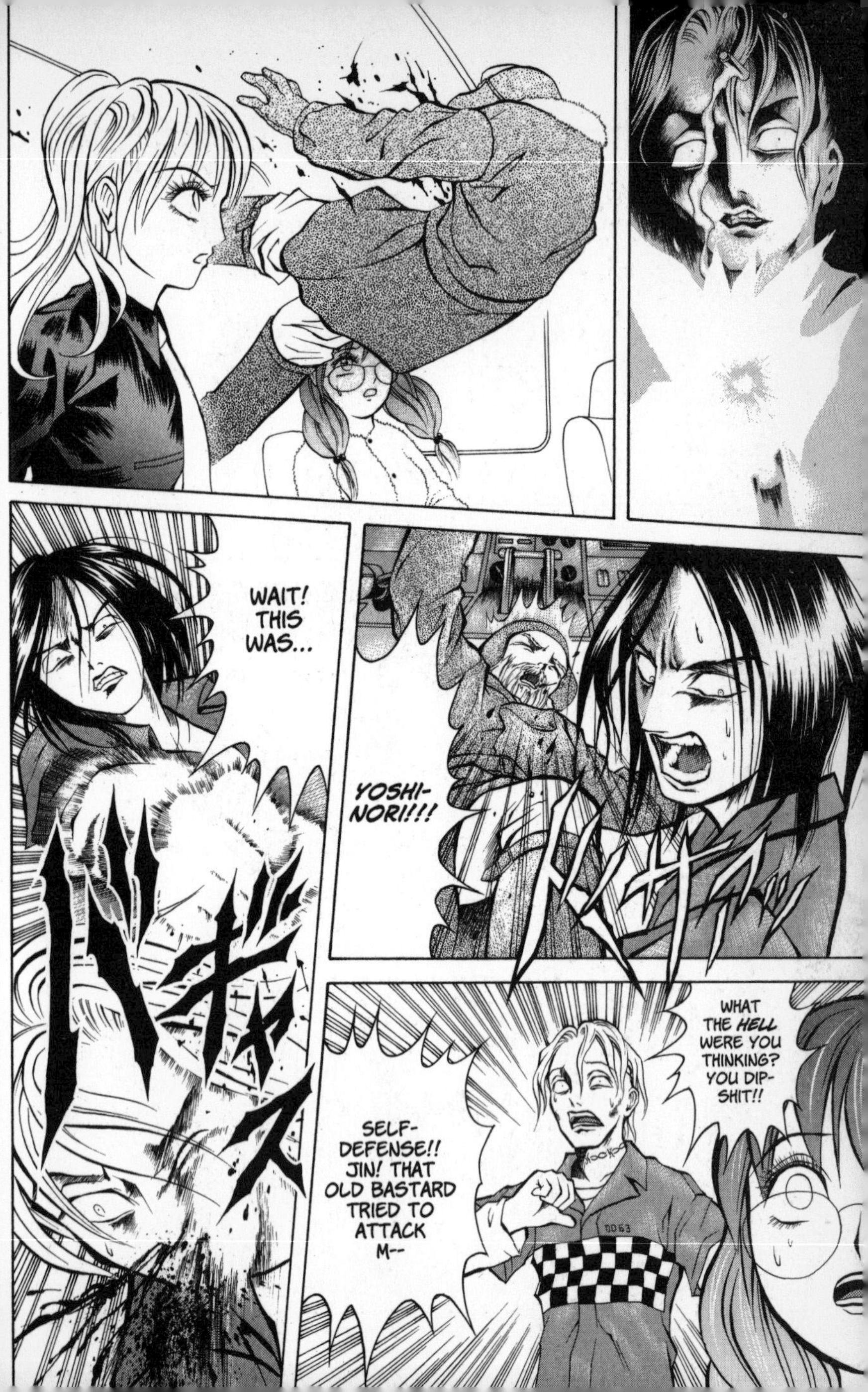
YOSHI-
NORI!!!
WHAT THE HELL WERE YOU THINKING? YOU DIP-SHIT!!
SELF-DEFENSE!! JIN! THAT OLD BASTARD TRIED TO ATTACK M--
WAIT! THIS WAS...

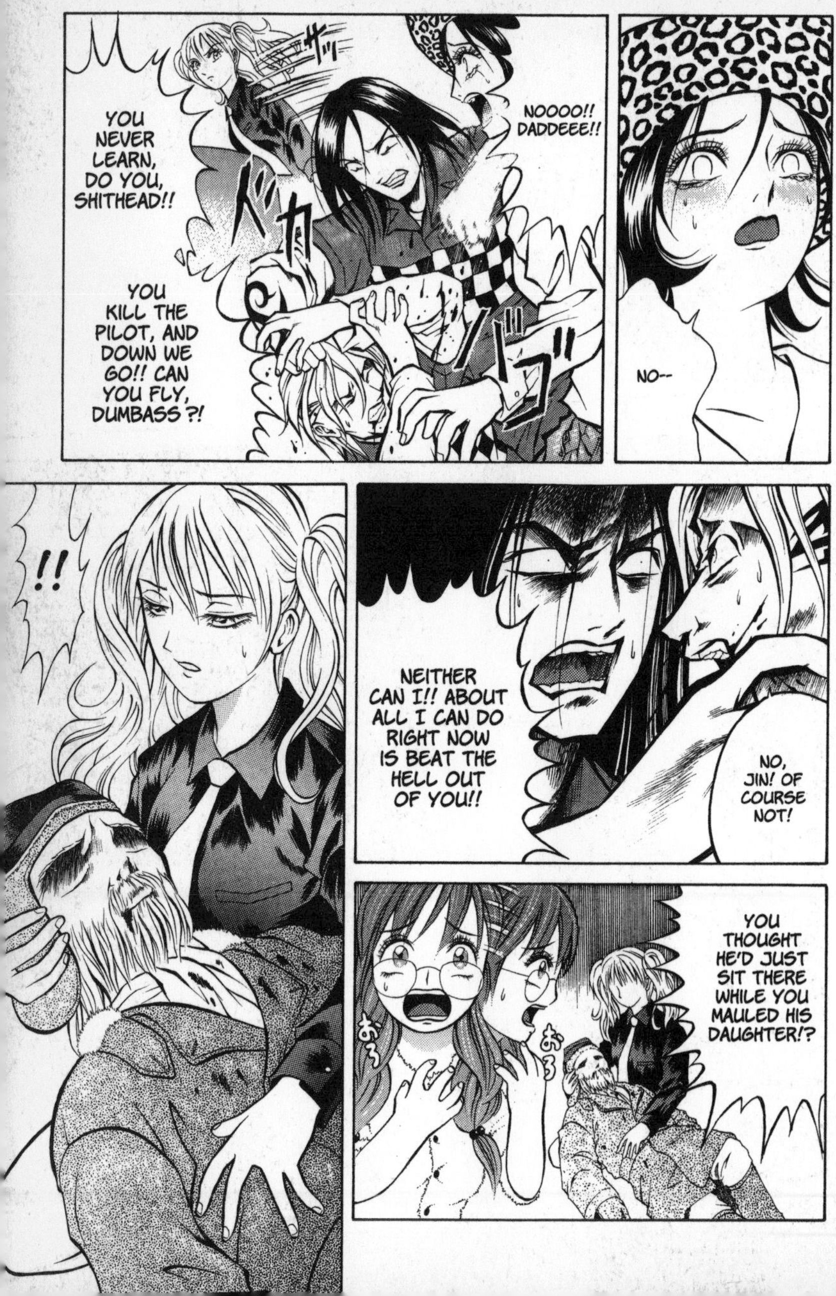
NO--
NOOOO!! DADDEEE!!
YOU NEVER LEARN, DO YOU, SHITHEAD!!
YOU KILL THE PILOT, AND DOWN WE GO!! CAN YOU FLY, DUMBASS?!
NO, JIN! OF COURSE NOT!
NEITHER CAN I!! ABOUT ALL I CAN DO RIGHT NOW IS BEAT THE HELL OUT OF YOU!!
YOU THOUGHT HE'D JUST SIT THERE WHILE YOU MAULED HIS DAUGHTER!?
おろ
おろ
!!

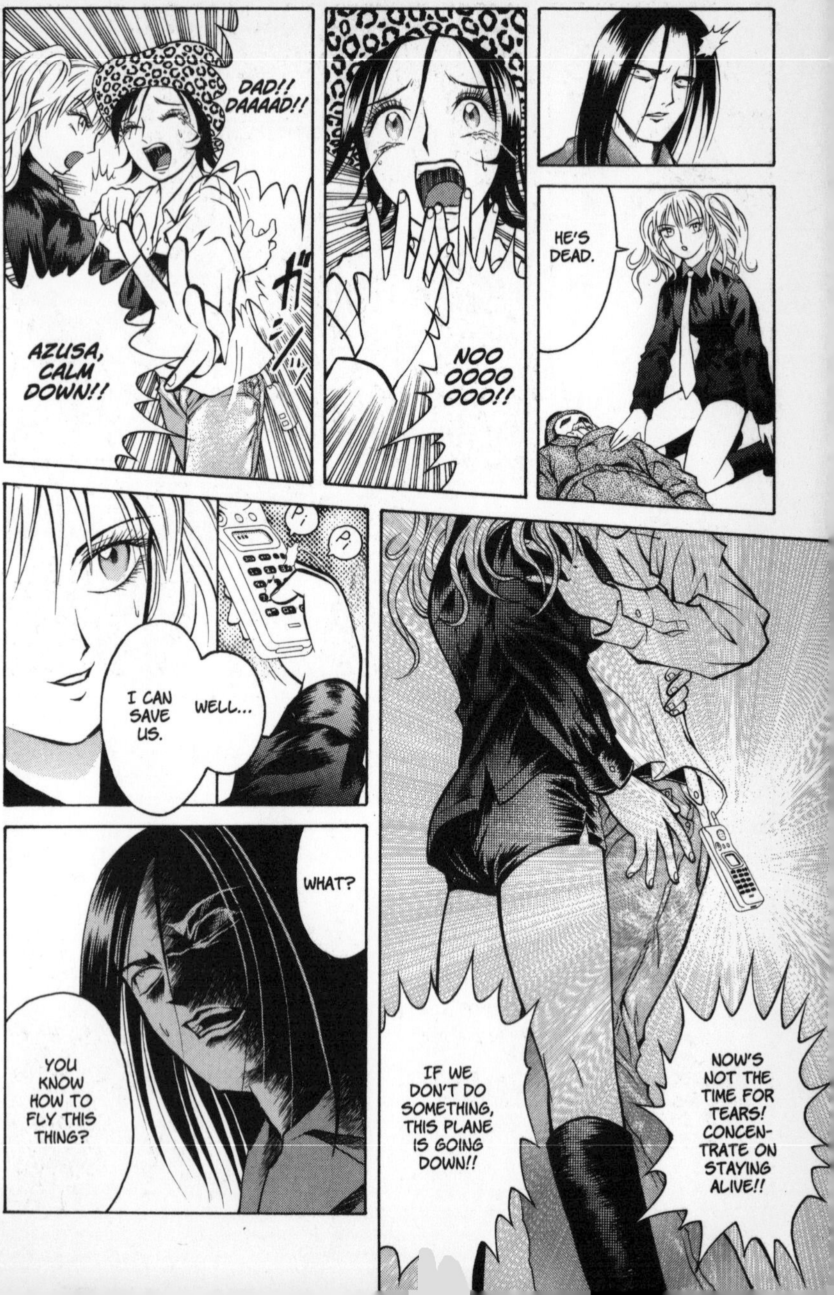
HE'S DEAD.
NOO OOOO OOO!!
DAD!! DAAAAD!!
ガシッ
AZUSA, CALM DOWN!!
NOW'S NOT THE TIME FOR TEARS! CONCEN-TRATE ON STAYING ALIVE!!
IF WE DON'T DO SOMETHING, THIS PLANE IS GOING DOWN!!
Pi
Pi
WELL...
I CAN SAVE US.
WHAT?
YOU KNOW HOW TO FLY THIS THING?

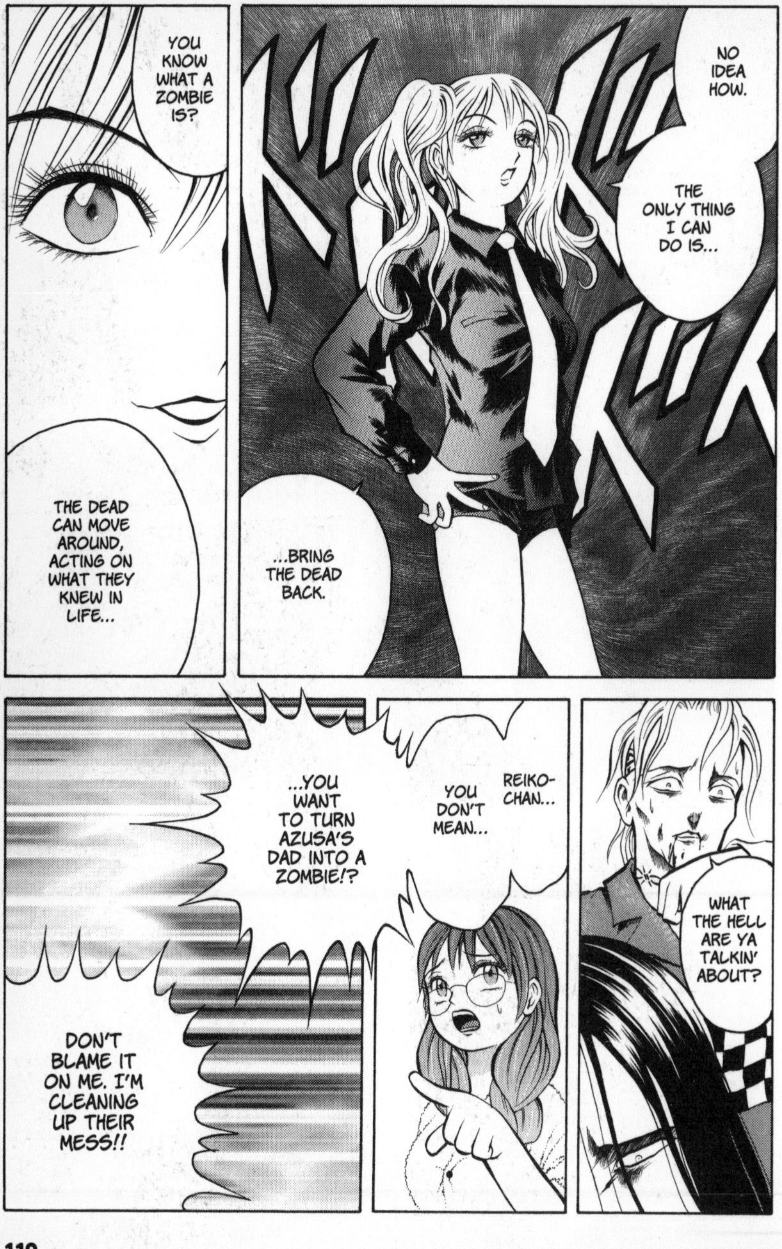
NO IDEA HOW.
THE ONLY THING I CAN DO IS...
...BRING THE DEAD BACK.
YOU KNOW WHAT A ZOMBIE IS?
THE DEAD CAN MOVE AROUND, ACTING ON WHAT THEY KNEW IN LIFE...
WHAT THE HELL ARE YA TALKIN' ABOUT?
REIKO-CHAN...
YOU DON'T MEAN...
...YOU WANT TO TURN AZUSA'S DAD INTO A ZOMBIE!?
DON'T BLAME IT ON ME. I'M CLEANING UP THEIR MESS!!

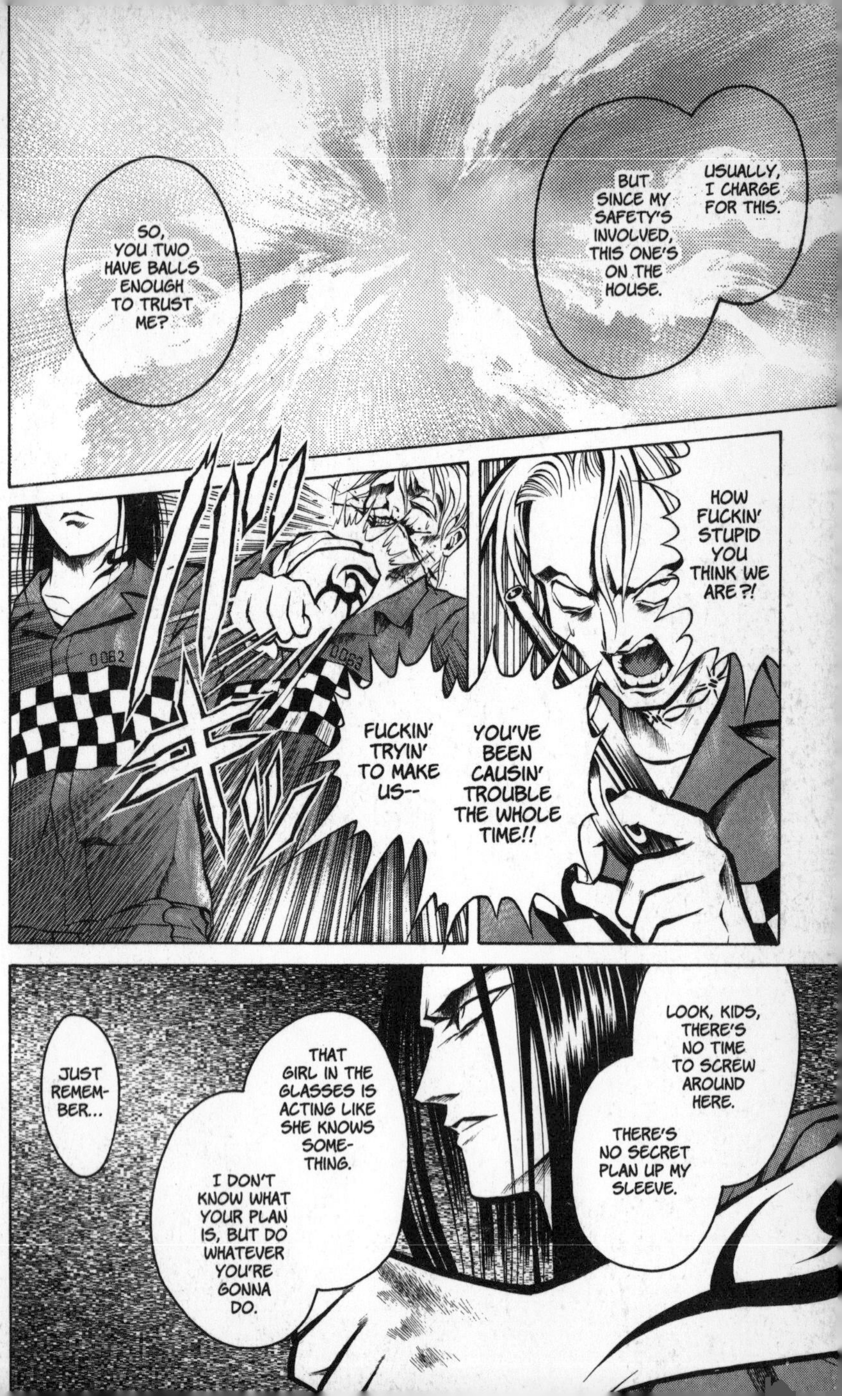
USUALLY, I CHARGE FOR THIS.
BUT SINCE MY SAFETY'S INVOLVED, THIS ONE'S ON THE HOUSE.
SO, YOU TWO HAVE BALLS ENOUGH TO TRUST ME?
HOW FUCKIN' STUPID YOU THINK WE ARE?!
YOU'VE BEEN CAUSIN' TROUBLE THE WHOLE TIME!!
FUCKIN' TRYIN' TO MAKE US--
LOOK, KIDS, THERE'S NO TIME TO SCREW AROUND HERE.
THERE'S NO SECRET PLAN UP MY SLEEVE.
THAT GIRL IN THE GLASSES IS ACTING LIKE SHE KNOWS SOME-THING.
I DON'T KNOW WHAT YOUR PLAN IS, BUT DO WHATEVER YOU'RE GONNA DO.
JUST REMEM-BER...

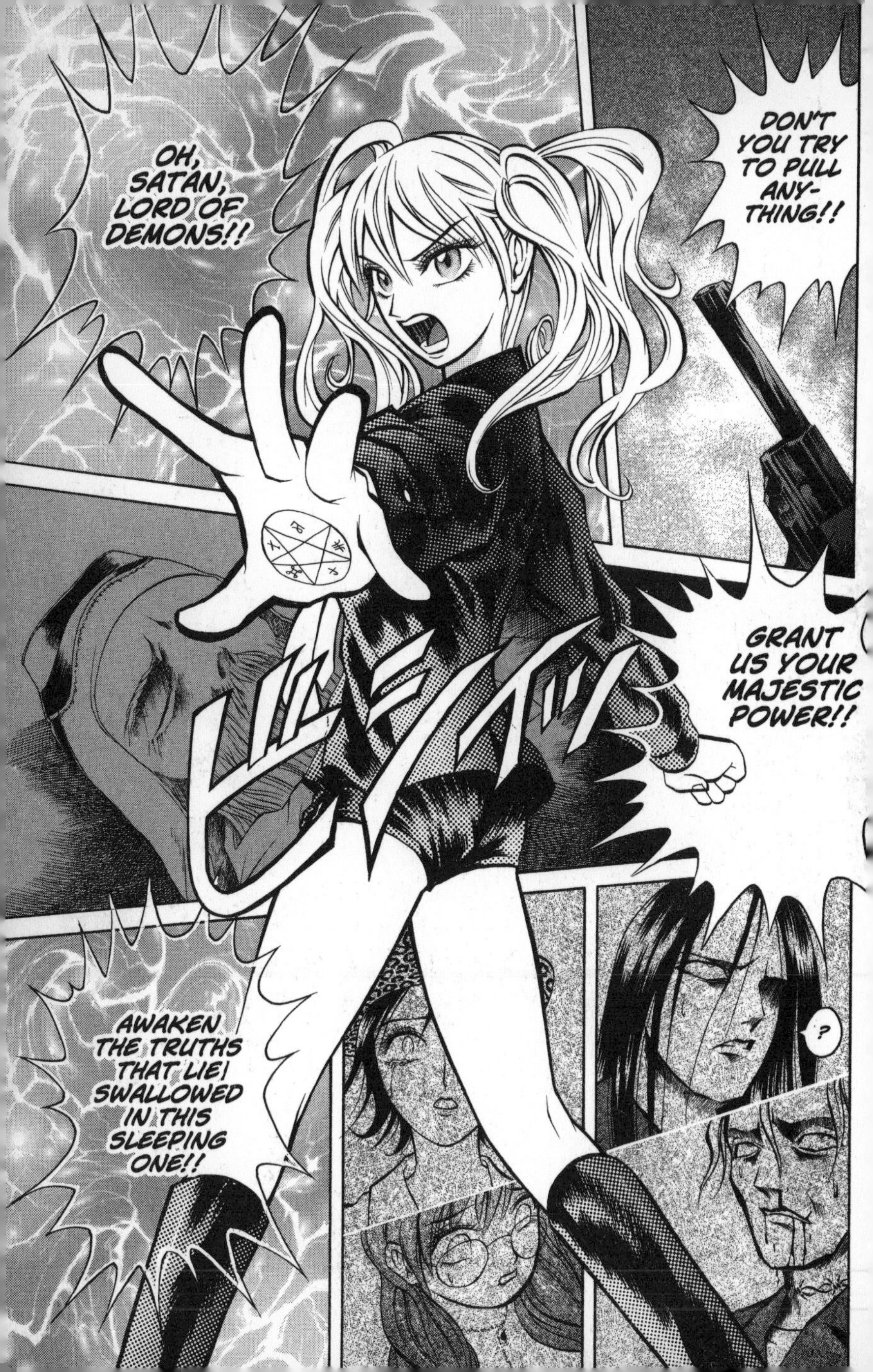
DON'T YOU TRY TO PULL ANY-THING!!
OH, SATAN, LORD OF DEMONS!!
GRANT US YOUR MAJESTIC POWER!!
?
AWAKEN THE TRUTHS THAT LIE SWALLOWED IN THIS SLEEPING ONE!!

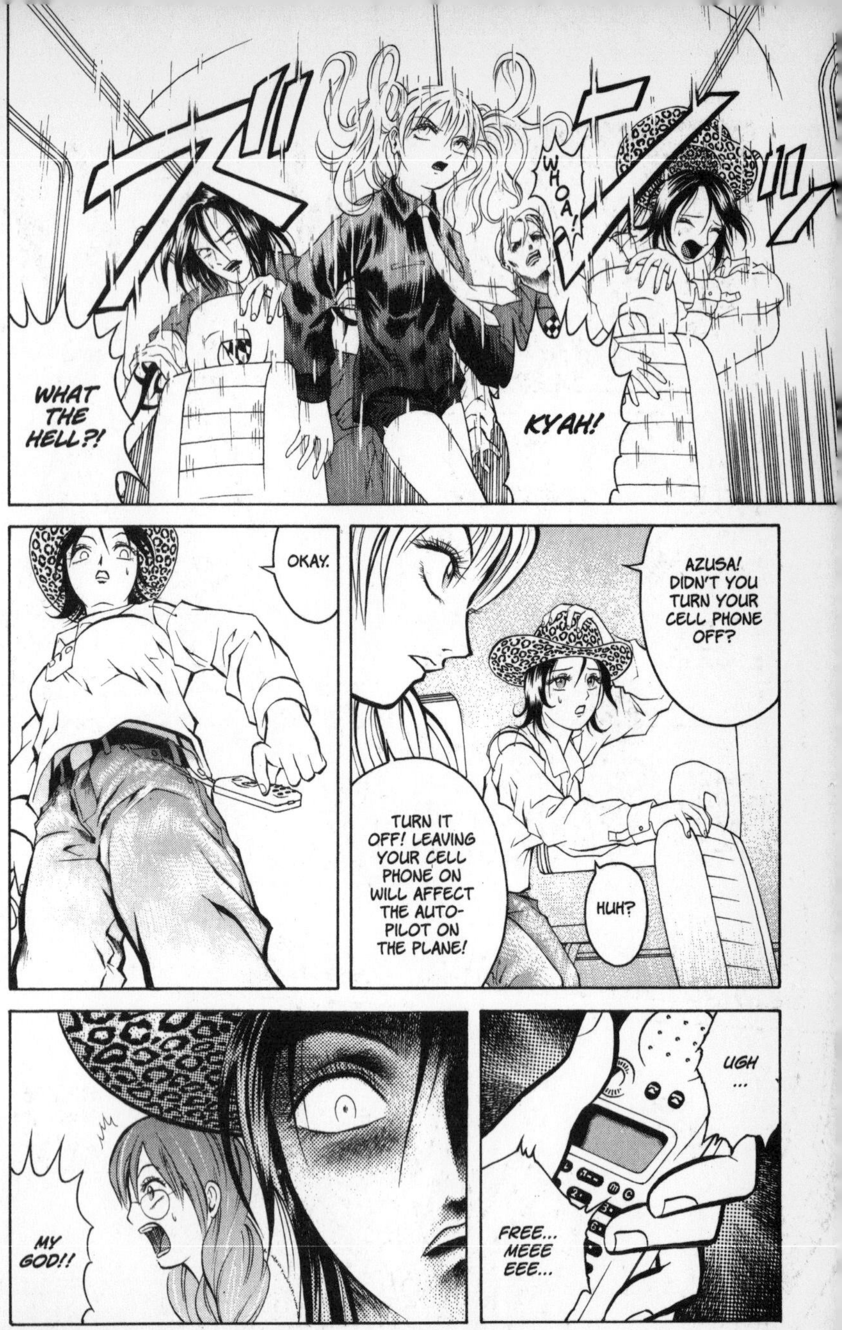
WHOA!
KYAH!
WHAT THE HELL?!
AZUSA! DIDN'T YOU TURN YOUR CELL PHONE OFF?
HUH?
TURN IT OFF! LEAVING YOUR CELL PHONE ON WILL AFFECT THE AUTO-PILOT ON THE PLANE!
OKAY.
UGH ...
FREE... MEEE EEE...
MY GOD!!

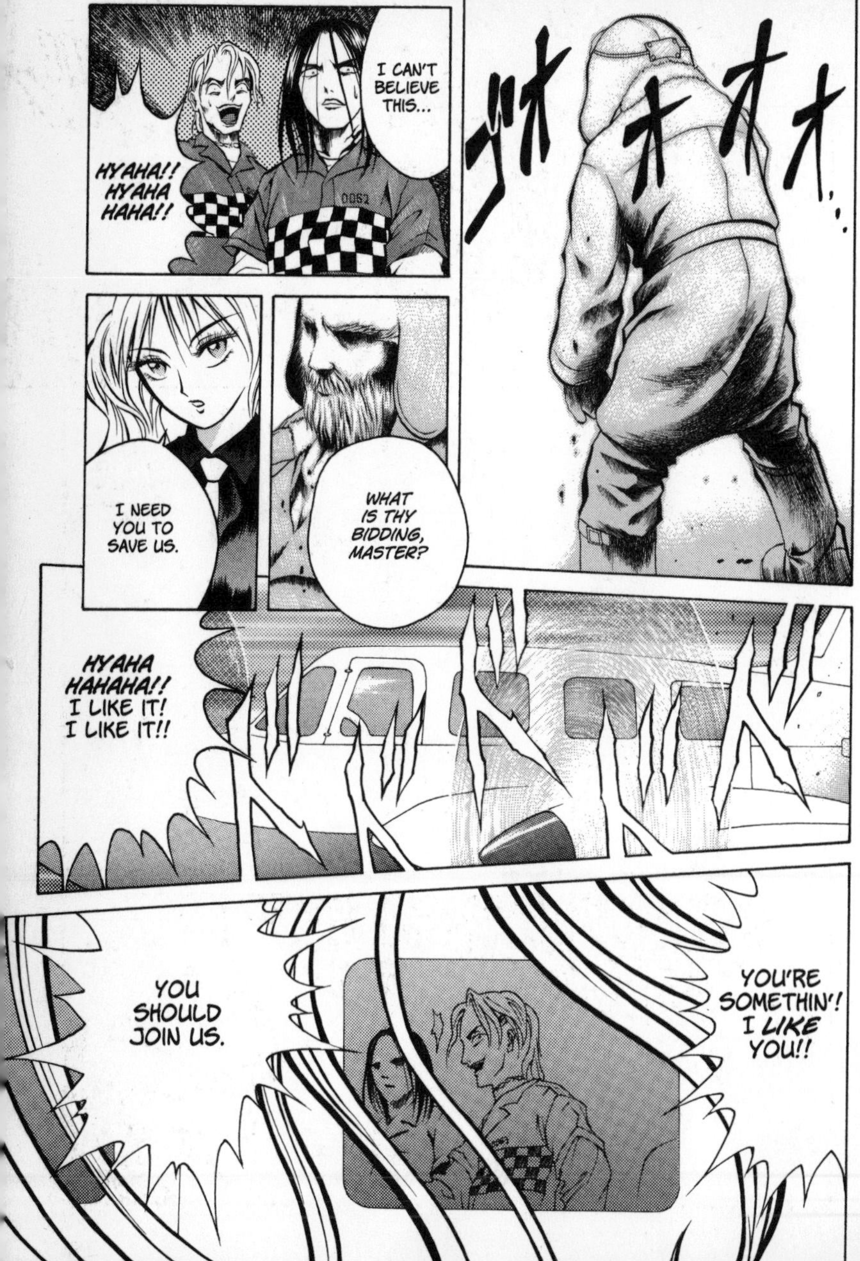
ゴオオオ
I CAN'T BELIEVE THIS...
HYAHA!! HYAHA HAHA!!
WHAT IS THY BIDDING, MASTER?
I NEED YOU TO SAVE US.
HYAHA HAHAHA!! I LIKE IT! I LIKE IT!!
YOU'RE SOMETHIN'! I *LIKE* YOU!!
YOU SHOULD JOIN US.

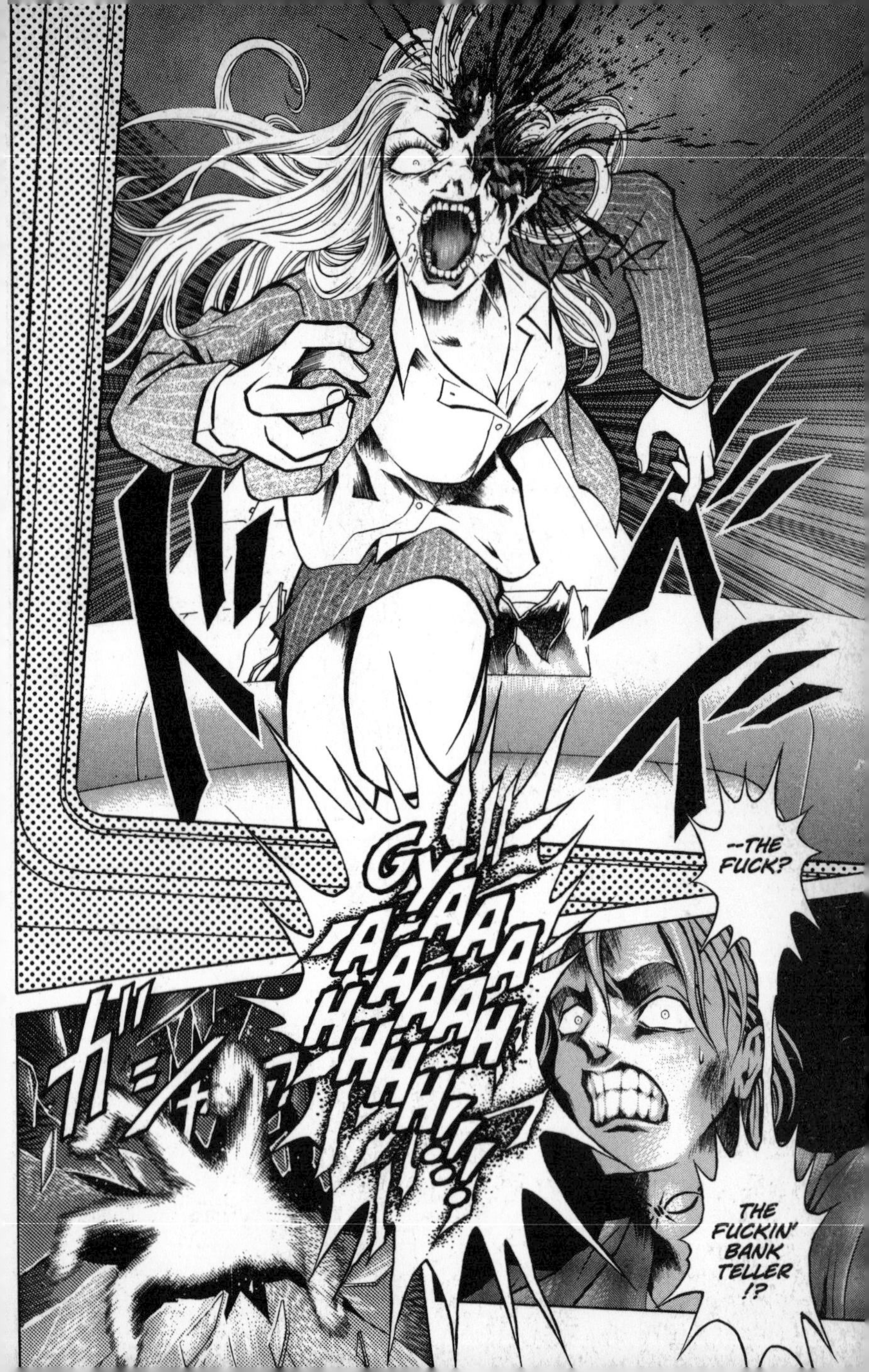
GYAAAAAAAAAAHHHHH!!!
--THE FUCK?
THE FUCKIN' BANK TELLER !?

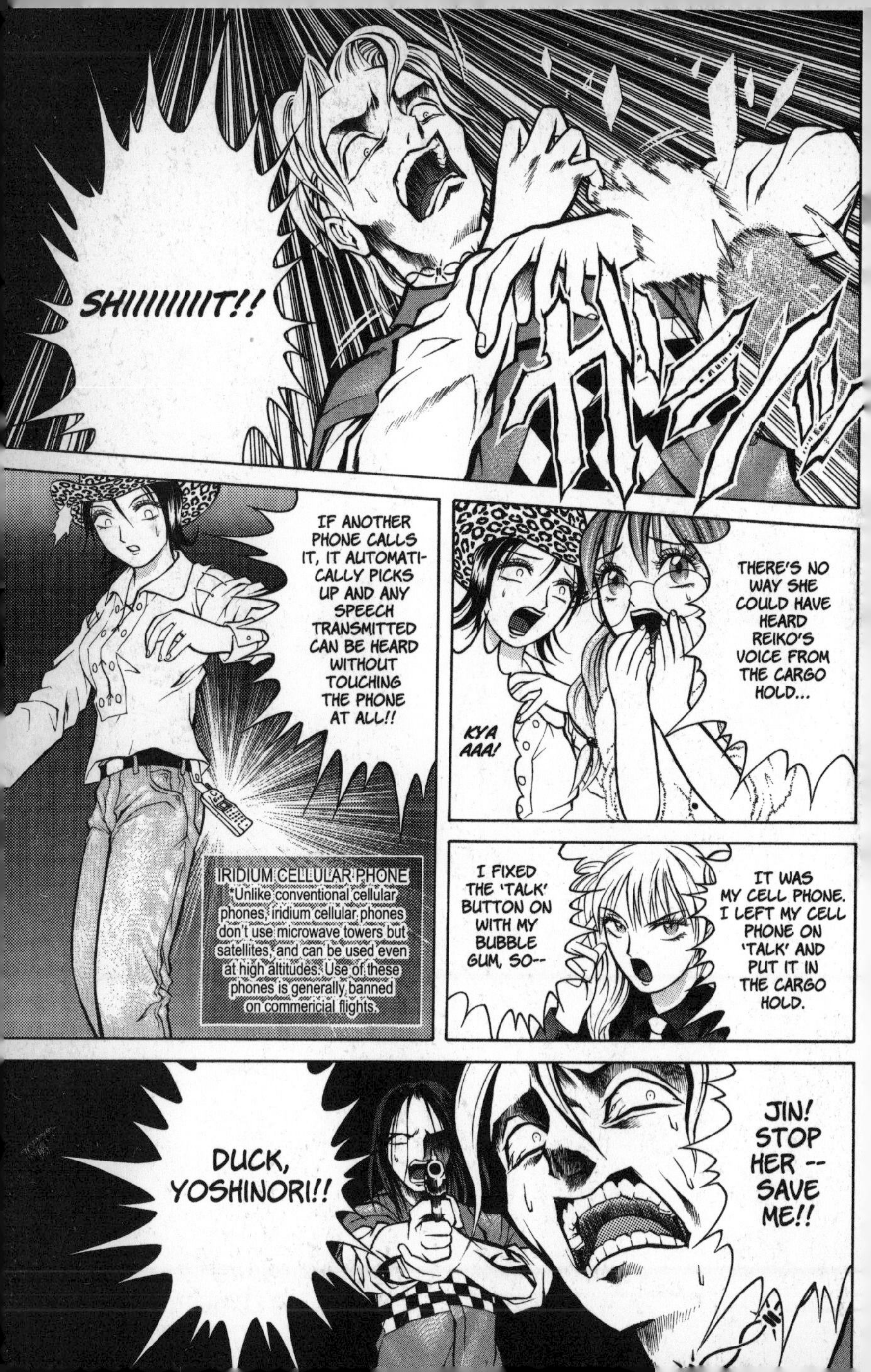
SHIIIIIIIIT!!
THERE'S NO WAY SHE COULD HAVE HEARD REIKO'S VOICE FROM THE CARGO HOLD...
KYA AAA!
IT WAS MY CELL PHONE. I LEFT MY CELL PHONE ON 'TALK' AND PUT IT IN THE CARGO HOLD.
I FIXED THE 'TALK' BUTTON ON WITH MY BUBBLE GUM, SO--
IF ANOTHER PHONE CALLS IT, IT AUTOMATI-CALLY PICKS UP AND ANY SPEECH TRANSMITTED CAN BE HEARD WITHOUT TOUCHING THE PHONE AT ALL!!
IRIDIUM CELLULAR PHONE
*Unlike conventional cellular phones, iridium cellular phones don't use microwave towers but satellites, and can be used even at high altitudes. Use of these phones is generally banned on commericial flights.
JIN! STOP HER -- SAVE ME!!
DUCK, YOSHINORI!!

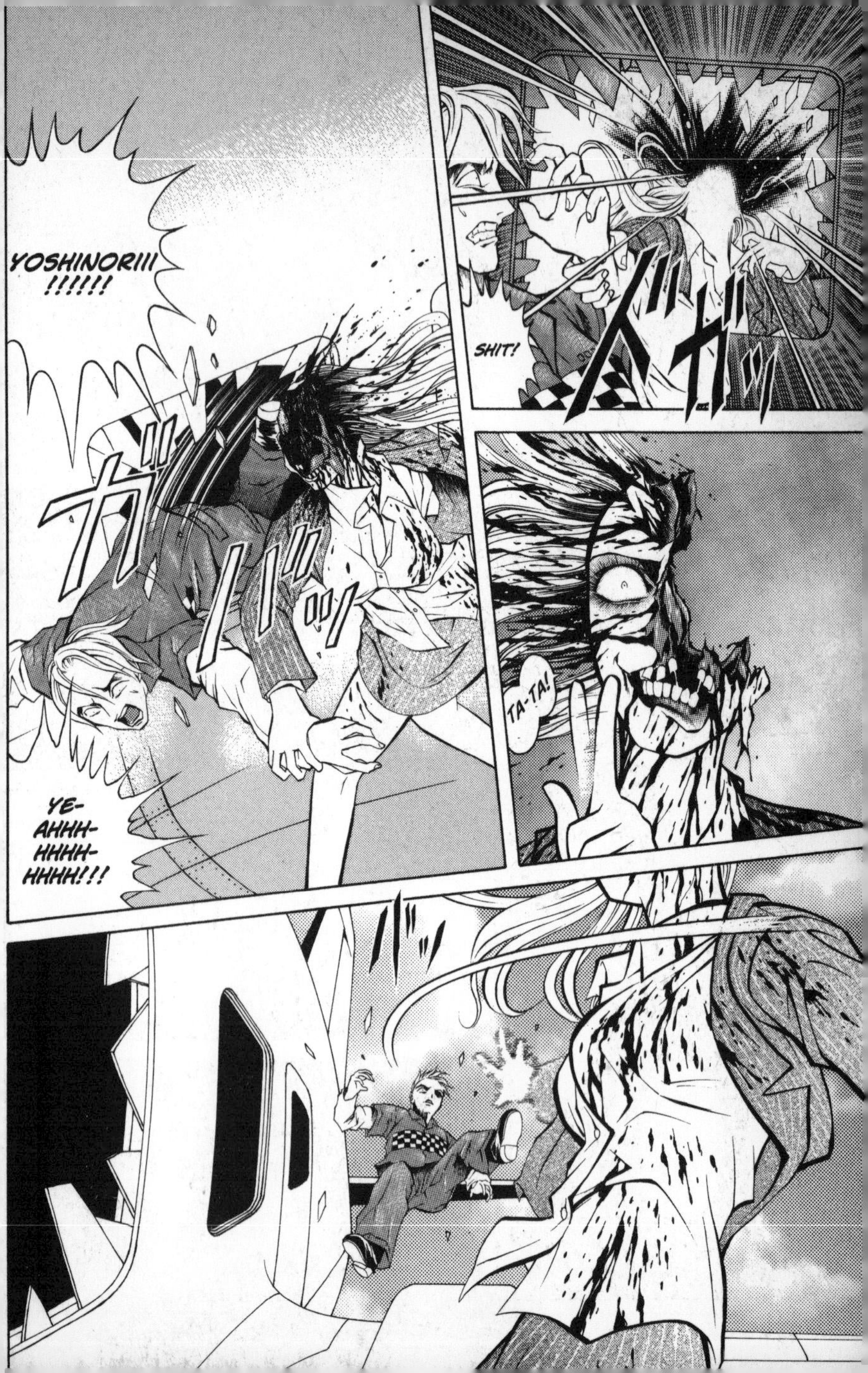
SHIT!
TA-TA!
YOSHINORIII !!!!!!
YE-AHHH-HHHH-HHHH!!!

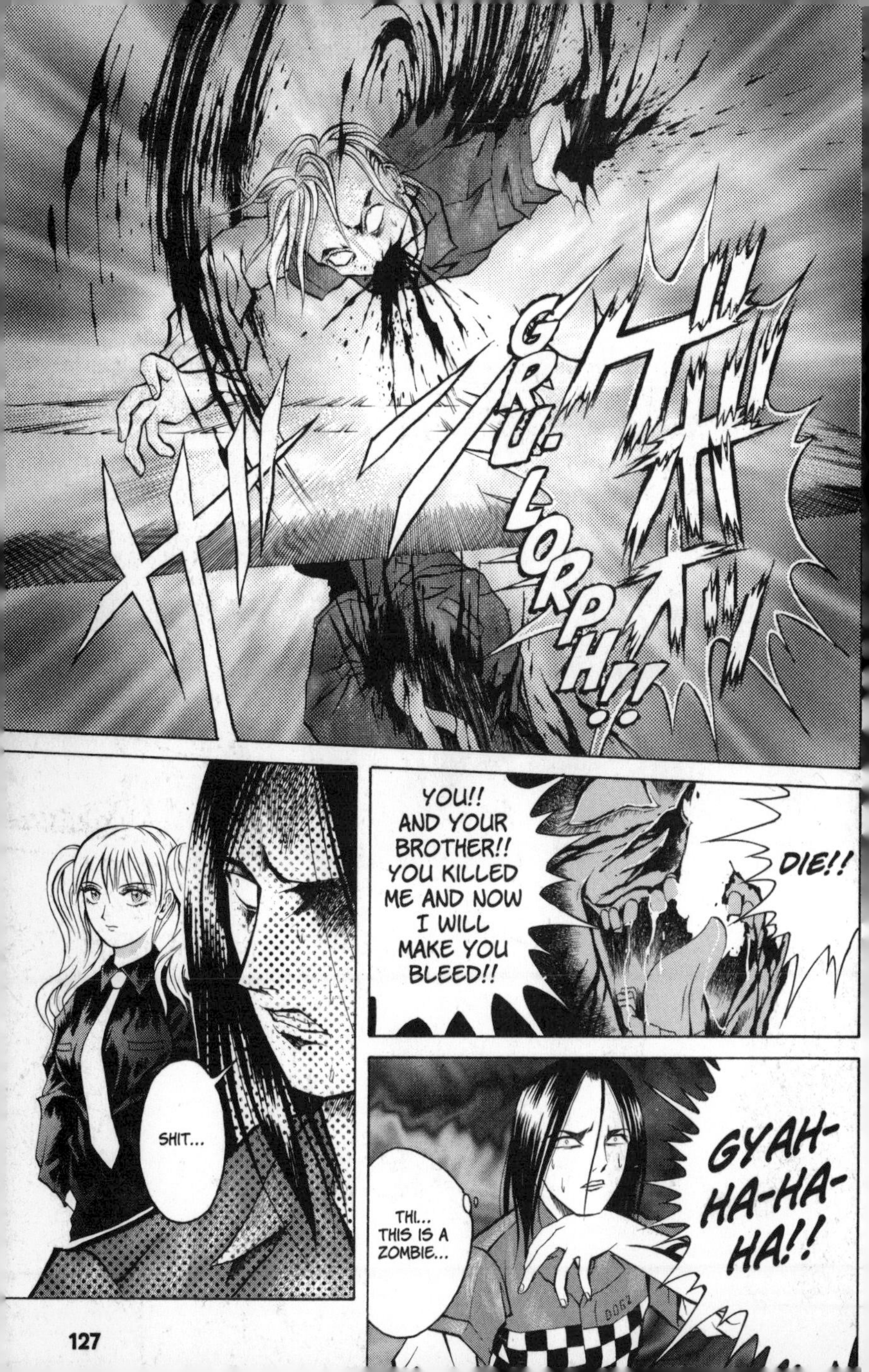
GRU-LORPH!!
YOU!! AND YOUR BROTHER!! YOU KILLED ME AND NOW I WILL MAKE YOU BLEED!!
DIE!!
GYAH-HA-HA-HA!!
THI... THIS IS A ZOMBIE...
SHIT...

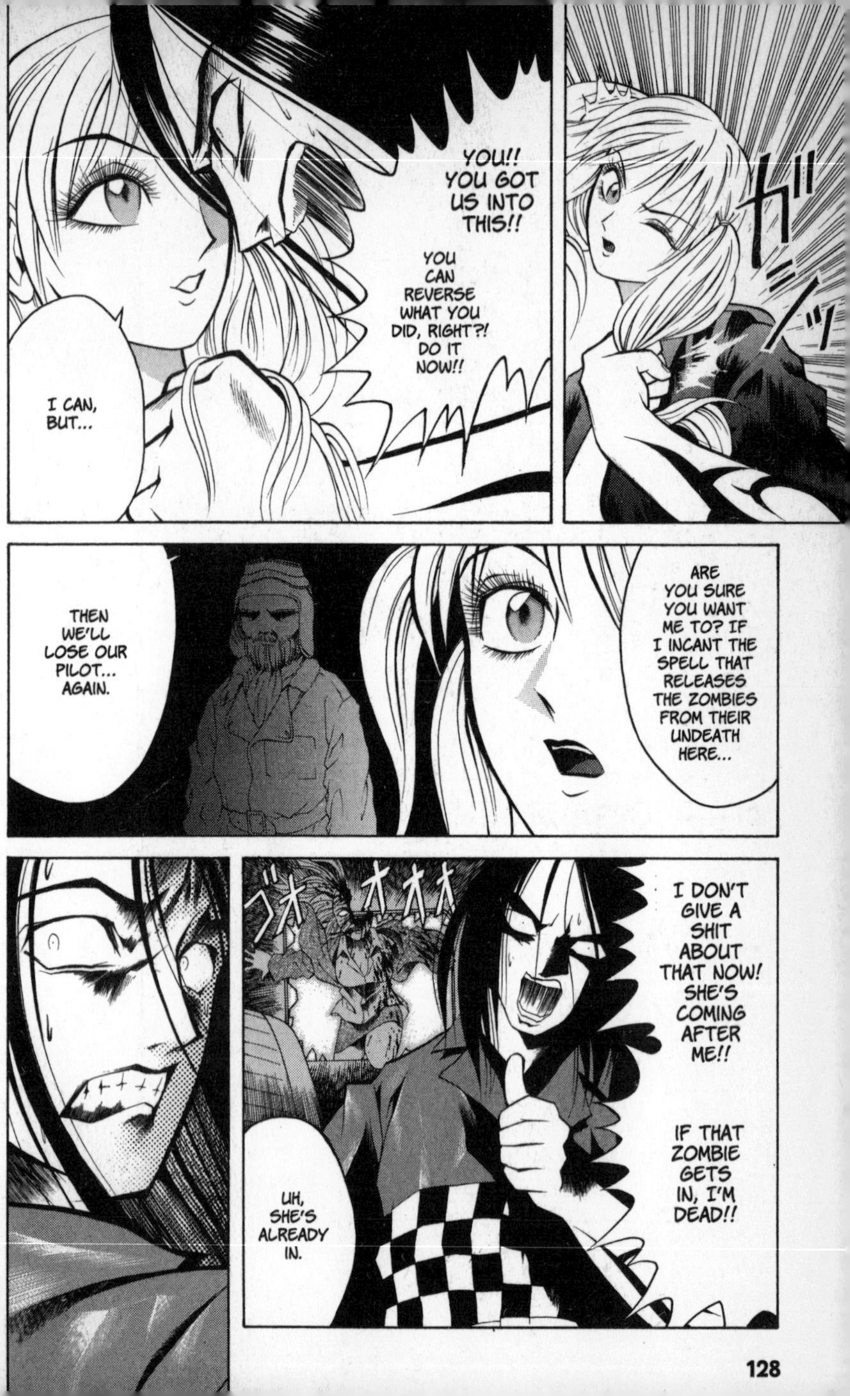
YOU!! YOU GOT US INTO THIS!!
YOU CAN REVERSE WHAT YOU DID, RIGHT?! DO IT NOW!!
I CAN, BUT...
ARE YOU SURE YOU WANT ME TO? IF I INCANT THE SPELL THAT RELEASES THE ZOMBIES FROM THEIR UNDEATH HERE...
THEN WE'LL LOSE OUR PILOT... AGAIN.
I DON'T GIVE A SHIT ABOUT THAT NOW! SHE'S COMING AFTER ME!!
IF THAT ZOMBIE GETS IN, I'M DEAD!!
ヴオオオ
UH, SHE'S ALREADY IN.

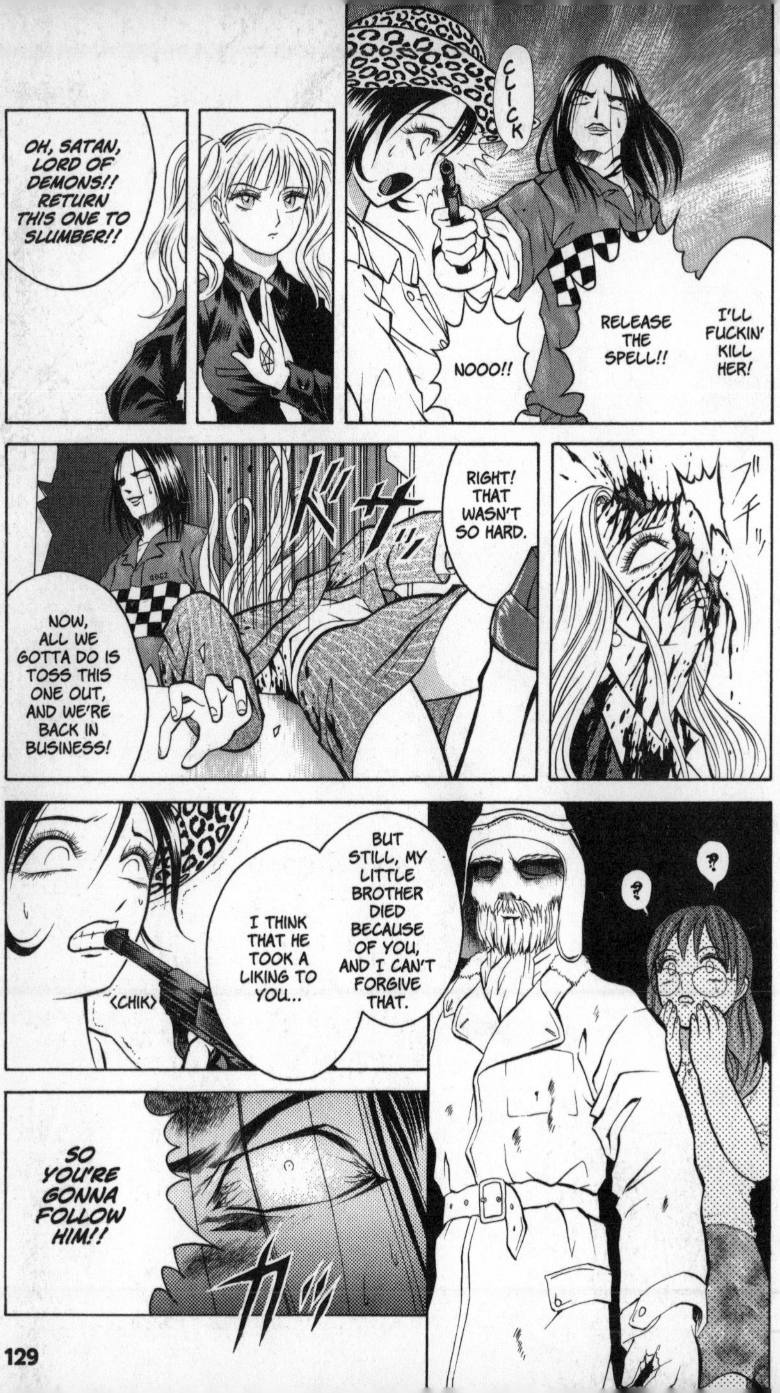
CLICK
I'LL FUCKIN' KILL HER!
RELEASE THE SPELL!!
NOOO!!
OH, SATAN, LORD OF DEMONS!! RETURN THIS ONE TO SLUMBER!!
ブチッ
RIGHT! THAT WASN'T SO HARD.
ドサッ
NOW, ALL WE GOTTA DO IS TOSS THIS ONE OUT, AND WE'RE BACK IN BUSINESS!
?
?
I THINK THAT HE TOOK A LIKING TO YOU...
BUT STILL, MY LITTLE BROTHER DIED BECAUSE OF YOU, AND I CAN'T FORGIVE THAT.
<CHIK>
SO YOU'RE GONNA FOLLOW HIM!!

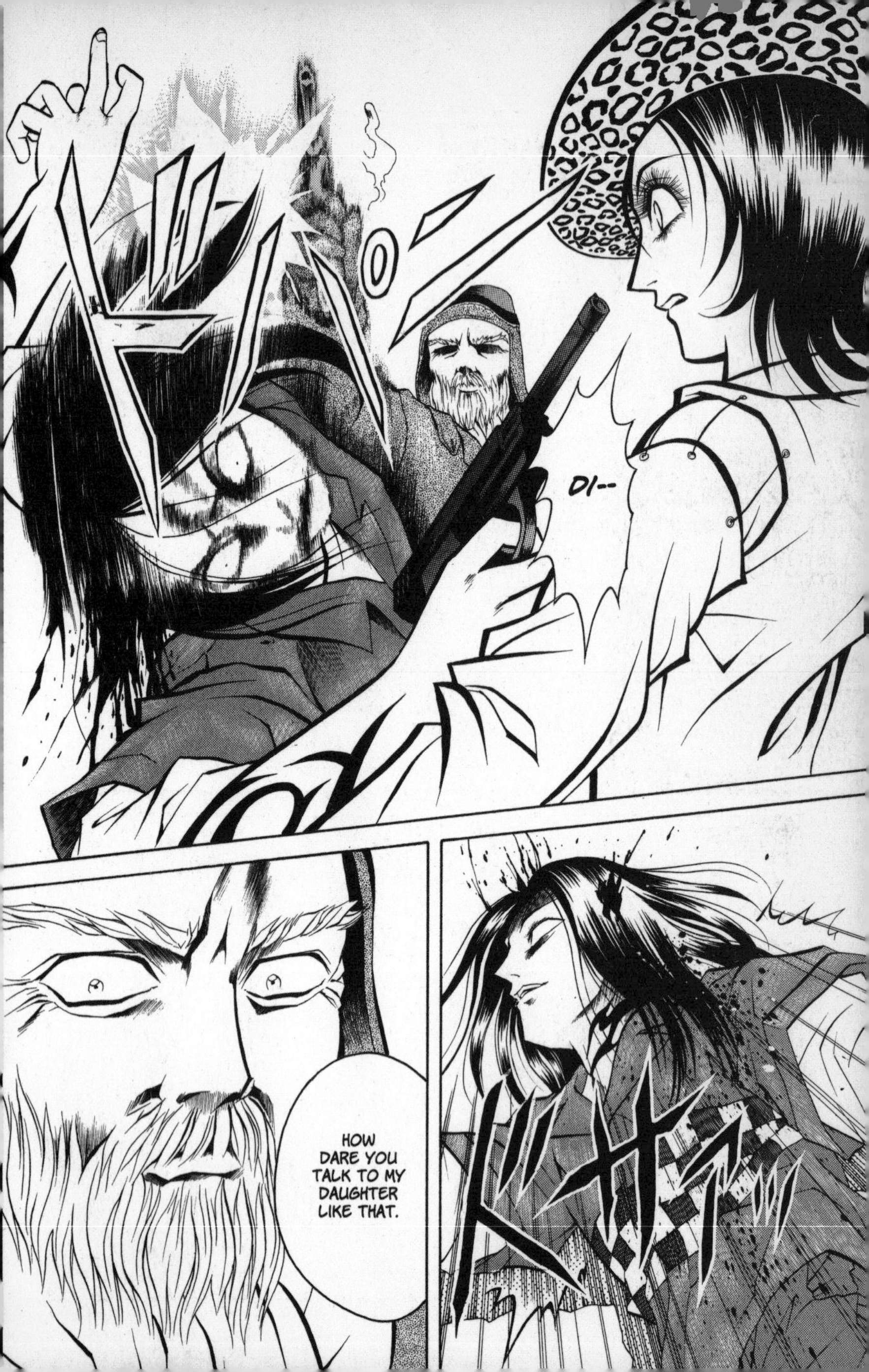
OI--
HOW DARE YOU TALK TO MY DAUGHTER LIKE THAT.

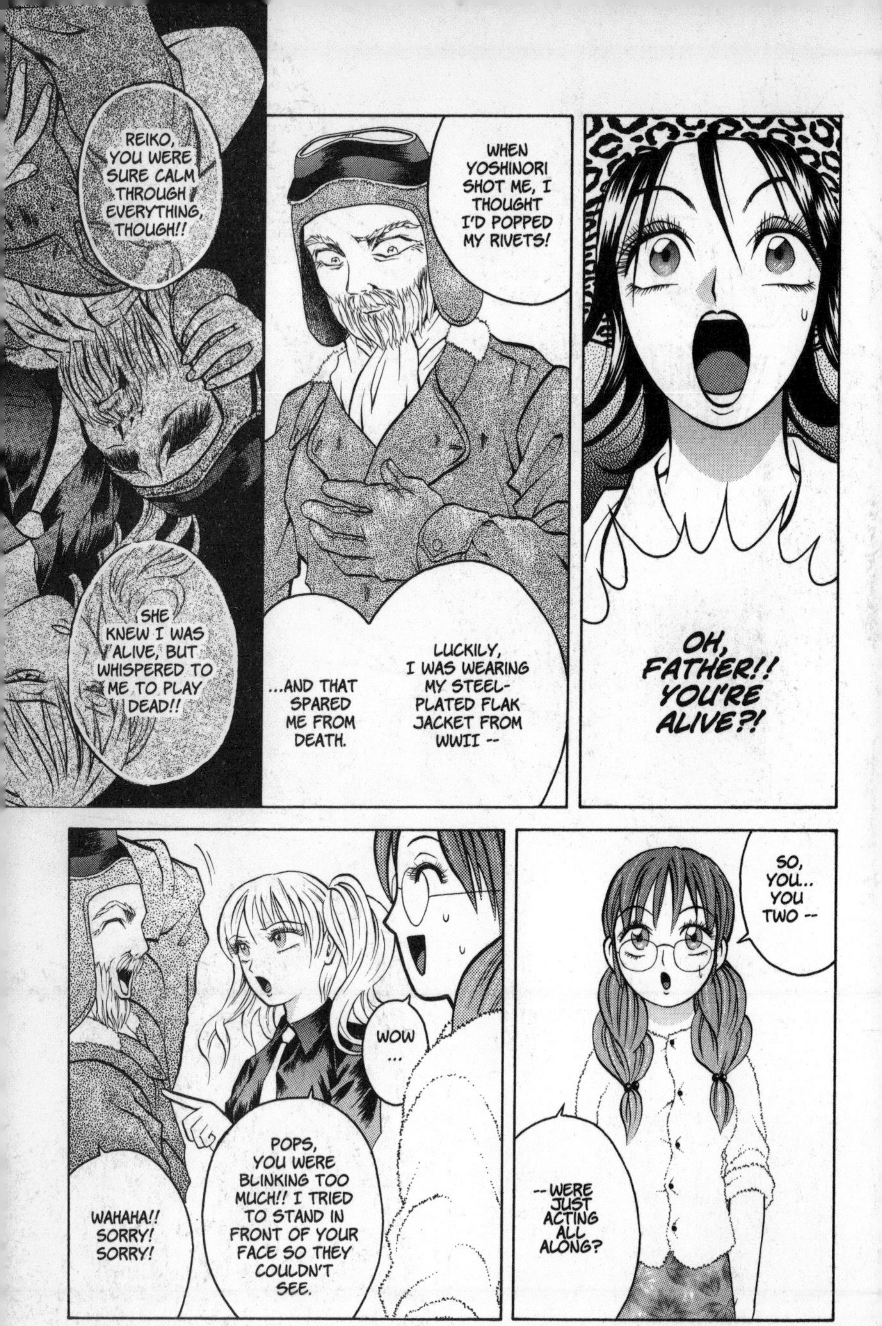
OH, FATHER!! YOU'RE ALIVE?!
WHEN YOSHINORI SHOT ME, I THOUGHT I'D POPPED MY RIVETS!
LUCKILY, I WAS WEARING MY STEEL-PLATED FLAK JACKET FROM WWII --
...AND THAT SPARED ME FROM DEATH.
REIKO, YOU WERE SURE CALM THROUGH EVERYTHING, THOUGH!!
SHE KNEW I WAS ALIVE, BUT WHISPERED TO ME TO PLAY DEAD!!
SO, YOU... YOU TWO --
-- WERE JUST ACTING ALL ALONG?
WOW ...
POPS, YOU WERE BLINKING TOO MUCH!! I TRIED TO STAND IN FRONT OF YOUR FACE SO THEY COULDN'T SEE.
WAHAHA!! SORRY! SORRY!

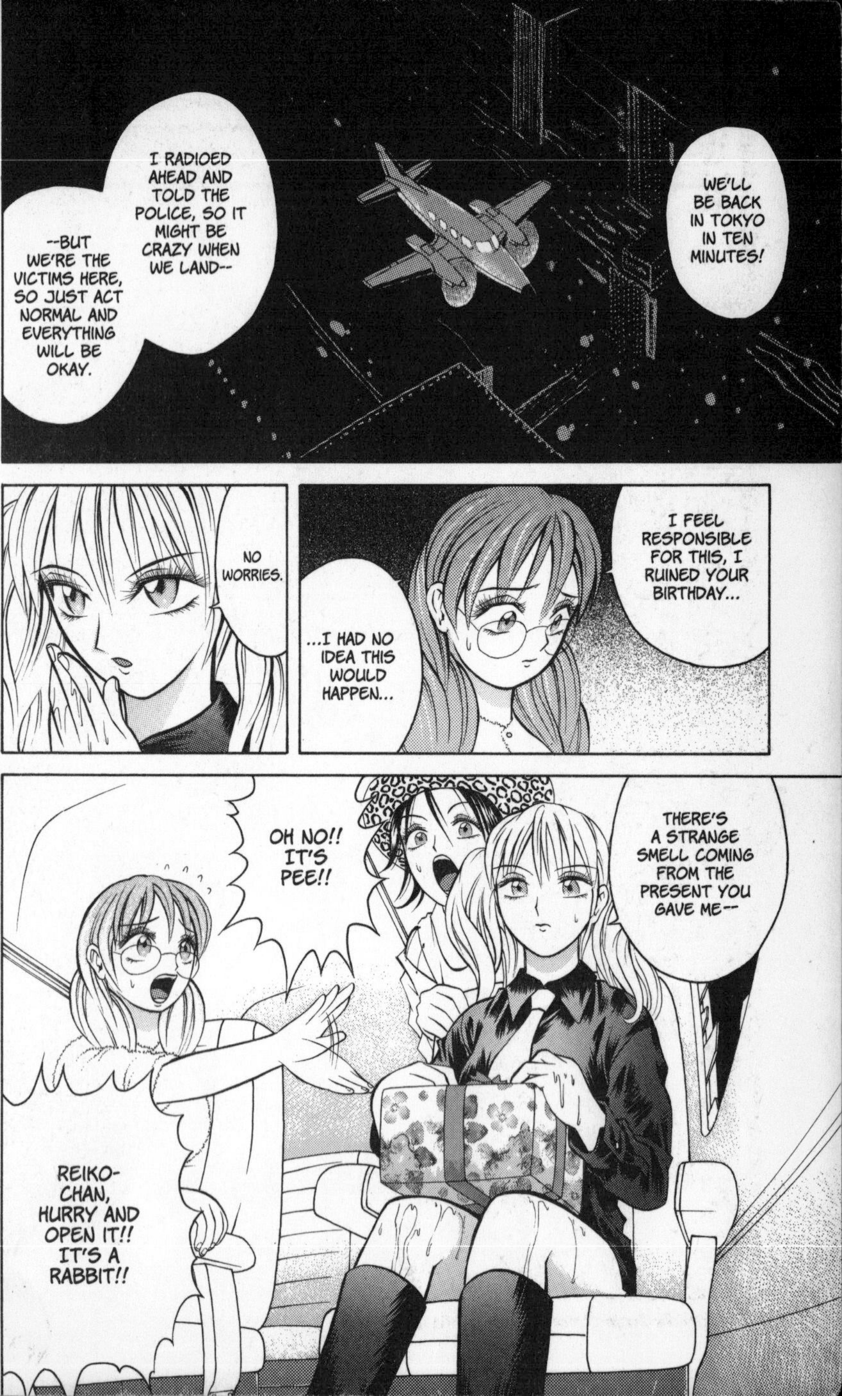
WE'LL BE BACK IN TOKYO IN TEN MINUTES!
I RADIOED AHEAD AND TOLD THE POLICE, SO IT MIGHT BE CRAZY WHEN WE LAND--
--BUT WE'RE THE VICTIMS HERE, SO JUST ACT NORMAL AND EVERYTHING WILL BE OKAY.
I FEEL RESPONSIBLE FOR THIS, I RUINED YOUR BIRTHDAY...
...I HAD NO IDEA THIS WOULD HAPPEN...
NO WORRIES.
THERE'S A STRANGE SMELL COMING FROM THE PRESENT YOU GAVE ME--
OH NO!! IT'S PEE!!
REIKO-CHAN, HURRY AND OPEN IT!! IT'S A RABBIT!!

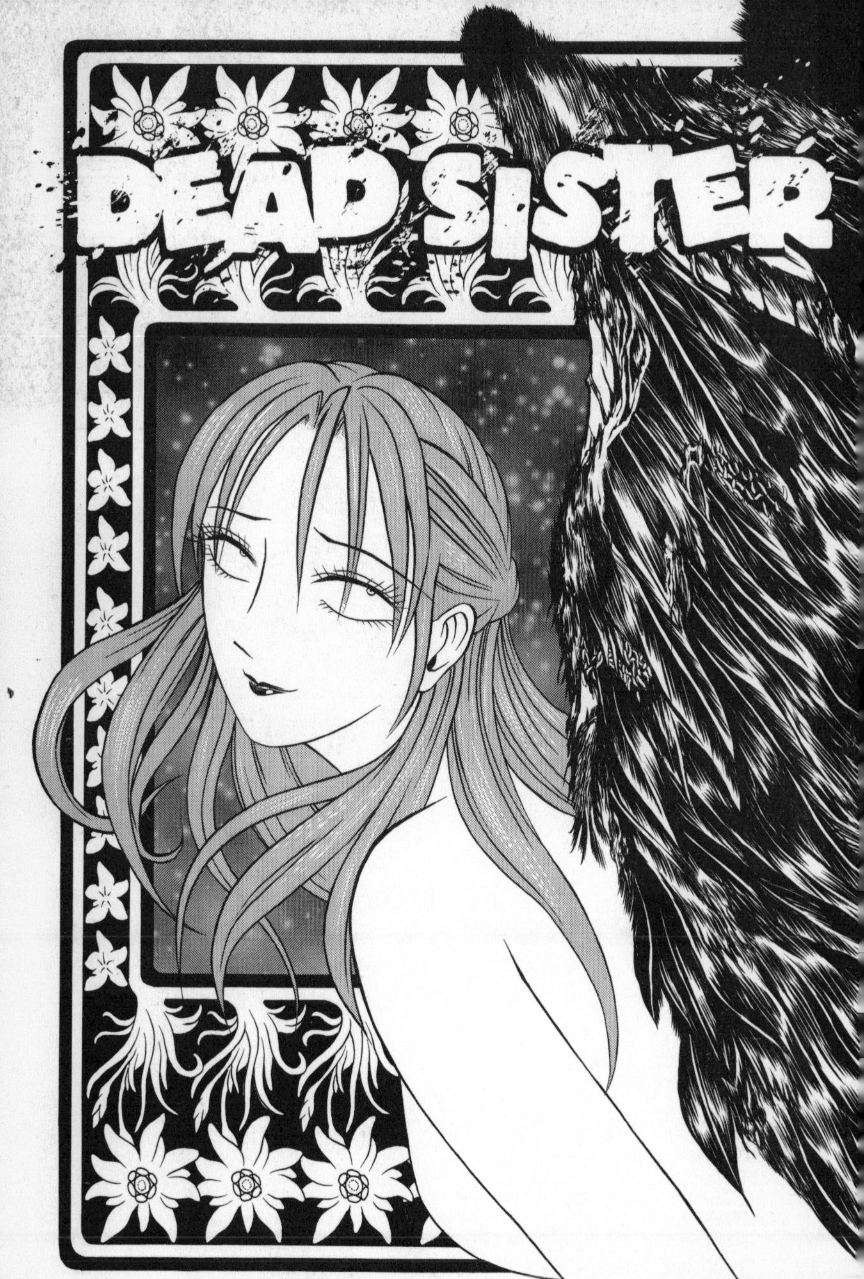
DEAD SISTER

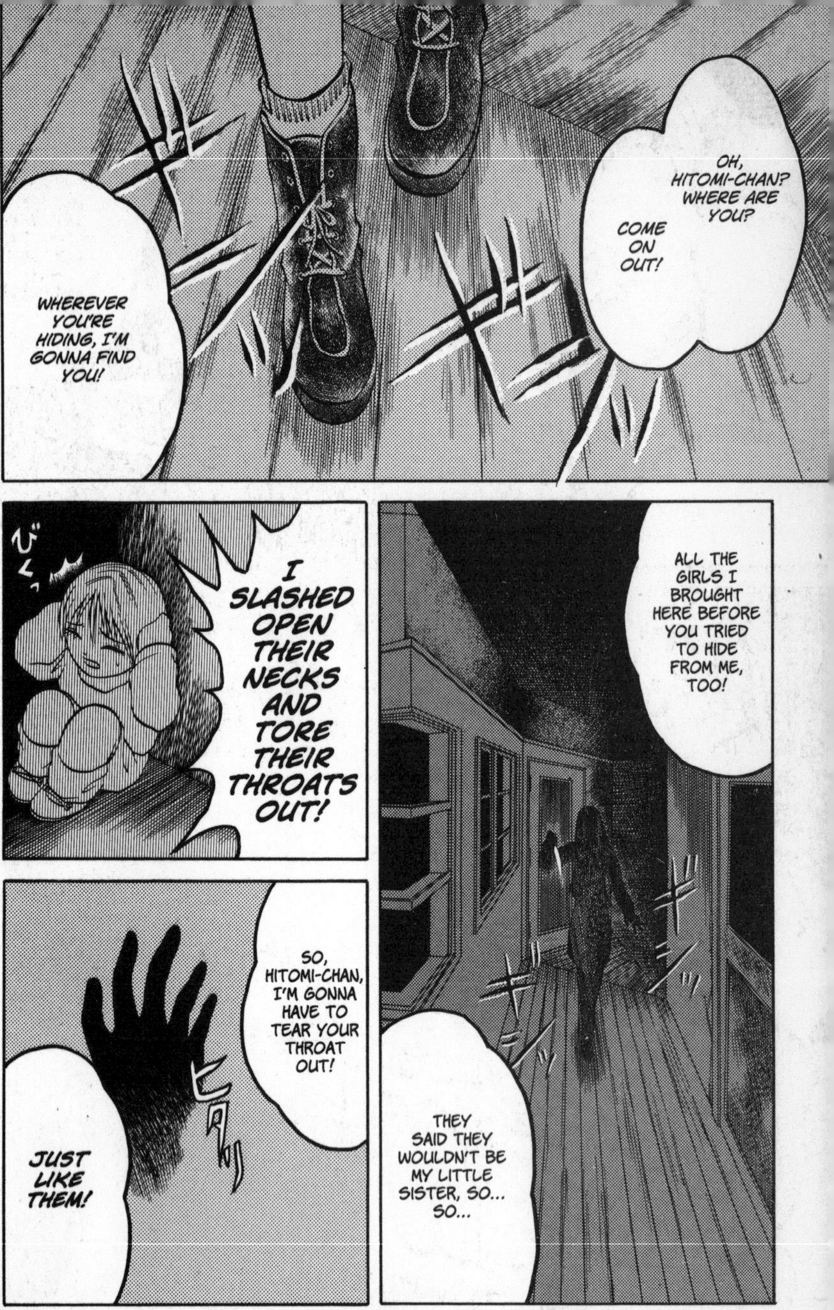
OH, HITOMI-CHAN? WHERE ARE YOU?
COME ON OUT!
WHEREVER YOU'RE HIDING, I'M GONNA FIND YOU!
ALL THE GIRLS I BROUGHT HERE BEFORE YOU TRIED TO HIDE FROM ME, TOO!
THEY SAID THEY WOULDN'T BE MY LITTLE SISTER, SO... SO...
I SLASHED OPEN THEIR NECKS AND TORE THEIR THROATS OUT!
SO, HITOMI-CHAN, I'M GONNA HAVE TO TEAR YOUR THROAT OUT!
JUST LIKE THEM!

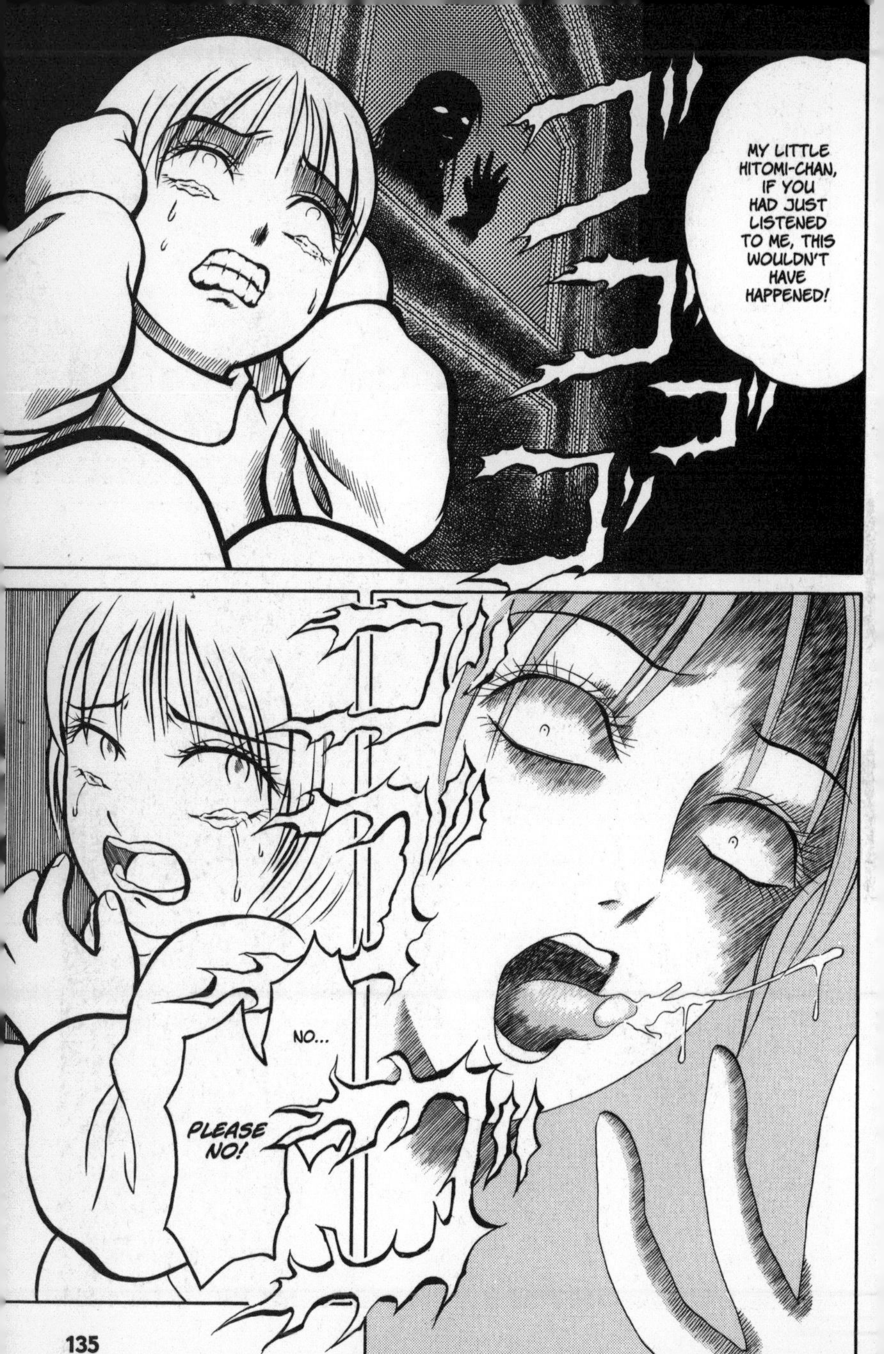
MY LITTLE HITOMI-CHAN, IF YOU HAD JUST LISTENED TO ME, THIS WOULDN'T HAVE HAPPENED!
NO...
PLEASE NO!

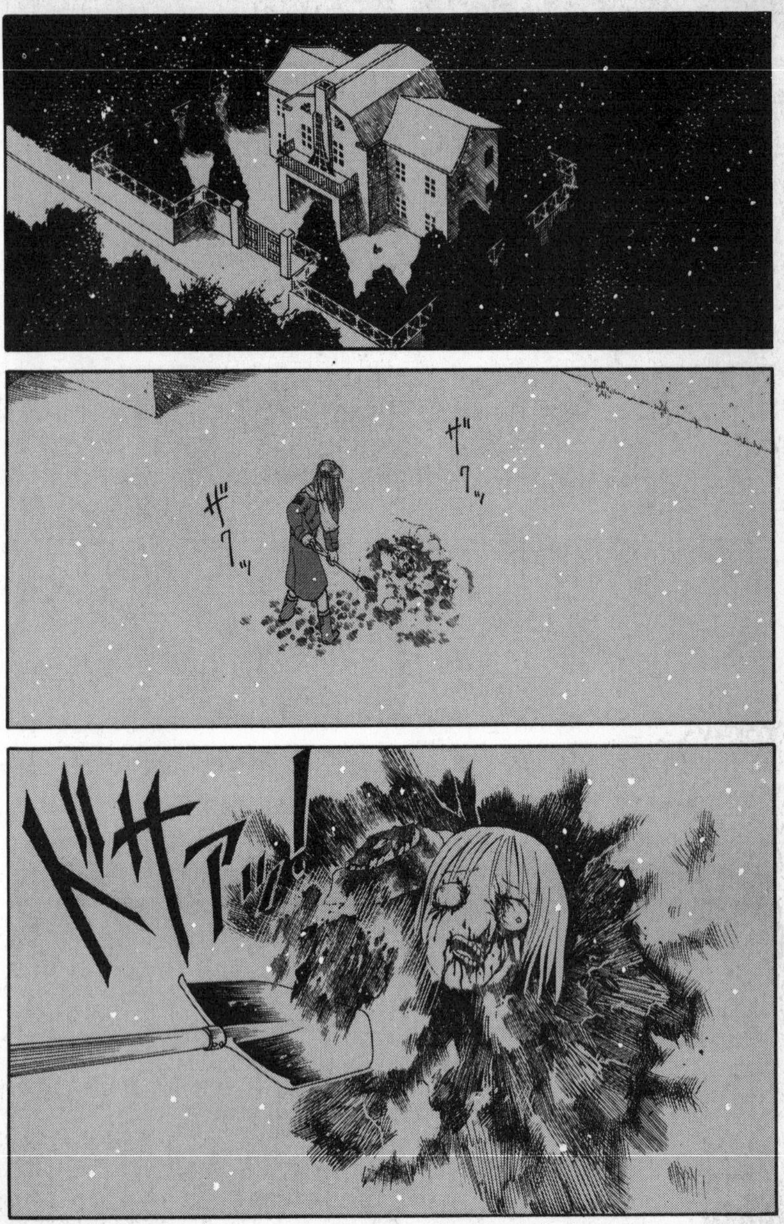
ザクッ
ザクッ
ドサァッ!

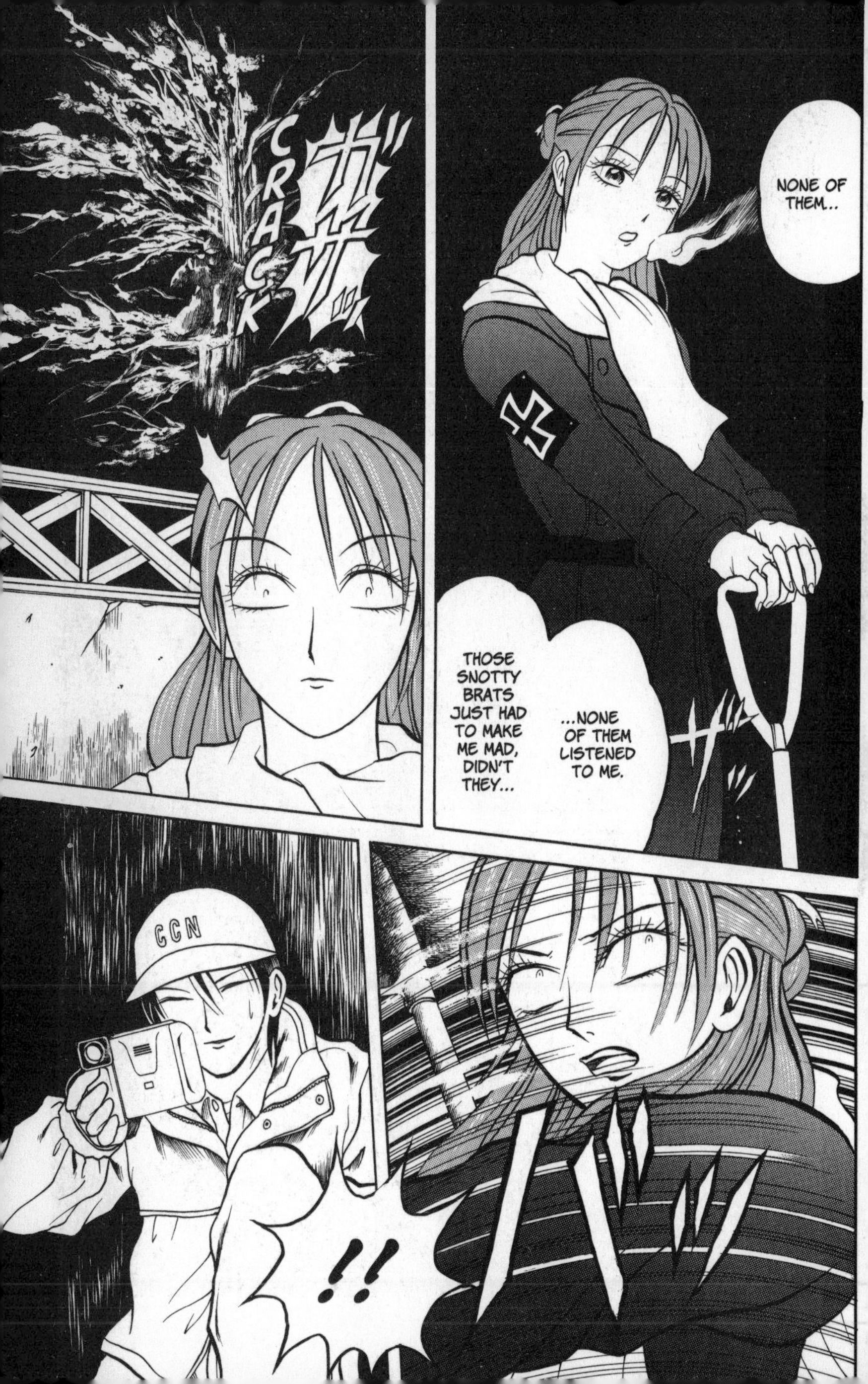
NONE OF THEM...
...NONE OF THEM LISTENED TO ME.
THOSE SNOTTY BRATS JUST HAD TO MAKE ME MAD, DIDN'T THEY...
CRACK
!!

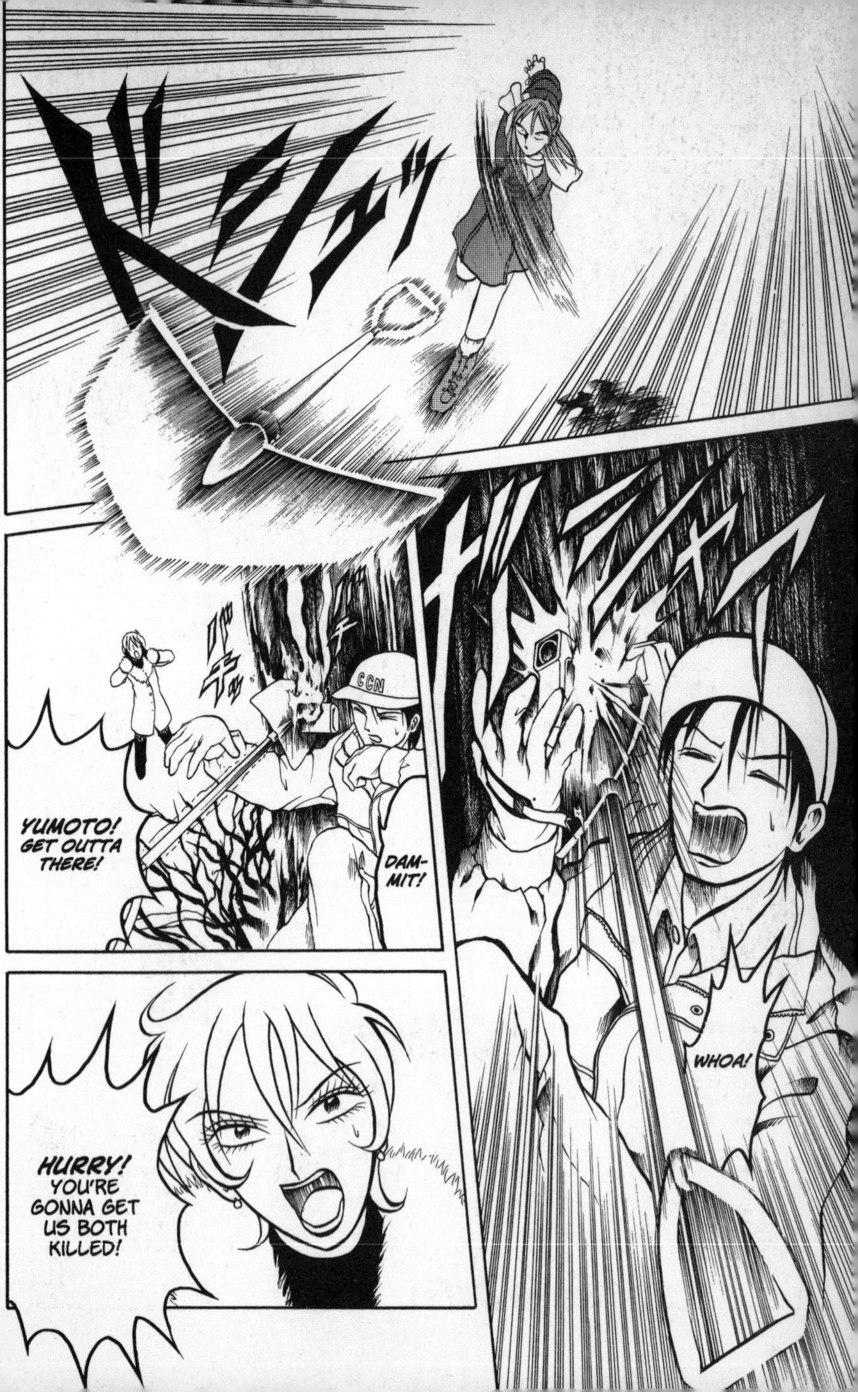
WHOA!
DAM-
MIT!
YUMOTO! GET OUTTA THERE!
HURRY! YOU'RE GONNA GET US BOTH KILLED!

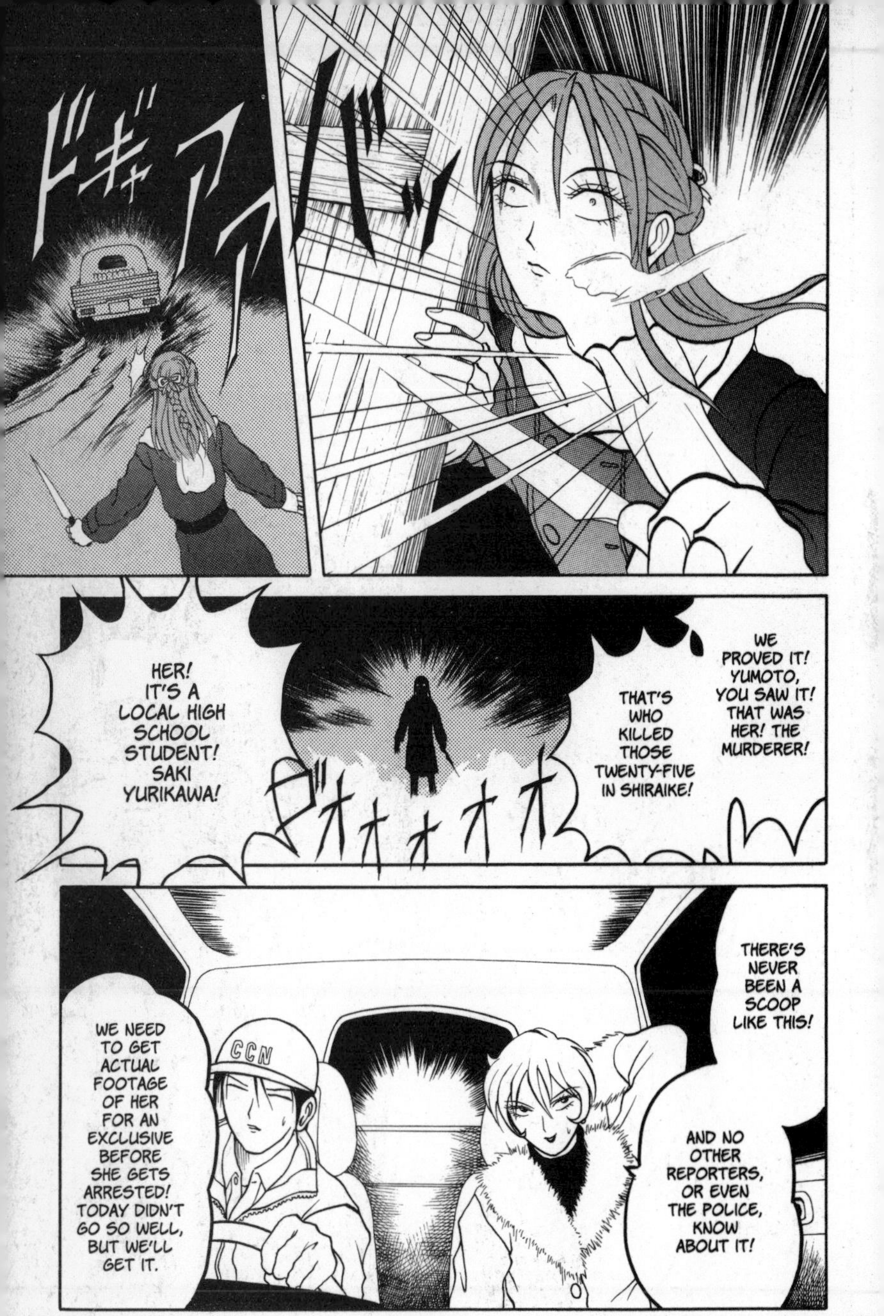
バッ
ドギャア
WE PROVED IT! YUMOTO, YOU SAW IT! THAT WAS HER! THE MURDERER!
THAT'S WHO KILLED THOSE TWENTY-FIVE IN SHIRAIKE!
HER! IT'S A LOCAL HIGH SCHOOL STUDENT! SAKI YURIKAWA!
ゾオオォオオ
THERE'S NEVER BEEN A SCOOP LIKE THIS!
AND NO OTHER REPORTERS, OR EVEN THE POLICE, KNOW ABOUT IT!
CCN
WE NEED TO GET ACTUAL FOOTAGE OF HER FOR AN EXCLUSIVE BEFORE SHE GETS ARRESTED! TODAY DIDN'T GO SO WELL, BUT WE'LL GET IT.

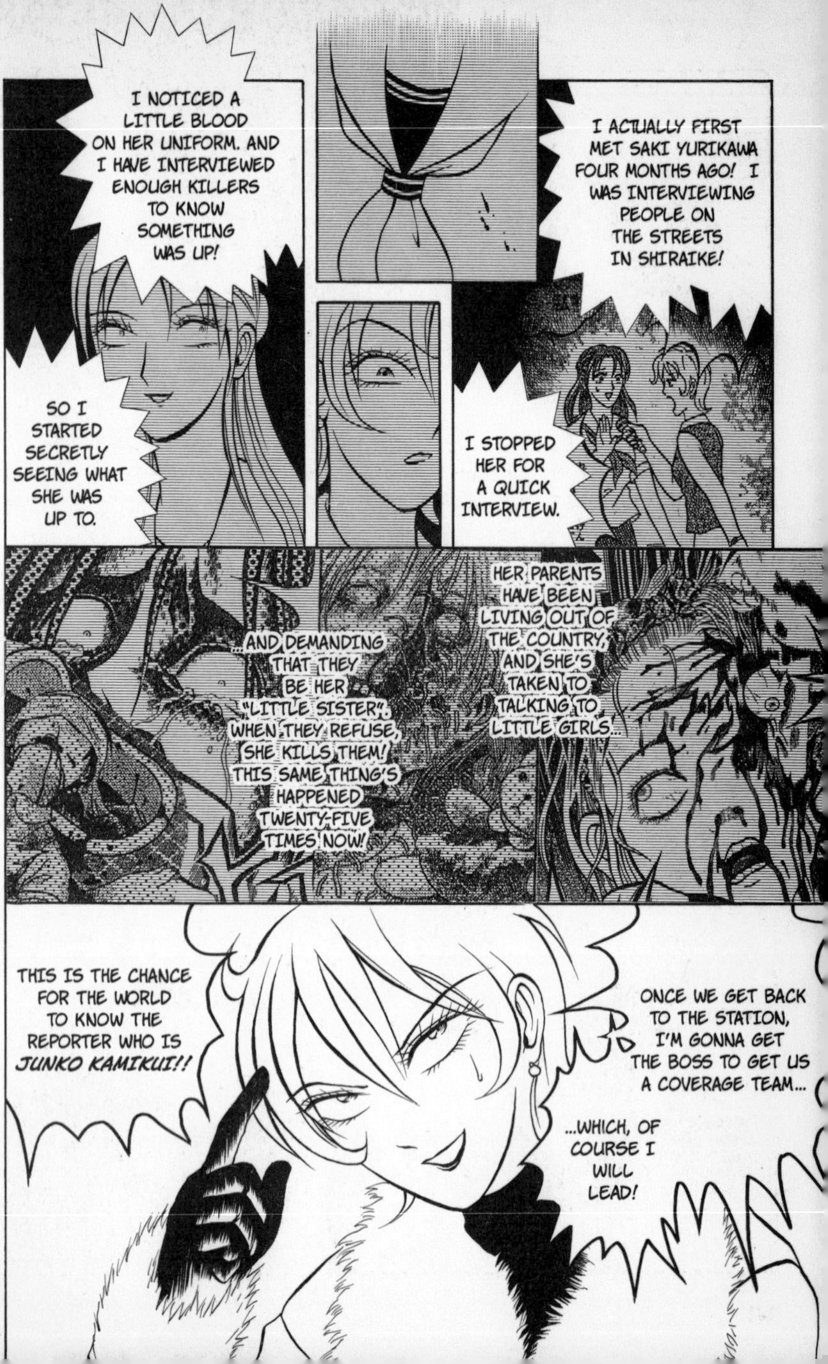
I ACTUALLY FIRST MET SAKI YURIKAWA FOUR MONTHS AGO! I WAS INTERVIEWING PEOPLE ON THE STREETS IN SHIRAIKE!
I STOPPED HER FOR A QUICK INTERVIEW.
I NOTICED A LITTLE BLOOD ON HER UNIFORM. AND I HAVE INTERVIEWED ENOUGH KILLERS TO KNOW SOMETHING WAS UP!
SO I STARTED SECRETLY SEEING WHAT SHE WAS UP TO.
HER PARENTS HAVE BEEN LIVING OUT OF THE COUNTRY, AND SHE'S TAKEN TO TALKING TO LITTLE GIRLS...
...AND DEMANDING THAT THEY BE HER "LITTLE SISTER". WHEN THEY REFUSE, SHE KILLS THEM! THIS SAME THING'S HAPPENED TWENTY-FIVE TIMES NOW!
ONCE WE GET BACK TO THE STATION, I'M GONNA GET THE BOSS TO GET US A COVERAGE TEAM...
...WHICH, OF COURSE I WILL LEAD!
THIS IS THE CHANCE FOR THE WORLD TO KNOW THE REPORTER WHO IS *JUNKO KAMIKUI!!*

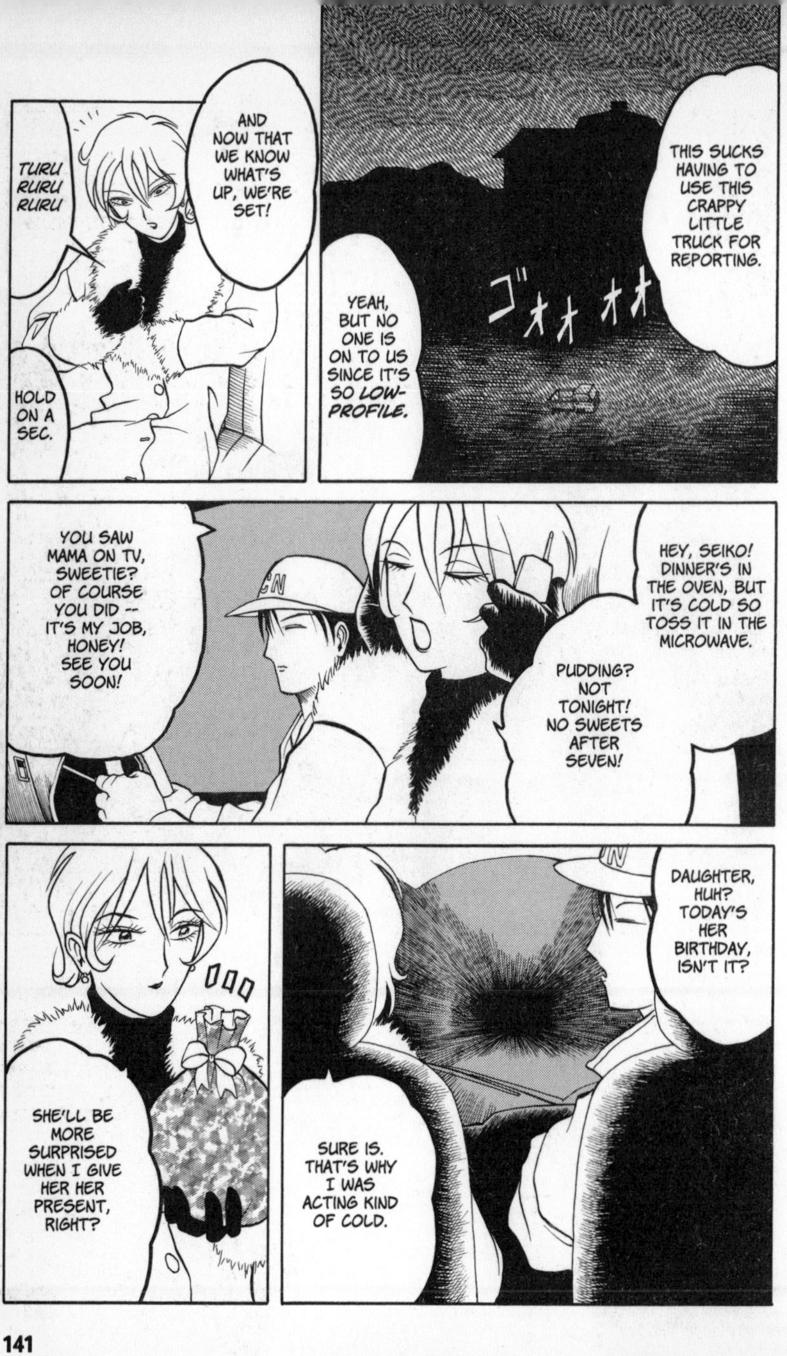
THIS SUCKS HAVING TO USE THIS CRAPPY LITTLE TRUCK FOR REPORTING.
ゴオオオオ
YEAH, BUT NO ONE IS ON TO US SINCE IT'S SO *LOW-PROFILE.*
AND NOW THAT WE KNOW WHAT'S UP, WE'RE SET!
*TURU RURU RURU*
HOLD ON A SEC.
HEY, SEIKO! DINNER'S IN THE OVEN, BUT IT'S COLD SO TOSS IT IN THE MICROWAVE.
PUDDING? NOT TONIGHT! NO SWEETS AFTER SEVEN!
YOU SAW MAMA ON TV, SWEETIE? OF COURSE YOU DID -- IT'S MY JOB, HONEY! SEE YOU SOON!
DAUGHTER, HUH? TODAY'S HER BIRTHDAY, ISN'T IT?
SURE IS. THAT'S WHY I WAS ACTING KIND OF COLD.
SHE'LL BE MORE SURPRISED WHEN I GIVE HER HER PRESENT, RIGHT?

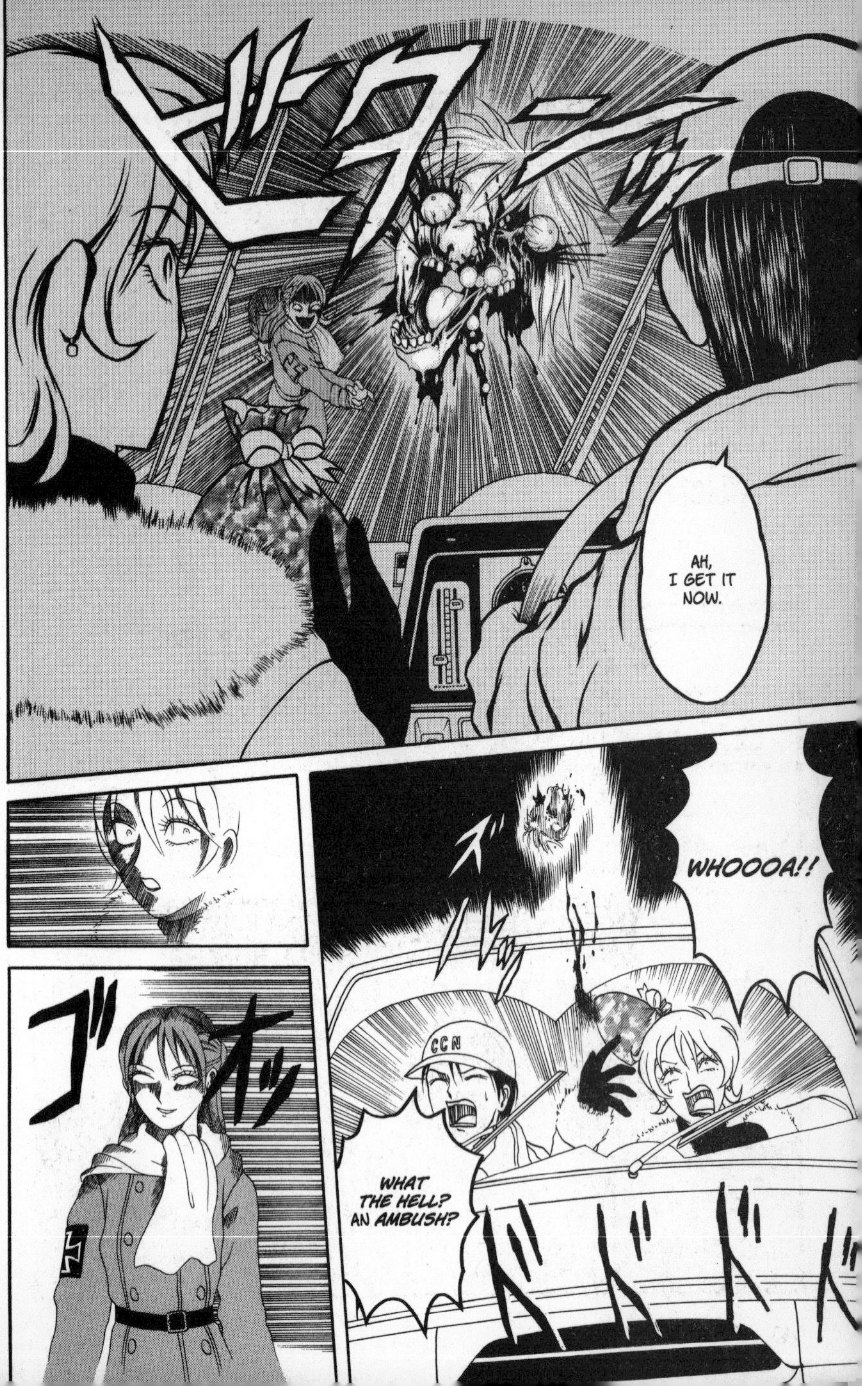
AH, I GET IT NOW.
WHOOOA!!
WHAT THE HELL? AN AMBUSH?

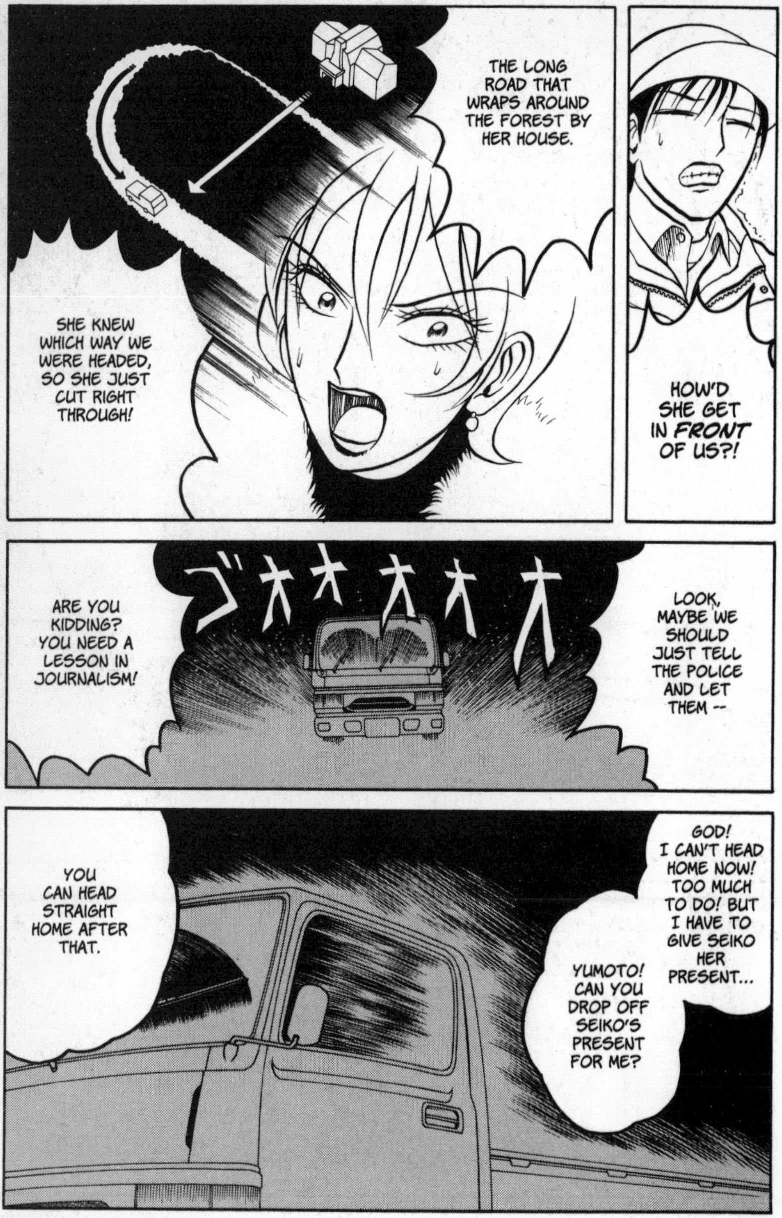
HOW'D SHE GET IN *FRONT* OF US?!
THE LONG ROAD THAT WRAPS AROUND THE FOREST BY HER HOUSE.
SHE KNEW WHICH WAY WE WERE HEADED, SO SHE JUST CUT RIGHT THROUGH!
LOOK, MAYBE WE SHOULD JUST TELL THE POLICE AND LET THEM --
ゴオオオオオ
ARE YOU KIDDING? YOU NEED A LESSON IN JOURNALISM!
GOD! I CAN'T HEAD HOME NOW! TOO MUCH TO DO! BUT I HAVE TO GIVE SEIKO HER PRESENT...
YUMOTO! CAN YOU DROP OFF SEIKO'S PRESENT FOR ME?
YOU CAN HEAD STRAIGHT HOME AFTER THAT.

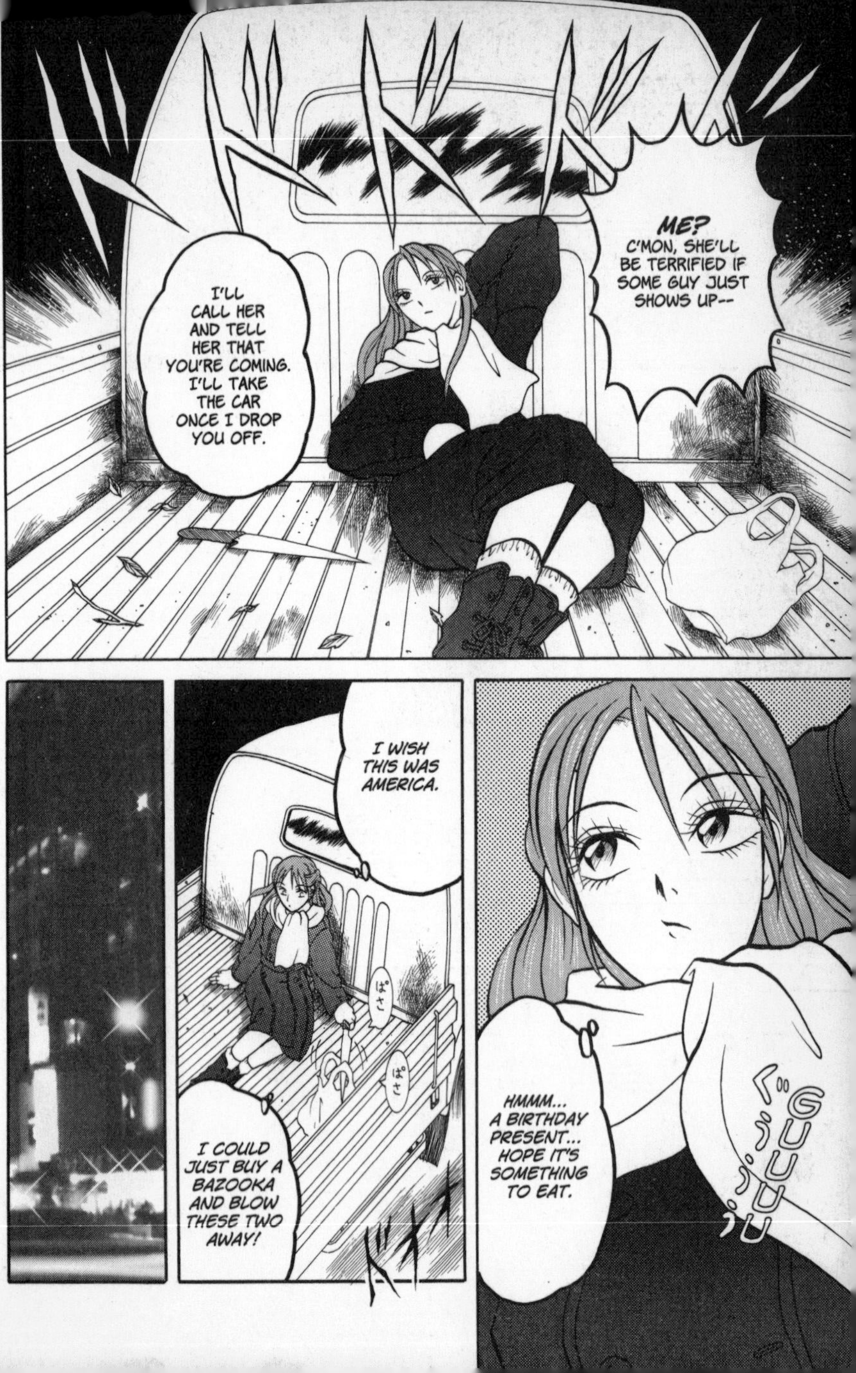
ME?
C'MON, SHE'LL BE TERRIFIED IF SOME GUY JUST SHOWS UP--
I'LL CALL HER AND TELL HER THAT YOU'RE COMING. I'LL TAKE THE CAR ONCE I DROP YOU OFF.
HMMM... A BIRTHDAY PRESENT... HOPE IT'S SOMETHING TO EAT.
GUUU
I WISH THIS WAS AMERICA.
ぱさ
ぱさ
I COULD JUST BUY A BAZOOKA AND BLOW THESE TWO AWAY!

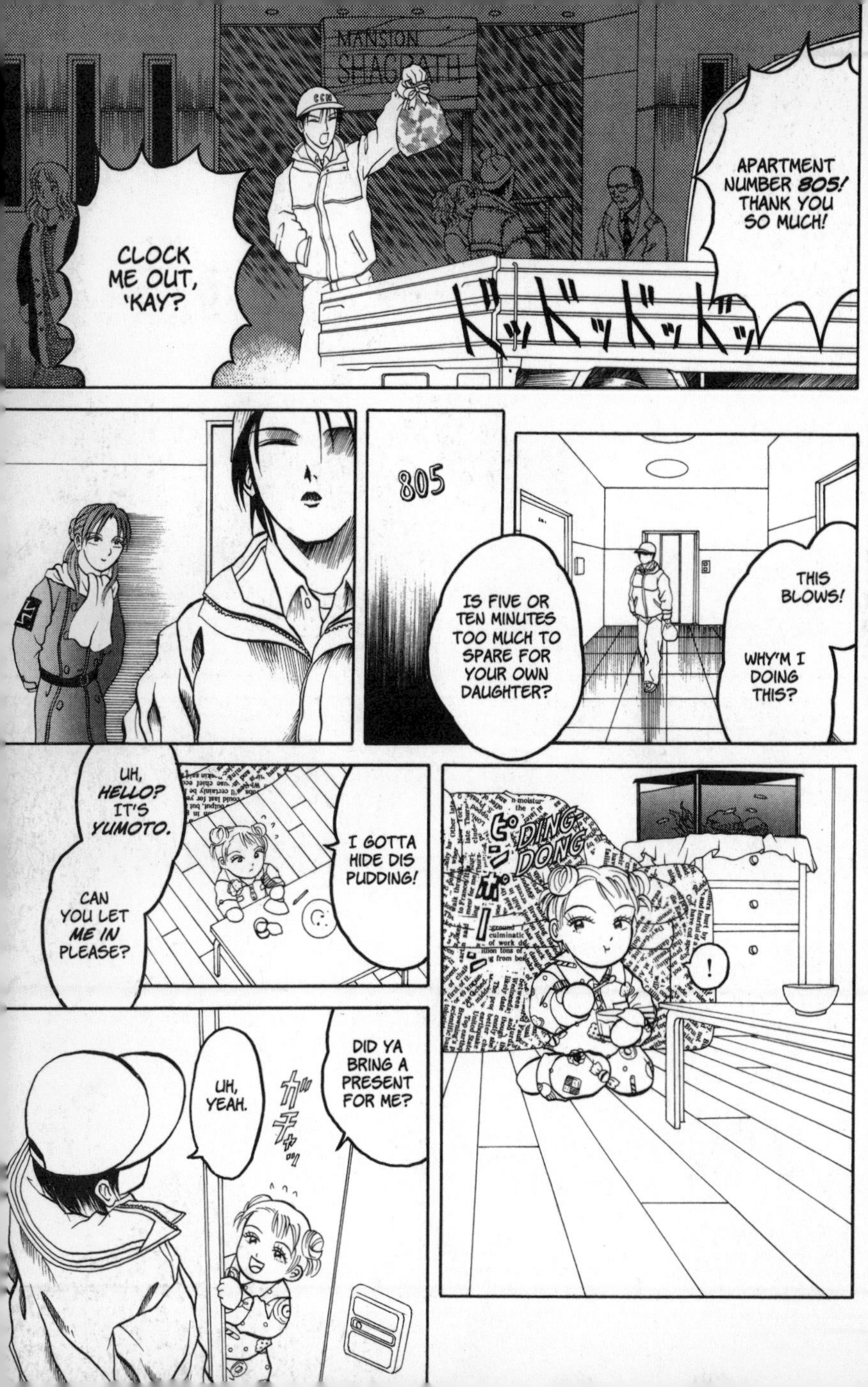
MANSION
SHAGRATH
APARTMENT NUMBER 805! THANK YOU SO MUCH!
CLOCK ME OUT, 'KAY?
ドッドッドッドッ
THIS BLOWS!
WHY'M I DOING THIS?
805
IS FIVE OR TEN MINUTES TOO MUCH TO SPARE FOR YOUR OWN DAUGHTER?
DING DONG
!
I GOTTA HIDE DIS PUDDING!
UH, *HELLO?* IT'S *YUMOTO.*
CAN YOU LET *ME IN* PLEASE?
DID YA BRING A PRESENT FOR ME?
ガチャ
UH, YEAH.

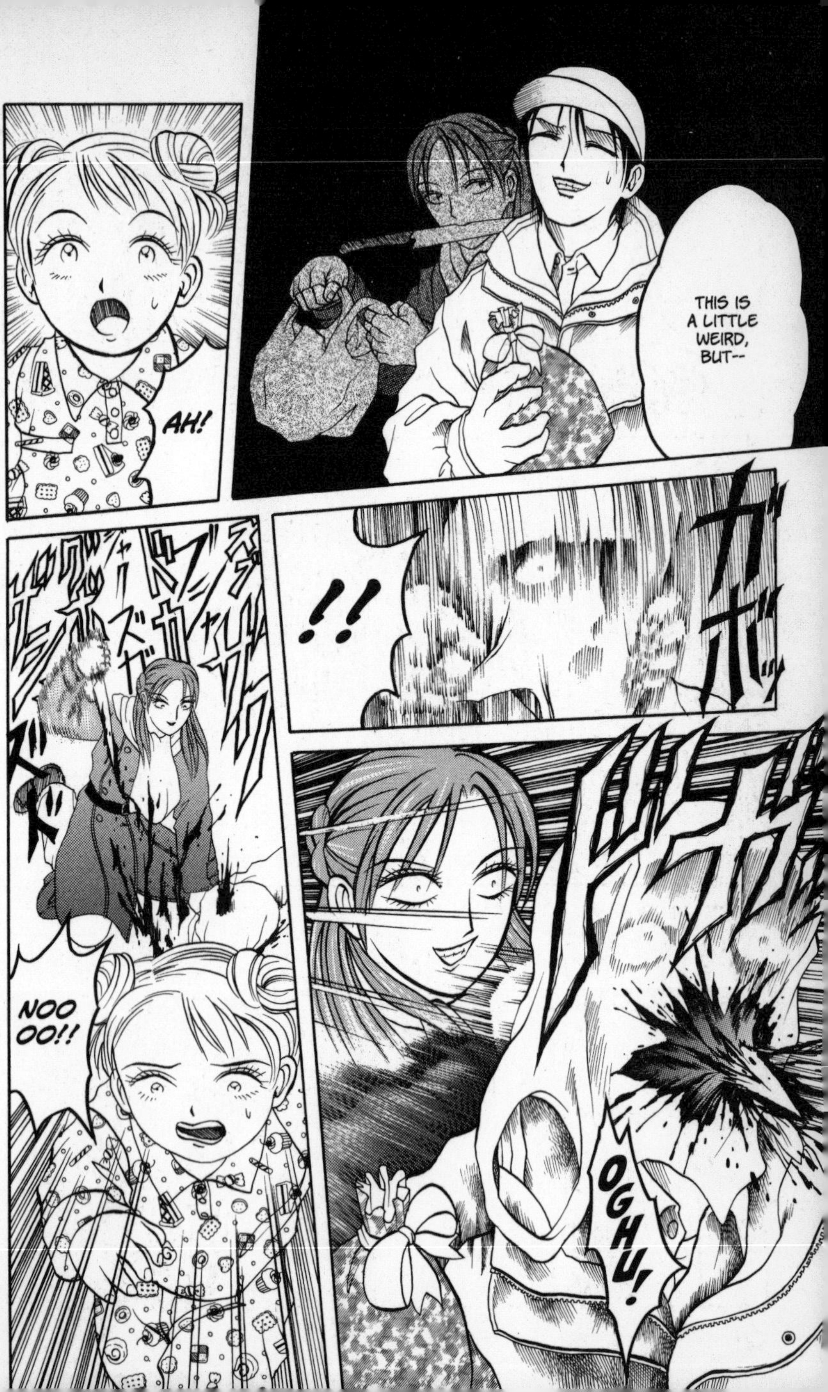
THIS IS A LITTLE WEIRD, BUT--
AH!
!!
ガボッ
OGHU!
NOOOO!!

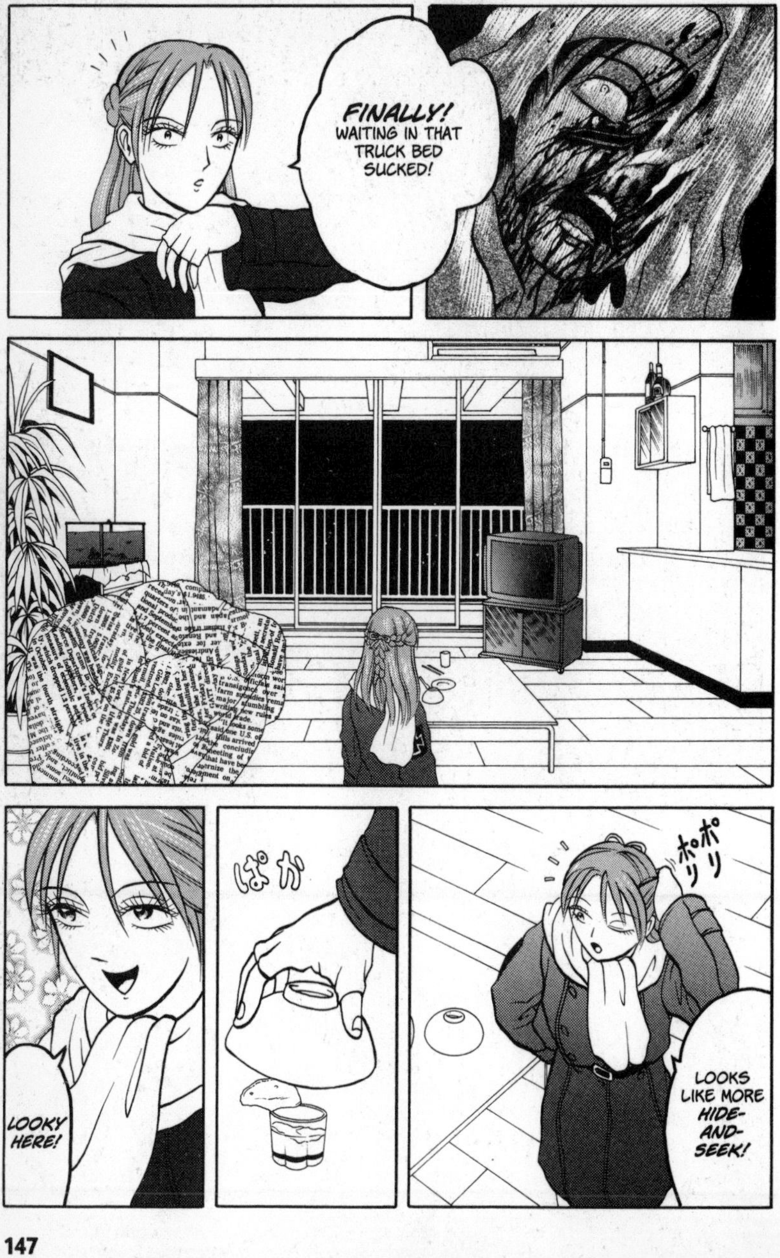
FINALLY! WAITING IN THAT TRUCK BED SUCKED!
ポリポリ
LOOKS LIKE MORE HIDE-AND-SEEK!
ぱか
LOOKY HERE!

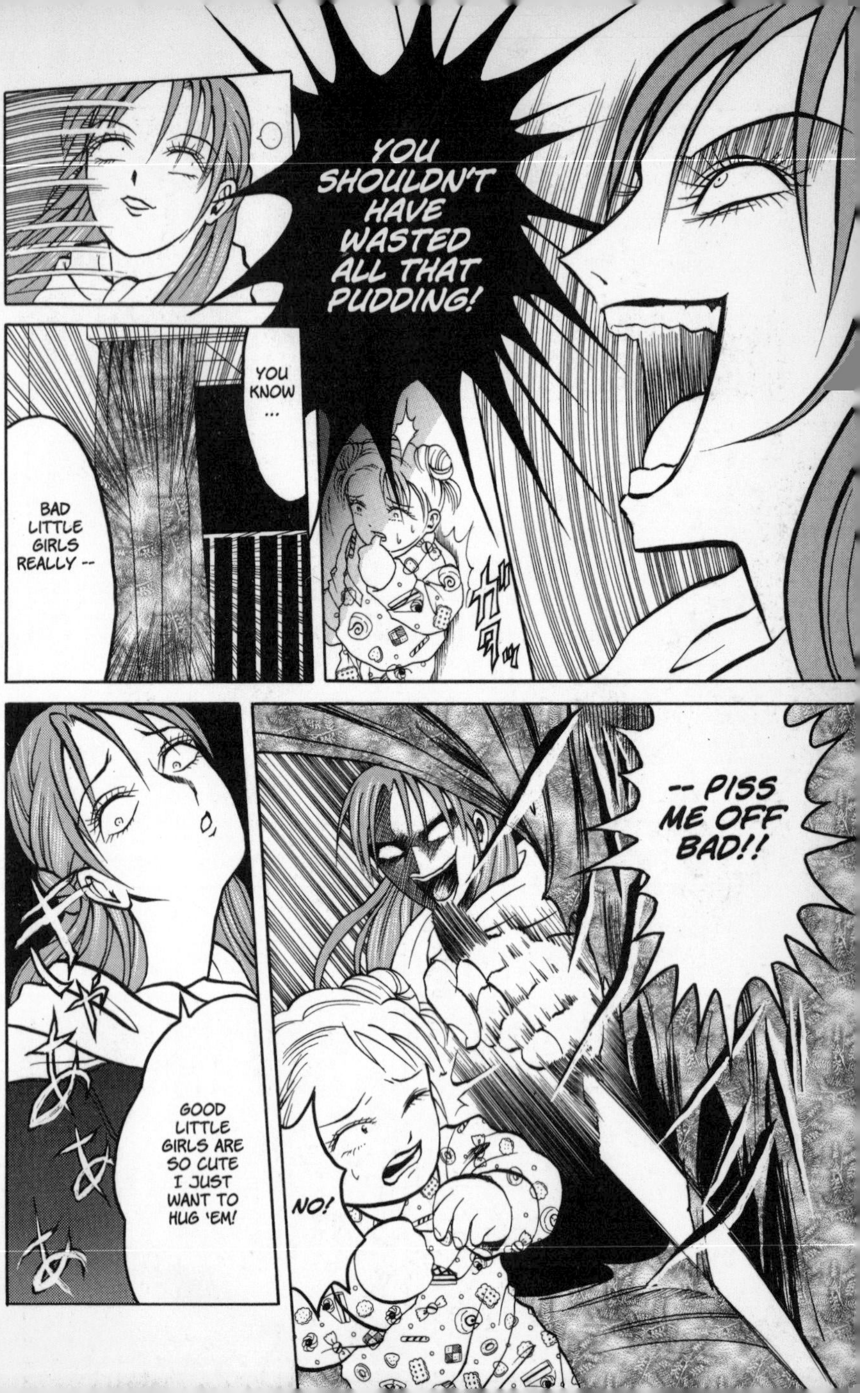
YOU SHOULDN'T HAVE WASTED ALL THAT PUDDING!
YOU KNOW ...
BAD LITTLE GIRLS REALLY --
-- PISS ME OFF BAD!!
NO!
GOOD LITTLE GIRLS ARE SO CUTE I JUST WANT TO HUG 'EM!

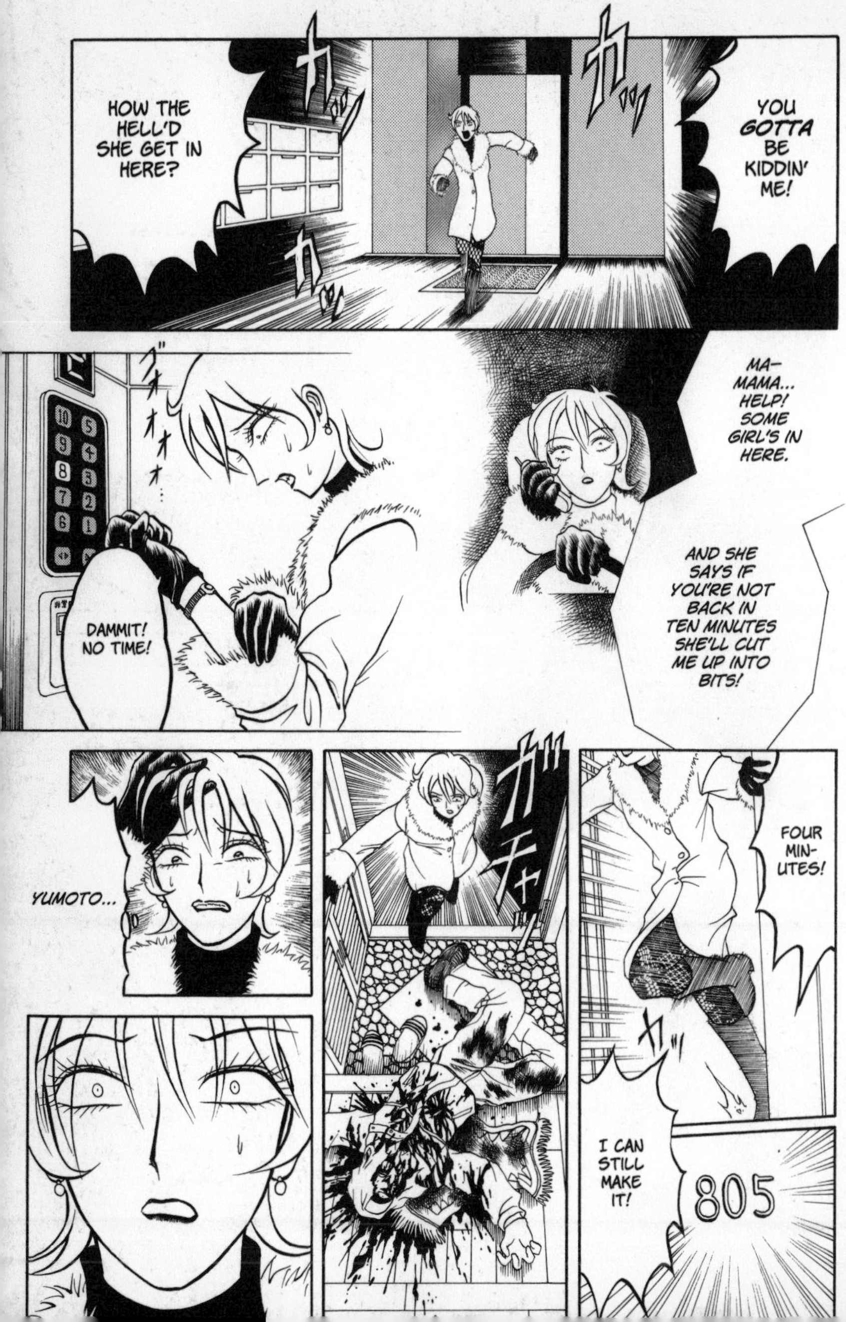
YOU GOTTA BE KIDDIN' ME!
HOW THE HELL'D SHE GET IN HERE?
MA-MAMA... HELP! SOME GIRL'S IN HERE.
AND SHE SAYS IF YOU'RE NOT BACK IN TEN MINUTES SHE'LL CUT ME UP INTO BITS!
DAMMIT! NO TIME!
FOUR MIN-UTES!
I CAN STILL MAKE IT!
805
YUMOTO...

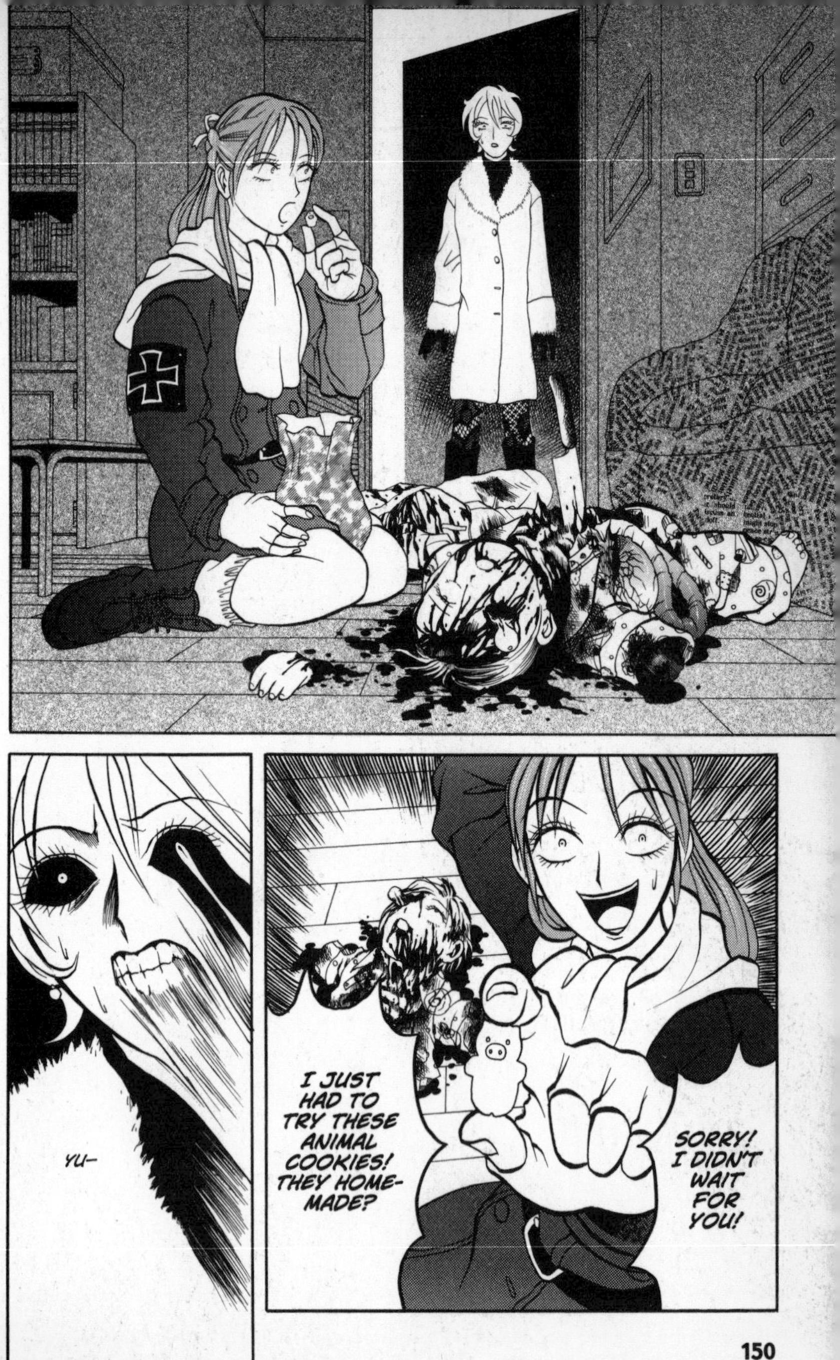
SORRY! I DIDN'T WAIT FOR YOU!
I JUST HAD TO TRY THESE ANIMAL COOKIES! THEY HOME-MADE?
YU-

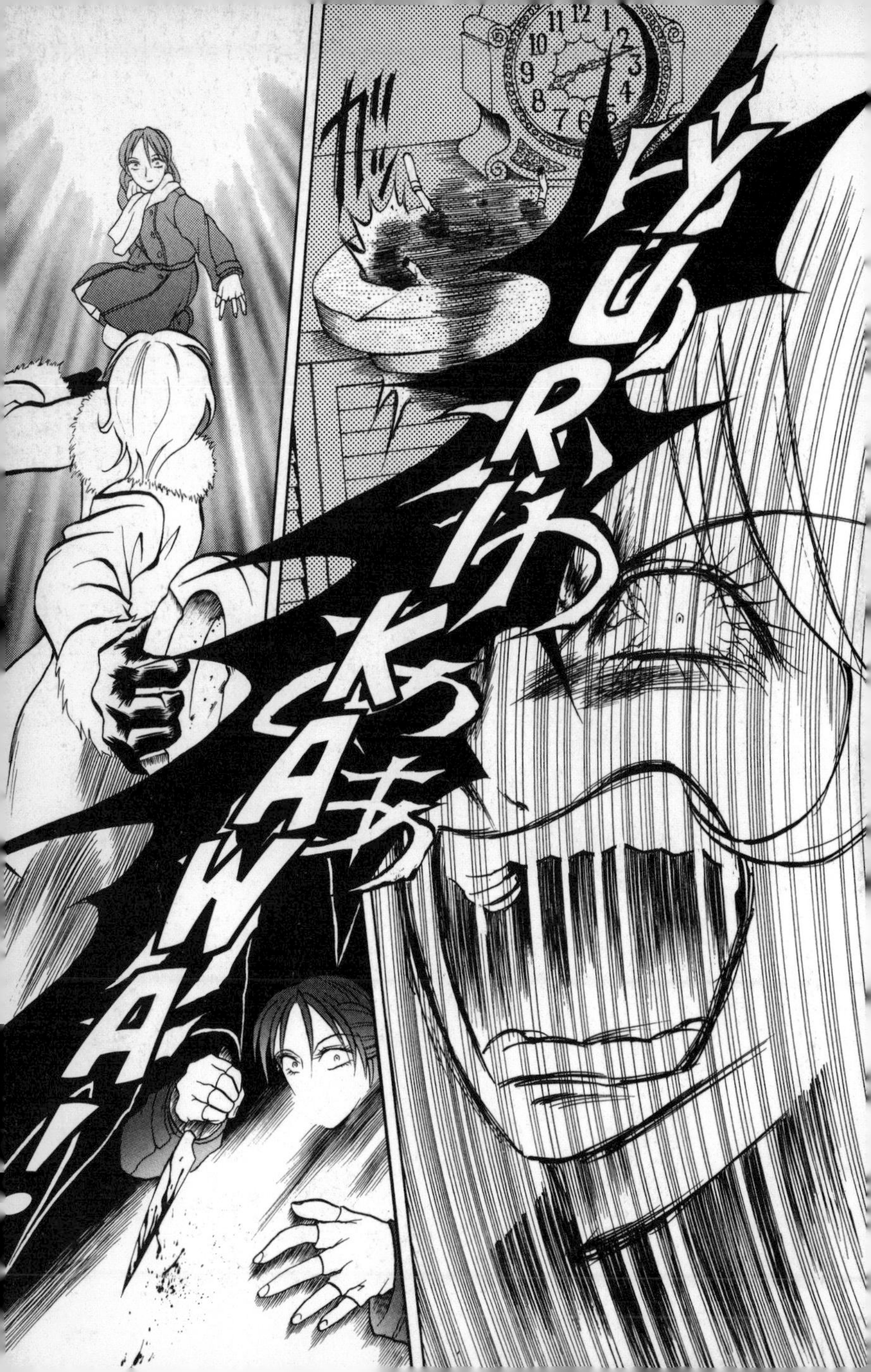
YURIKAWAA!!

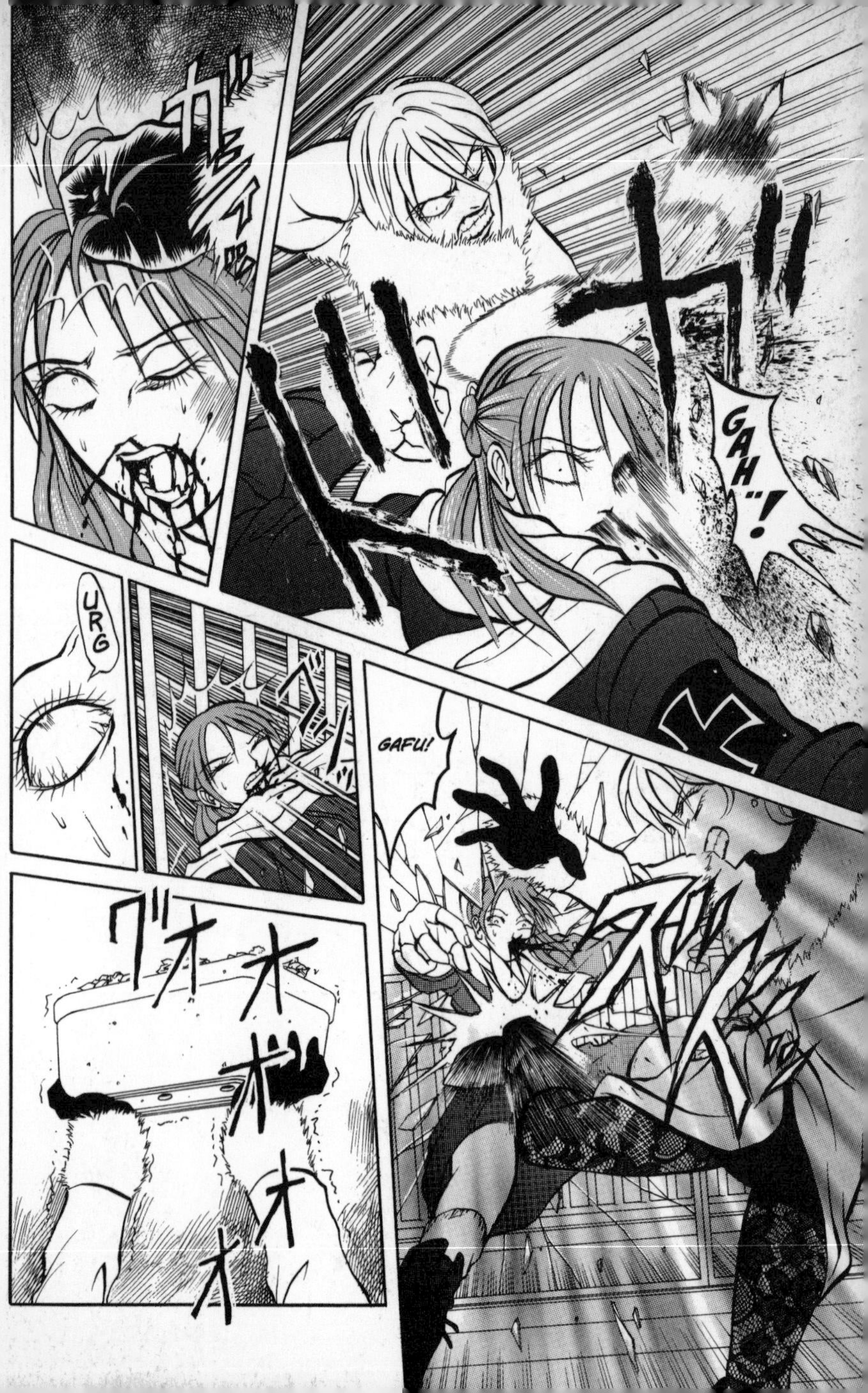
GAH...!
URG
GAFU!

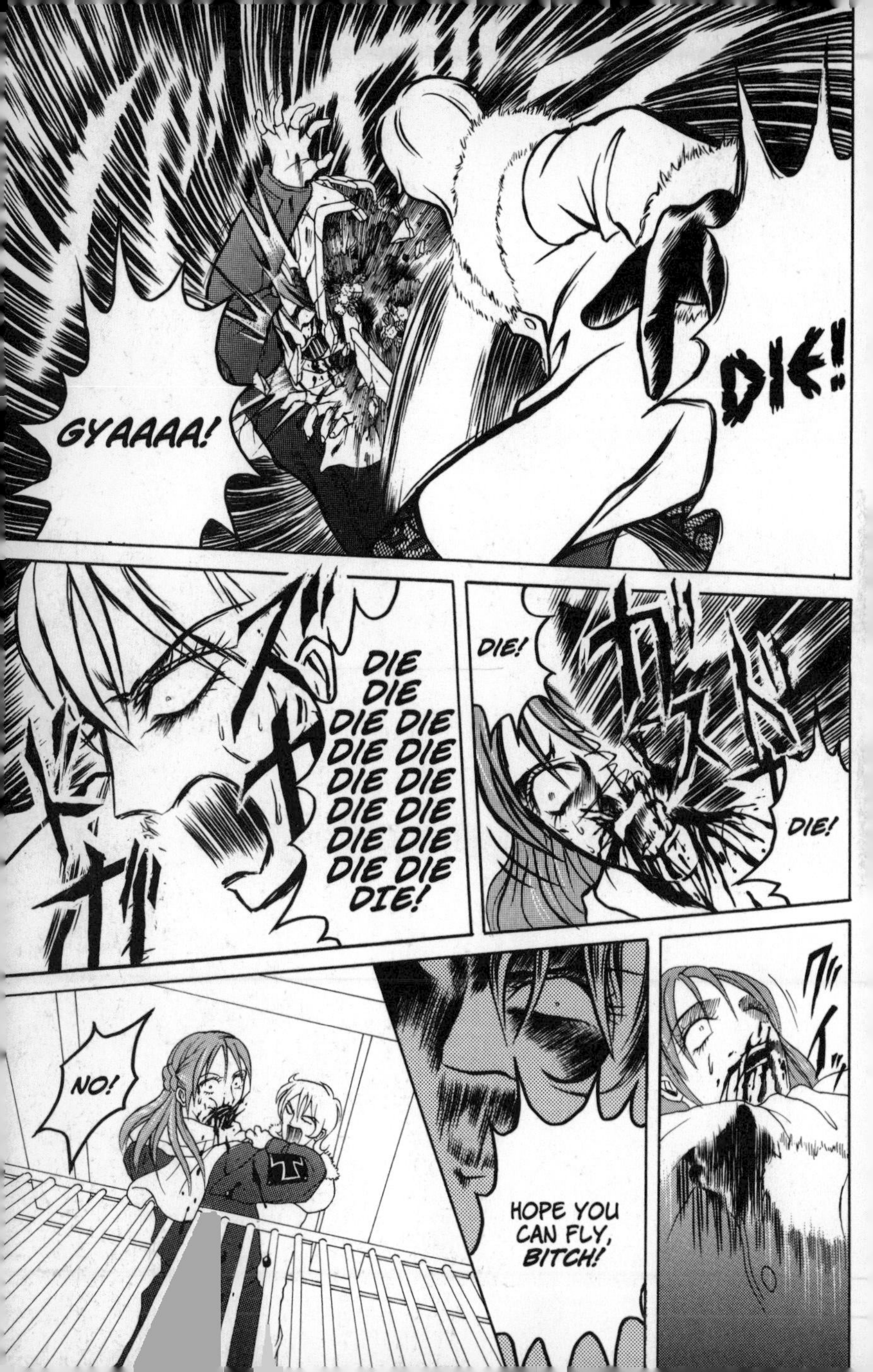
DIE!!
GYAAAA!
DIE!
DIE!
DIE DIE DIE DIE DIE DIE DIE DIE DIE DIE DIE DIE DIE DIE DIE!
HOPE YOU CAN FLY, BITCH!
NO!

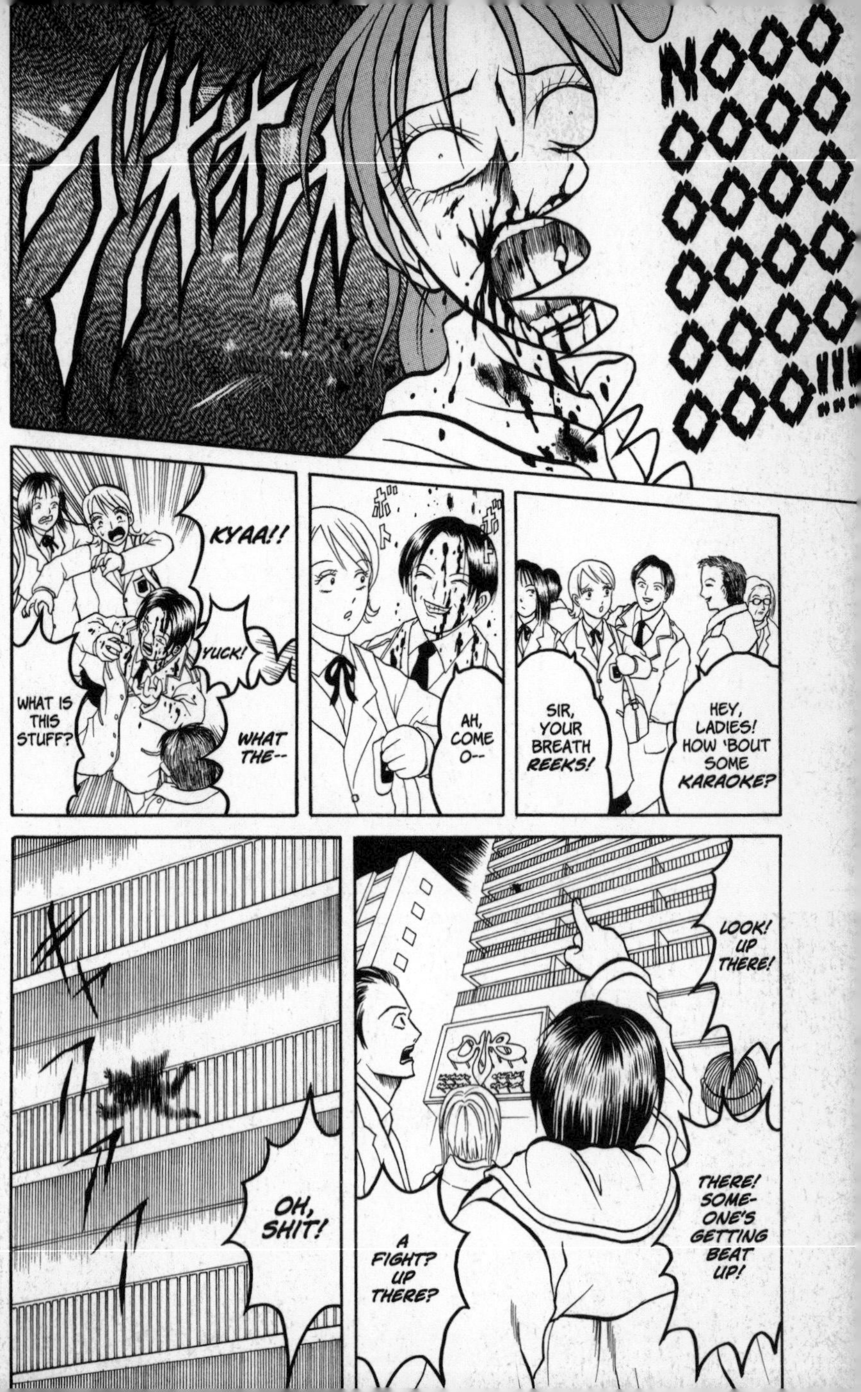
NOOOOOOOOOOOOOOOOOOOOOO!!!
HEY, LADIES! HOW 'BOUT SOME KARAOKE?
SIR, YOUR BREATH REEKS!
AH, COME O--
KYAA!!
YUCK!
WHAT THE--
WHAT IS THIS STUFF?
LOOK! UP THERE!
THERE! SOME-ONE'S GETTING BEAT UP!
A FIGHT? UP THERE?
OH, SHIT!

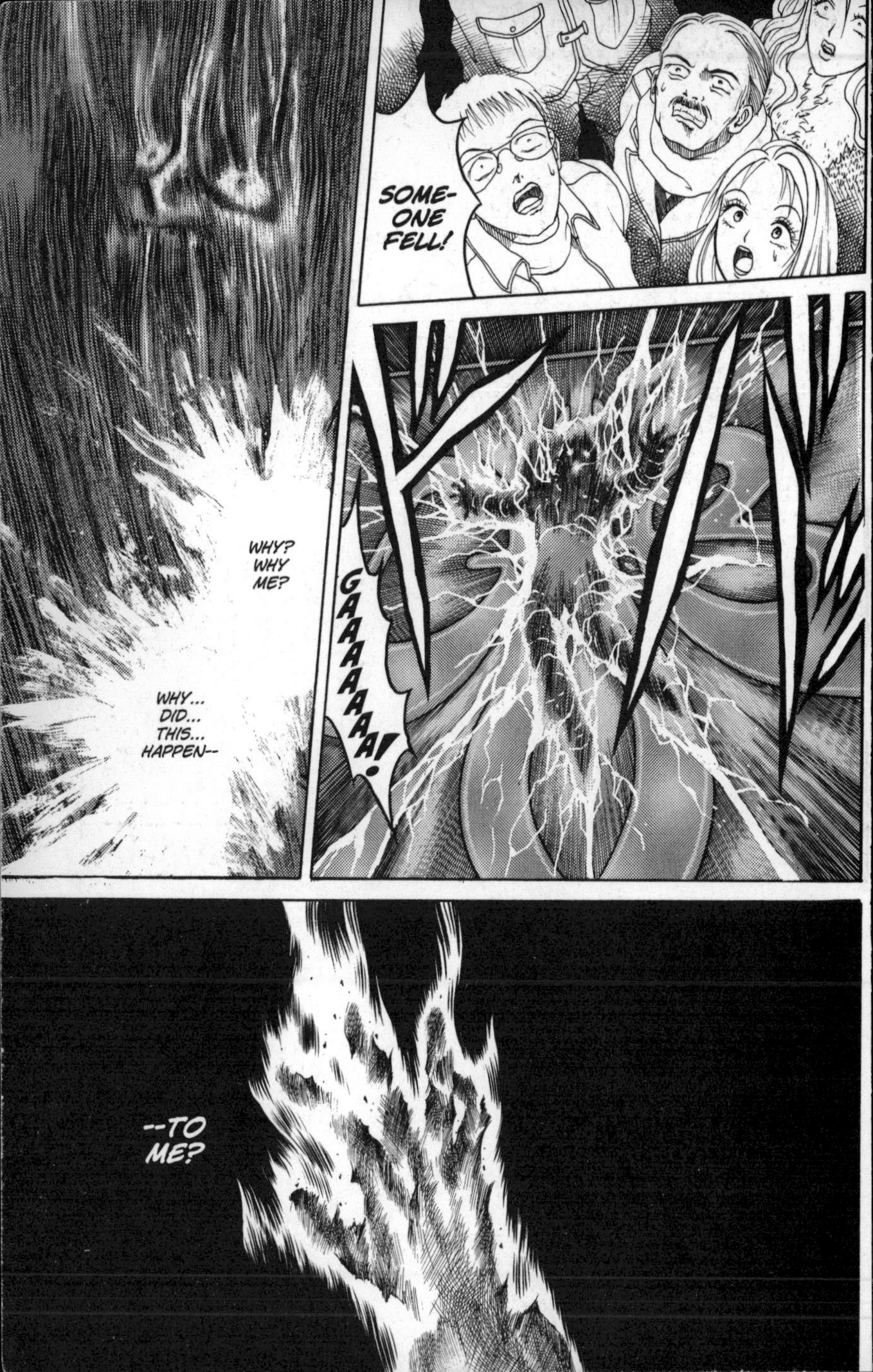
SOME-ONE FELL!
GAAAAAAA!
WHY? WHY ME?
WHY... DID... THIS... HAPPEN--
--TO ME?

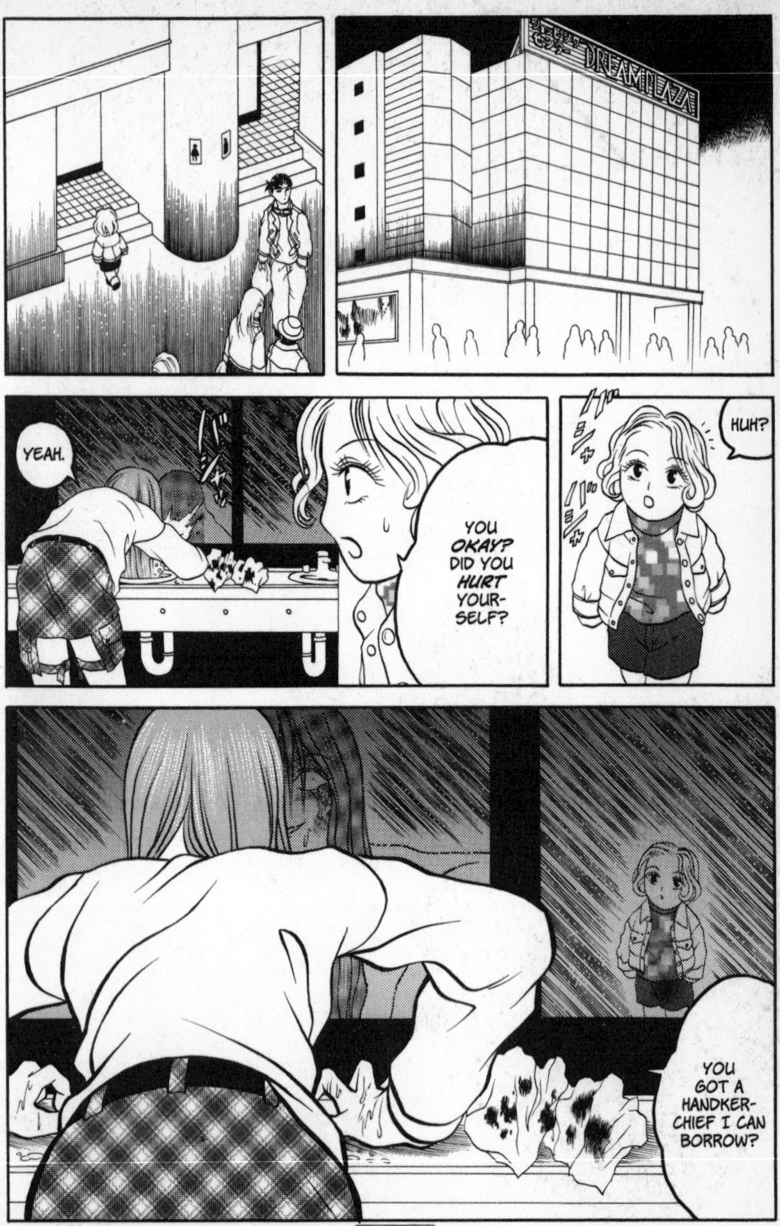
DREAM PLAZA
バシャ
バシャ
HUH?
YOU OKAY? DID YOU HURT YOURSELF?
バシャ
YEAH.
YOU GOT A HANDKERCHIEF I CAN BORROW?

おわり

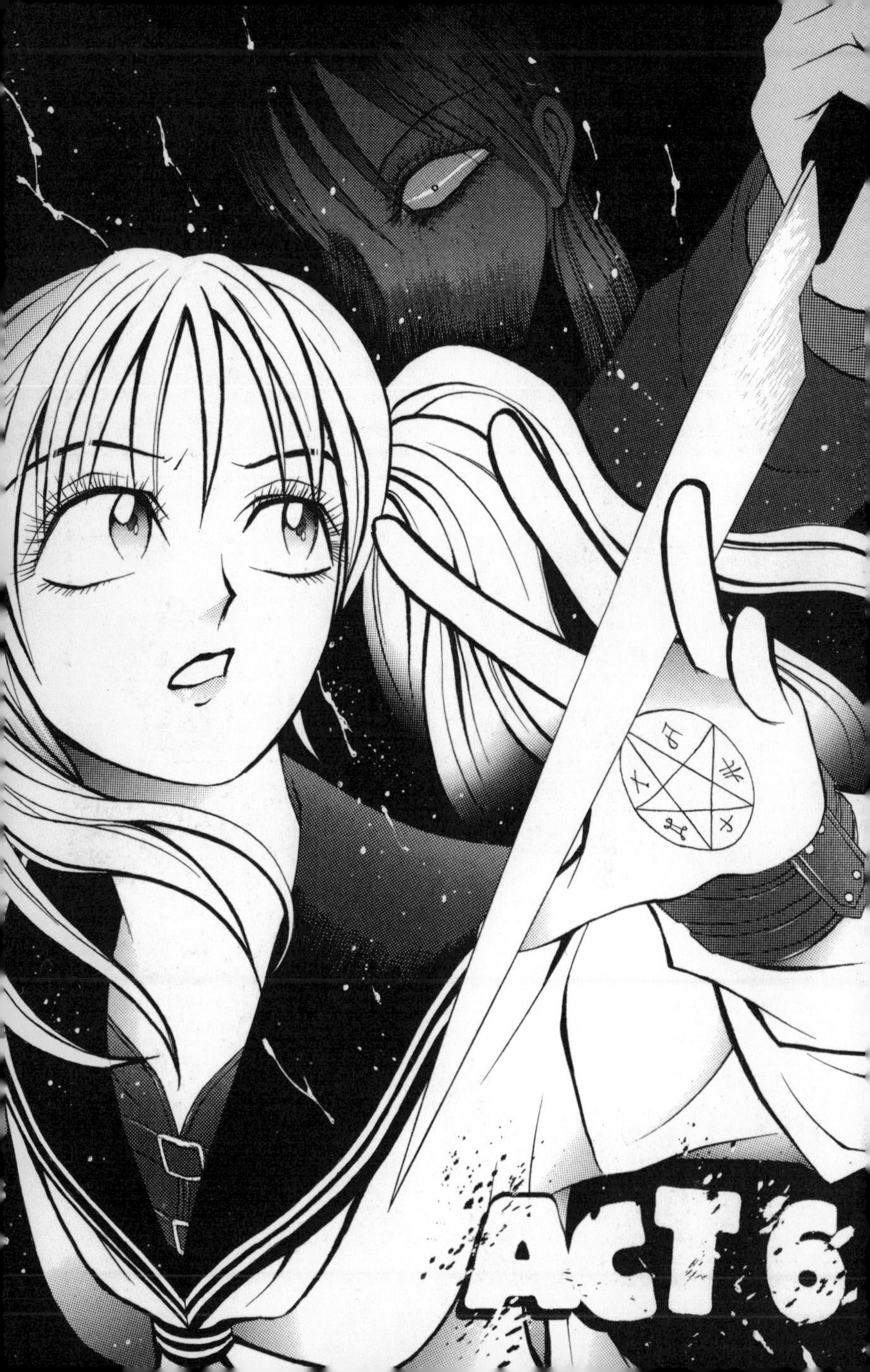
ACT 6

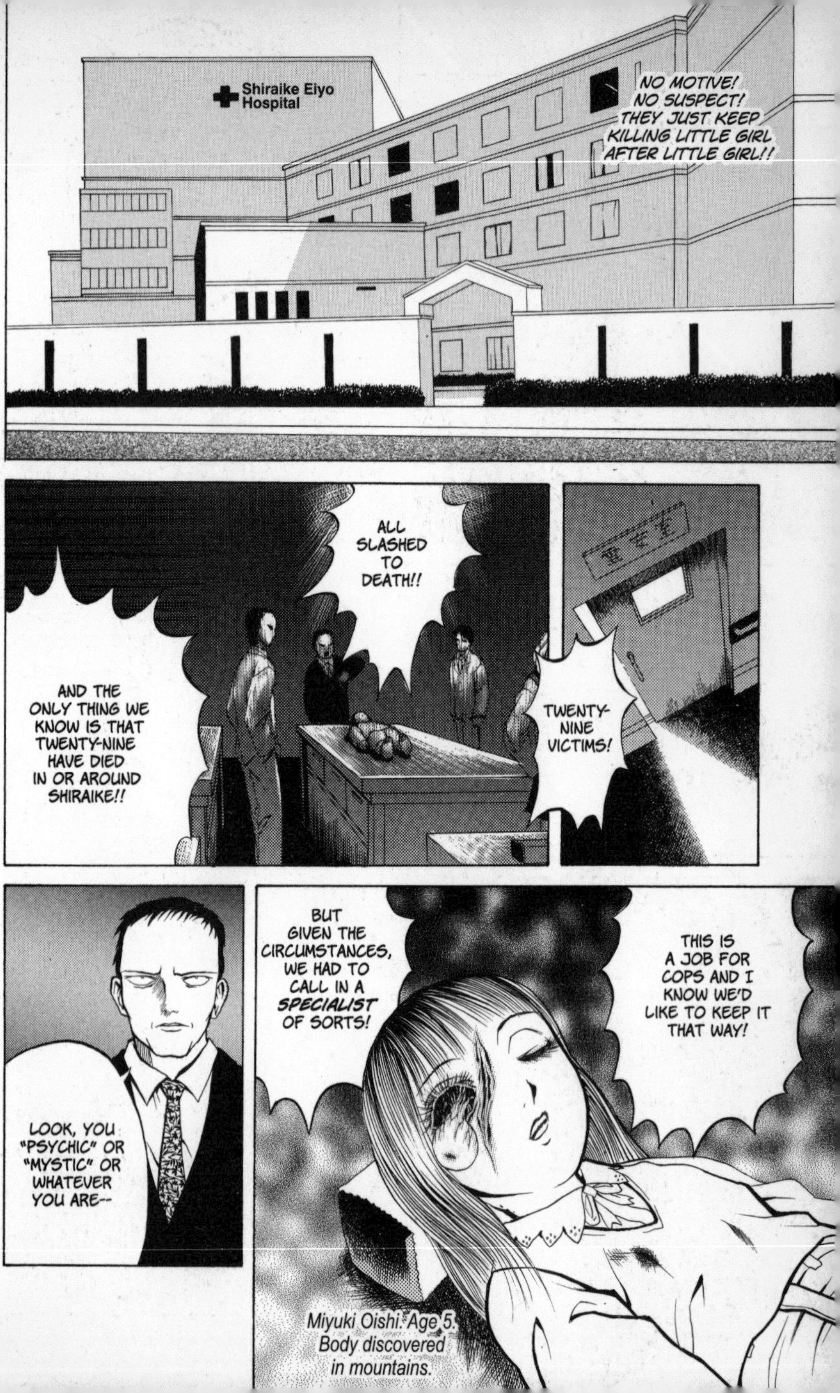
Shiraike Eiyo Hospital
NO MOTIVE! NO SUSPECT! THEY JUST KEEP KILLING LITTLE GIRL AFTER LITTLE GIRL!!
TWENTY-NINE VICTIMS!
ALL SLASHED TO DEATH!!
AND THE ONLY THING WE KNOW IS THAT TWENTY-NINE HAVE DIED IN OR AROUND SHIRAIKE!!
THIS IS A JOB FOR COPS AND I KNOW WE'D LIKE TO KEEP IT THAT WAY!
BUT GIVEN THE CIRCUMSTANCES, WE HAD TO CALL IN A SPECIALIST OF SORTS!
Miyuki Oishi. Age 5. Body discovered in mountains.
LOOK, YOU "PSYCHIC" OR "MYSTIC" OR WHATEVER YOU ARE--

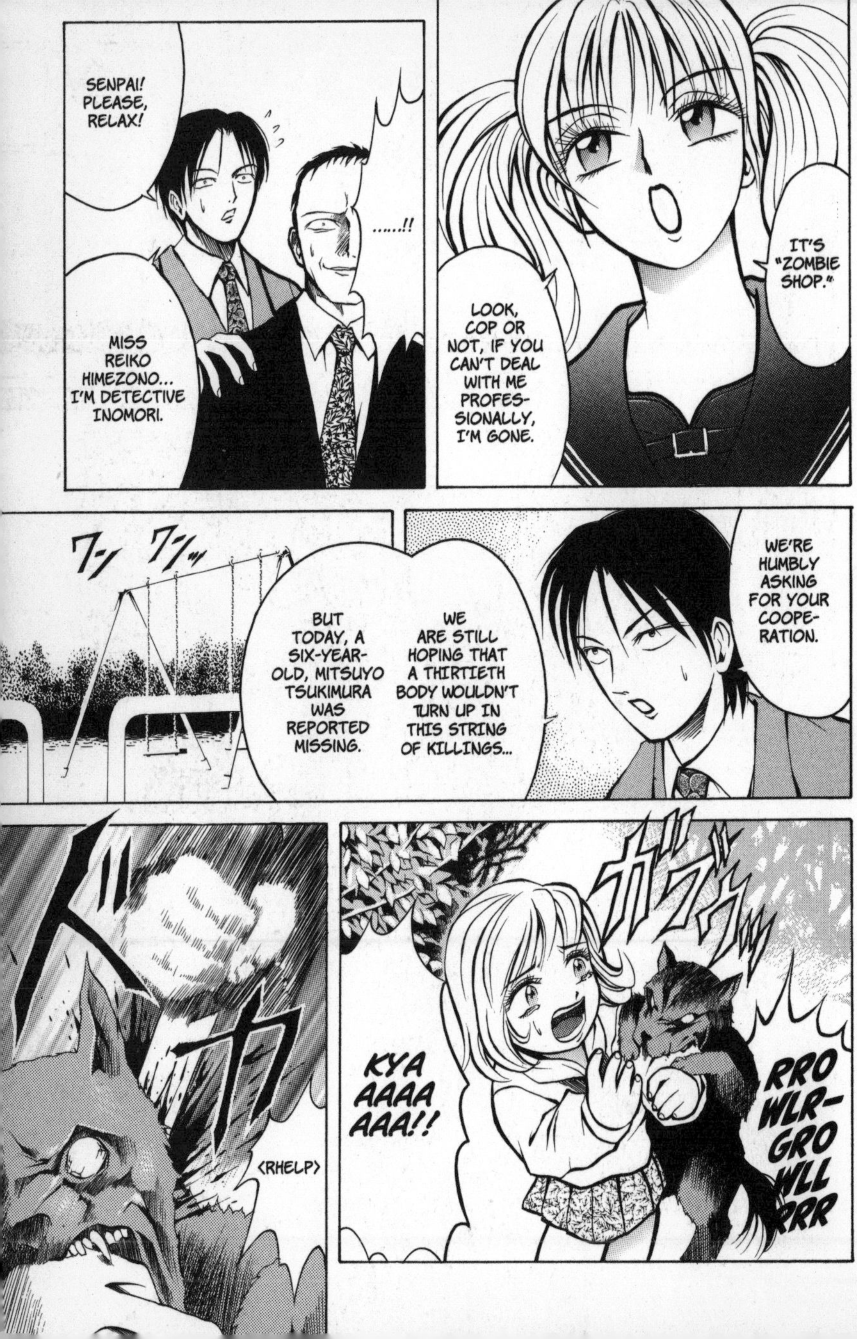
IT'S "ZOMBIE SHOP."
LOOK, COP OR NOT, IF YOU CAN'T DEAL WITH ME PROFES-SIONALLY, I'M GONE.
......!!
SENPAI! PLEASE, RELAX!
MISS REIKO HIMEZONO... I'M DETECTIVE INOMORI.
WE'RE HUMBLY ASKING FOR YOUR COOPE-RATION.
WE ARE STILL HOPING THAT A THIRTIETH BODY WOULDN'T TURN UP IN THIS STRING OF KILLINGS...
BUT TODAY, A SIX-YEAR-OLD, MITSUYO TSUKIMURA WAS REPORTED MISSING.
ワーン ワーンッ
RRO WLR-GRO WLL RRR
KYA AAAA AAA!!
<RHELP>

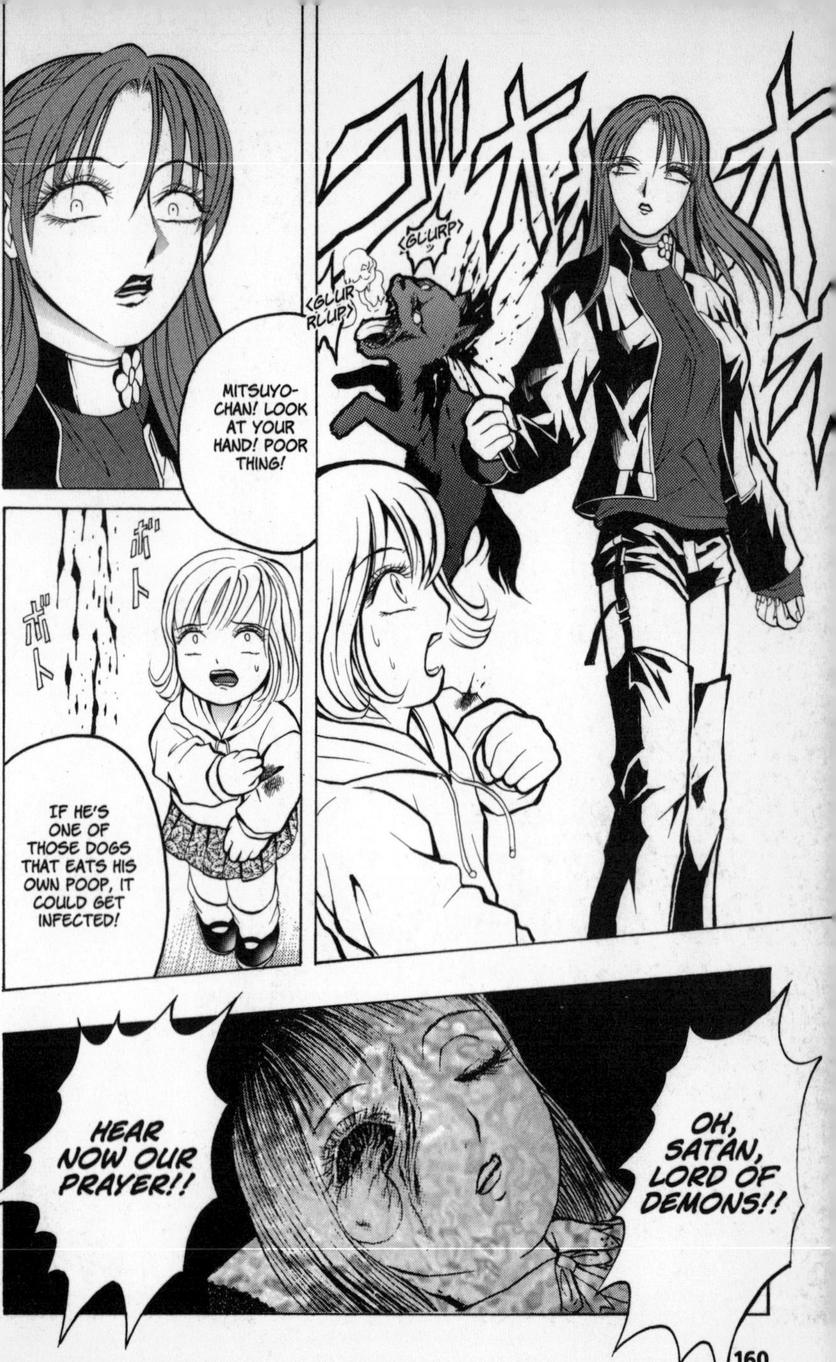
<GLURP>
<GLURRLUP>
MITSUYO-CHAN! LOOK AT YOUR HAND! POOR THING!
ボト
ボト
IF HE'S ONE OF THOSE DOGS THAT EATS HIS OWN POOP, IT COULD GET INFECTED!
OH, SATAN, LORD OF DEMONS!!
HEAR NOW OUR PRAYER!!

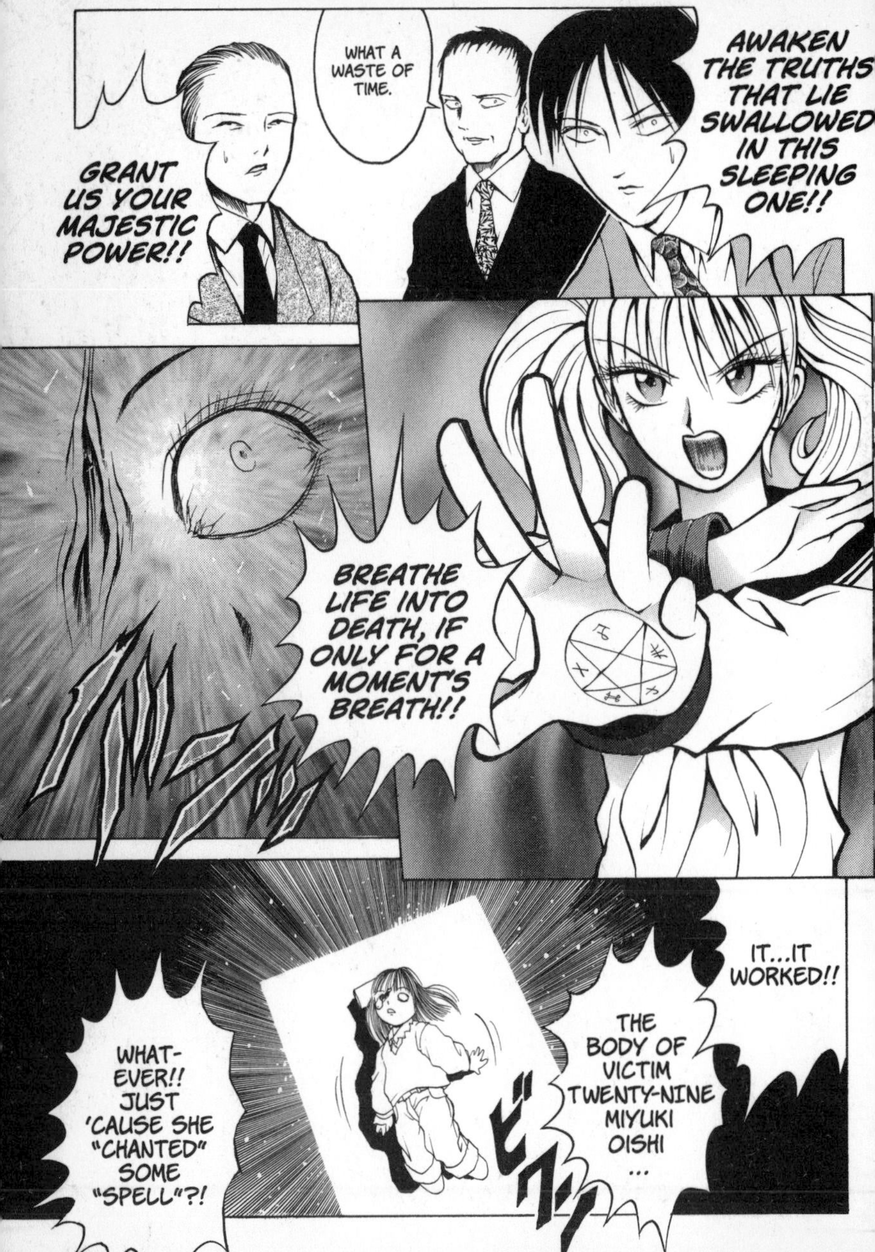
AWAKEN THE TRUTHS THAT LIE SWALLOWED IN THIS SLEEPING ONE!!
WHAT A WASTE OF TIME.
GRANT US YOUR MAJESTIC POWER!!
BREATHE LIFE INTO DEATH, IF ONLY FOR A MOMENT'S BREATH!!
IT...IT WORKED!!
THE BODY OF VICTIM TWENTY-NINE MIYUKI OISHI ...
WHAT-EVER!! JUST 'CAUSE SHE "CHANTED" SOME "SPELL"?!

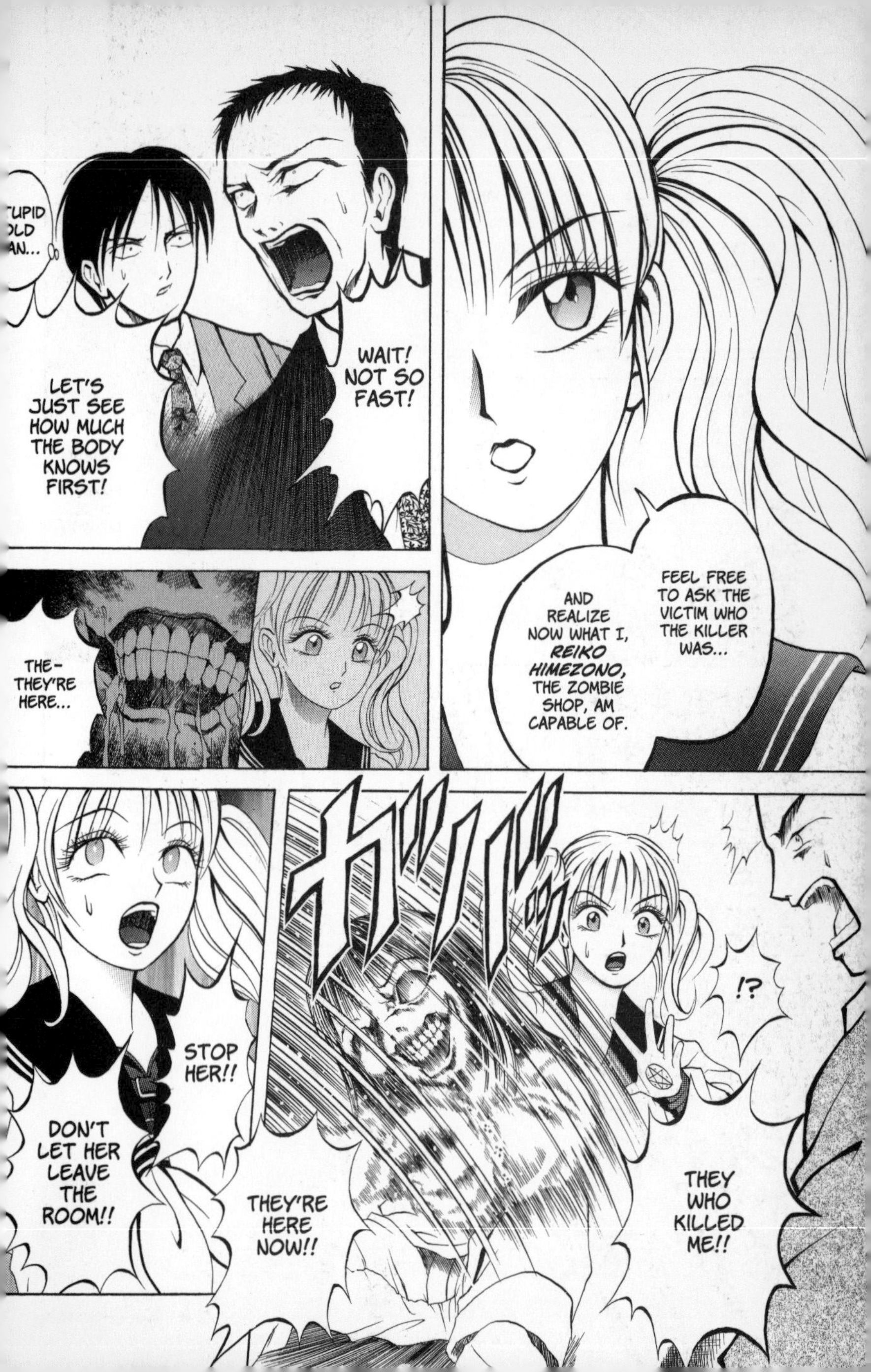
FEEL FREE TO ASK THE VICTIM WHO THE KILLER WAS...
AND REALIZE NOW WHAT I, *REIKO HIMEZONO*, THE ZOMBIE SHOP, AM CAPABLE OF.
WAIT! NOT SO FAST!
LET'S JUST SEE HOW MUCH THE BODY KNOWS FIRST!
TUPID OLD AN...
THE- THEY'RE HERE...
!?
THEY WHO KILLED ME!!
THEY'RE HERE NOW!!
STOP HER!!
DON'T LET HER LEAVE THE ROOM!!

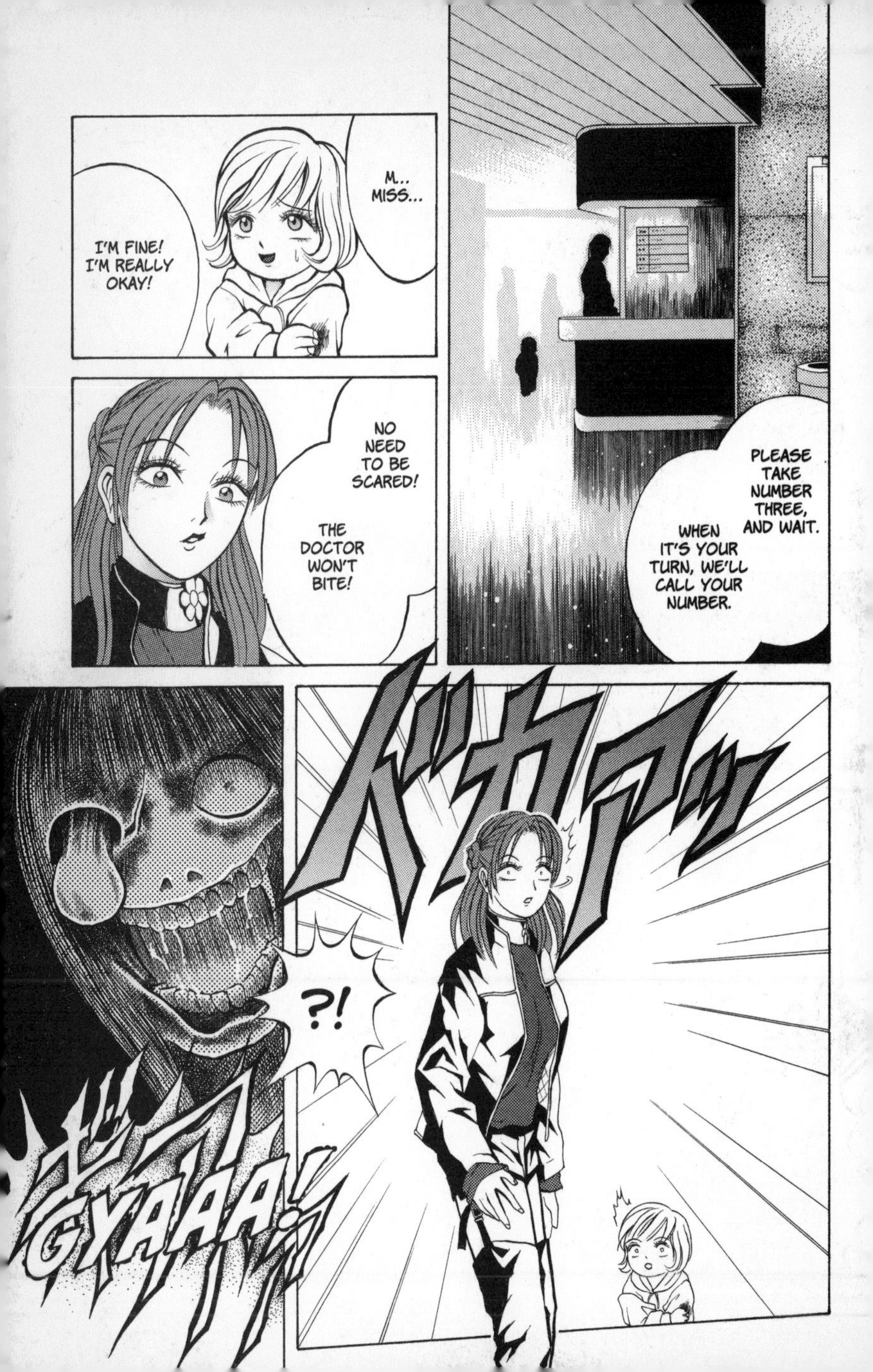
PLEASE TAKE NUMBER THREE, AND WAIT.
WHEN IT'S YOUR TURN, WE'LL CALL YOUR NUMBER.
M... MISS...
I'M FINE! I'M REALLY OKAY!
NO NEED TO BE SCARED!
THE DOCTOR WON'T BITE!
?!
GYAAA!

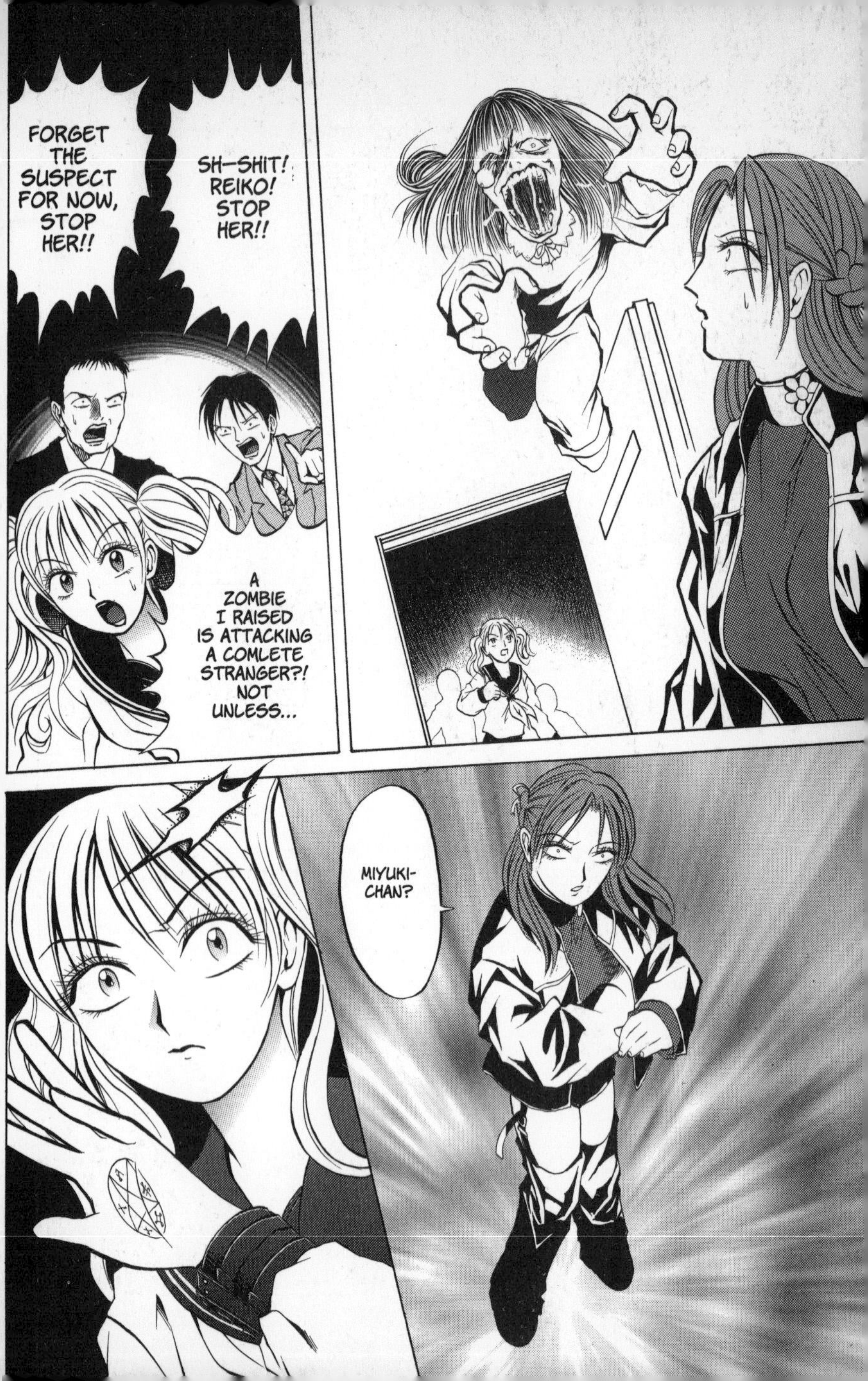
SH–SHIT! REIKO! STOP HER!!
FORGET THE SUSPECT FOR NOW, STOP HER!!
A ZOMBIE I RAISED IS ATTACKING A COMLETE STRANGER?! NOT UNLESS...
MIYUKI-CHAN?

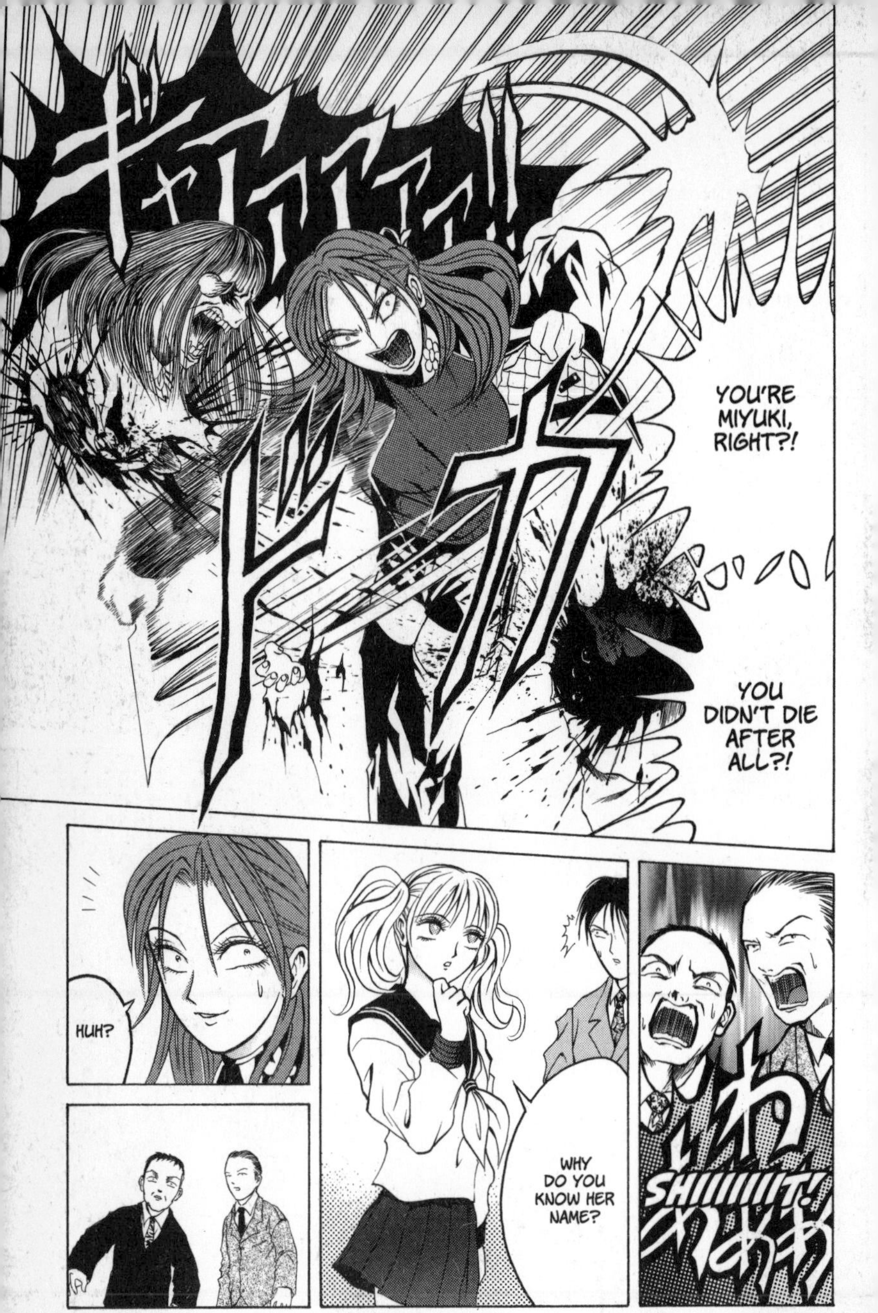
YOU'RE MIYUKI, RIGHT?!
YOU DIDN'T DIE AFTER ALL?!
SHIIIIIIT!
WHY DO YOU KNOW HER NAME?
HUH?

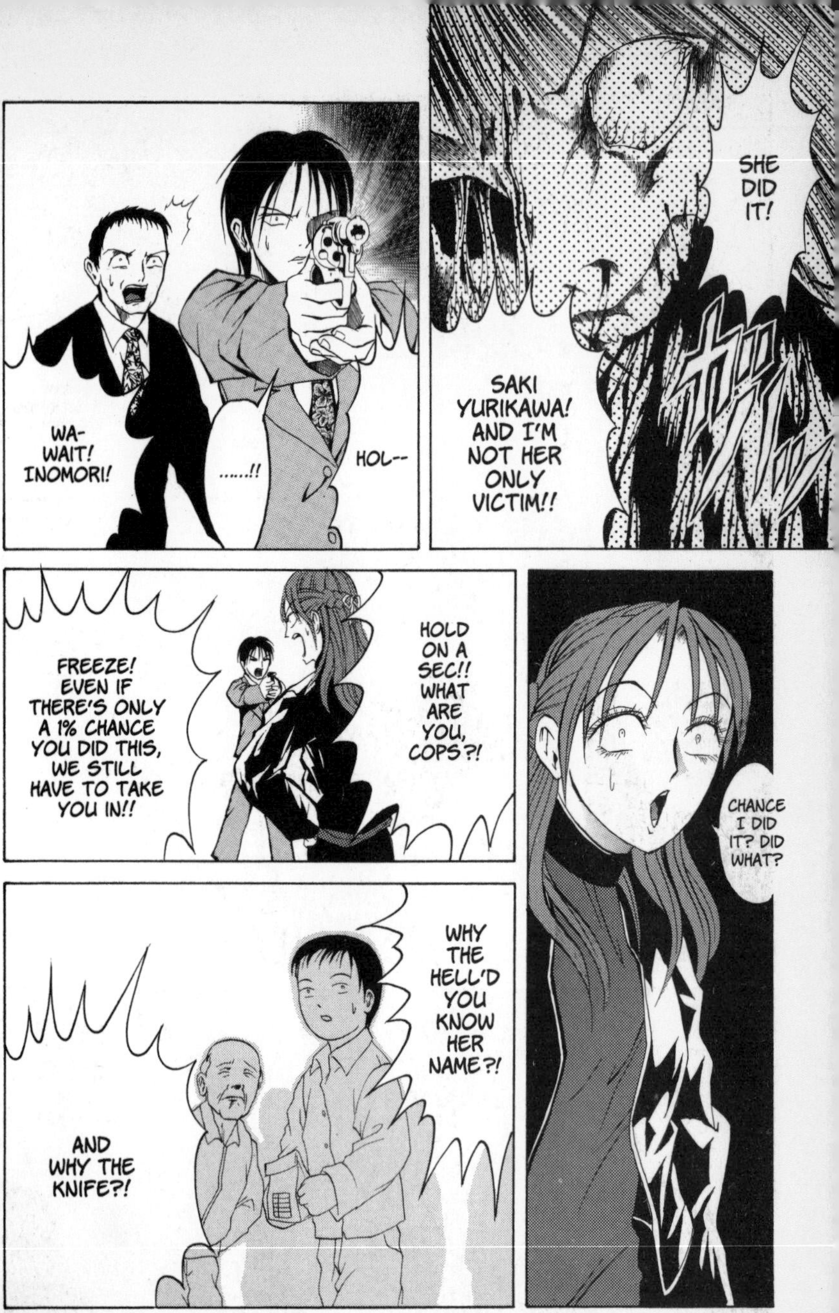
SHE DID IT!
SAKI YURIKAWA! AND I'M NOT HER ONLY VICTIM!!
HOL--
......!!
WA-WAIT! INOMORI!
CHANCE I DID IT? DID WHAT?
HOLD ON A SEC!! WHAT ARE YOU, COPS?!
FREEZE! EVEN IF THERE'S ONLY A 1% CHANCE YOU DID THIS, WE STILL HAVE TO TAKE YOU IN!!
WHY THE HELL'D YOU KNOW HER NAME?!
AND WHY THE KNIFE?!

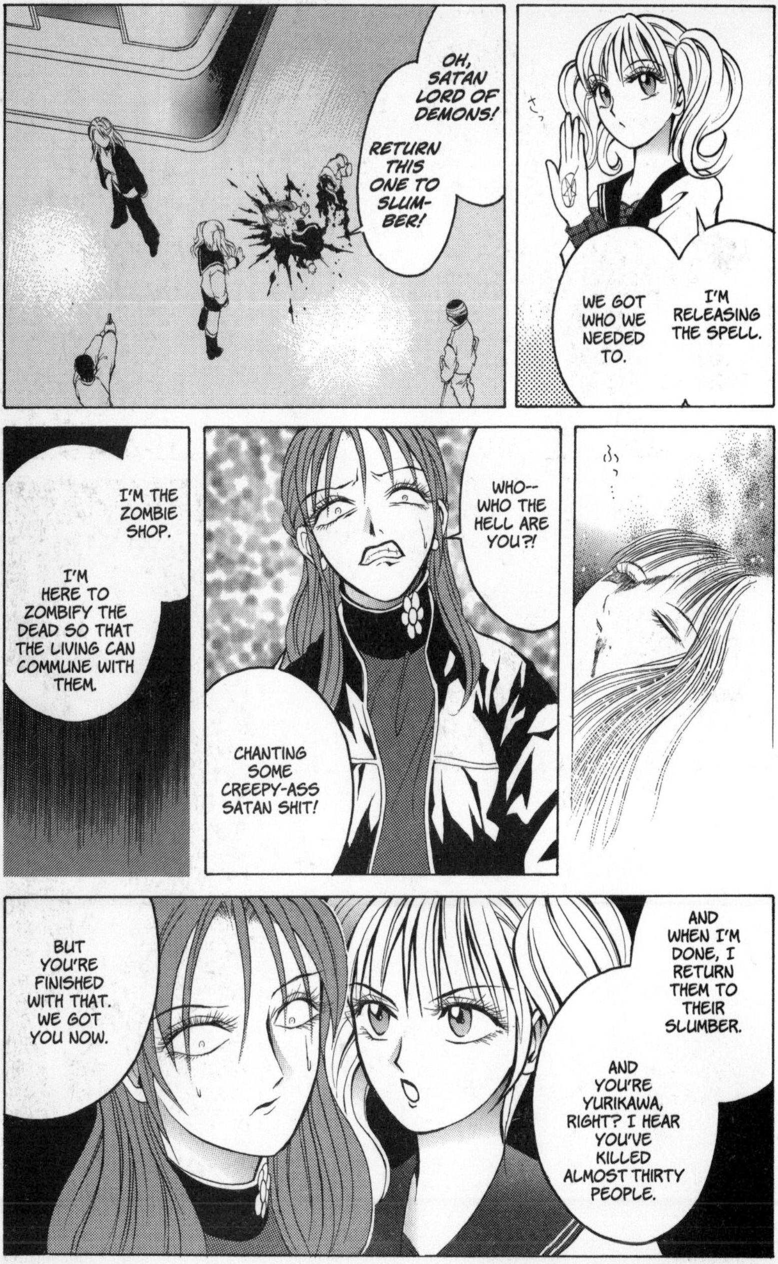
さっ
I'M RELEASING THE SPELL.
WE GOT WHO WE NEEDED TO.
OH, SATAN LORD OF DEMONS!
RETURN THIS ONE TO SLUM-BER!
ふっ…
WHO-- WHO THE HELL ARE YOU?!
CHANTING SOME CREEPY-ASS SATAN SHIT!
I'M THE ZOMBIE SHOP.
I'M HERE TO ZOMBIFY THE DEAD SO THAT THE LIVING CAN COMMUNE WITH THEM.
AND WHEN I'M DONE, I RETURN THEM TO THEIR SLUMBER.
AND YOU'RE YURIKAWA, RIGHT? I HEAR YOU'VE KILLED ALMOST THIRTY PEOPLE.
BUT YOU'RE FINISHED WITH THAT. WE GOT YOU NOW.

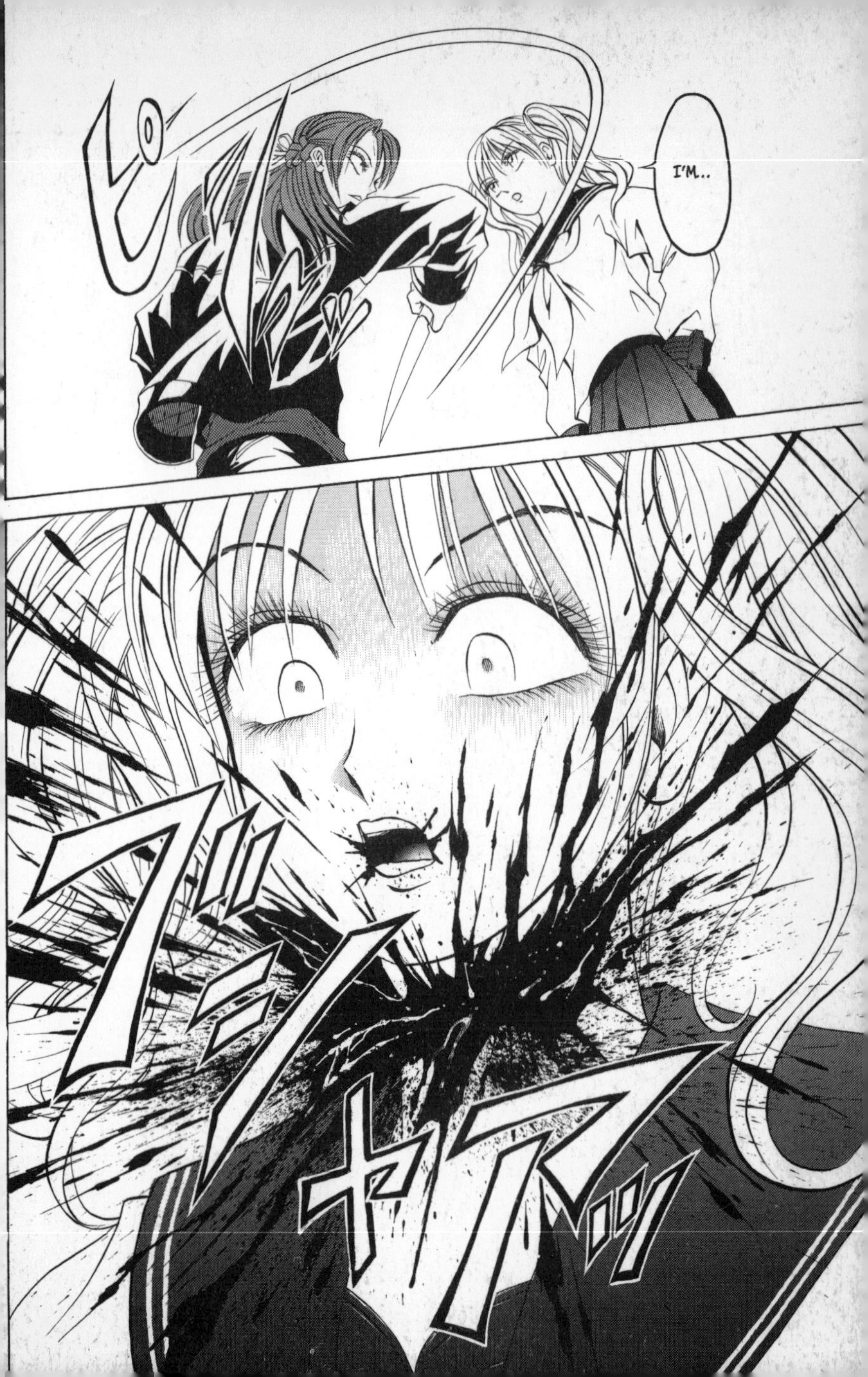
I'M..

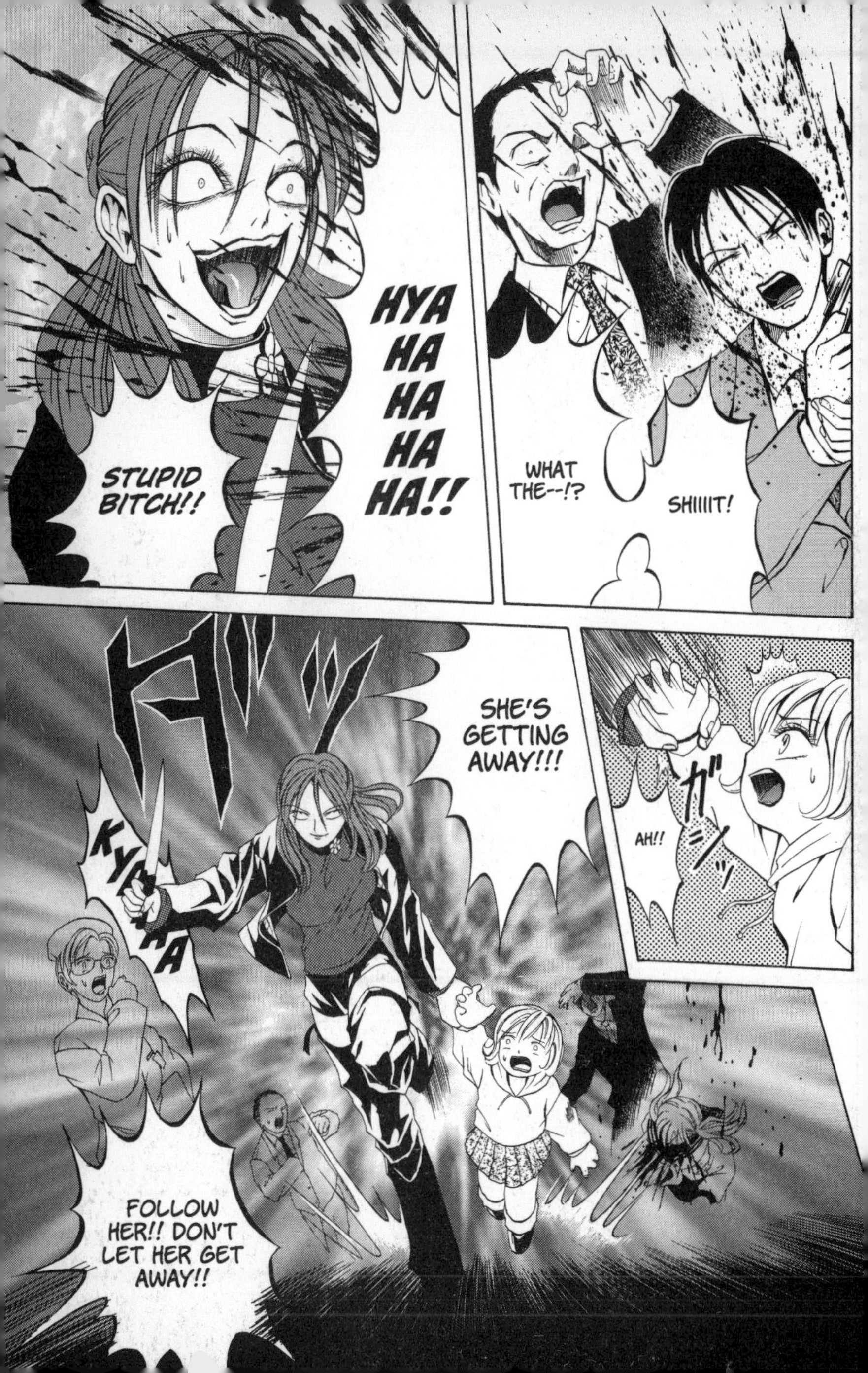
SHIIIIT!
WHAT THE--!?
HYA HA HA HA HA!!
STUPID BITCH!!
AH!!
SHE'S GETTING AWAY!!!
FOLLOW HER!! DON'T LET HER GET AWAY!!

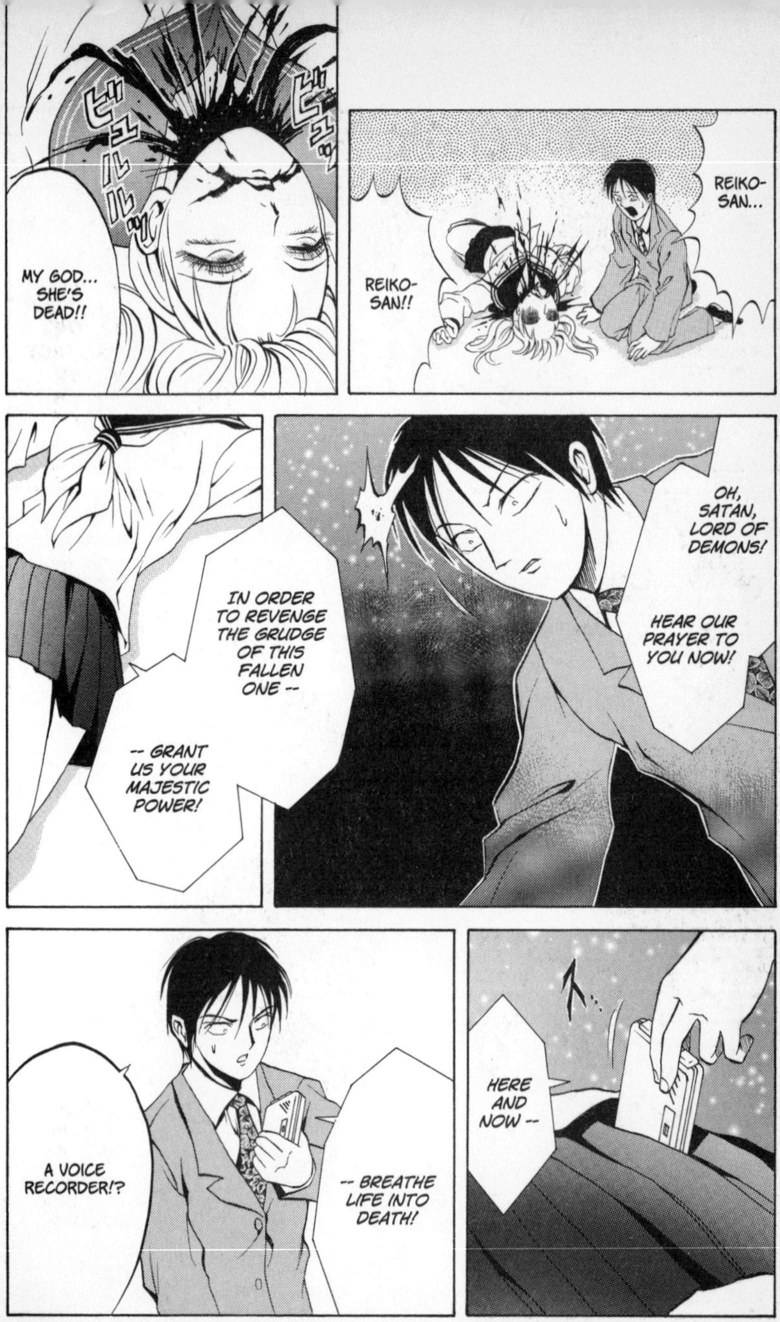
REIKO-SAN...
REIKO-SAN!!
MY GOD... SHE'S DEAD!!
OH, SATAN, LORD OF DEMONS!
HEAR OUR PRAYER TO YOU NOW!
IN ORDER TO REVENGE THE GRUDGE OF THIS FALLEN ONE --
-- GRANT US YOUR MAJESTIC POWER!
HERE AND NOW --
-- BREATHE LIFE INTO DEATH!
A VOICE RECORDER!?

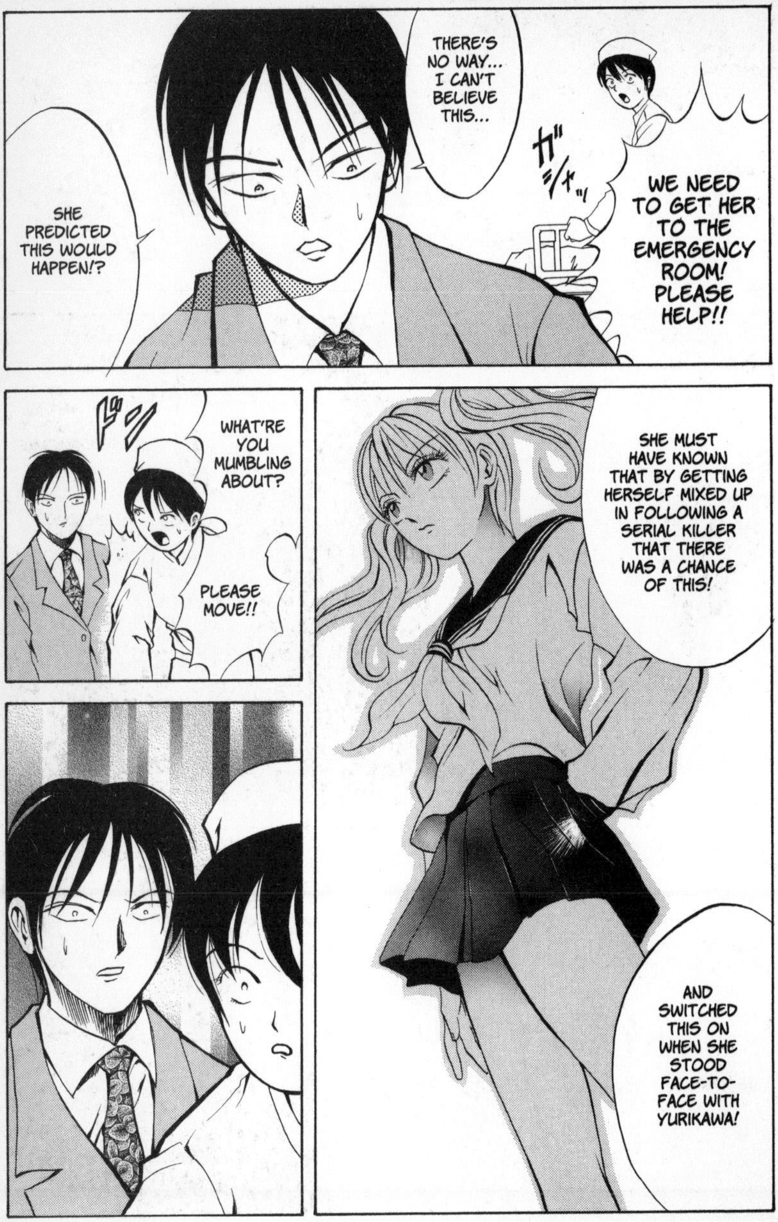
WE NEED TO GET HER TO THE EMERGENCY ROOM! PLEASE HELP!!
ガシャッ
THERE'S NO WAY... I CAN'T BELIEVE THIS...
SHE PREDICTED THIS WOULD HAPPEN!?
SHE MUST HAVE KNOWN THAT BY GETTING HERSELF MIXED UP IN FOLLOWING A SERIAL KILLER THAT THERE WAS A CHANCE OF THIS!
AND SWITCHED THIS ON WHEN SHE STOOD FACE-TO-FACE WITH YURIKAWA!
ドン
WHAT'RE YOU MUMBLING ABOUT?
PLEASE MOVE!!

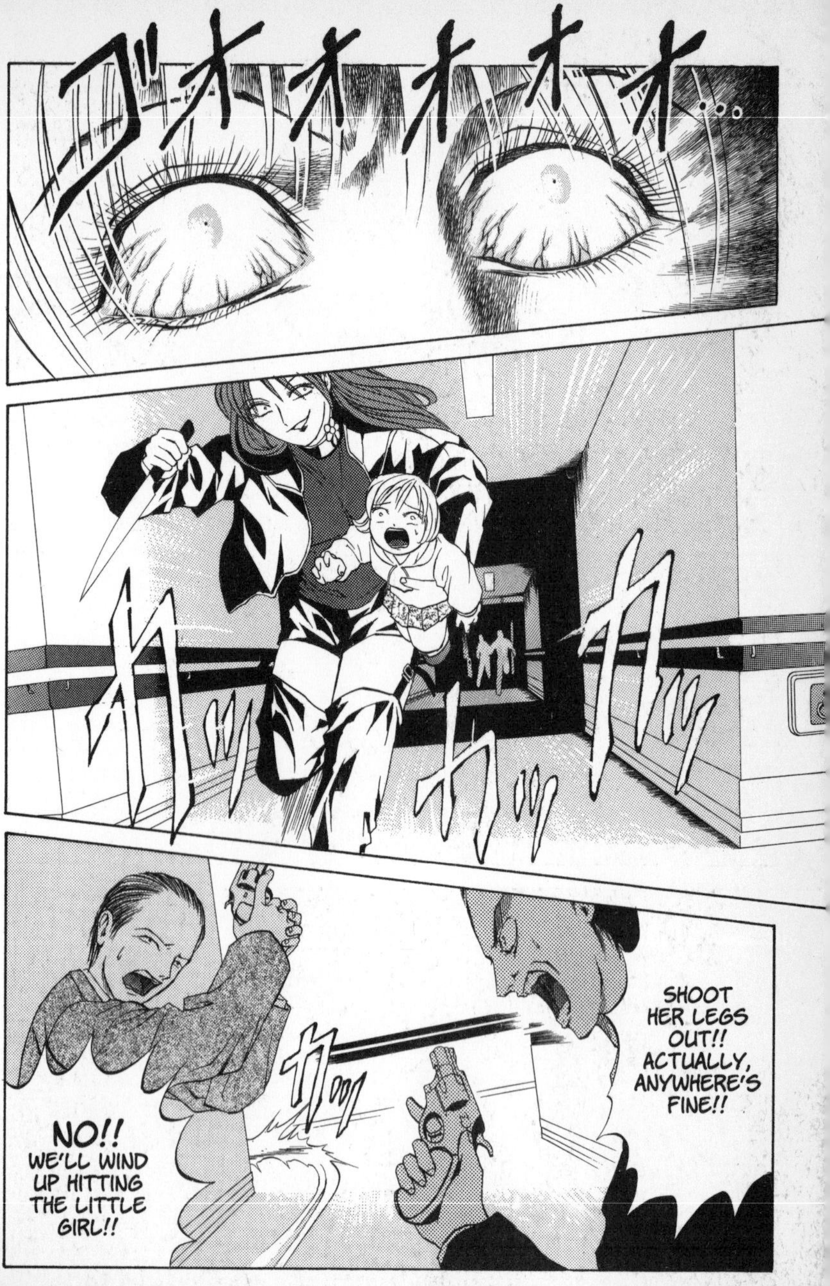
SHOOT HER LEGS OUT!! ACTUALLY, ANYWHERE'S FINE!!
NO!! WE'LL WIND UP HITTING THE LITTLE GIRL!!

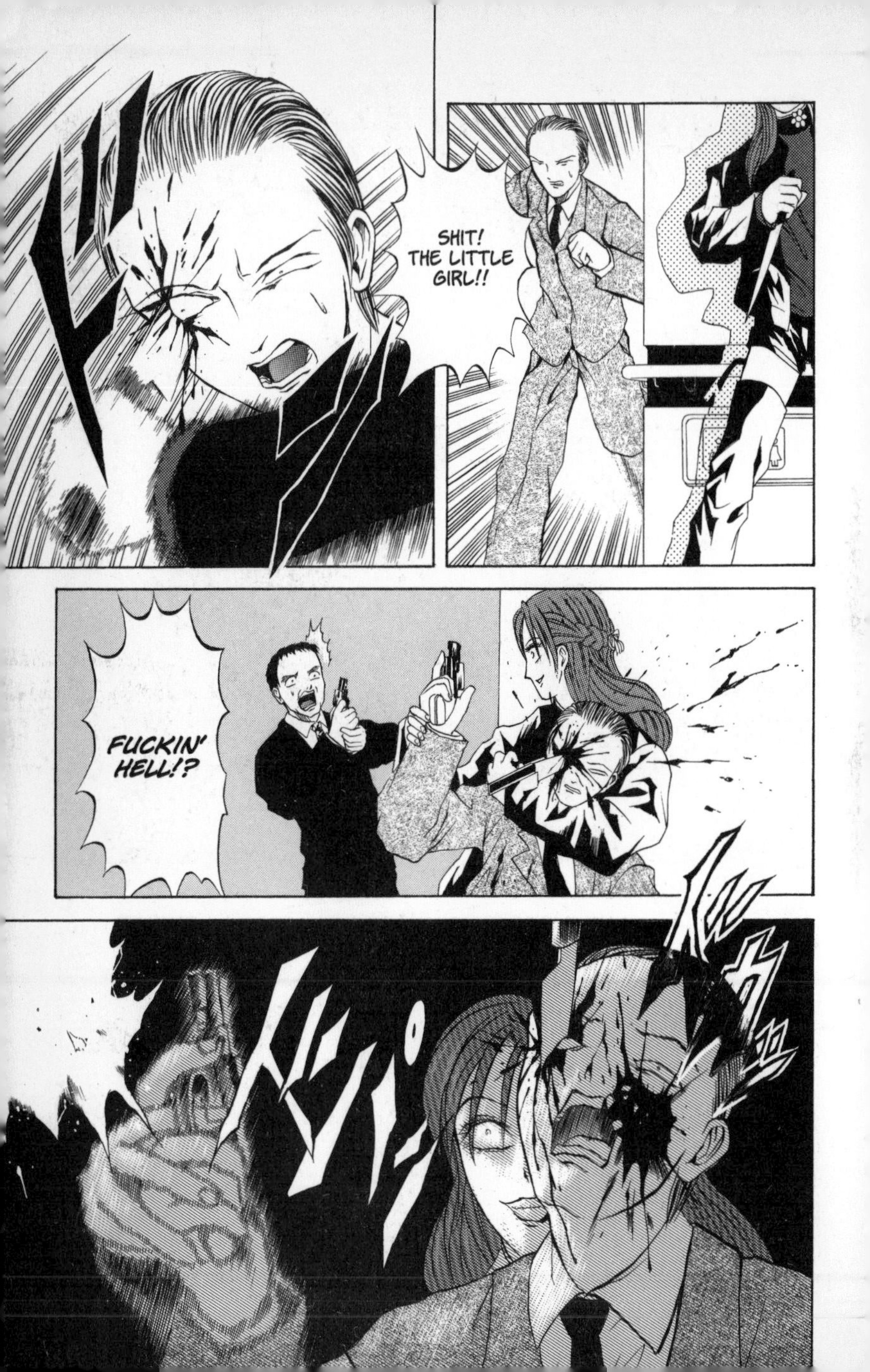
SHIT! THE LITTLE GIRL!!
FUCKIN' HELL!?

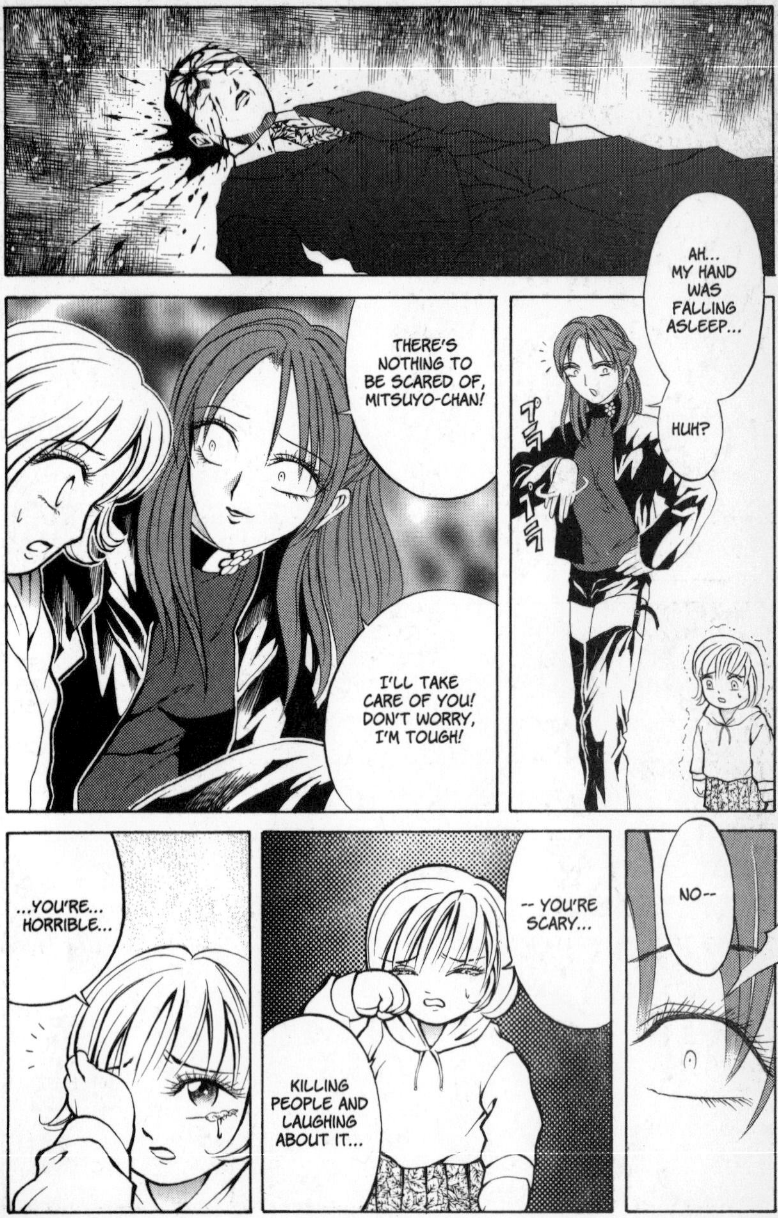
AH... MY HAND WAS FALLING ASLEEP...
HUH?
THERE'S NOTHING TO BE SCARED OF, MITSUYO-CHAN!
I'LL TAKE CARE OF YOU! DON'T WORRY, I'M TOUGH!
NO--
-- YOU'RE SCARY...
KILLING PEOPLE AND LAUGHING ABOUT IT...
...YOU'RE... HORRIBLE...

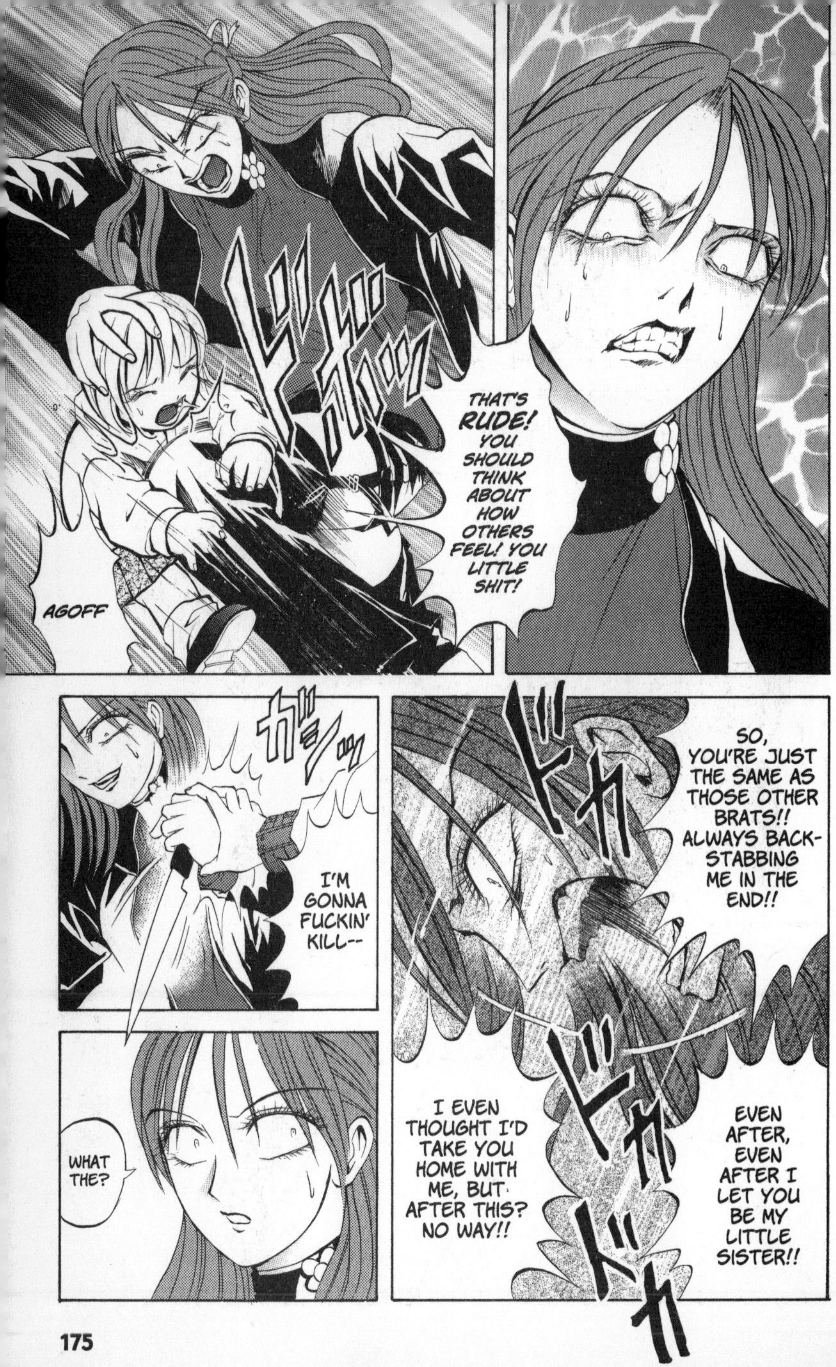
THAT'S RUDE! YOU SHOULD THINK ABOUT HOW OTHERS FEEL! YOU LITTLE SHIT!
AGOFF
SO, YOU'RE JUST THE SAME AS THOSE OTHER BRATS!! ALWAYS BACK-STABBING ME IN THE END!!
EVEN AFTER, EVEN AFTER I LET YOU BE MY LITTLE SISTER!!
I EVEN THOUGHT I'D TAKE YOU HOME WITH ME, BUT AFTER THIS? NO WAY!!
I'M GONNA FUCKIN' KILL--
WHAT THE?

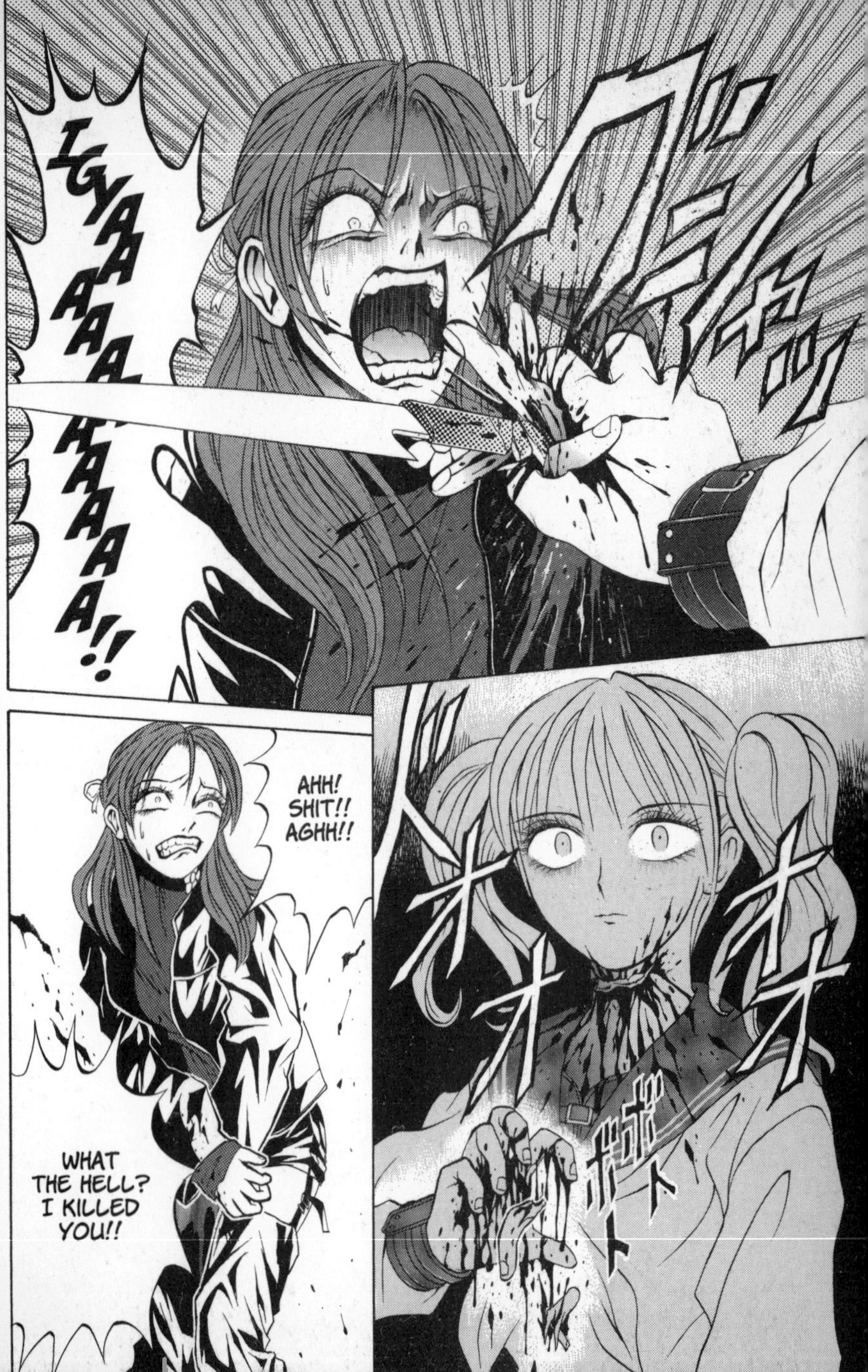
IGYAAAAAAAAAAA!!
AHH! SHIT!! AGHH!!
WHAT THE HELL? I KILLED YOU!!

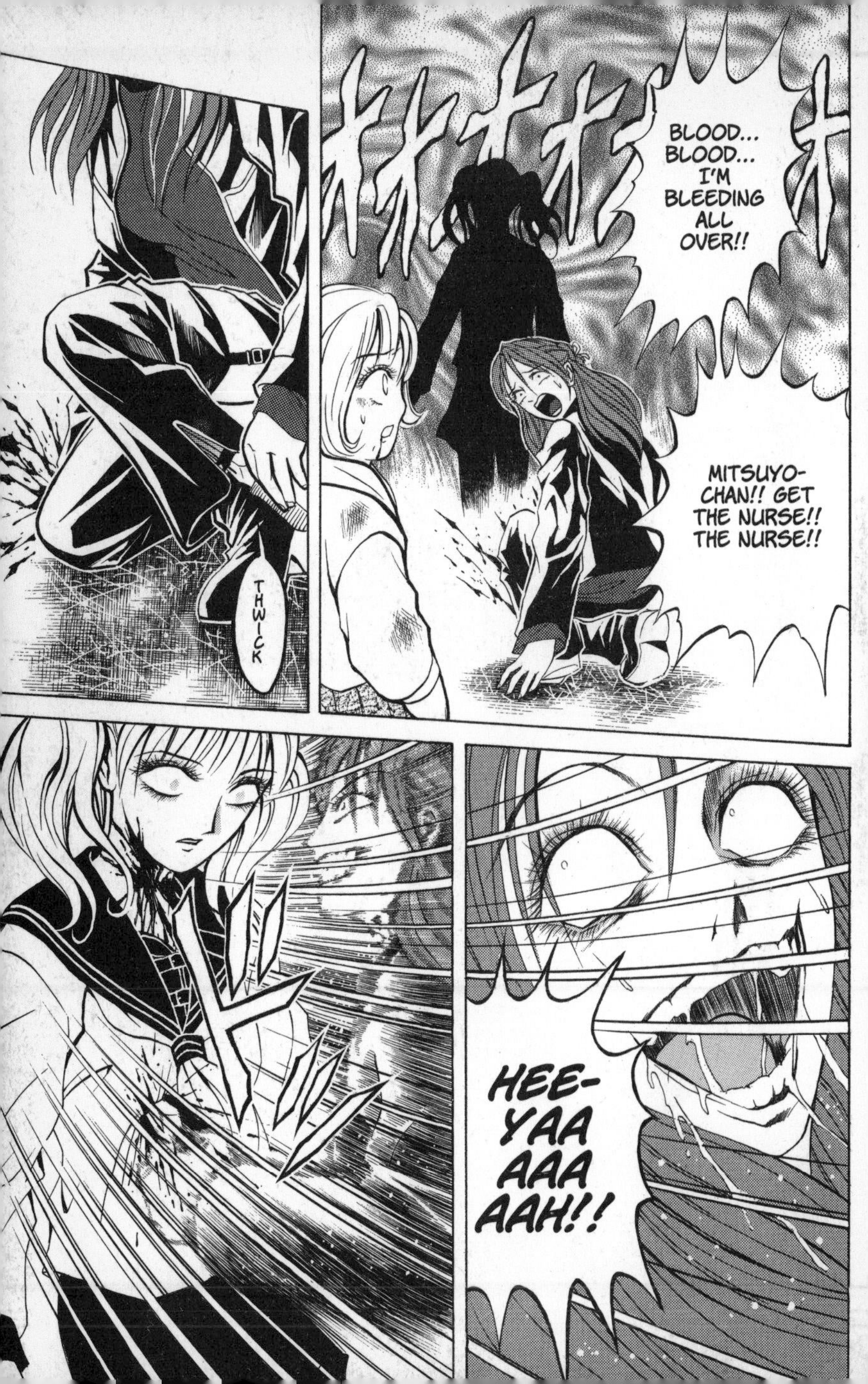
BLOOD... BLOOD... I'M BLEEDING ALL OVER!!
MITSUYO-CHAN!! GET THE NURSE!! THE NURSE!!
THWICK
HEE-YAAAAAAAH!!

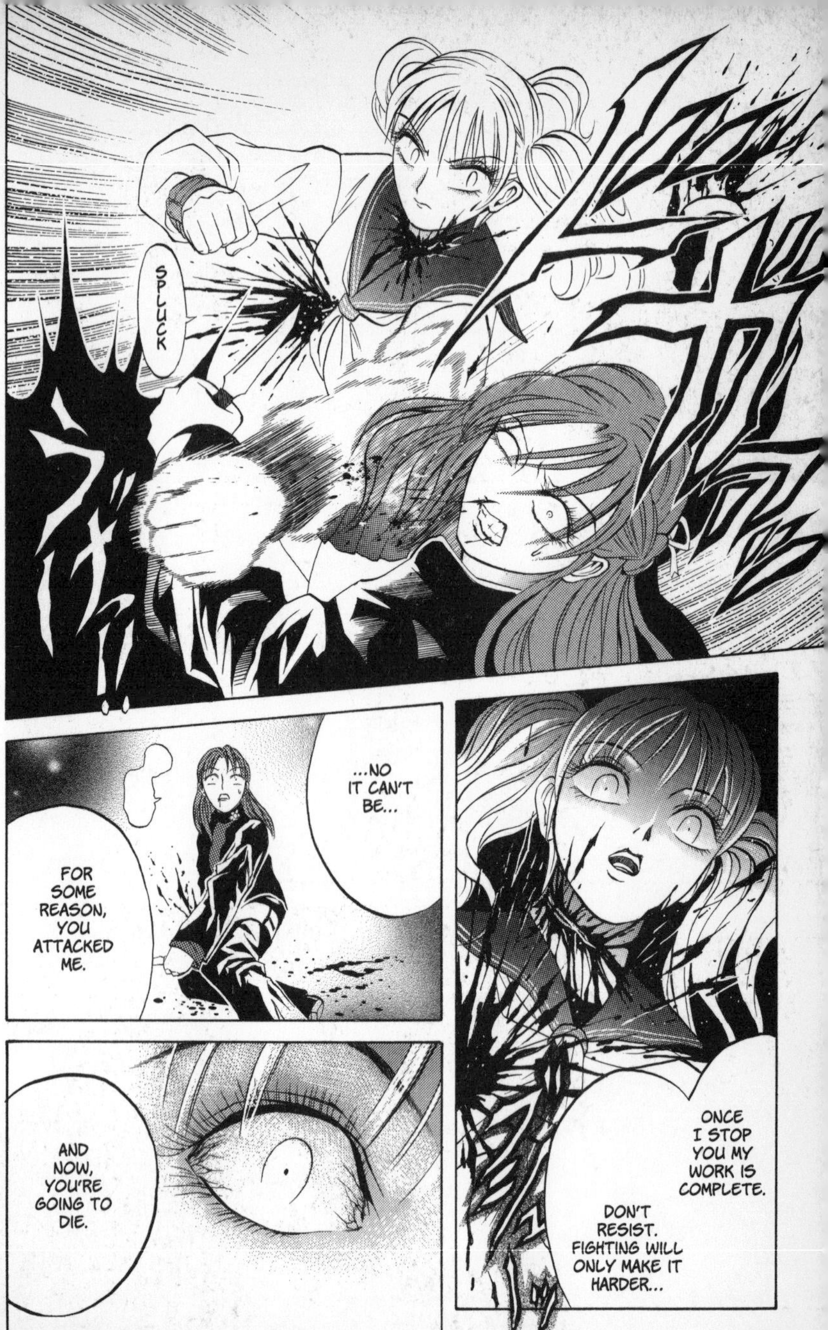
SPLUCK
ONCE I STOP YOU MY WORK IS COMPLETE.
DON'T RESIST. FIGHTING WILL ONLY MAKE IT HARDER...
...NO IT CAN'T BE...
FOR SOME REASON, YOU ATTACKED ME.
AND NOW, YOU'RE GOING TO DIE.

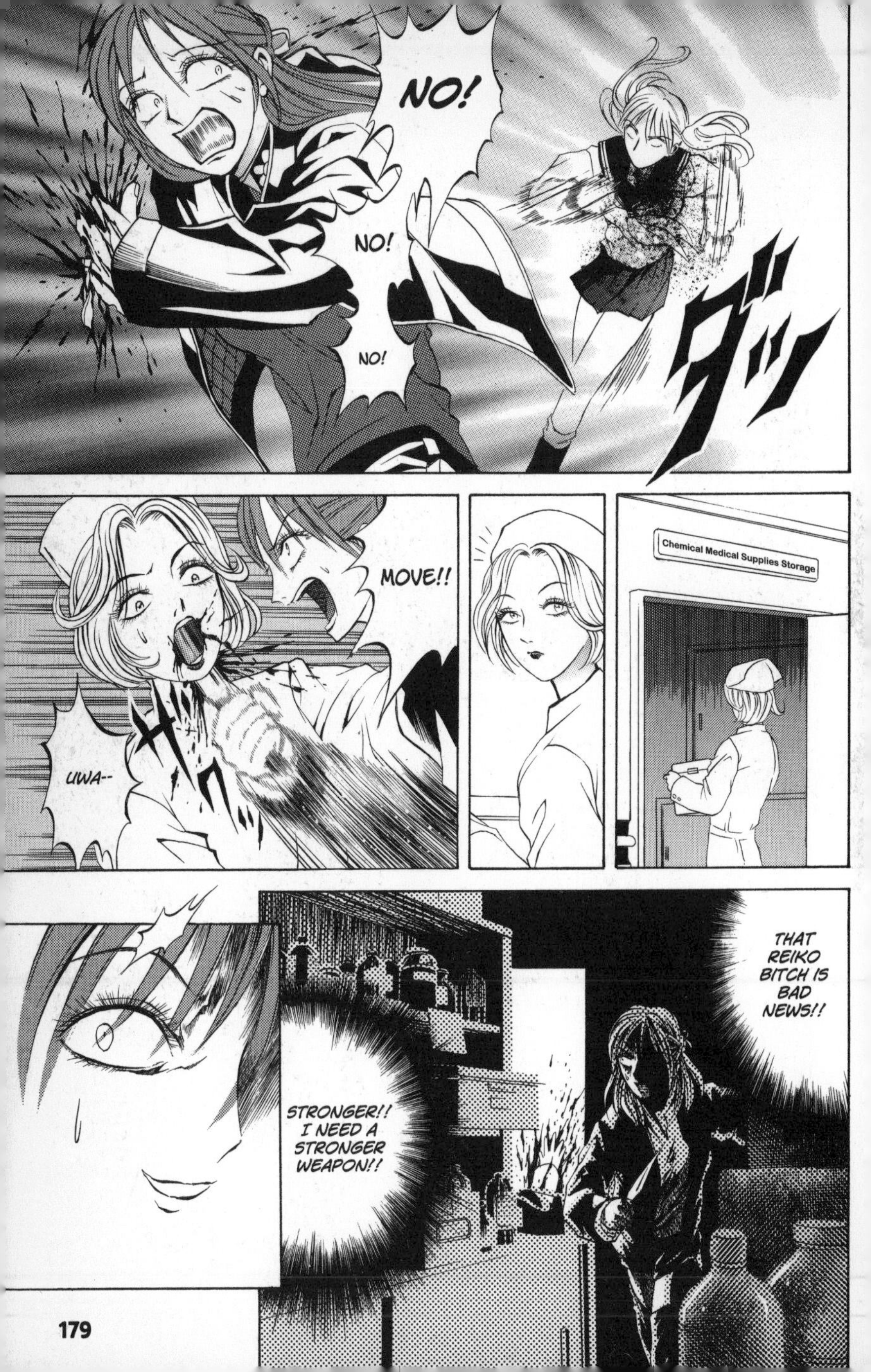
NO!
NO!
NO!
ヅッ
Chemical Medical Supplies Storage
MOVE!!
UWA--
THAT REIKO BITCH IS BAD NEWS!!
STRONGER!! I NEED A STRONGER WEAPON!!

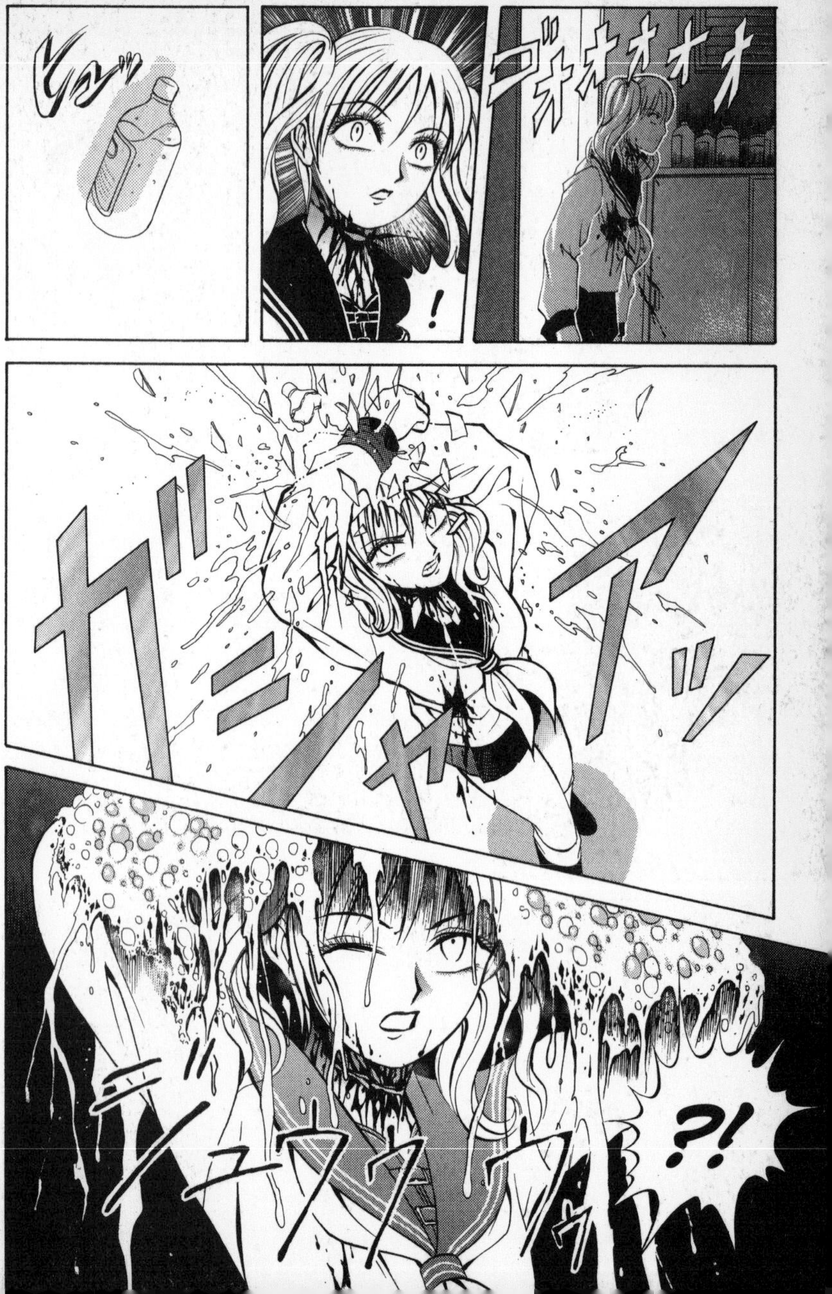
ゴオオオオオ
!
ガシャアアッ
ジュウウウウ
?!

CONCEN-
TRATED
SULPHURIC
ACID!!

LOOKIT
YOUR
CUTE
WITTLE
HANDS
MELT!!

HOW
DARE YOU
THINK YOU
CAN STOP ME,
BITCH!!
HYAHA
HAHAHA!!

UW...
UWAHH...

MAMA!

MITSUYO-
CHAN ♥
WHERE'RE
YOU GOING?

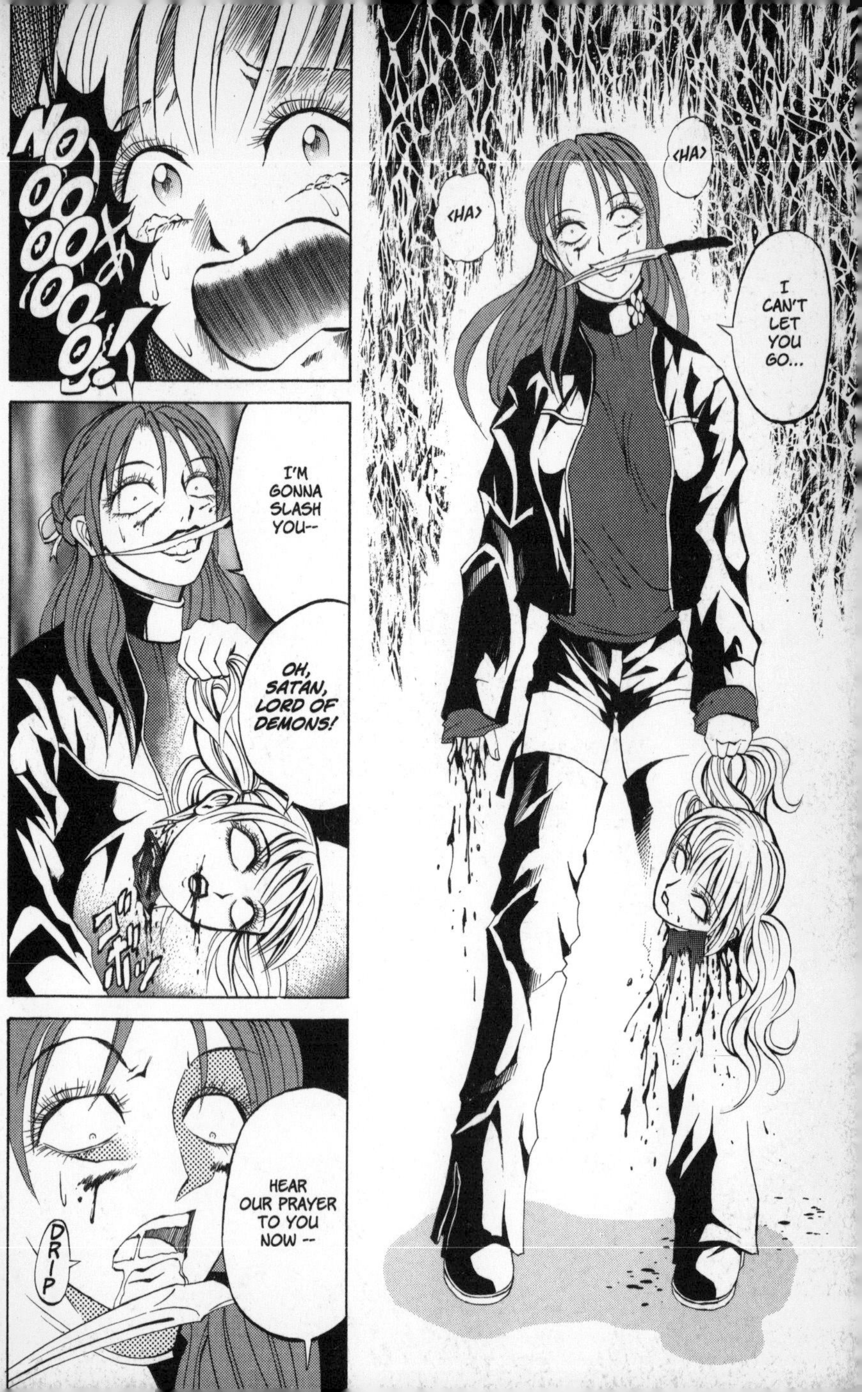
<HA>
<HA>
I CAN'T LET YOU GO...
NOOOOOOOO!
I'M GONNA SLASH YOU--
OH, SATAN, LORD OF DEMONS!
HEAR OUR PRAYER TO YOU NOW --
DRIP

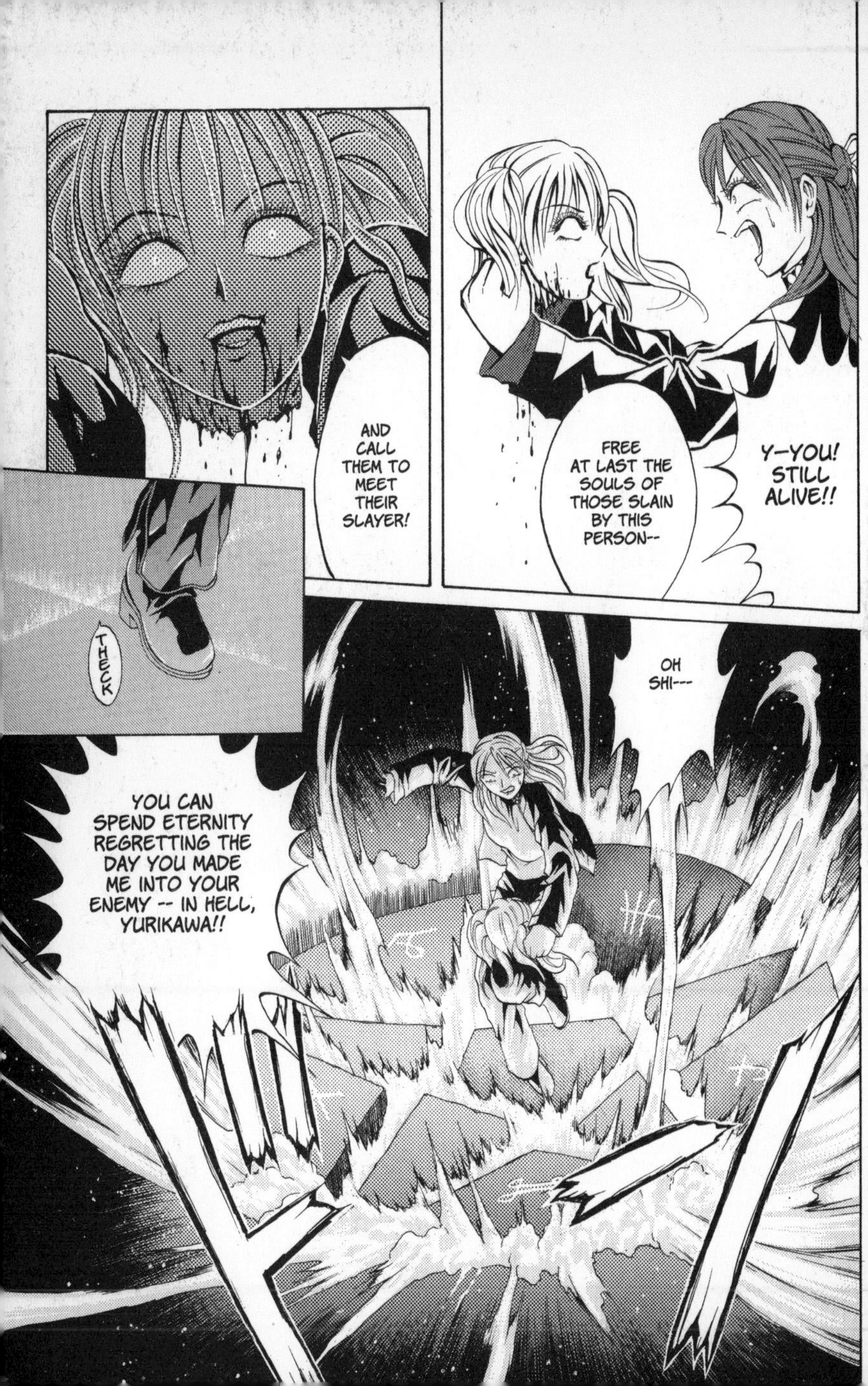
Y--YOU! STILL ALIVE!!
FREE AT LAST THE SOULS OF THOSE SLAIN BY THIS PERSON--
AND CALL THEM TO MEET THEIR SLAYER!
THECK
OH SHI---
YOU CAN SPEND ETERNITY REGRETTING THE DAY YOU MADE ME INTO YOUR ENEMY -- IN HELL, YURIKAWA!!

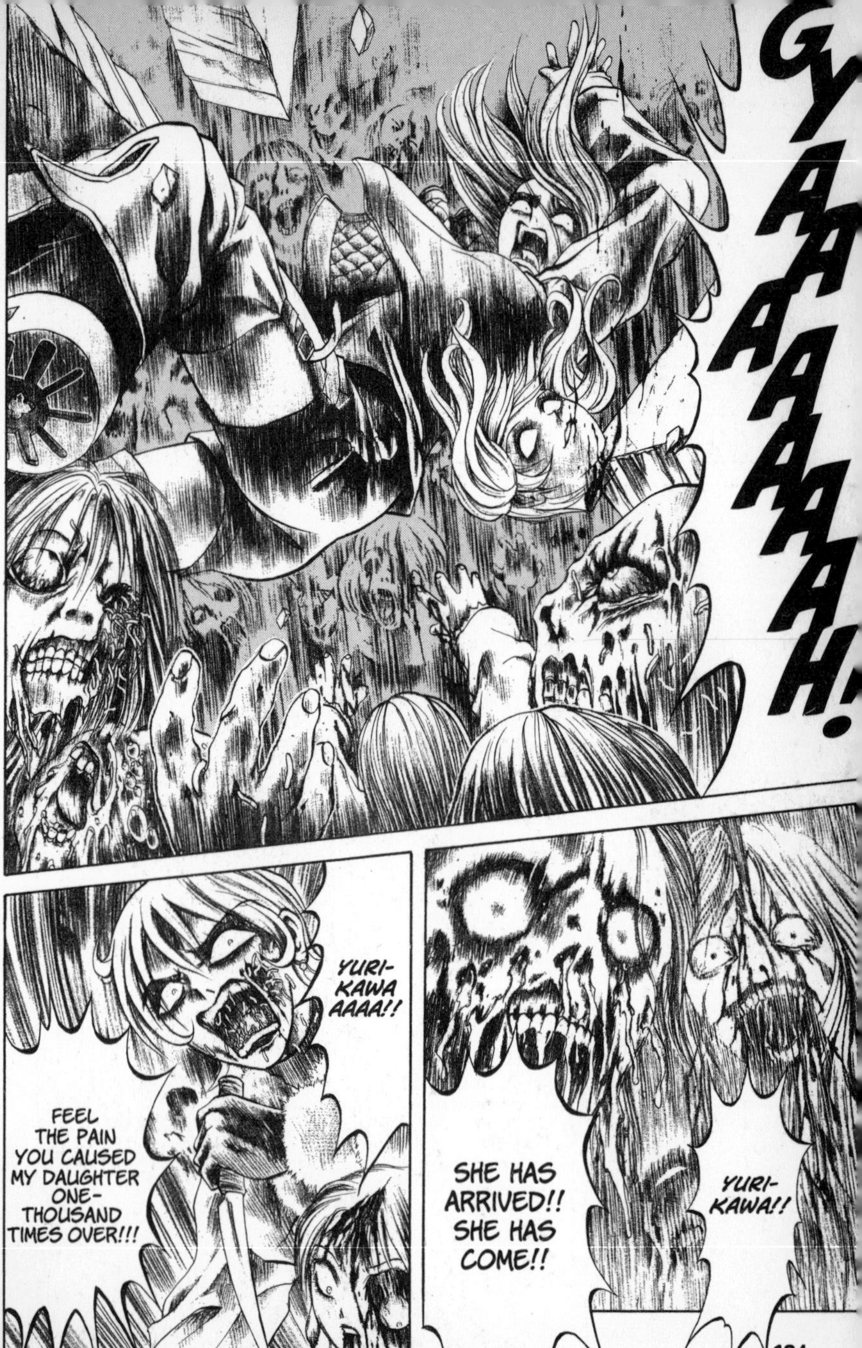
GYAAAAAAAH!
YURI-KAWA!!
SHE HAS ARRIVED!! SHE HAS COME!!
YURI-KAWA AAAA!!
FEEL THE PAIN YOU CAUSED MY DAUGHTER ONE-THOUSAND TIMES OVER!!!

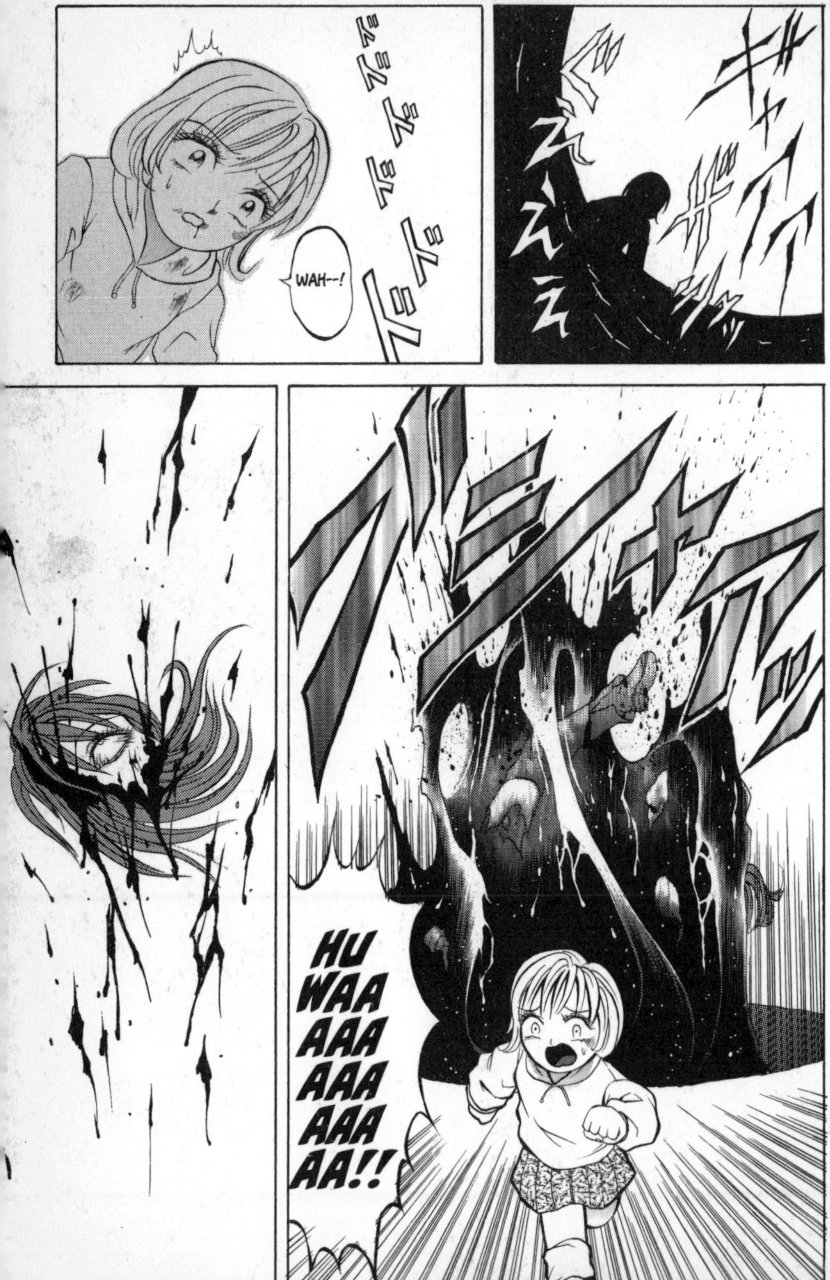
WAH--!
HUWAAAAAAAAAAAAAAAAA!!

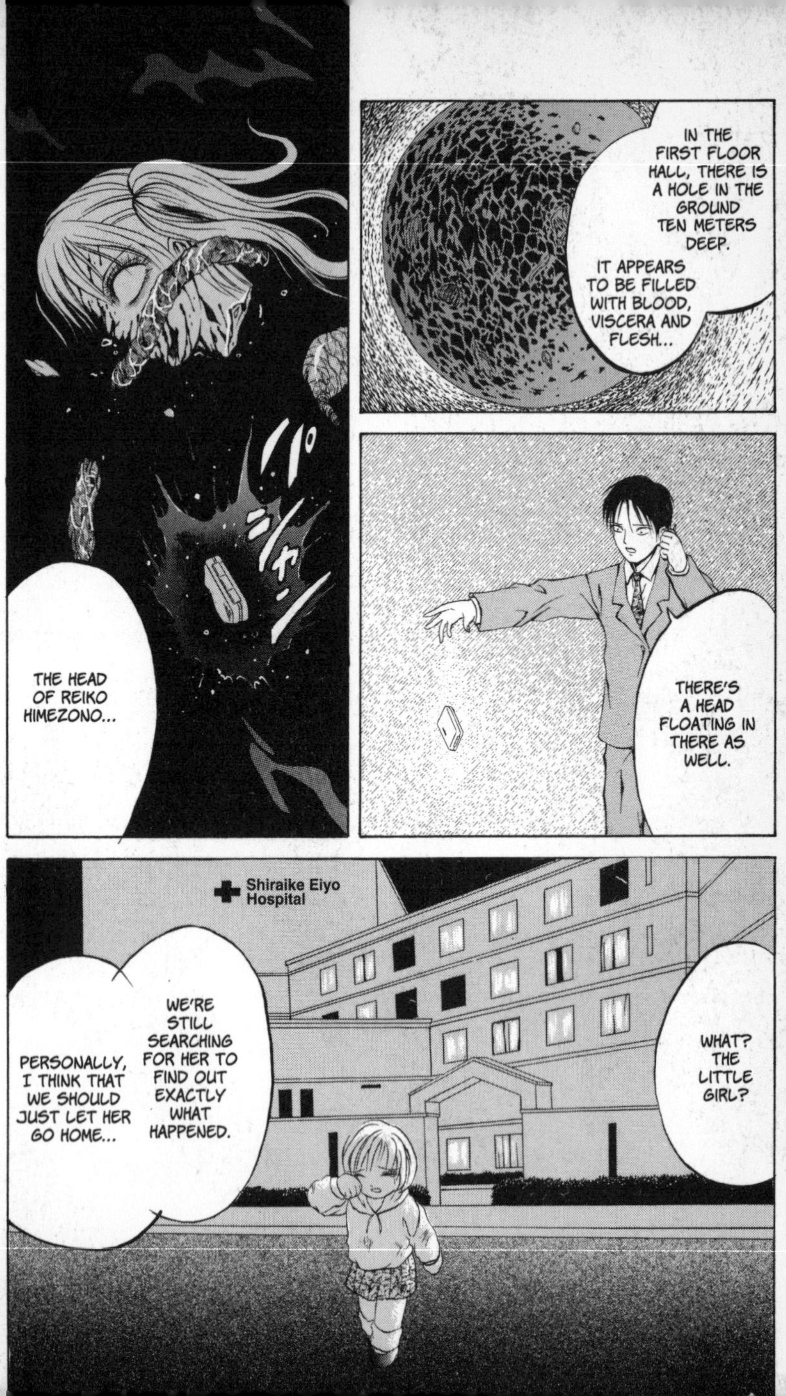
IN THE FIRST FLOOR HALL, THERE IS A HOLE IN THE GROUND TEN METERS DEEP.
IT APPEARS TO BE FILLED WITH BLOOD, VISCERA AND FLESH...
THERE'S A HEAD FLOATING IN THERE AS WELL.
パシャ
THE HEAD OF REIKO HIMEZONO...
Shiraike Eiyo Hospital
WHAT? THE LITTLE GIRL?
WE'RE STILL SEARCHING FOR HER TO FIND OUT EXACTLY WHAT HAPPENED.
PERSONALLY, I THINK THAT WE SHOULD JUST LET HER GO HOME...

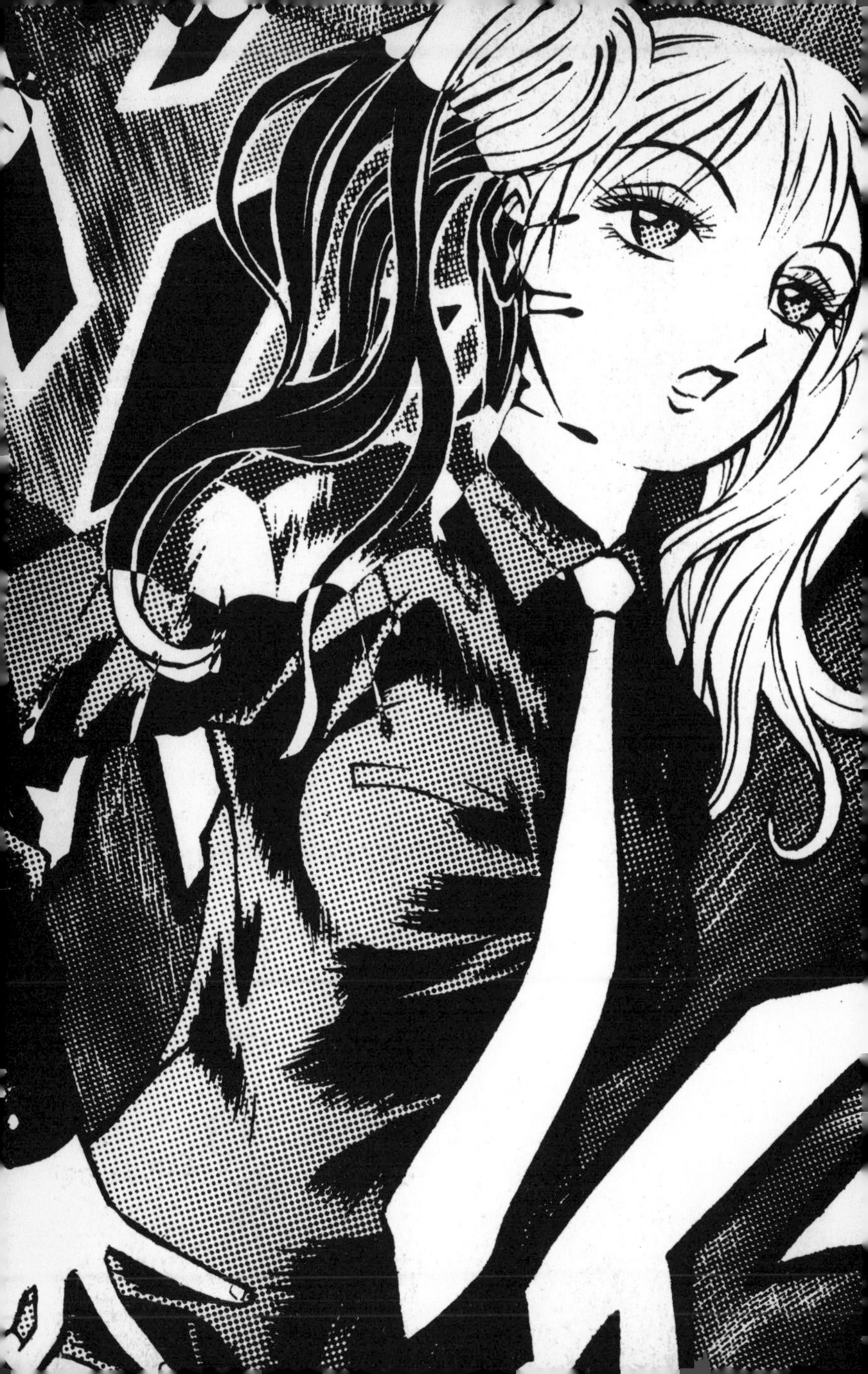

# the ZOMBIE SHOP GALLERY

GRAND OPENING!!

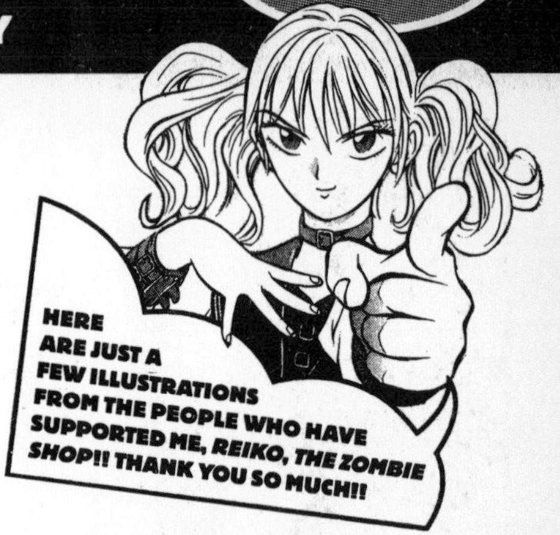
HERE ARE JUST A FEW ILLUSTRATIONS FROM THE PEOPLE WHO HAVE SUPPORTED ME, *REIKO, THE ZOMBIE SHOP*!! THANK YOU SO MUCH!!

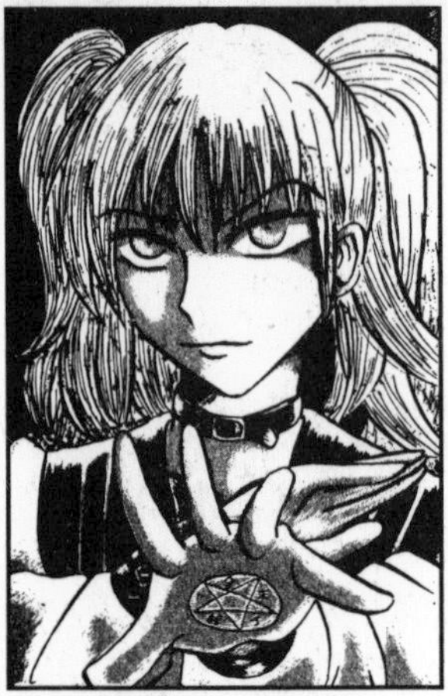

**MIYUKI SETA • AGE 14**
**KANAGAWA PREFECTURE**
VERY NICE USE OF DIFFERENT TONES!!

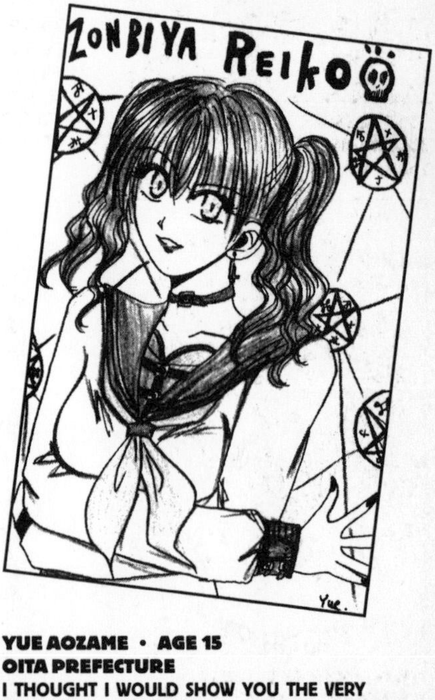
ZONBIYA REIKO
Yue.

**YUE AOZAME • AGE 15**
**OITA PREFECTURE**
I THOUGHT I WOULD SHOW YOU THE VERY FIRST PIECE OF FAN ART THAT I GOT FOLLOWING *REIKO, THE ZOMBIE SHOP'S* RELEASE ♡ (MIKAMOTO)

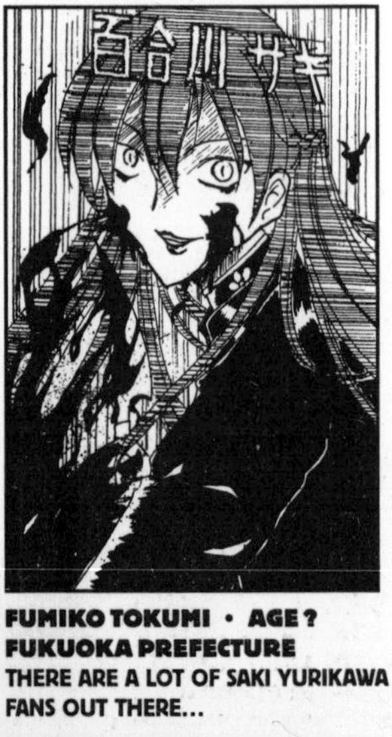
百合川サキ

**FUMIKO TOKUMI • AGE ?**
**FUKUOKA PREFECTURE**
THERE ARE A LOT OF SAKI YURIKAWA FANS OUT THERE...

IF YOU WANT TO SUBMIT YOUR ART, WE'RE WAITING TO HEAR FROM YOU. ♡

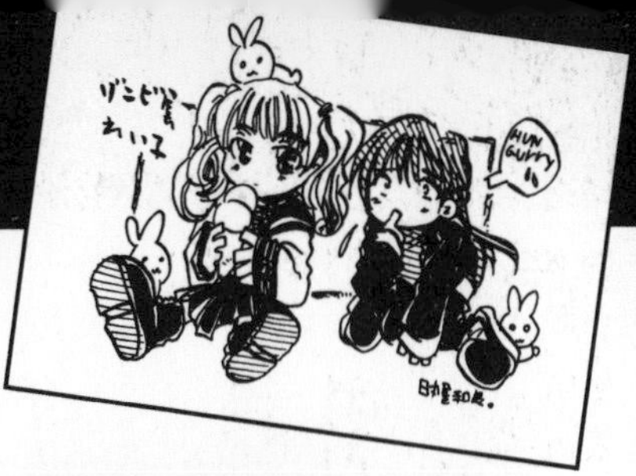

**KAZURA HINOMARUYA • AGE ?**
**FUKUSHIMA PREFECTURE**
REIKO'S FAVORITE ICE CREAM, BY THE WAY, IS RUM-RAISIN ♡

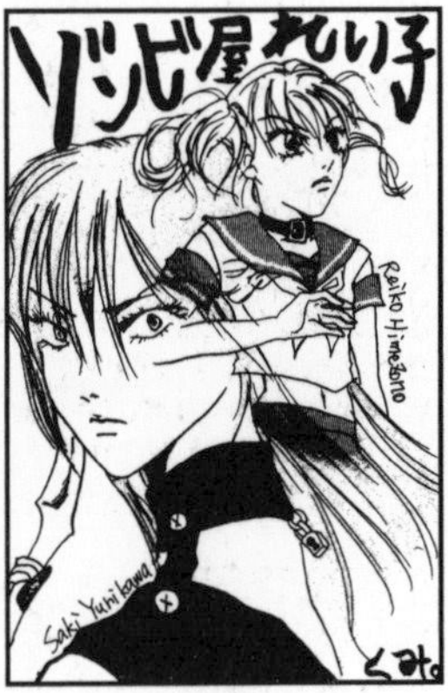
ゾンビ屋れい子
Reiko Himezono

**KUMIKO MATSUMOTO**
**AGE ? • TOKYO**
THE FATE-DECIDING BATTLE: REIKO VERSUS SAKI!!

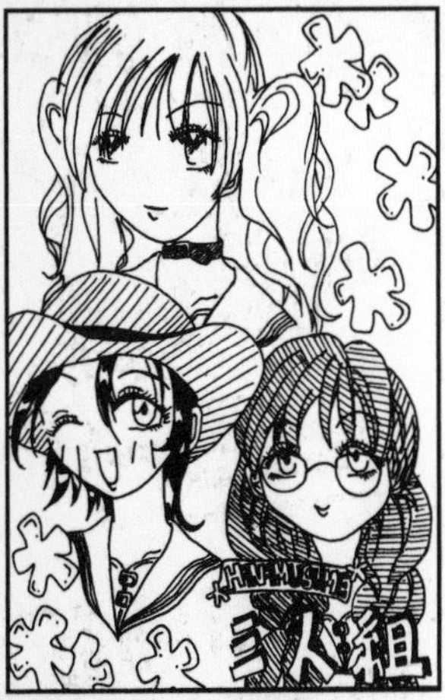
三人組

**MAMI ENDOH • AGE ?**
**KANAGAWA PREFECTURE**
THOSE THREE—BEST FRIENDS FOREVER!!

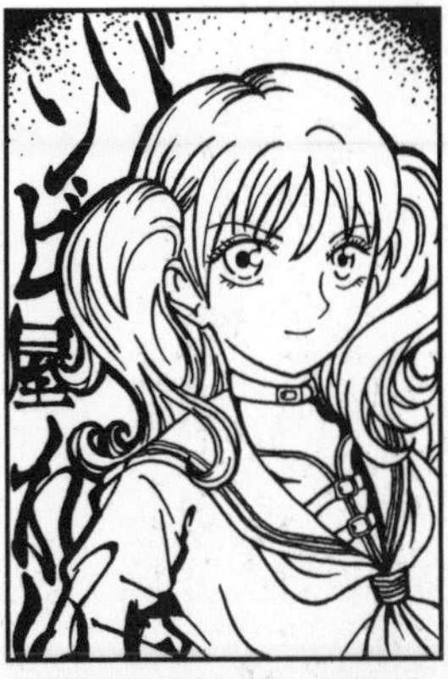

**MASARU SASAKI • AGE 14**
**HOKKAIDO PREFECTURE**
CALM, COOL, AND IN CONTROL—THAT'S REIKO!!

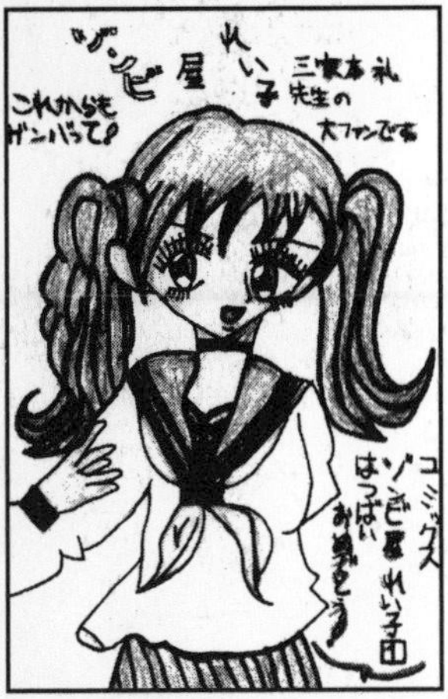
ゾンビ屋れい子
三家本礼先生の大ファンです
これからもガンバって!

**RYOKA MANIWA • AGE 8**
**TOCHIGI PREFECTURE**
THIS ONE WAS DONE REALLY WELL IN BEAUTIFUL COLORS. BUT, UNFORTUNATELY IT'S HARD TO TELL IN BLACK AND WHITE...

FOUR PANEL FREEBIE

# REIKO THE ZOMBIE SHOP

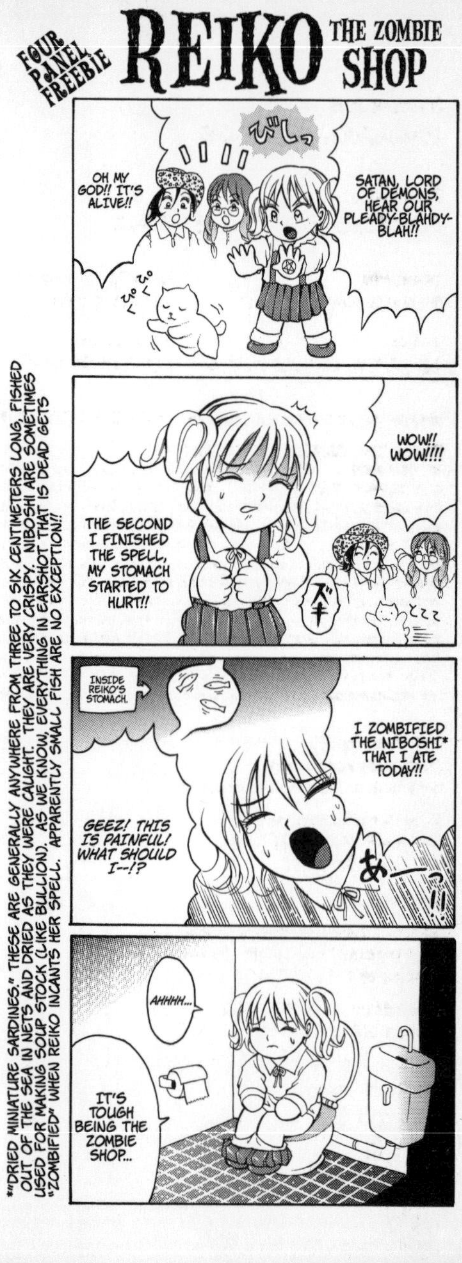
びしっ
SATAN, LORD OF DEMONS, HEAR OUR PLEADY-BLAHDY-BLAH!!
OH MY GOD!! IT'S ALIVE!!
WOW!! WOW!!!!
THE SECOND I FINISHED THE SPELL, MY STOMACH STARTED TO HURT!!
ズキ
とてて
I ZOMBIFIED THE NIBOSHI* THAT I ATE TODAY!!
INSIDE REIKO'S STOMACH.
GEEZ! THIS IS PAINFUL! WHAT SHOULD I--!?
あーっ!!
AHHHH...
IT'S TOUGH BEING THE ZOMBIE SHOP...

*"DRIED MINIATURE SARDINES." THESE ARE GENERALLY ANYWHERE FROM THREE TO SIX CENTIMETERS LONG, FISHED OUT OF THE SEA IN NETS AND DRIED AS THEY WERE CAUGHT. THEY ARE VERY CRISPY. NIBOSHI ARE SOMETIMES USED FOR MAKING SOUP STOCK (LIKE BULLION). AS WE KNOW, EVERYTHING IN EARSHOT THAT IS DEAD GETS "ZOMBIFIED" WHEN REIKO INCANTS HER SPELL. APPARENTLY SMALL FISH ARE NO EXCEPTION!!

translation
**MICHAEL GOMBOS**

lettering
**MICHAEL DAVID THOMAS**

publisher
**MIKE RICHARDSON**

editor
**MICHAEL CARRIGLITTO**

collection designer
**APRIL GRAY**

art director
**LIA RIBACCHI**

English-language version produced by DARK HORSE COMICS.

REIKO, THE ZOMBIE SHOP VOL. 1


published by
**Dark Horse Manga**
a division of Dark Horse Comics, Inc.

Dark Horse Comics, Inc.
10956 S.E. Main Street
Milwaukie, OR 97222

darkhorse.com

To find a comics shop in your area,
call the Comic Shop Locator Service
toll-free at 1-888-266-4226

First edition: December 2005
ISBN: 1-59307-413-1

10 9 8 7 6 5 4 3 2 1
Printed in Canada

TM

# STOP

## THIS IS THE BACK OF THE BOOK

**This manga collection is translated into English but oriented in right-to-left reading format at the creator's request, maintaining the artwork's visual orientation as originally published in Japan. If you've never read manga in this way before, take a look at the diagram below to give yourself an idea of how to go about it. Basically, you'll be starting in the upper right corner and will read each balloon and panel moving right to left. It may take some getting used to, but you should get the hang of it very quickly. Have fun!**

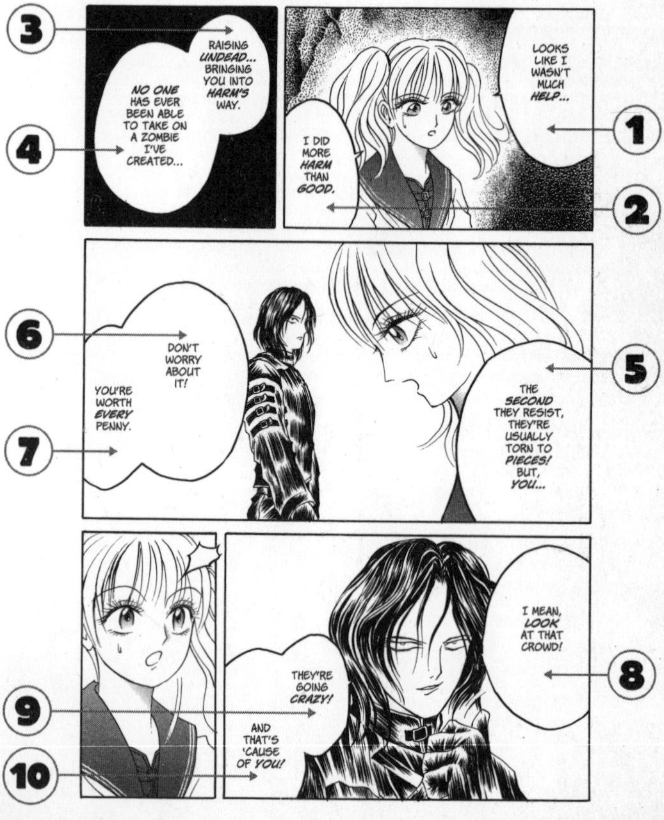
1
LOOKS LIKE I WASN'T MUCH HELP...
2
I DID MORE HARM THAN GOOD.
3
RAISING UNDEAD... BRINGING YOU INTO HARM'S WAY.
4
NO ONE HAS EVER BEEN ABLE TO TAKE ON A ZOMBIE I'VE CREATED...
5
THE SECOND THEY RESIST, THEY'RE USUALLY TORN TO PIECES! BUT, YOU...
6
DON'T WORRY ABOUT IT!
7
YOU'RE WORTH EVERY PENNY.
8
I MEAN, LOOK AT THAT CROWD!
9
THEY'RE GOING CRAZY!
10
AND THAT'S 'CAUSE OF YOU!